THE SILE[illegible]ER

HELL-IDAY ROAD

VOL. 2

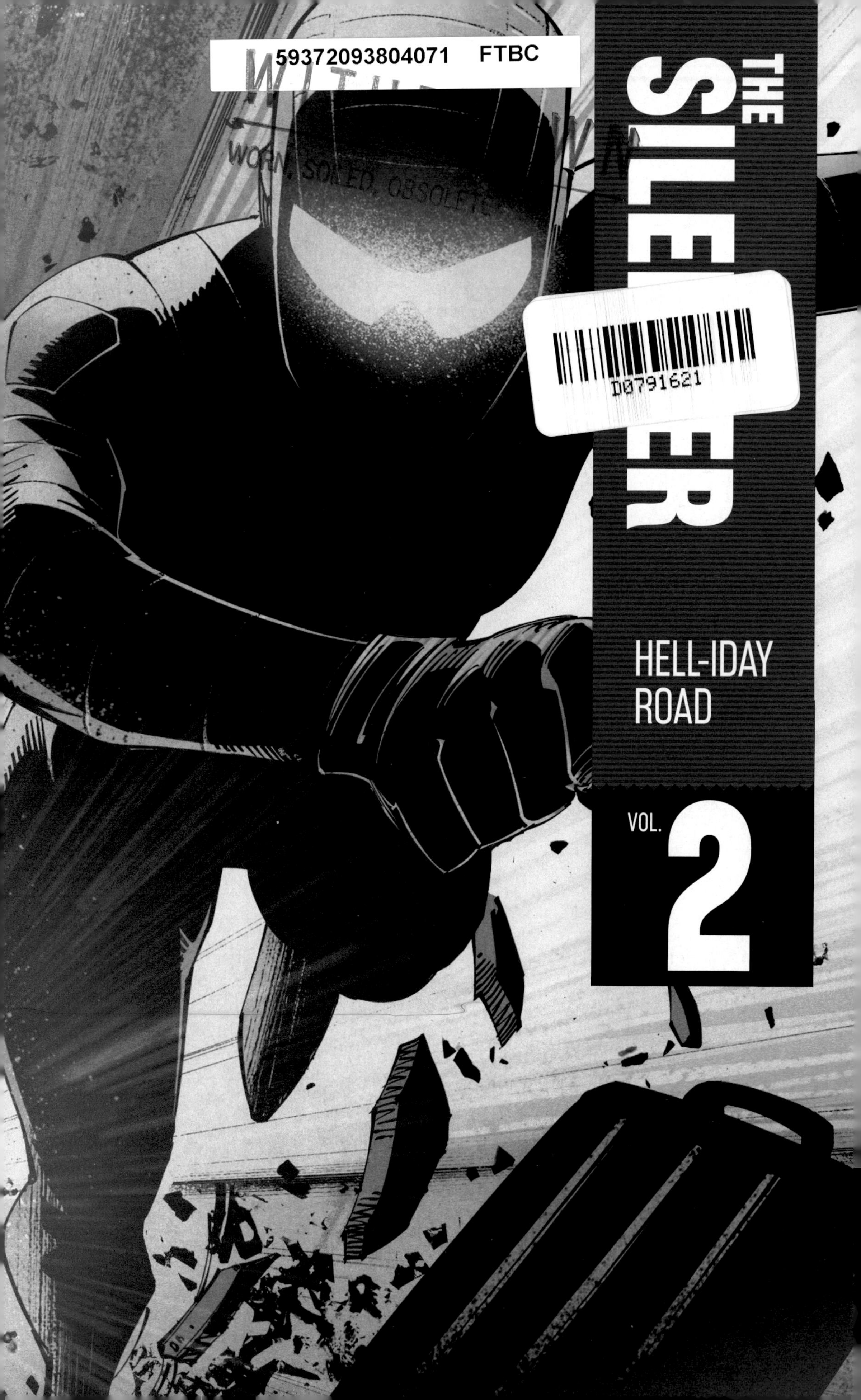

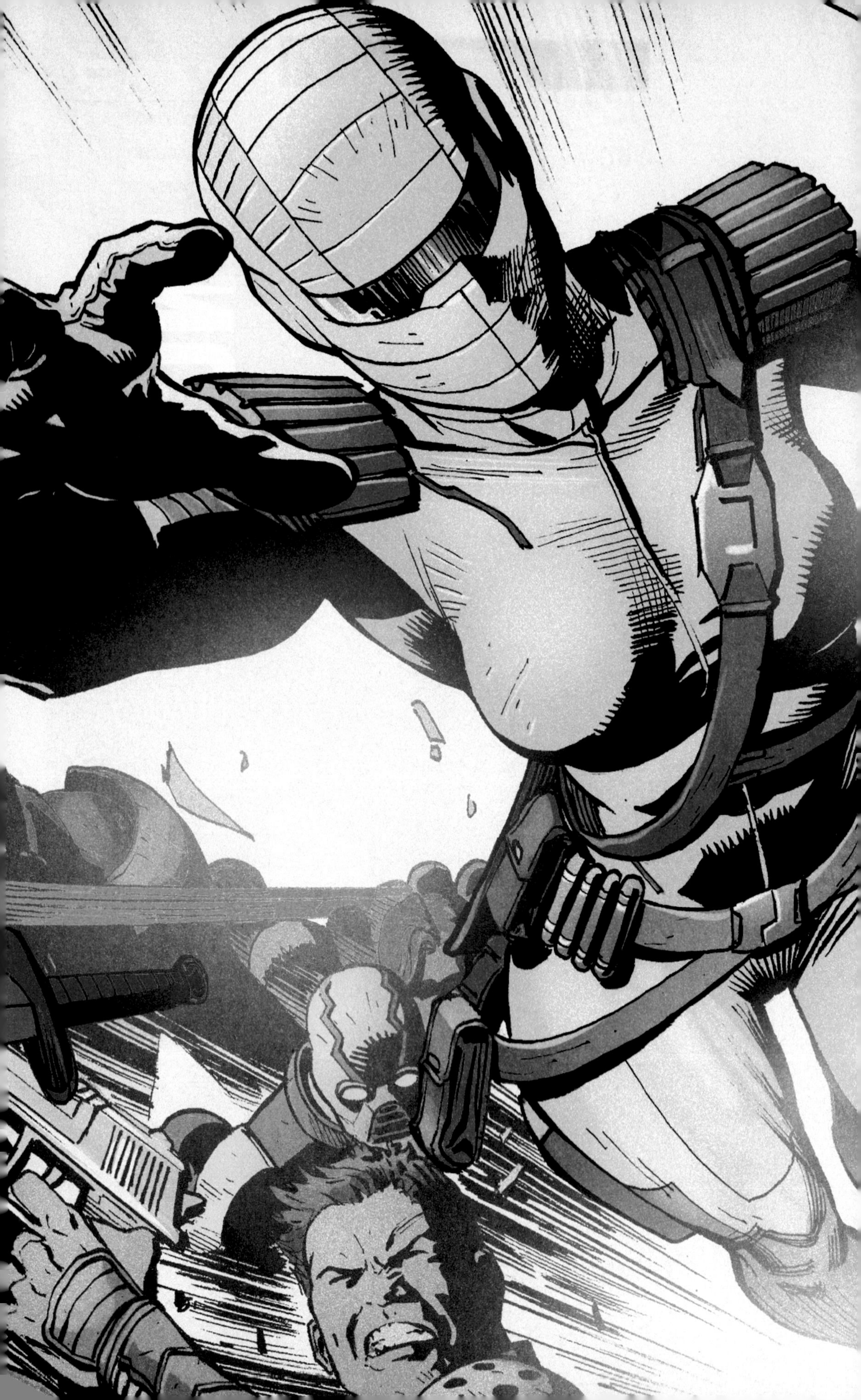

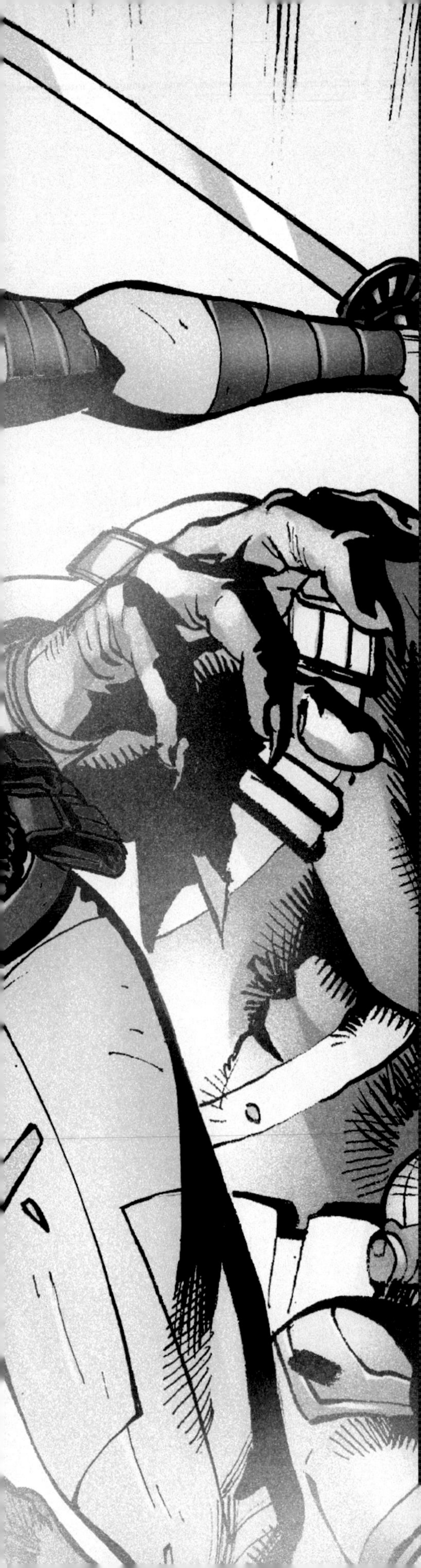

THE SILENCER
HELL-IDAY ROAD

artists

JACK HERBERT \ PATCH ZIRCHER
VIKTOR BOGDANOVIC
TOM DERENICK \ JONATHAN GLAPION

writer

DAN ABNETT

colorists

MIKE SPICER
HI-FI

letterer

TOM NAPOLITANO

collection cover artists

TYLER KIRKHAM and ARIF PRIANTO

VOL. 2

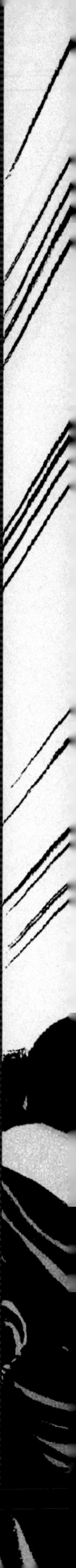

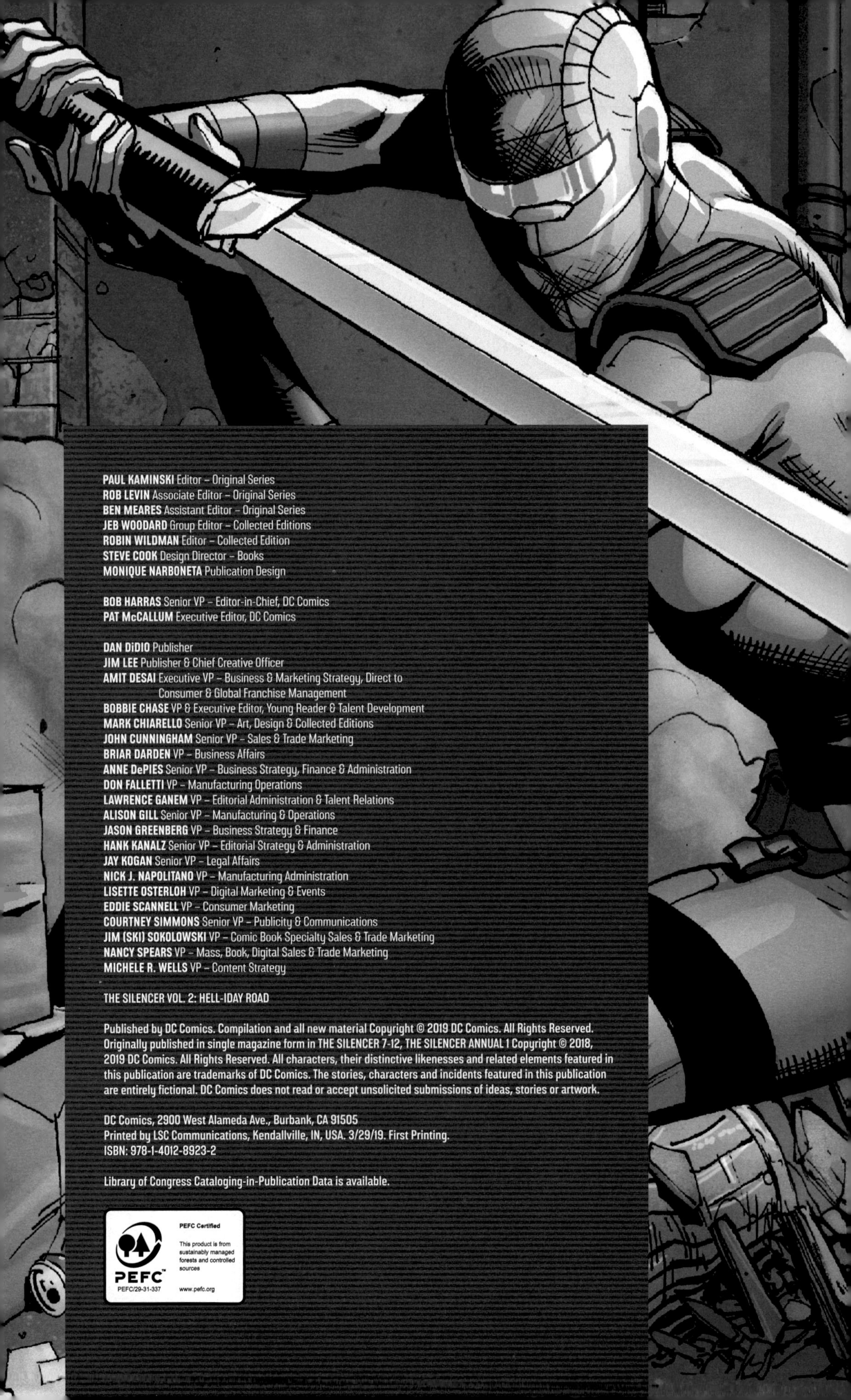

PAUL KAMINSKI Editor – Original Series
ROB LEVIN Associate Editor – Original Series
BEN MEARES Assistant Editor – Original Series
JEB WOODARD Group Editor – Collected Editions
ROBIN WILDMAN Editor – Collected Edition
STEVE COOK Design Director – Books
MONIQUE NARBONETA Publication Design

BOB HARRAS Senior VP – Editor-in-Chief, DC Comics
PAT McCALLUM Executive Editor, DC Comics

DAN DiDIO Publisher
JIM LEE Publisher & Chief Creative Officer
AMIT DESAI Executive VP – Business & Marketing Strategy, Direct to Consumer & Global Franchise Management
BOBBIE CHASE VP & Executive Editor, Young Reader & Talent Development
MARK CHIARELLO Senior VP – Art, Design & Collected Editions
JOHN CUNNINGHAM Senior VP – Sales & Trade Marketing
BRIAR DARDEN VP – Business Affairs
ANNE DePIES Senior VP – Business Strategy, Finance & Administration
DON FALLETTI VP – Manufacturing Operations
LAWRENCE GANEM VP – Editorial Administration & Talent Relations
ALISON GILL Senior VP – Manufacturing & Operations
JASON GREENBERG VP – Business Strategy & Finance
HANK KANALZ Senior VP – Editorial Strategy & Administration
JAY KOGAN Senior VP – Legal Affairs
NICK J. NAPOLITANO VP – Manufacturing Administration
LISETTE OSTERLOH VP – Digital Marketing & Events
EDDIE SCANNELL VP – Consumer Marketing
COURTNEY SIMMONS Senior VP – Publicity & Communications
JIM (SKI) SOKOLOWSKI VP – Comic Book Specialty Sales & Trade Marketing
NANCY SPEARS VP – Mass, Book, Digital Sales & Trade Marketing
MICHELE R. WELLS VP – Content Strategy

THE SILENCER VOL. 2: HELL-IDAY ROAD

DC Comics, 2900 West Alameda Ave., Burbank, CA 91505
Printed by LSC Communications, Kendallville, IN, USA. 3/29/19. First Printing.
ISBN: 978-1-4012-8923-2

Library of Congress Cataloging-in-Publication Data is available.

PEFC Certified
This product is from sustainably managed forests and controlled sources
PEFC
PEFC/29-31-337
www.pefc.org

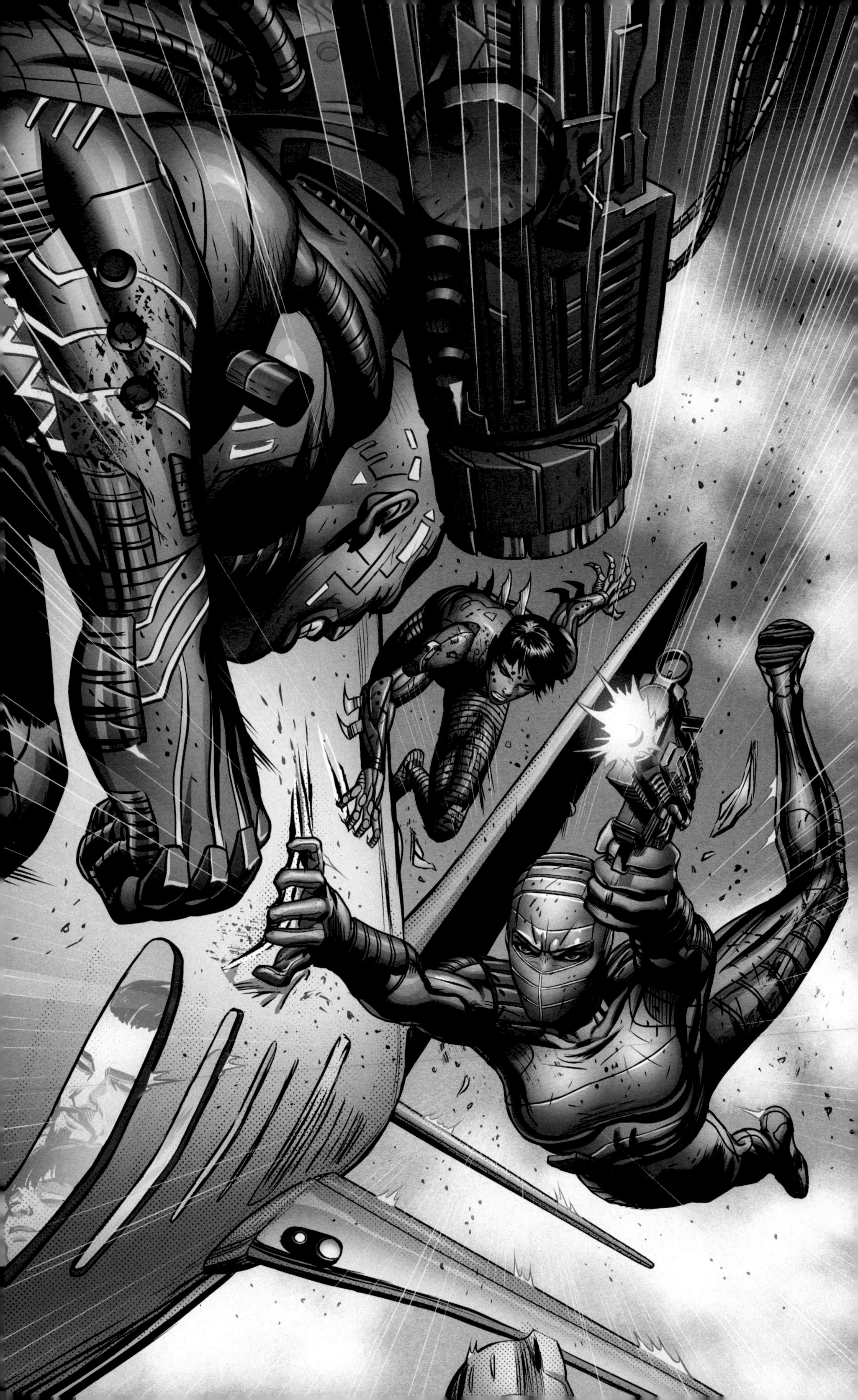

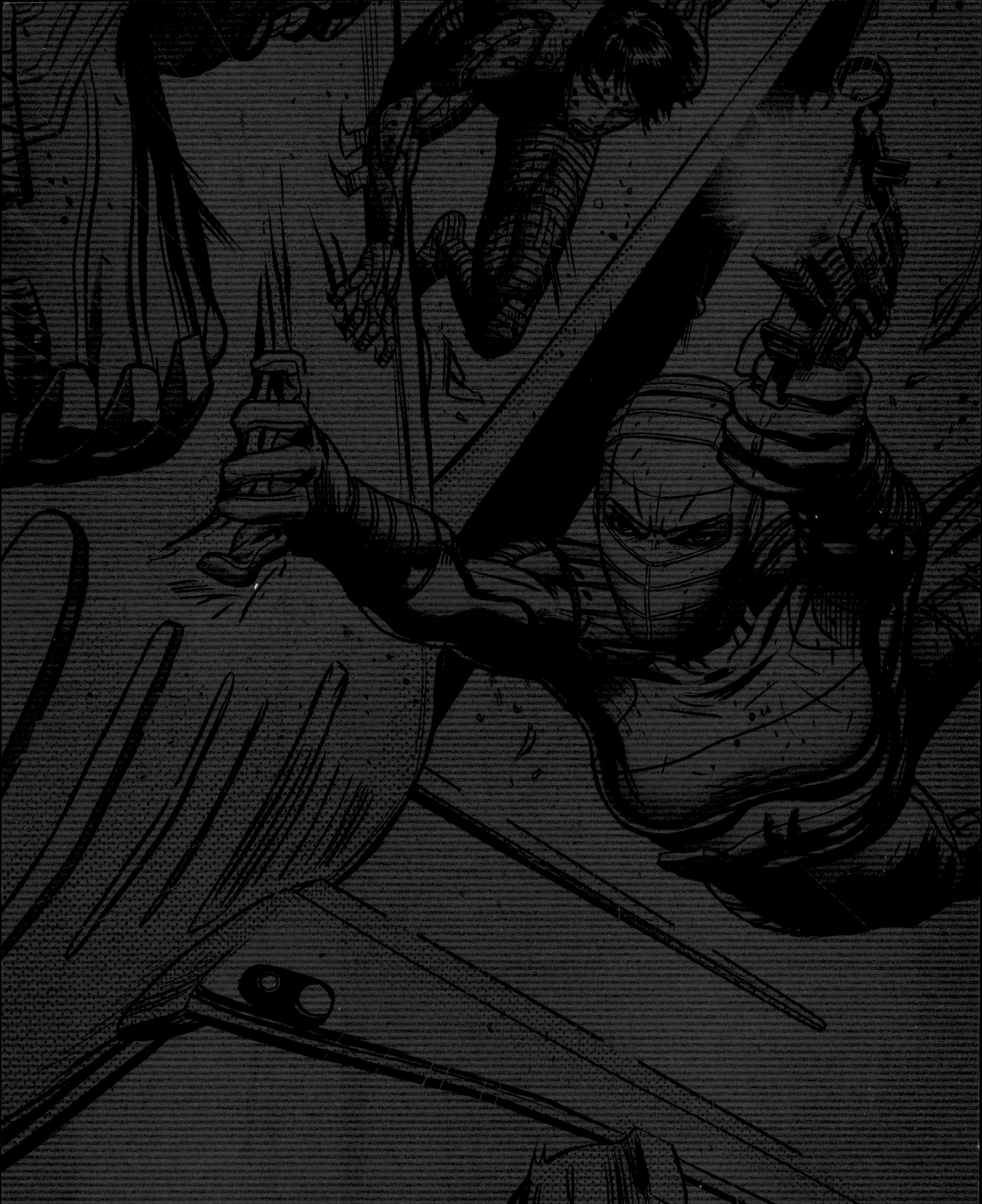

THE SILENCER
#7

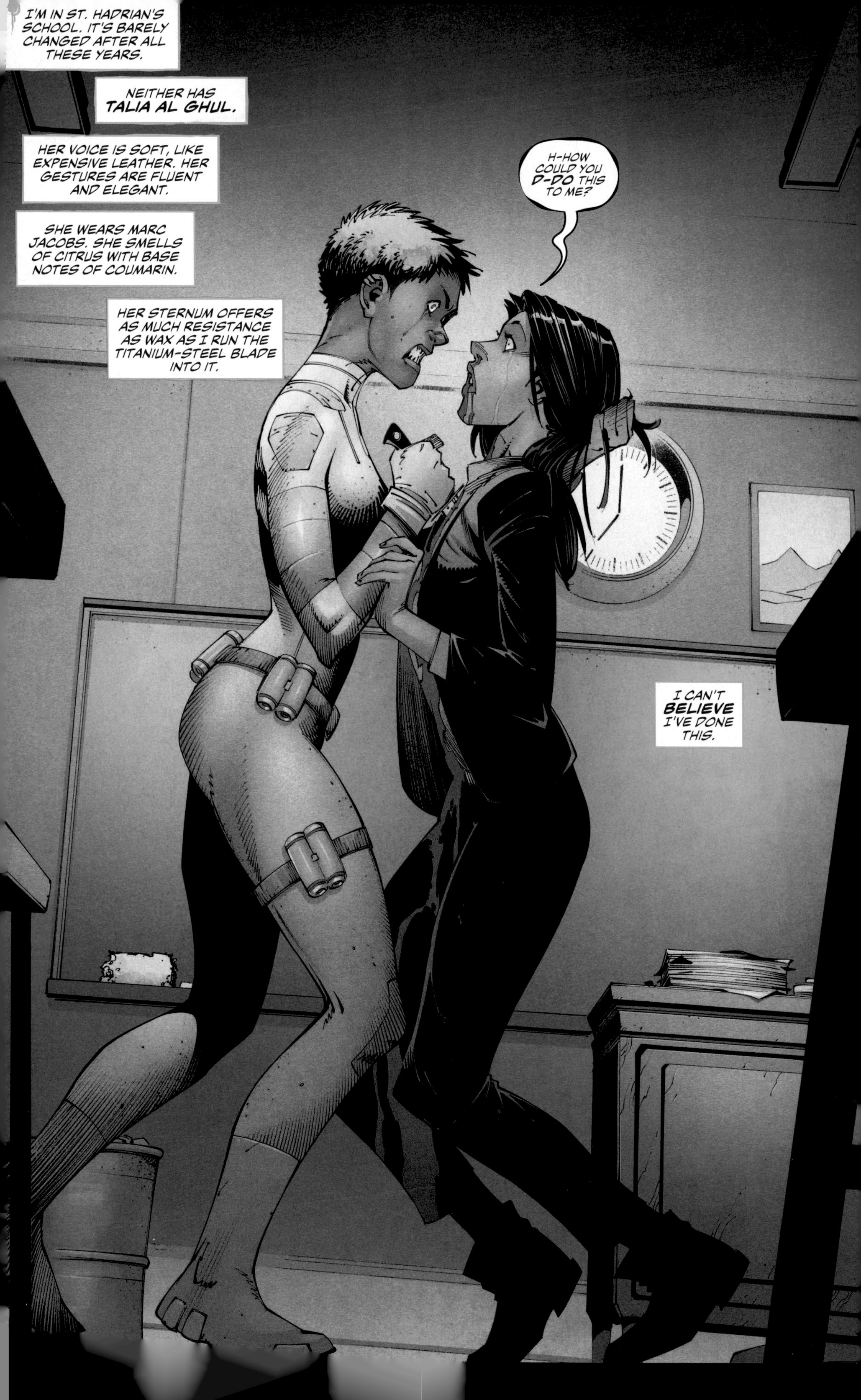
I'M IN ST. HADRIAN'S SCHOOL. IT'S BARELY CHANGED AFTER ALL THESE YEARS.
NEITHER HAS TALIA AL GHUL.
HER VOICE IS SOFT, LIKE EXPENSIVE LEATHER. HER GESTURES ARE FLUENT AND ELEGANT.
SHE WEARS MARC JACOBS. SHE SMELLS OF CITRUS WITH BASE NOTES OF COUMARIN.
H-HOW COULD YOU D-DO THIS TO ME?
HER STERNUM OFFERS AS MUCH RESISTANCE AS WAX AS I RUN THE TITANIUM-STEEL BLADE INTO IT.
I CAN'T BELIEVE I'VE DONE THIS.

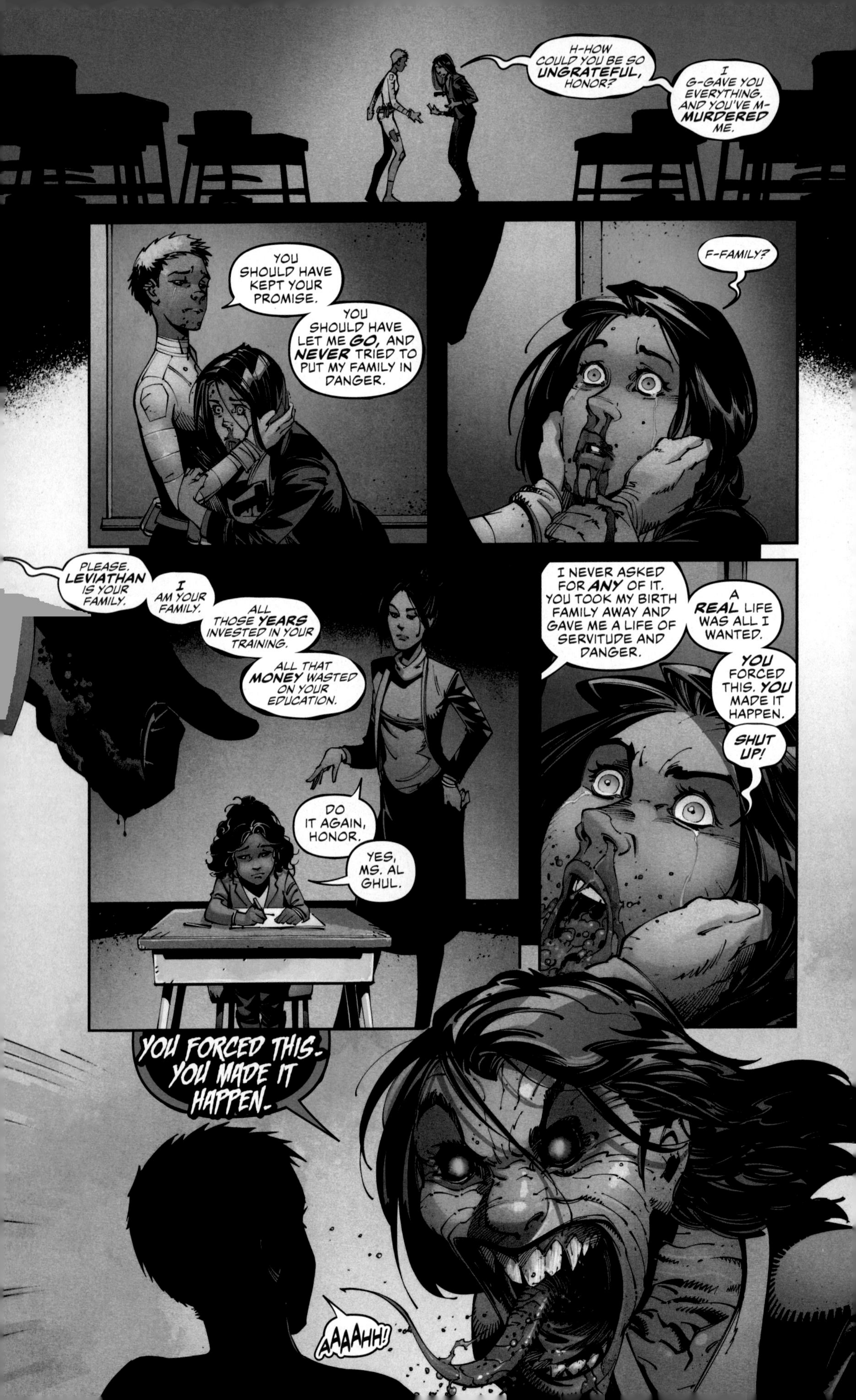
H-HOW COULD YOU BE SO UNGRATEFUL, HONOR?
I G-GAVE YOU EVERYTHING. AND YOU'VE M-MURDERED ME.
YOU SHOULD HAVE KEPT YOUR PROMISE.
YOU SHOULD HAVE LET ME GO, AND NEVER TRIED TO PUT MY FAMILY IN DANGER.
F-FAMILY?
PLEASE. LEVIATHAN IS YOUR FAMILY.
I AM YOUR FAMILY.
ALL THOSE YEARS INVESTED IN YOUR TRAINING.
ALL THAT MONEY WASTED ON YOUR EDUCATION.
DO IT AGAIN, HONOR.
YES, MS. AL GHUL.
I NEVER ASKED FOR ANY OF IT. YOU TOOK MY BIRTH FAMILY AWAY AND GAVE ME A LIFE OF SERVITUDE AND DANGER.
A REAL LIFE WAS ALL I WANTED.
YOU FORCED THIS. YOU MADE IT HAPPEN.
SHUT UP!
YOU FORCED THIS. YOU MADE IT HAPPEN.
AAAAHH!

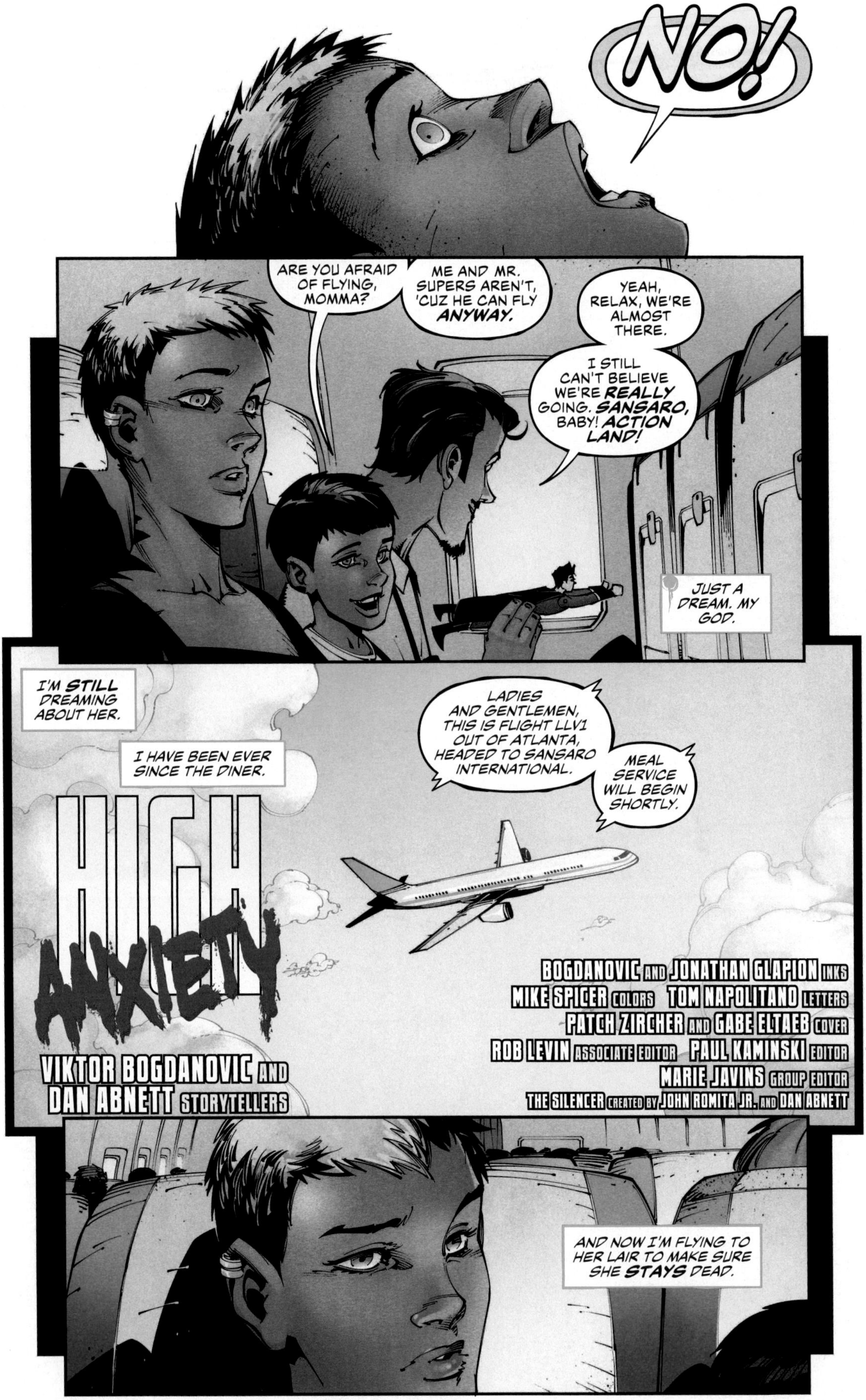
NO!
ARE YOU AFRAID OF FLYING, MOMMA?
ME AND MR. SUPERS AREN'T, 'CUZ HE CAN FLY ANYWAY.
YEAH, RELAX, WE'RE ALMOST THERE.
I STILL CAN'T BELIEVE WE'RE REALLY GOING. SANSARO, BABY! ACTION LAND!
JUST A DREAM. MY GOD.
I'M STILL DREAMING ABOUT HER.
I HAVE BEEN EVER SINCE THE DINER.
LADIES AND GENTLEMEN, THIS IS FLIGHT LLV1 OUT OF ATLANTA, HEADED TO SANSARO INTERNATIONAL.
MEAL SERVICE WILL BEGIN SHORTLY.
HIGH ANXIETY
VIKTOR BOGDANOVIC AND DAN ABNETT STORYTELLERS
BOGDANOVIC AND JONATHAN GLAPION INKS
MIKE SPICER COLORS TOM NAPOLITANO LETTERS
PATCH ZIRCHER AND GABE ELTAEB COVER
ROB LEVIN ASSOCIATE EDITOR PAUL KAMINSKI EDITOR
MARIE JAVINS GROUP EDITOR
THE SILENCER CREATED BY JOHN ROMITA JR. AND DAN ABNETT
AND NOW I'M FLYING TO HER LAIR TO MAKE SURE SHE STAYS DEAD.

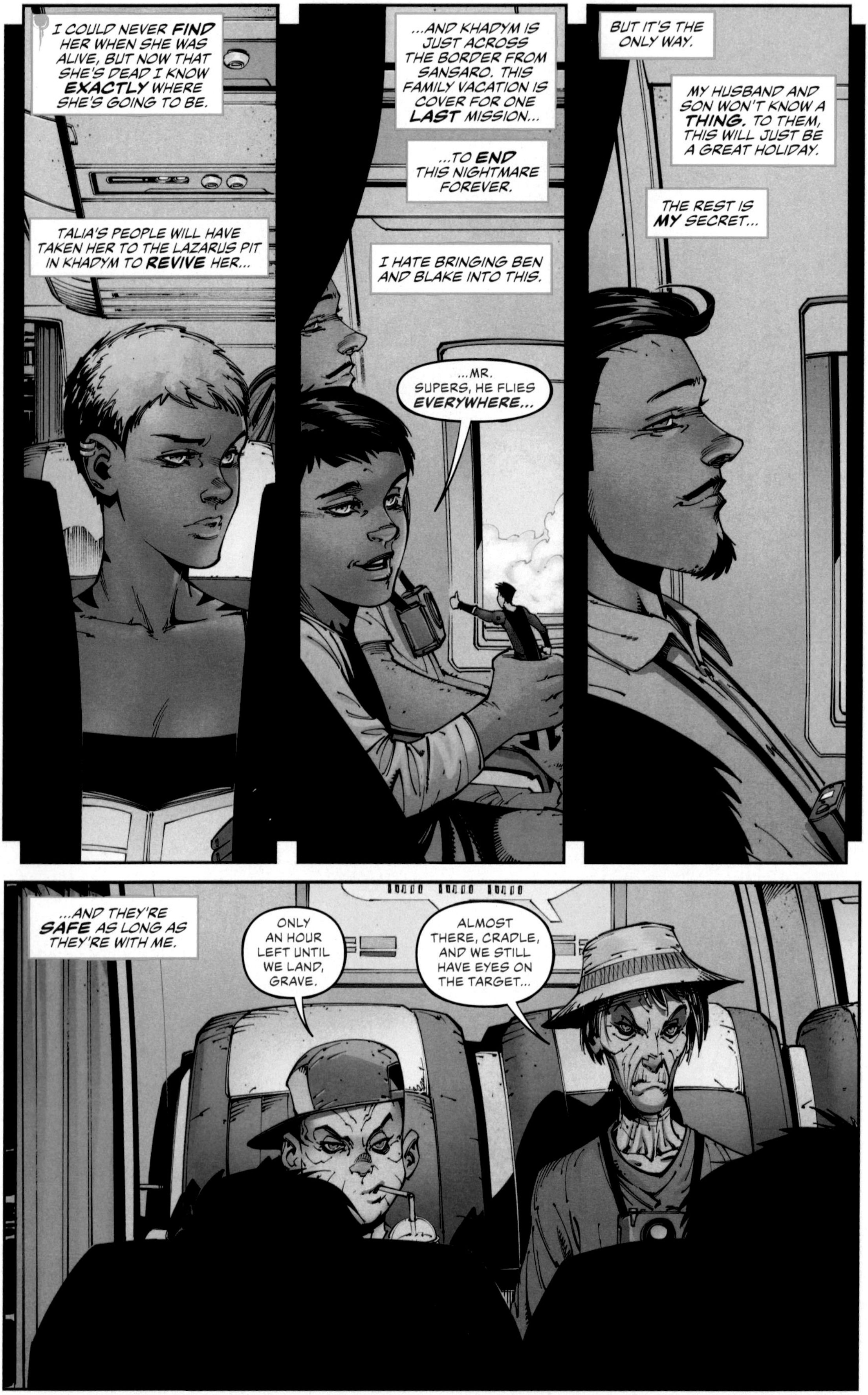

I COULD NEVER FIND HER WHEN SHE WAS ALIVE, BUT NOW THAT SHE'S DEAD I KNOW EXACTLY WHERE SHE'S GOING TO BE.
TALIA'S PEOPLE WILL HAVE TAKEN HER TO THE LAZARUS PIT IN KHADYM TO REVIVE HER...
...AND KHADYM IS JUST ACROSS THE BORDER FROM SANSARO. THIS FAMILY VACATION IS COVER FOR ONE LAST MISSION...
...TO END THIS NIGHTMARE FOREVER.
I HATE BRINGING BEN AND BLAKE INTO THIS.
...MR. SUPERS, HE FLIES EVERYWHERE...
BUT IT'S THE ONLY WAY.
MY HUSBAND AND SON WON'T KNOW A THING. TO THEM, THIS WILL JUST BE A GREAT HOLIDAY.
THE REST IS MY SECRET...
...AND THEY'RE SAFE AS LONG AS THEY'RE WITH ME.
ONLY AN HOUR LEFT UNTIL WE LAND, GRAVE.
ALMOST THERE, CRADLE, AND WE STILL HAVE EYES ON THE TARGET...

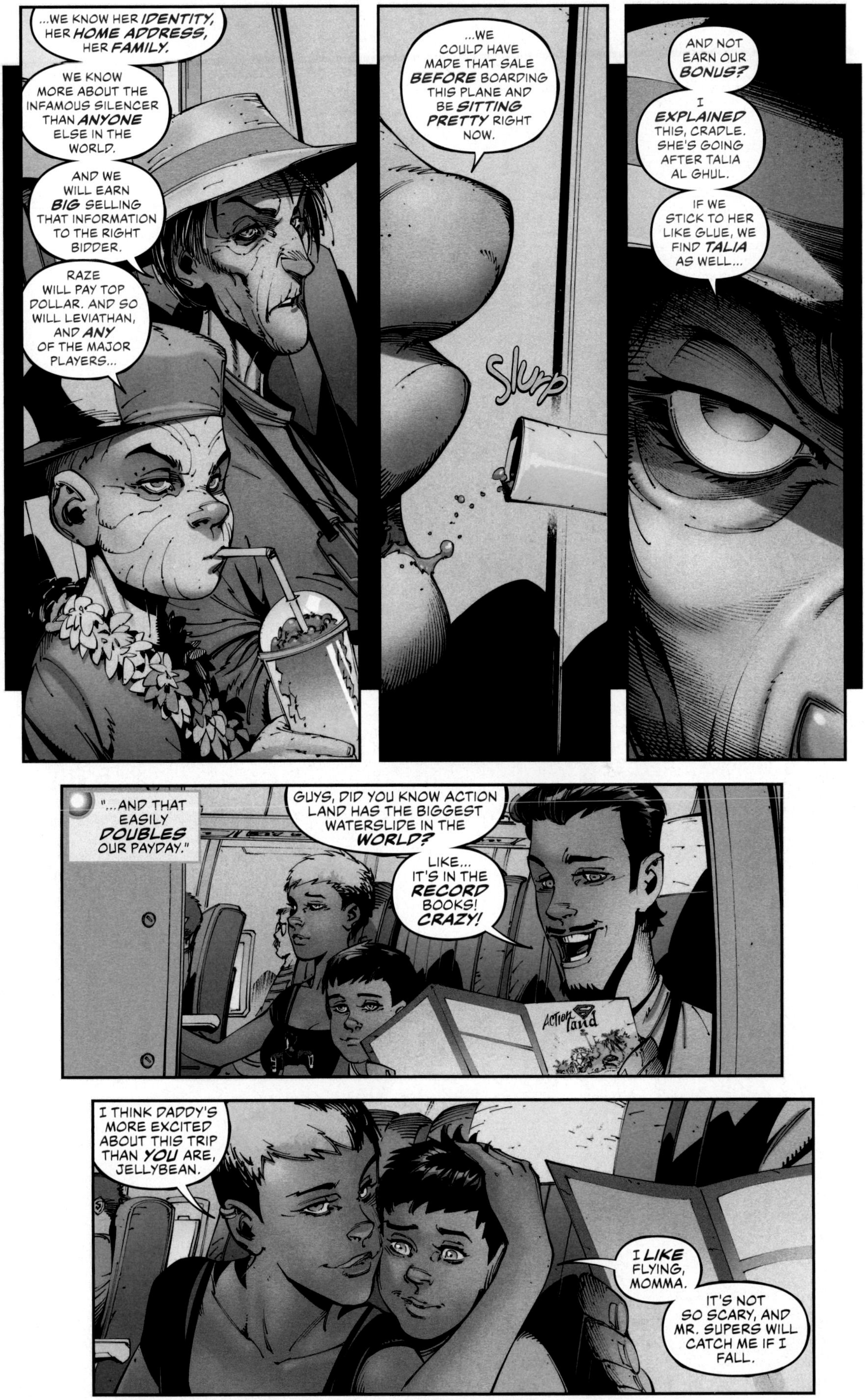
...WE KNOW HER IDENTITY, HER HOME ADDRESS, HER FAMILY.
WE KNOW MORE ABOUT THE INFAMOUS SILENCER THAN ANYONE ELSE IN THE WORLD.
AND WE WILL EARN BIG SELLING THAT INFORMATION TO THE RIGHT BIDDER.
RAZE WILL PAY TOP DOLLAR. AND SO WILL LEVIATHAN, AND ANY OF THE MAJOR PLAYERS...
...WE COULD HAVE MADE THAT SALE BEFORE BOARDING THIS PLANE AND BE SITTING PRETTY RIGHT NOW.
SLURP
AND NOT EARN OUR BONUS?
I EXPLAINED THIS, CRADLE. SHE'S GOING AFTER TALIA AL GHUL.
IF WE STICK TO HER LIKE GLUE, WE FIND TALIA AS WELL...
"...AND THAT EASILY DOUBLES OUR PAYDAY."
GUYS, DID YOU KNOW ACTION LAND HAS THE BIGGEST WATERSLIDE IN THE WORLD?
LIKE... IT'S IN THE RECORD BOOKS! CRAZY!
ACTION LAND
I THINK DADDY'S MORE EXCITED ABOUT THIS TRIP THAN YOU ARE, JELLYBEAN.
I LIKE FLYING, MOMMA.
IT'S NOT SO SCARY, AND MR. SUPERS WILL CATCH ME IF I FALL.

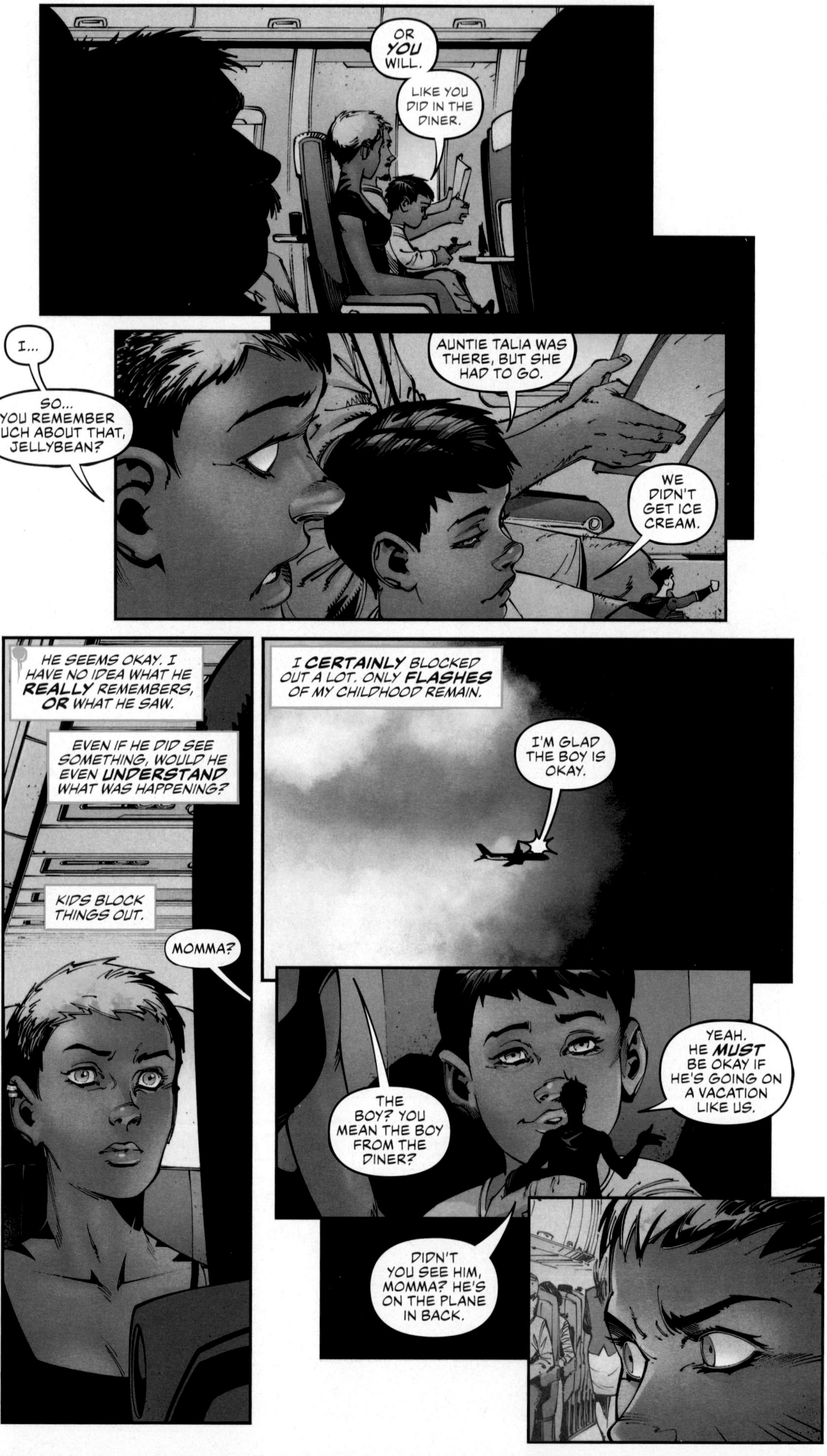

OR YOU WILL.
LIKE YOU DID IN THE DINER.
I...
SO... YOU REMEMBER MUCH ABOUT THAT, JELLYBEAN?
AUNTIE TALIA WAS THERE, BUT SHE HAD TO GO.
WE DIDN'T GET ICE CREAM.
HE SEEMS OKAY. I HAVE NO IDEA WHAT HE REALLY REMEMBERS, OR WHAT HE SAW.
EVEN IF HE DID SEE SOMETHING, WOULD HE EVEN UNDERSTAND WHAT WAS HAPPENING?
KIDS BLOCK THINGS OUT.
MOMMA?
I CERTAINLY BLOCKED OUT A LOT. ONLY FLASHES OF MY CHILDHOOD REMAIN.
I'M GLAD THE BOY IS OKAY.
THE BOY? YOU MEAN THE BOY FROM THE DINER?
YEAH. HE MUST BE OKAY IF HE'S GOING ON A VACATION LIKE US.
DIDN'T YOU SEE HIM, MOMMA? HE'S ON THE PLANE IN BACK.

NO.

MOMMA'S JUST GOT TO VISIT THE TOILET, OKAY?

HOW COULD ANYBODY BE ON--

NO.

CRADLE AND GRAVE.

FREELANCE BODY-MOD ASSASSINS, WEARING THEIR HUMAN FACES. STONE KILLERS.

THIS IS BAD. VERY BAD.

IF THEY'RE HERE, IT CAN MEAN ONLY ONE THING.

THEY'VE MADE ME.

THEY KNOW WHO I AM. THEY KNOW MY FAMILY.

THEY MUST HAVE IDENTIFIED BEN DURING THE CHAOS AT THE DINER.

AND NOW THEY'RE TAILING ME.

KLANK

I HAVE ZERO CHOICE. I NEED TO SILENCE THEM FAST BEFORE THEY GIVE THE GAME AWAY.

BUT FIRST I NEED TO KNOW IF THEY'VE TOLD ANYONE.

I GRAB THE NANODE...

...AND LET IT WEAVE MY GEAR.

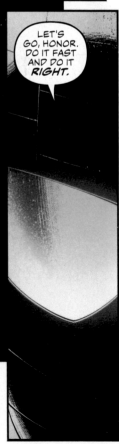

LET'S GO, HONOR. DO IT FAST AND DO IT RIGHT.

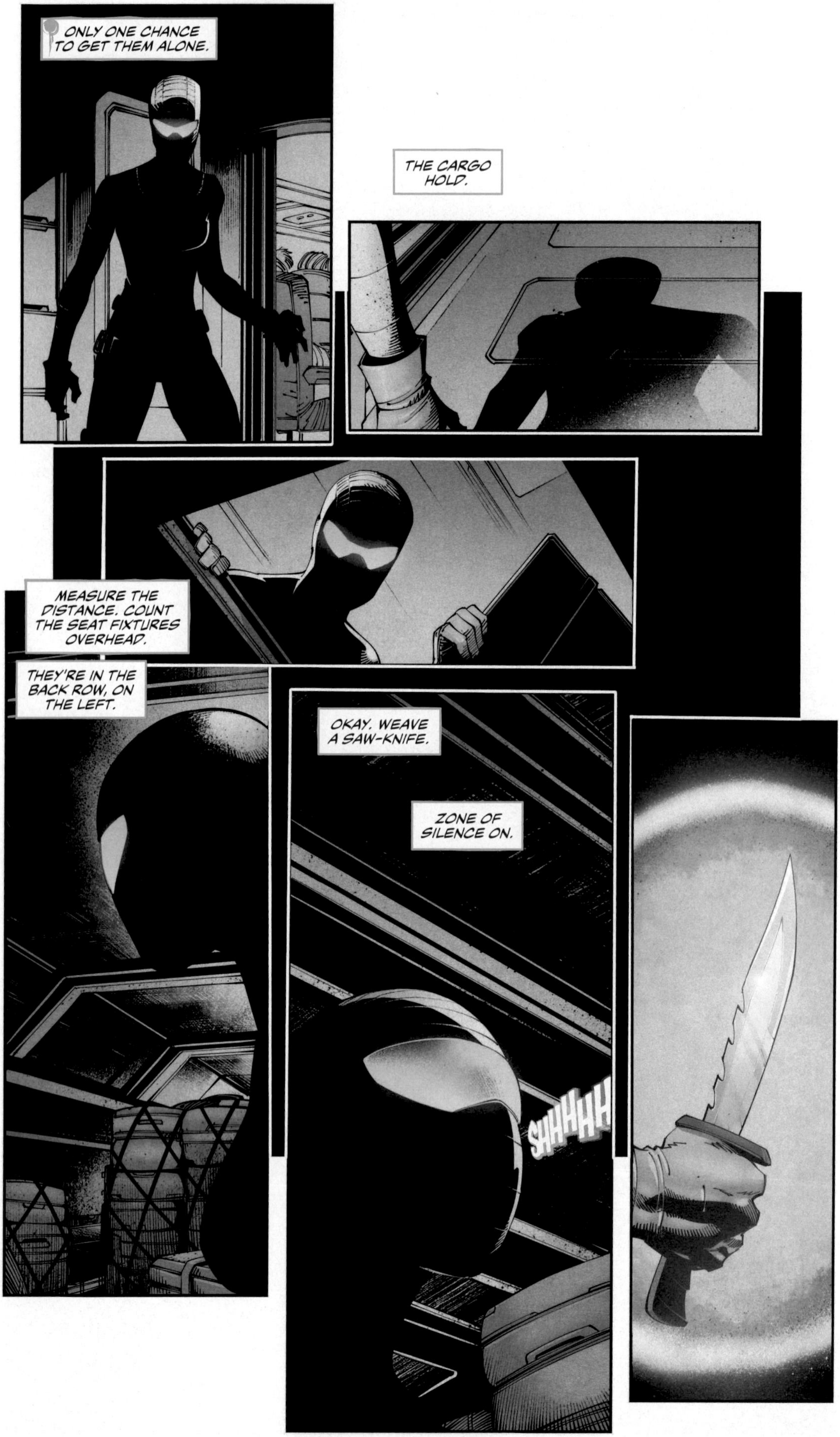
ONLY ONE CHANCE TO GET THEM ALONE.
THE CARGO HOLD.
MEASURE THE DISTANCE. COUNT THE SEAT FIXTURES OVERHEAD.
THEY'RE IN THE BACK ROW, ON THE LEFT.
OKAY. WEAVE A SAW-KNIFE.
ZONE OF SILENCE ON.
SHHHHH

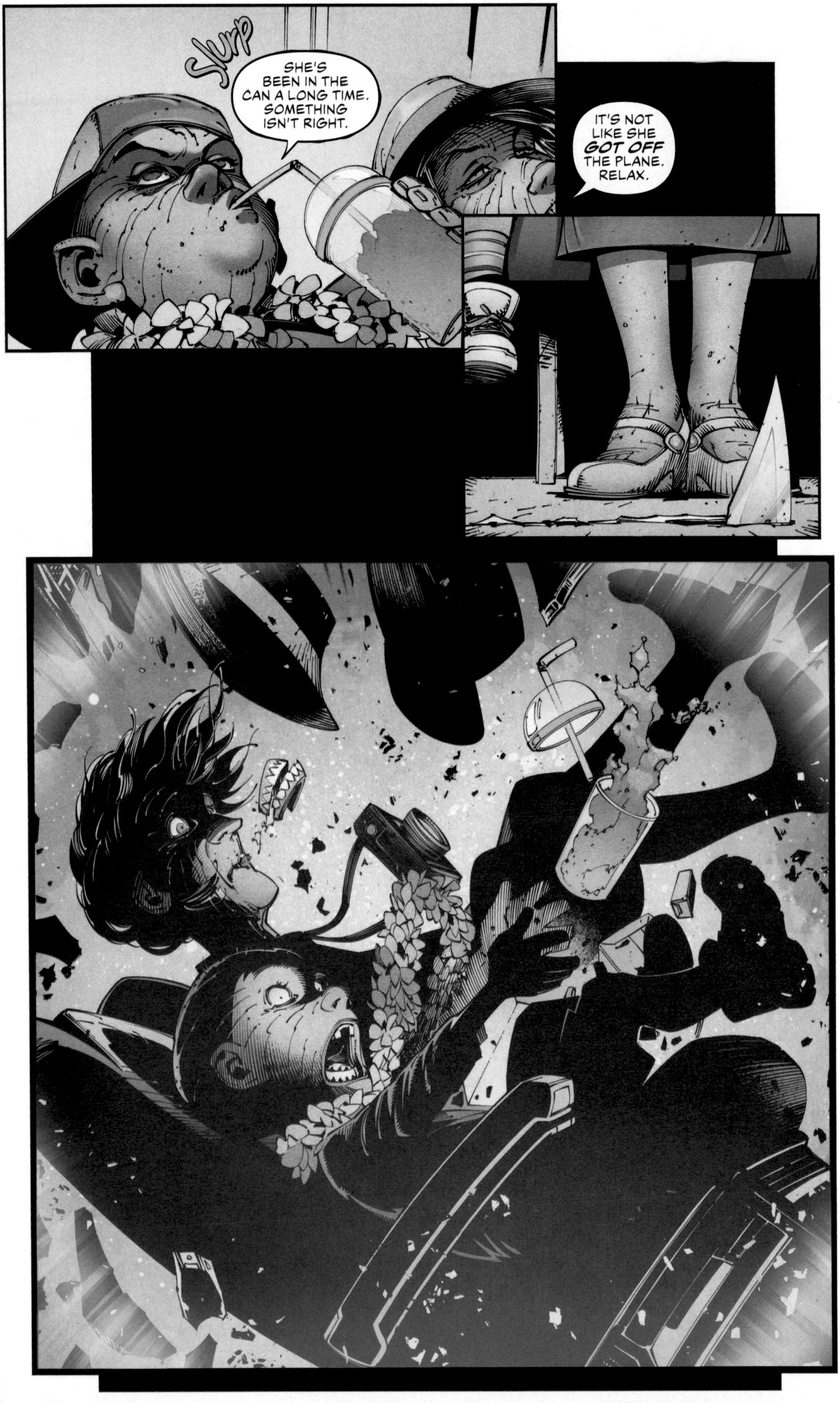
SLURP
SHE'S BEEN IN THE CAN A LONG TIME. SOMETHING ISN'T RIGHT.
IT'S NOT LIKE SHE GOT OFF THE PLANE. RELAX.

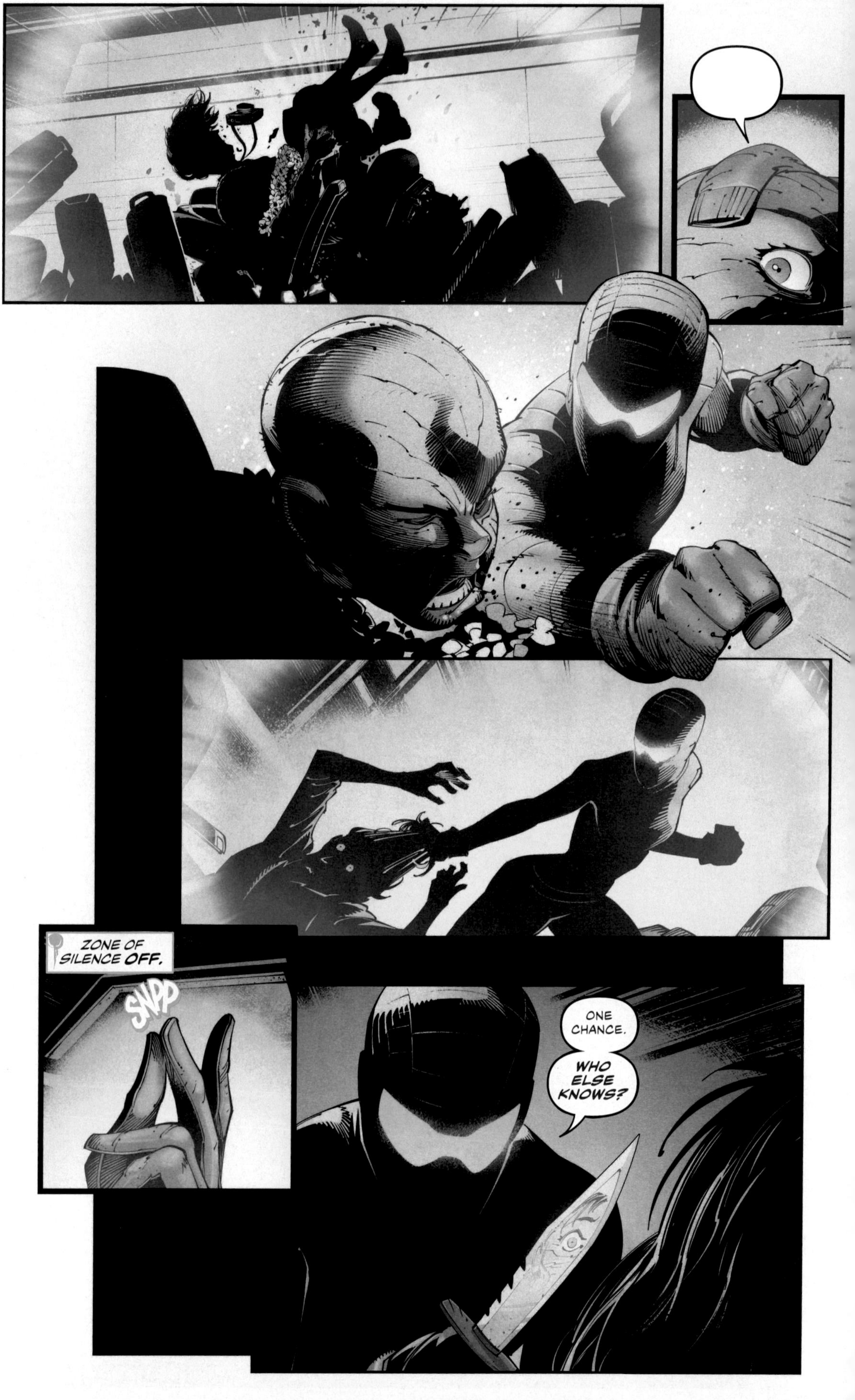
ZONE OF SILENCE OFF.
SNPP
ONE CHANCE.
WHO ELSE KNOWS?

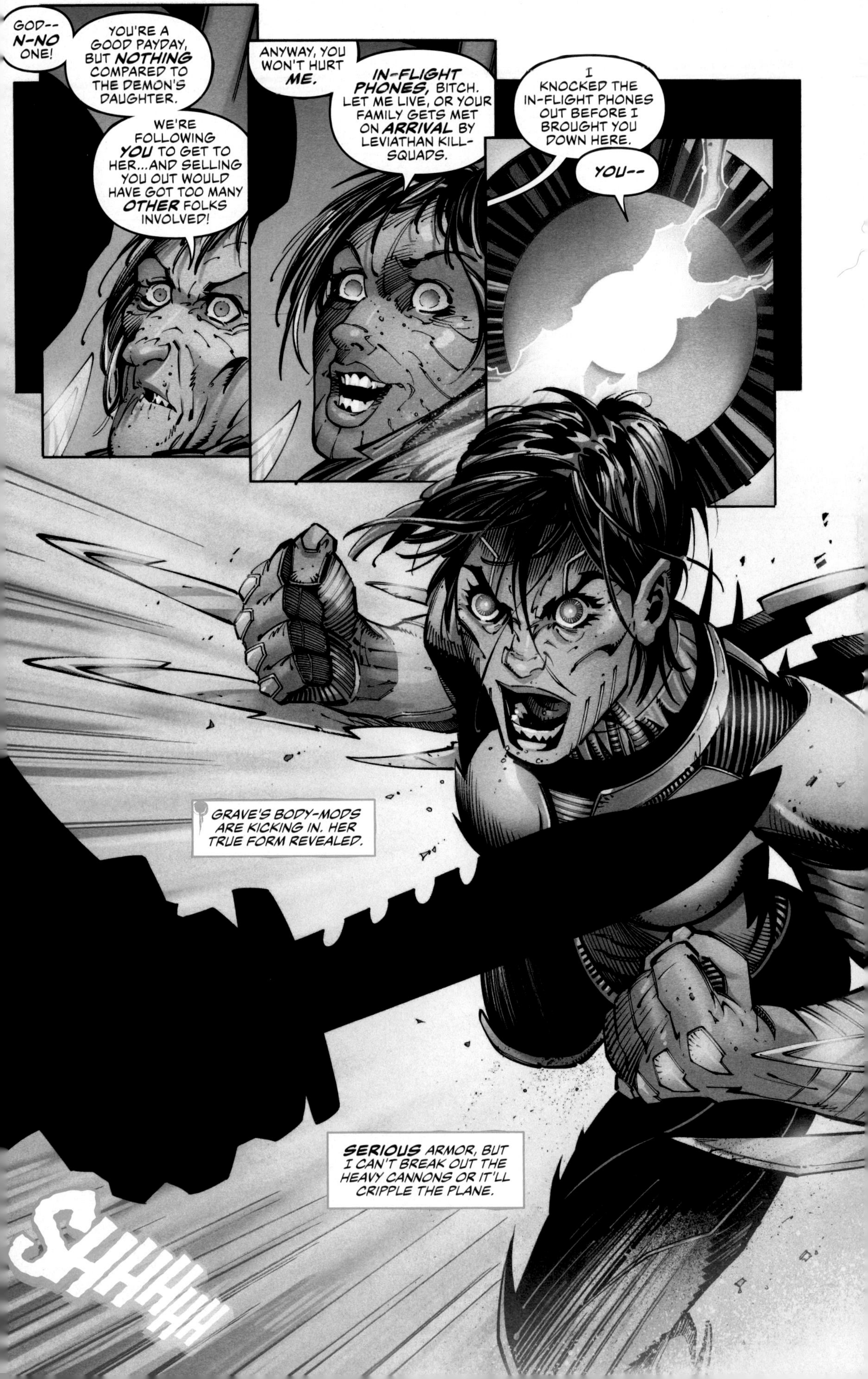
GOD-- N-NO ONE!
YOU'RE A GOOD PAYDAY, BUT NOTHING COMPARED TO THE DEMON'S DAUGHTER.
WE'RE FOLLOWING YOU TO GET TO HER...AND SELLING YOU OUT WOULD HAVE GOT TOO MANY OTHER FOLKS INVOLVED!
ANYWAY, YOU WON'T HURT ME.
IN-FLIGHT PHONES, BITCH. LET ME LIVE, OR YOUR FAMILY GETS MET ON ARRIVAL BY LEVIATHAN KILL-SQUADS.
I KNOCKED THE IN-FLIGHT PHONES OUT BEFORE I BROUGHT YOU DOWN HERE.
YOU--
GRAVE'S BODY-MODS ARE KICKING IN. HER TRUE FORM REVEALED.
SERIOUS ARMOR, BUT I CAN'T BREAK OUT THE HEAVY CANNONS OR IT'LL CRIPPLE THE PLANE.
SHHHH

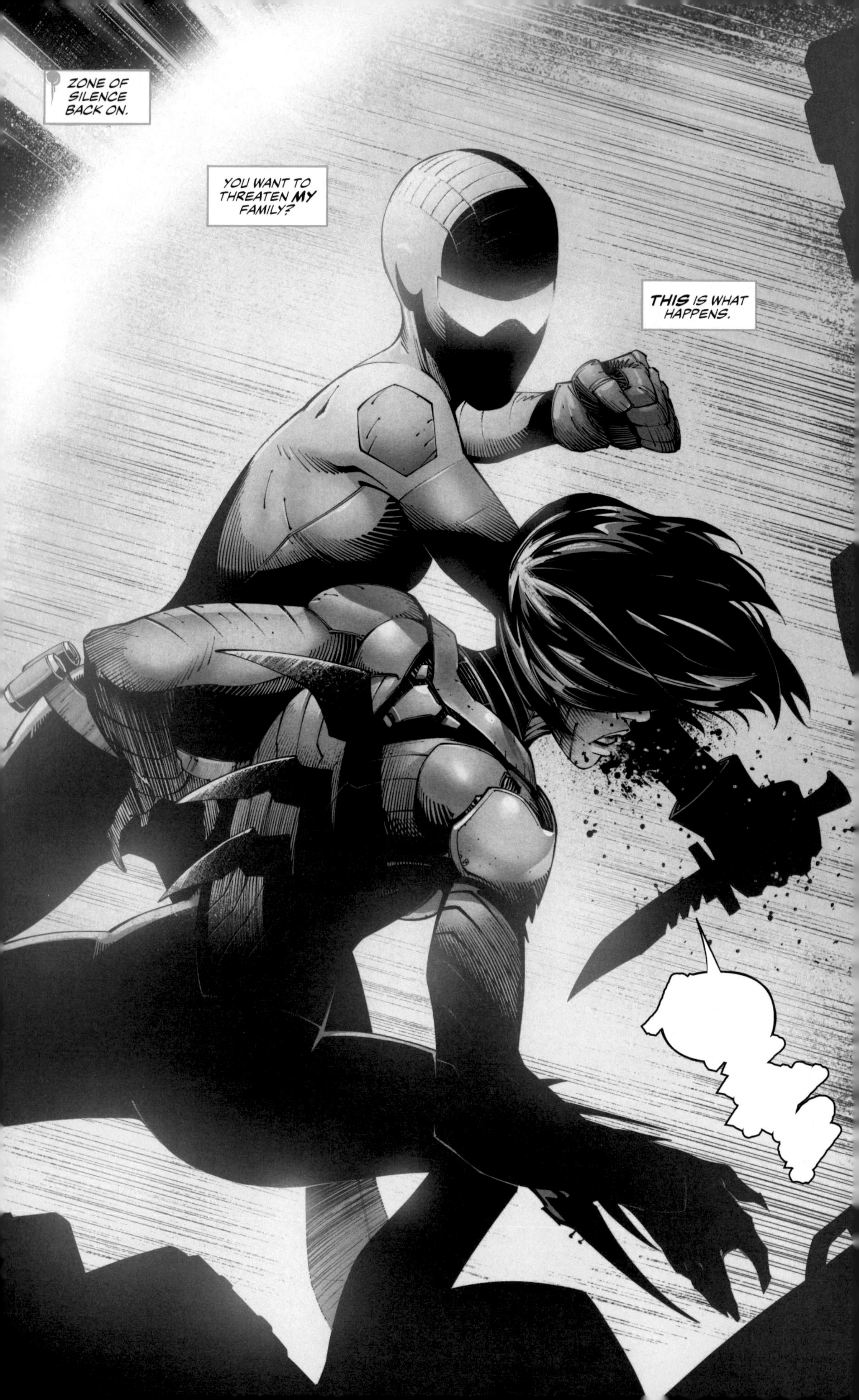
ZONE OF SILENCE BACK ON.
YOU WANT TO THREATEN MY FAMILY?
THIS IS WHAT HAPPENS.

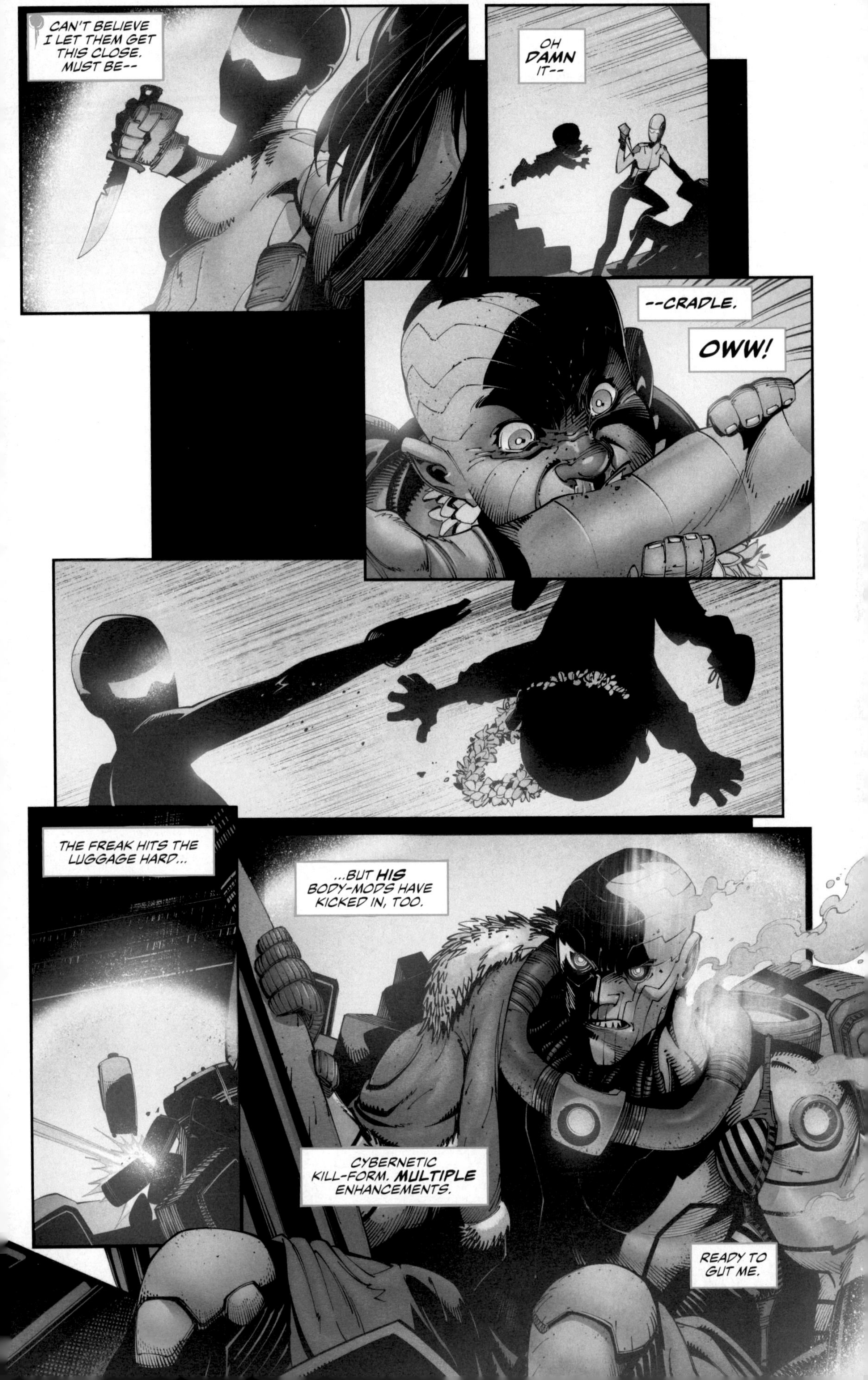
CAN'T BELIEVE I LET THEM GET THIS CLOSE. MUST BE--
OH DAMN IT--
--CRADLE.
OWW!
THE FREAK HITS THE LUGGAGE HARD...
...BUT HIS BODY-MODS HAVE KICKED IN, TOO.
CYBERNETIC KILL-FORM. MULTIPLE ENHANCEMENTS.
READY TO GUT ME.

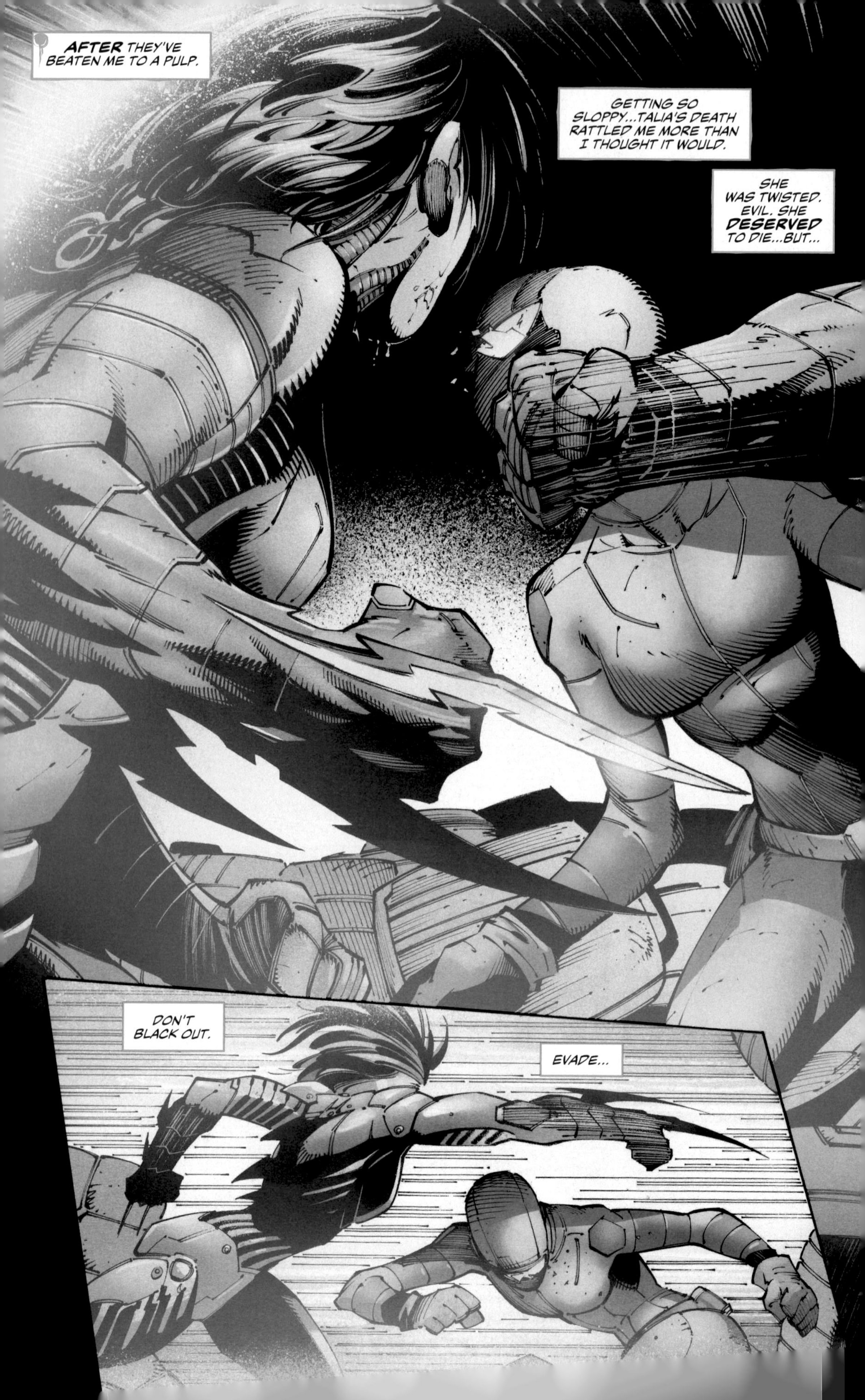
AFTER THEY'VE BEATEN ME TO A PULP.
GETTING SO SLOPPY...TALIA'S DEATH RATTLED ME MORE THAN I THOUGHT IT WOULD.
SHE WAS TWISTED. EVIL. SHE DESERVED TO DIE...BUT...
DON'T BLACK OUT.
EVADE...

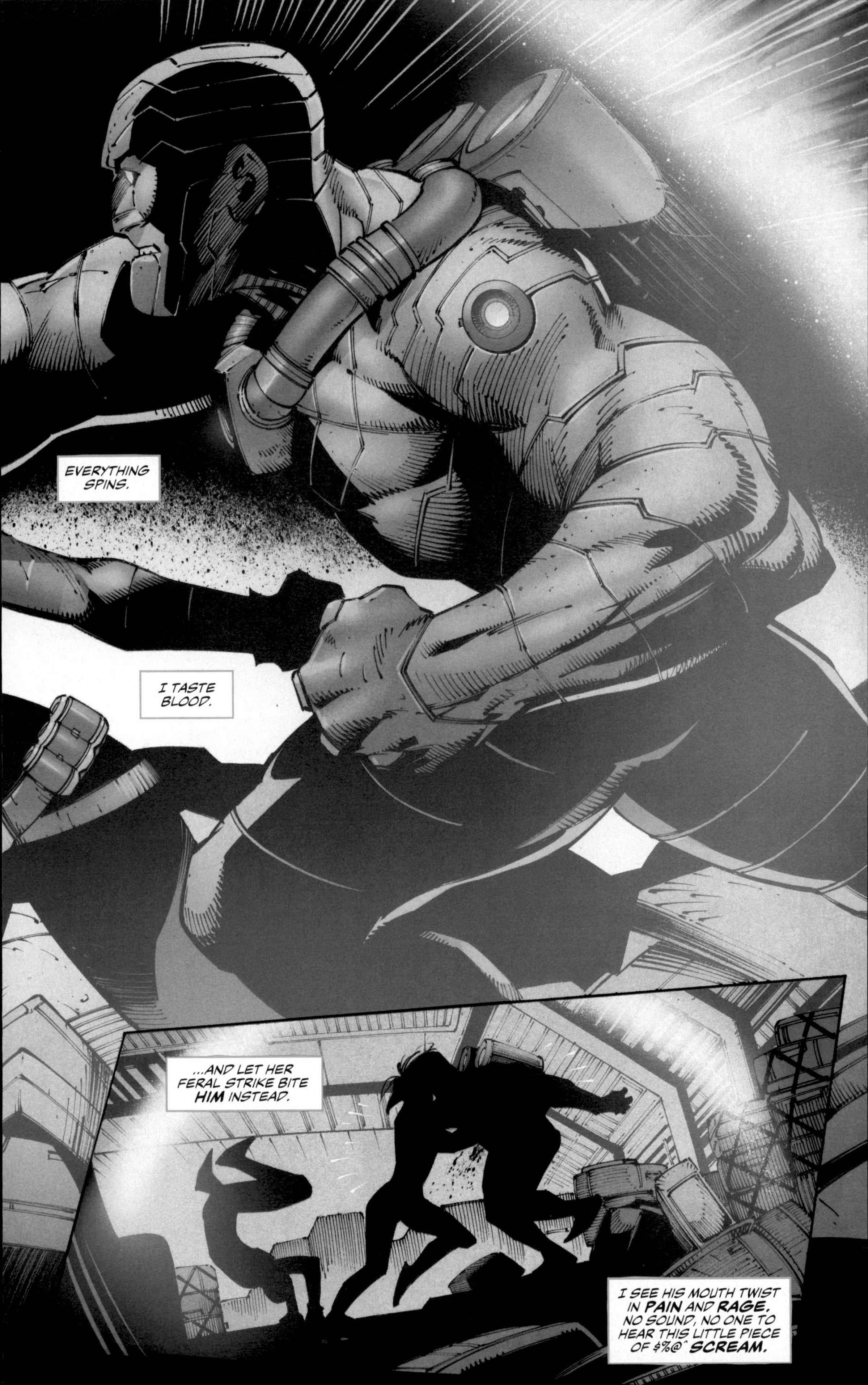
EVERYTHING SPINS.
I TASTE BLOOD.
...AND LET HER FERAL STRIKE BITE HIM INSTEAD.
I SEE HIS MOUTH TWIST IN PAIN AND RAGE. NO SOUND, NO ONE TO HEAR THIS LITTLE PIECE OF $%@^ SCREAM.

ANGER'S GOT THE BETTER OF HIM. HE WANTS GRAVE TO GET OUT OF THE WAY--

OH GOD, THE IDIOT...

...HE'S DEPLOYING HIS BODY CANNONS.

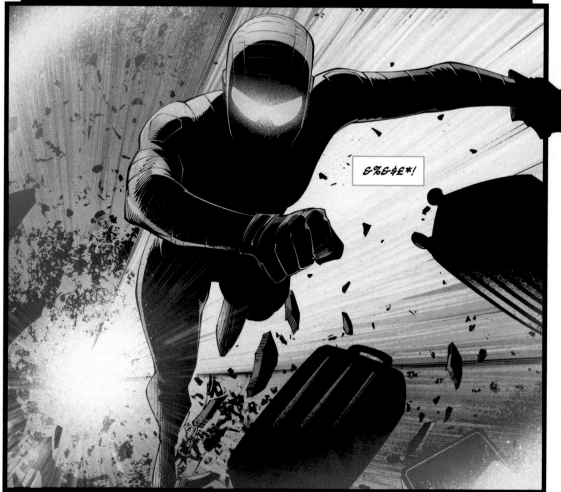

&%&$£*!

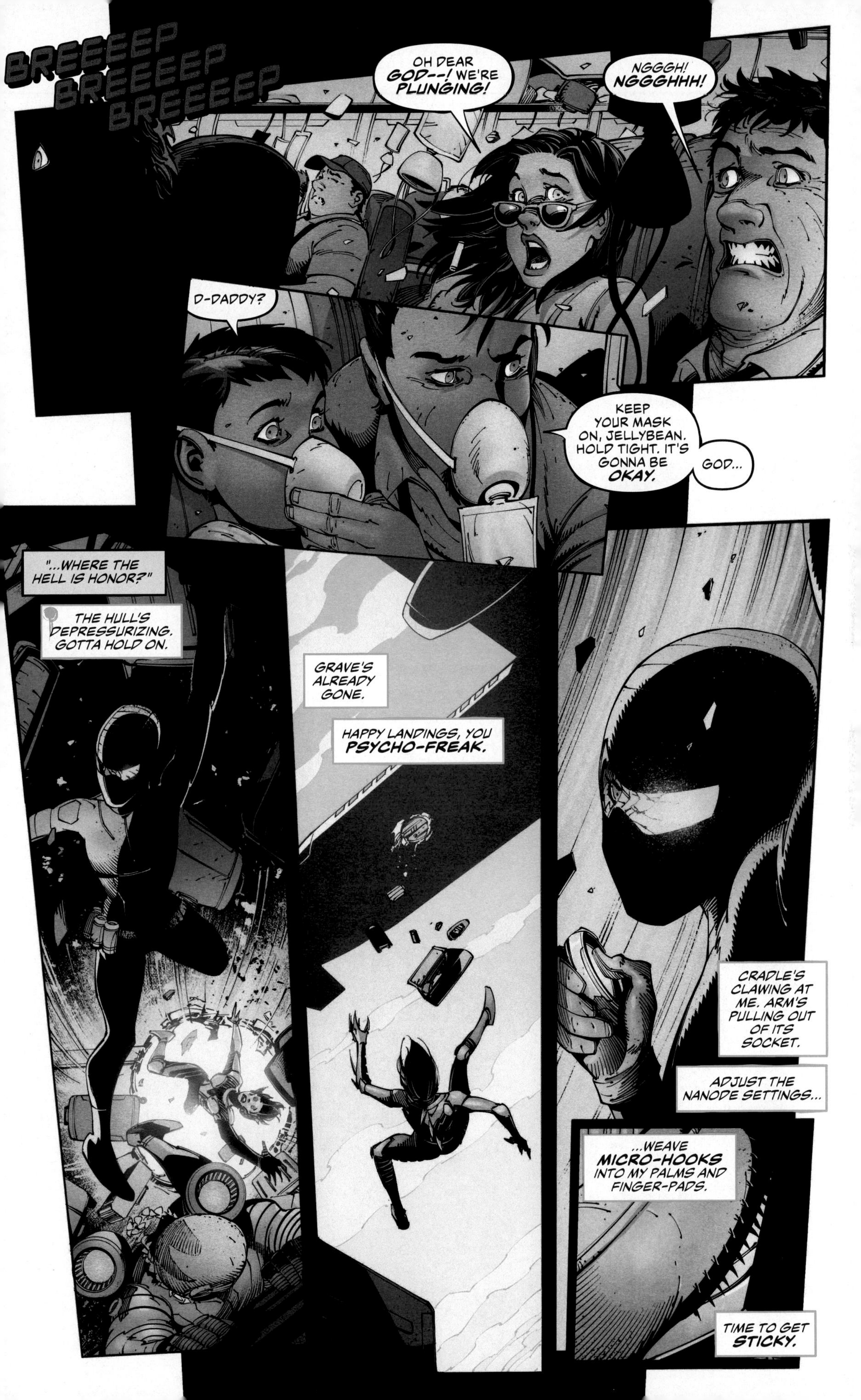
BREEEEEP BREEEEEP BREEEEEP
OH DEAR GOD--! WE'RE PLUNGING!
NGGGH! NGGGHHH!
D-DADDY?
KEEP YOUR MASK ON, JELLYBEAN. HOLD TIGHT. IT'S GONNA BE OKAY.
GOD...
"...WHERE THE HELL IS HONOR?"
THE HULL'S DEPRESSURIZING. GOTTA HOLD ON.
GRAVE'S ALREADY GONE.
HAPPY LANDINGS, YOU PSYCHO-FREAK.
CRADLE'S CLAWING AT ME. ARM'S PULLING OUT OF ITS SOCKET.
ADJUST THE NANODE SETTINGS...
...WEAVE MICRO-HOOKS INTO MY PALMS AND FINGER-PADS.
TIME TO GET STICKY.

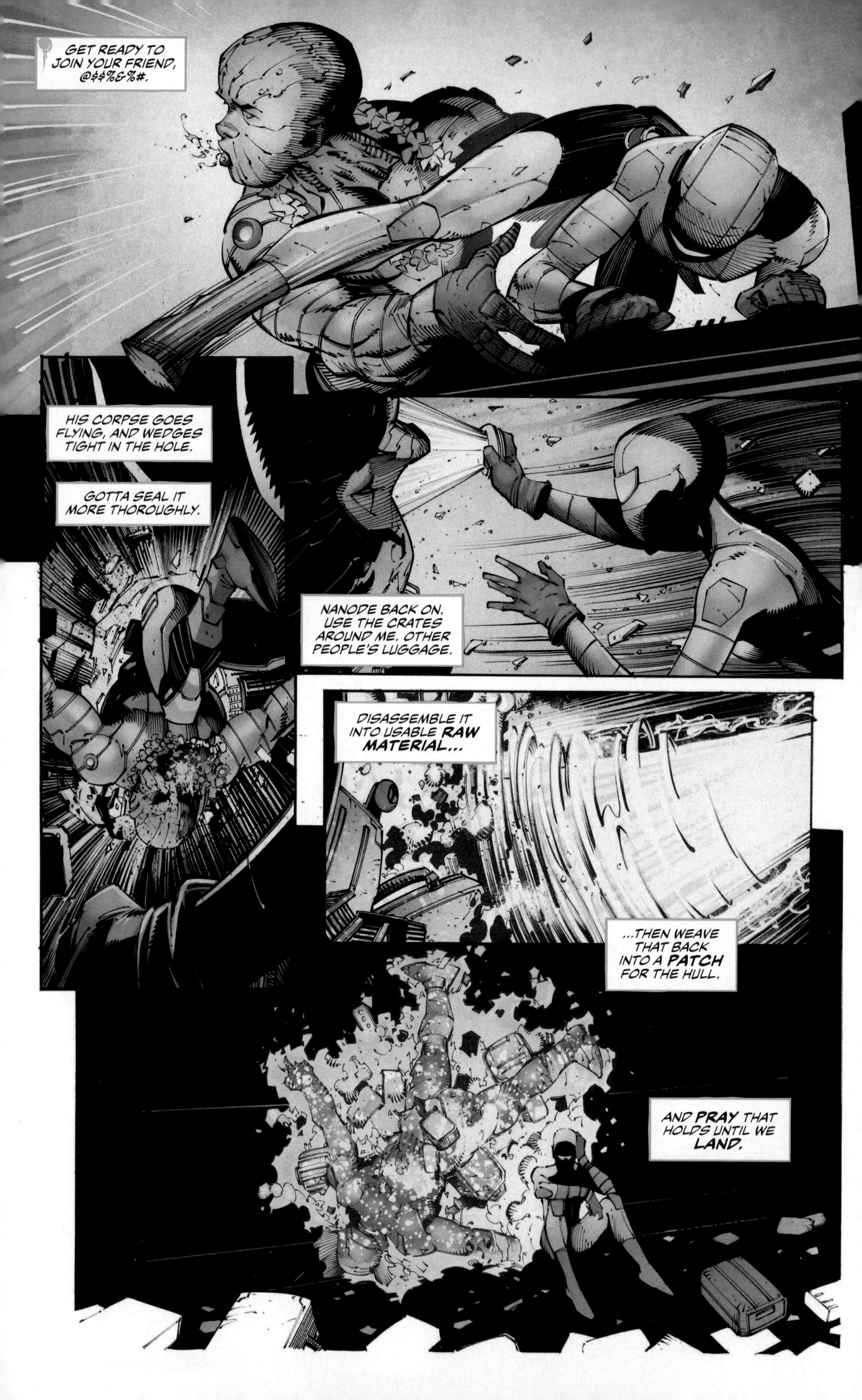
GET READY TO JOIN YOUR FRIEND, @$$%&%#.
HIS CORPSE GOES FLYING, AND WEDGES TIGHT IN THE HOLE.
GOTTA SEAL IT MORE THOROUGHLY.
NANODE BACK ON. USE THE CRATES AROUND ME. OTHER PEOPLE'S LUGGAGE.
DISASSEMBLE IT INTO USABLE RAW MATERIAL...
...THEN WEAVE THAT BACK INTO A PATCH FOR THE HULL.
AND PRAY THAT HOLDS UNTIL WE LAND.

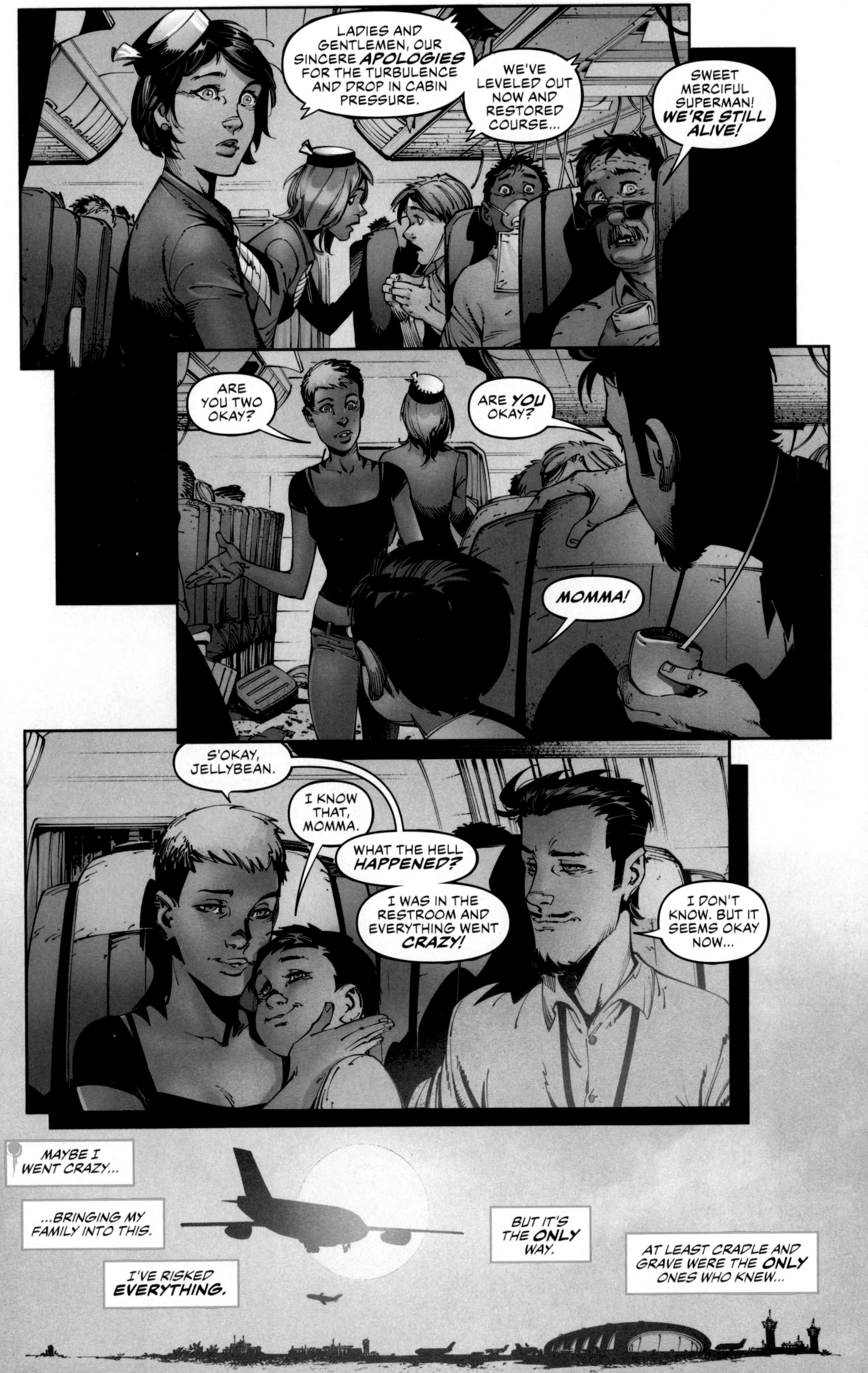
LADIES AND GENTLEMEN, OUR SINCERE APOLOGIES FOR THE TURBULENCE AND DROP IN CABIN PRESSURE.
WE'VE LEVELED OUT NOW AND RESTORED COURSE...
SWEET MERCIFUL SUPERMAN! WE'RE STILL ALIVE!
ARE YOU TWO OKAY?
ARE YOU OKAY?
MOMMA!
S'OKAY, JELLYBEAN.
I KNOW THAT, MOMMA.
WHAT THE HELL HAPPENED?
I WAS IN THE RESTROOM AND EVERYTHING WENT CRAZY!
I DON'T KNOW. BUT IT SEEMS OKAY NOW...
MAYBE I WENT CRAZY...
...BRINGING MY FAMILY INTO THIS.
I'VE RISKED EVERYTHING.
BUT IT'S THE ONLY WAY.
AT LEAST CRADLE AND GRAVE WERE THE ONLY ONES WHO KNEW...

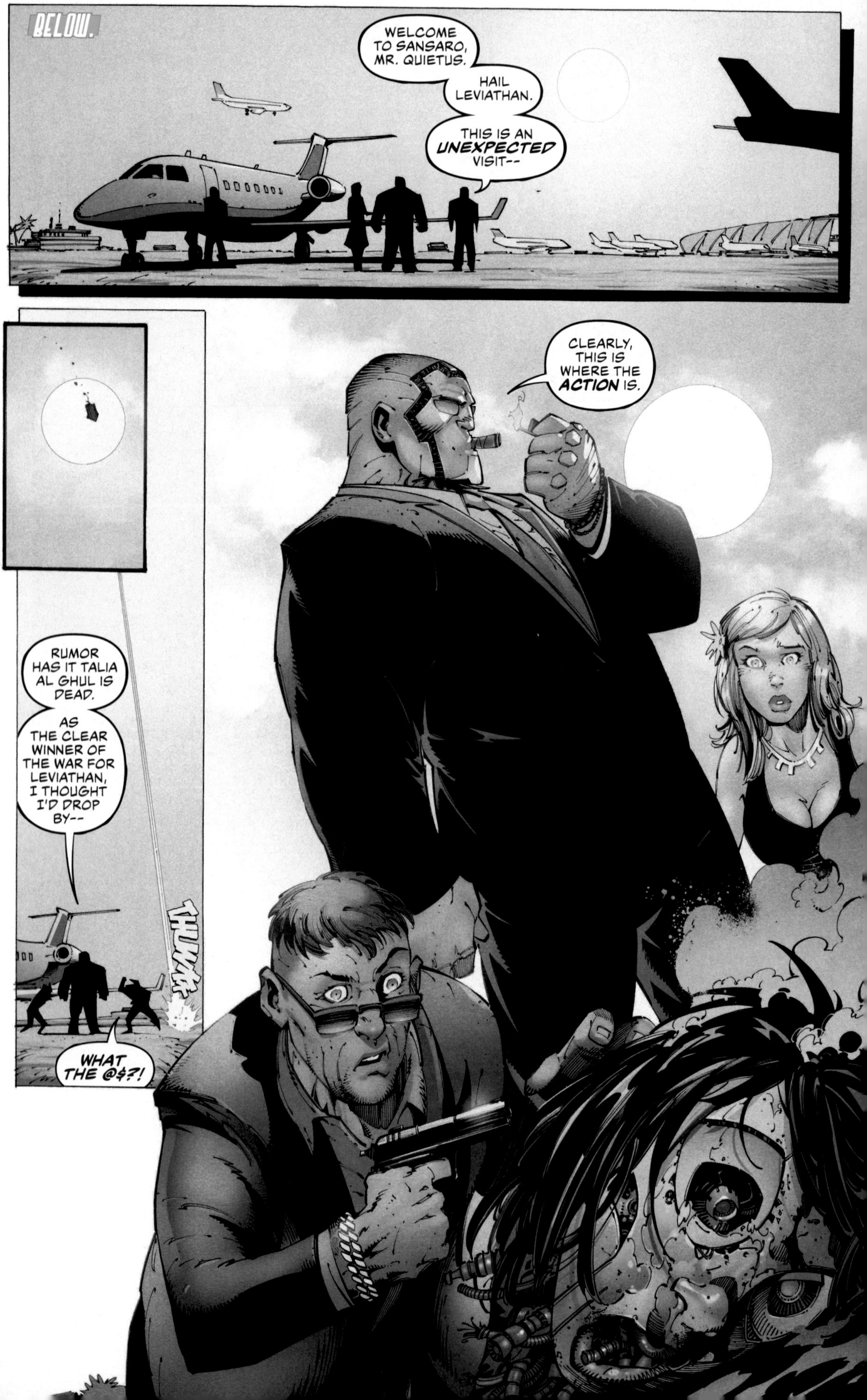
BELOW.
WELCOME TO SANSARO, MR. QUIETUS.
HAIL LEVIATHAN.
THIS IS AN UNEXPECTED VISIT--
CLEARLY, THIS IS WHERE THE ACTION IS.
RUMOR HAS IT TALIA AL GHUL IS DEAD.
AS THE CLEAR WINNER OF THE WAR FOR LEVIATHAN, I THOUGHT I'D DROP BY--
THUWAK
WHAT THE @$?!

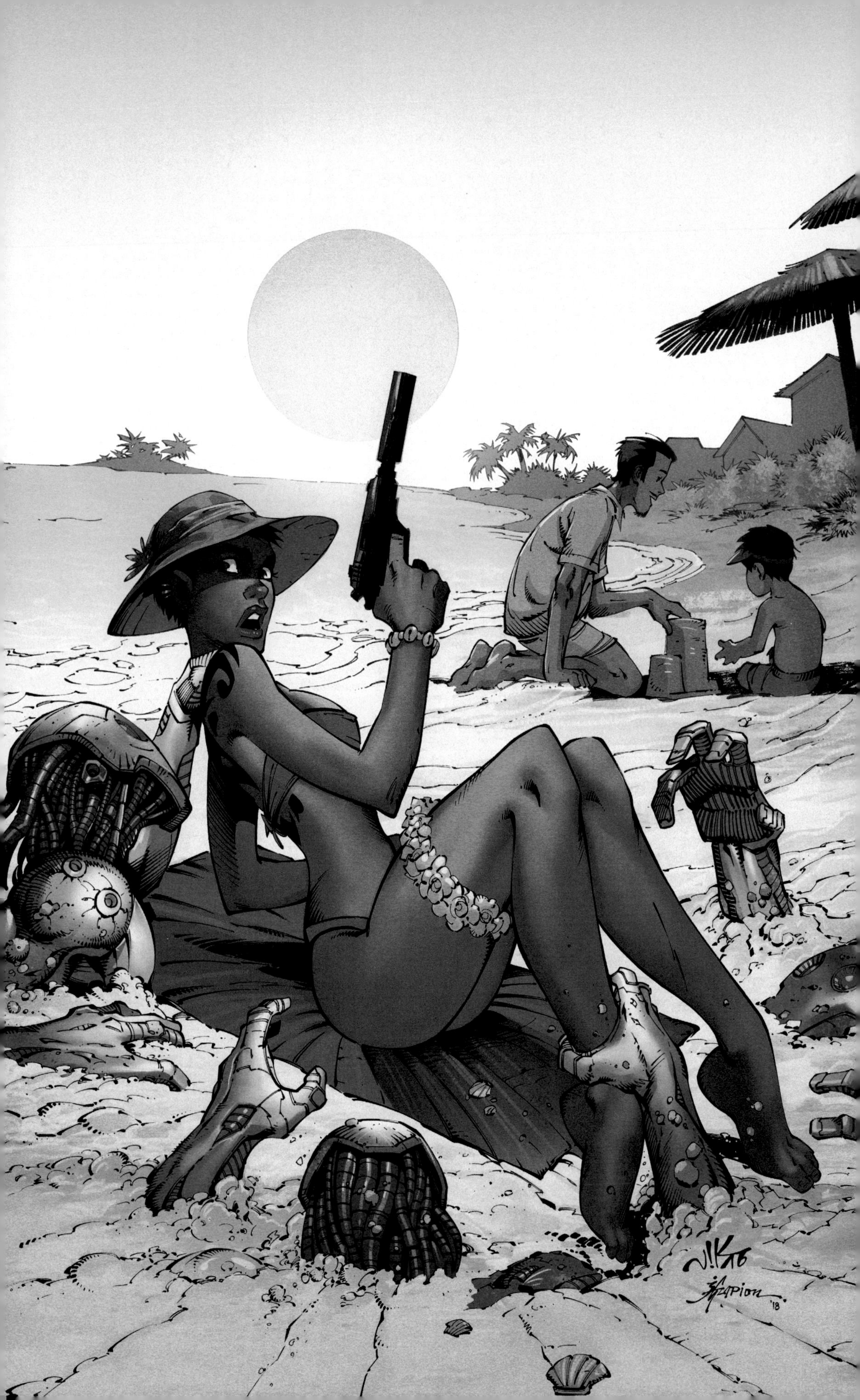

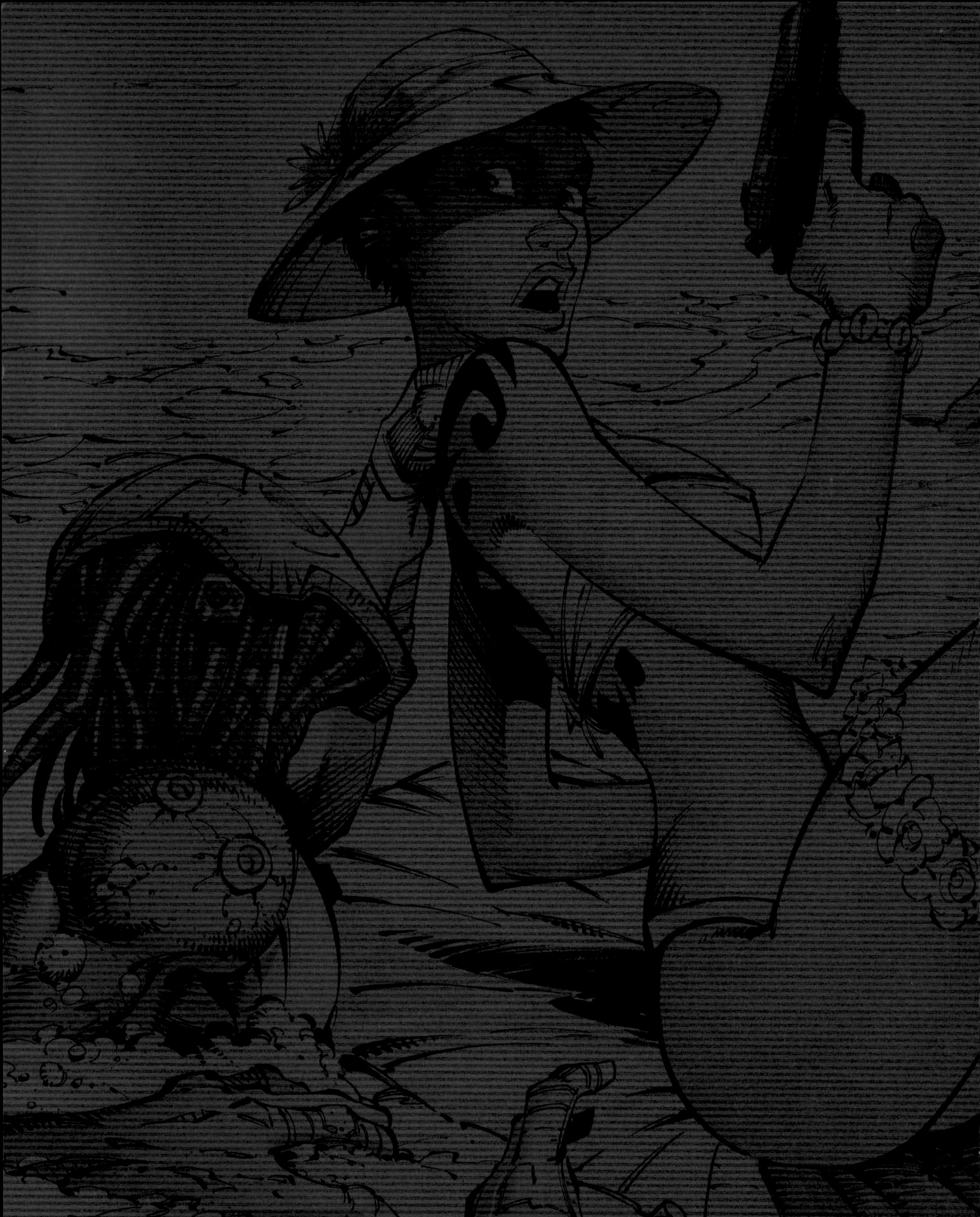

THE SILENCER
#8

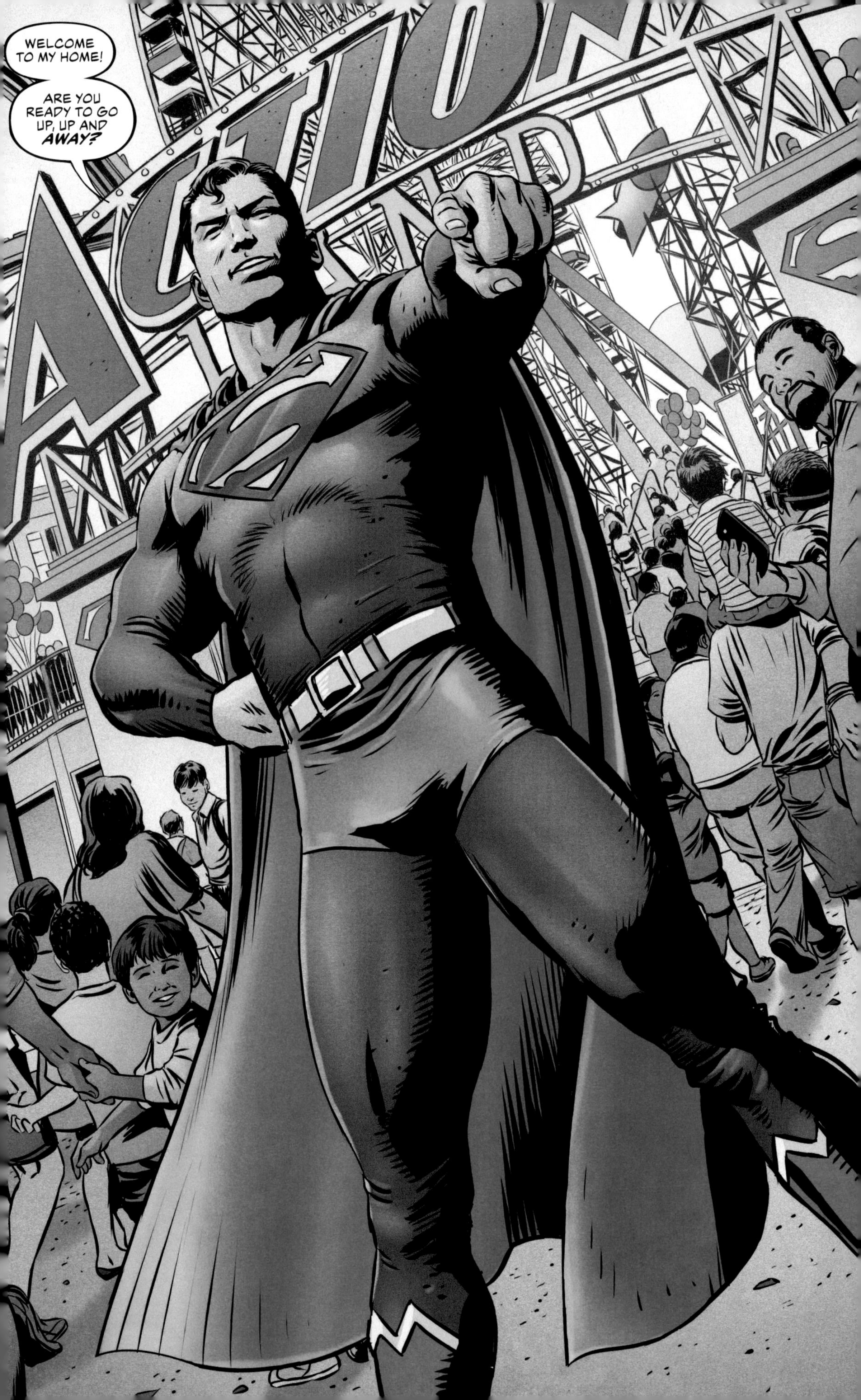
WELCOME TO MY HOME!
ARE YOU READY TO GO UP, UP AND ***AWAY?***

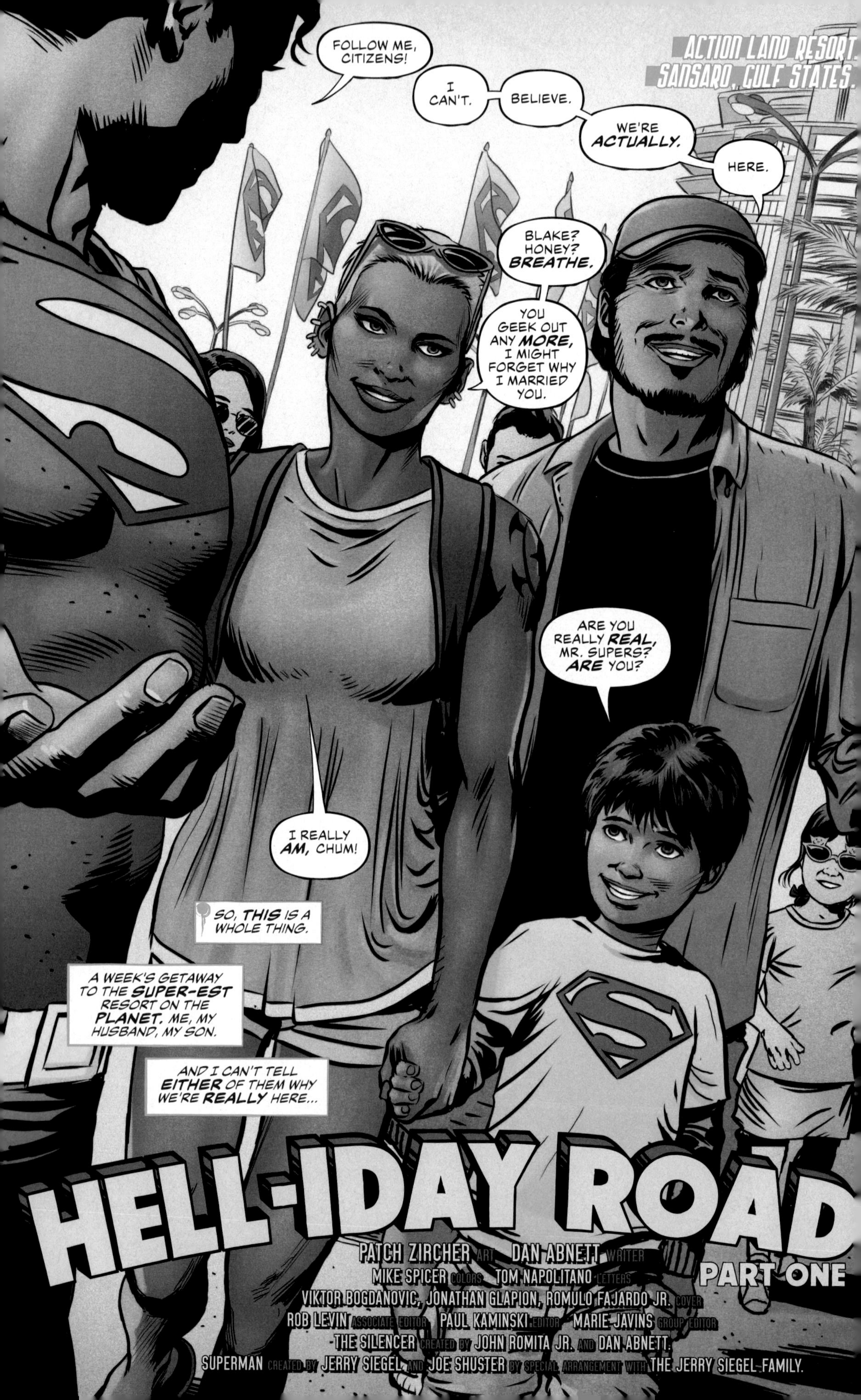
ACTION LAND RESORT. SANSARO, GULF STATES.
FOLLOW ME, CITIZENS!
I CAN'T.
BELIEVE.
WE'RE ACTUALLY.
HERE.
BLAKE? HONEY? BREATHE.
YOU GEEK OUT ANY MORE, I MIGHT FORGET WHY I MARRIED YOU.
ARE YOU REALLY REAL, MR. SUPERS? ARE YOU?
I REALLY AM, CHUM!
SO, THIS IS A WHOLE THING.
A WEEK'S GETAWAY TO THE SUPER-EST RESORT ON THE PLANET. ME, MY HUSBAND, MY SON.
AND I CAN'T TELL EITHER OF THEM WHY WE'RE REALLY HERE...
HELL-IDAY ROAD
PART ONE
PATCH ZIRCHER ART DAN ABNETT WRITER
MIKE SPICER COLORS TOM NAPOLITANO LETTERS
VIKTOR BOGDANOVIC, JONATHAN GLAPION, ROMULO FAJARDO JR. COVER
ROB LEVIN ASSOCIATE EDITOR PAUL KAMINSKI EDITOR MARIE JAVINS GROUP EDITOR
THE SILENCER CREATED BY JOHN ROMITA JR. AND DAN ABNETT.
SUPERMAN CREATED BY JERRY SIEGEL AND JOE SHUSTER BY SPECIAL ARRANGEMENT WITH THE JERRY SIEGEL FAMILY.

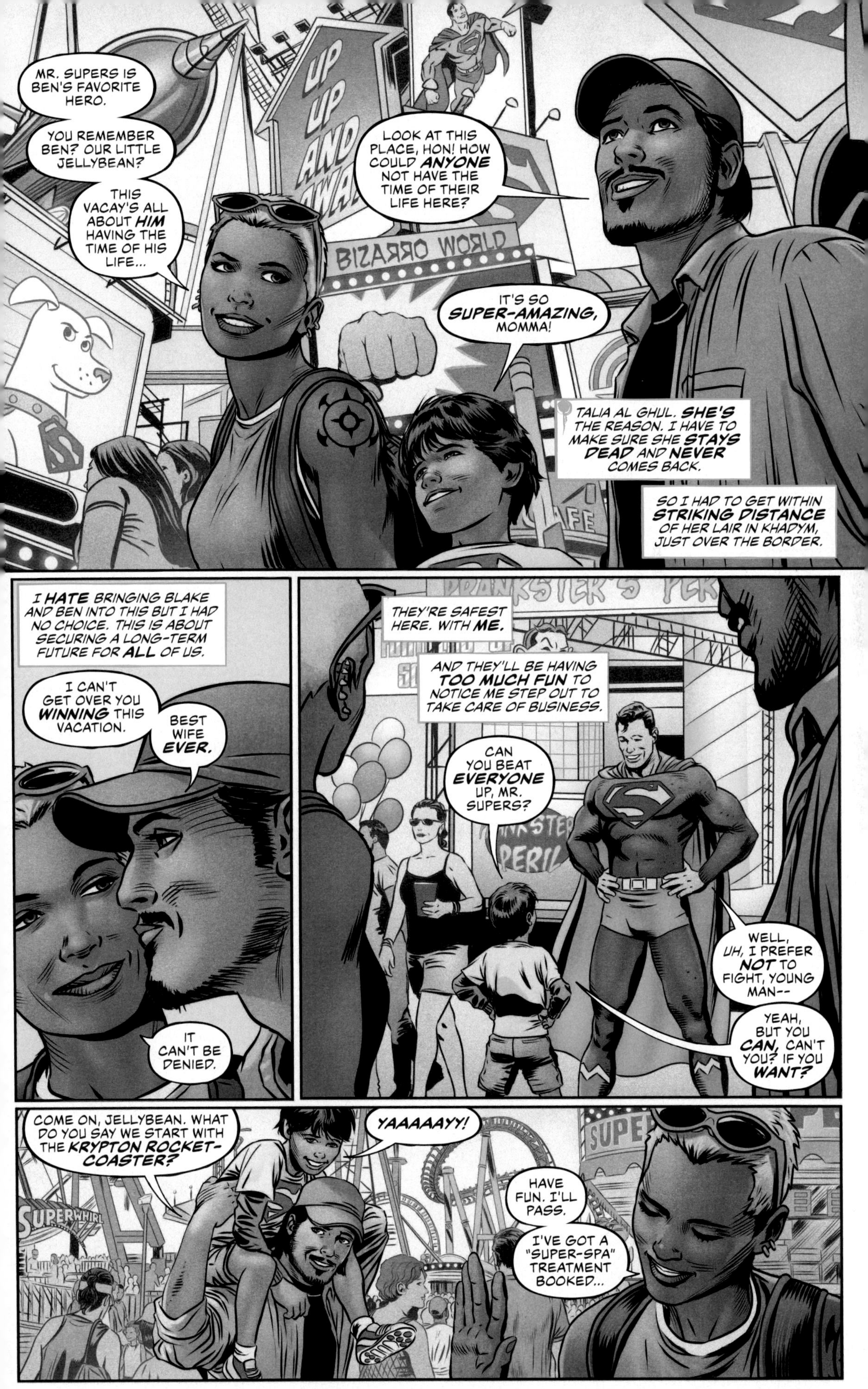
MR. SUPERS IS BEN'S FAVORITE HERO.
YOU REMEMBER BEN? OUR LITTLE JELLYBEAN?
THIS VACAY'S ALL ABOUT HIM HAVING THE TIME OF HIS LIFE...
UP UP AND AWAY
LOOK AT THIS PLACE, HON! HOW COULD ANYONE NOT HAVE THE TIME OF THEIR LIFE HERE?
BIZARRO WORLD
IT'S SO SUPER-AMAZING, MOMMA!
TALIA AL GHUL. SHE'S THE REASON. I HAVE TO MAKE SURE SHE STAYS DEAD AND NEVER COMES BACK.
SO I HAD TO GET WITHIN STRIKING DISTANCE OF HER LAIR IN KHADYM, JUST OVER THE BORDER.
I HATE BRINGING BLAKE AND BEN INTO THIS BUT I HAD NO CHOICE. THIS IS ABOUT SECURING A LONG-TERM FUTURE FOR ALL OF US.
I CAN'T GET OVER YOU WINNING THIS VACATION.
BEST WIFE EVER.
IT CAN'T BE DENIED.
THEY'RE SAFEST HERE. WITH ME.
AND THEY'LL BE HAVING TOO MUCH FUN TO NOTICE ME STEP OUT TO TAKE CARE OF BUSINESS.
CAN YOU BEAT EVERYONE UP, MR. SUPERS?
WELL, UH, I PREFER NOT TO FIGHT, YOUNG MAN--
YEAH, BUT YOU CAN, CAN'T YOU? IF YOU WANT?
COME ON, JELLYBEAN. WHAT DO YOU SAY WE START WITH THE KRYPTON ROCKET-COASTER?
YAAAAAYY!
SUPERWHIRL
HAVE FUN. I'LL PASS.
I'VE GOT A "SUPER-SPA" TREATMENT BOOKED...

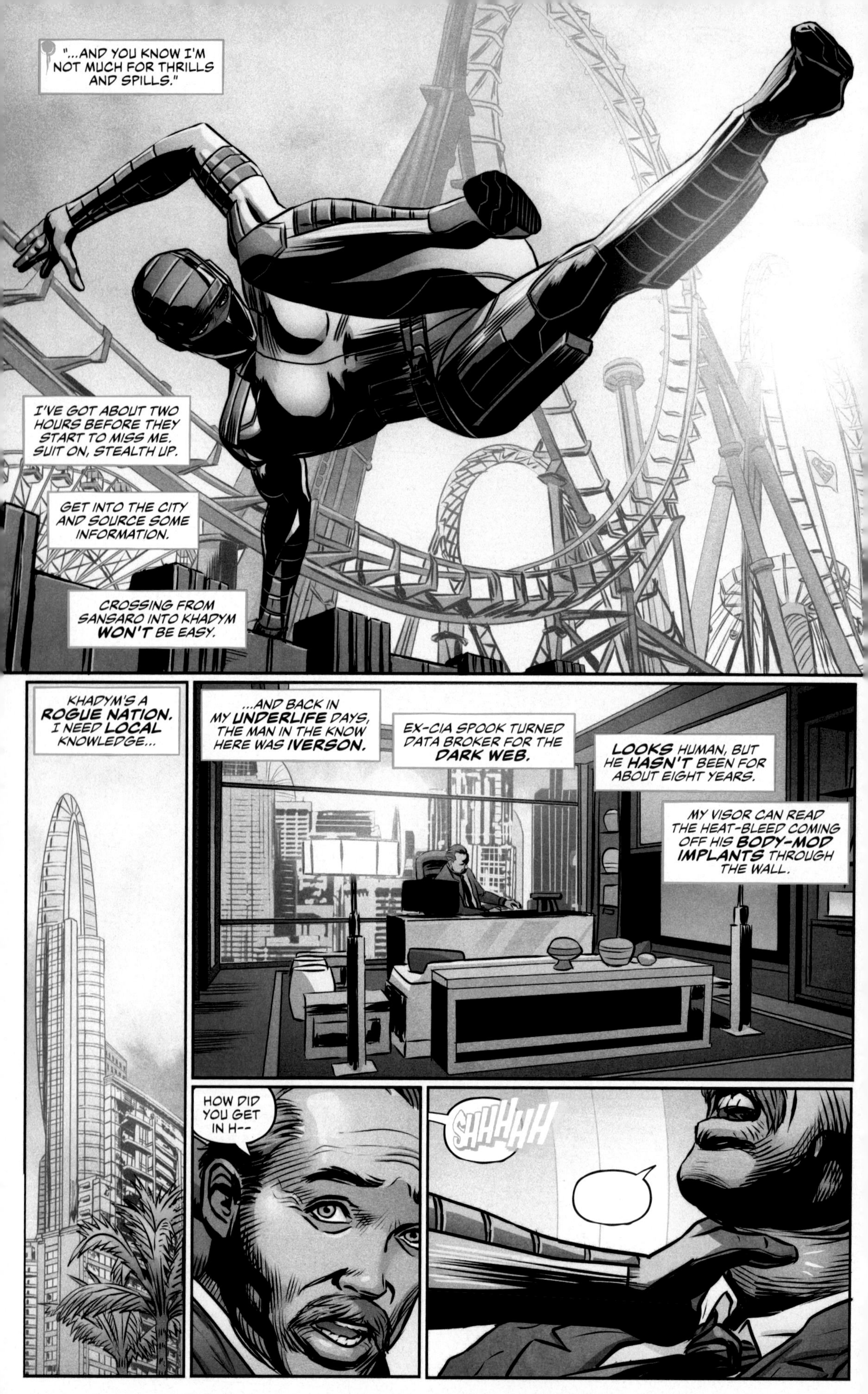
"...AND YOU KNOW I'M NOT MUCH FOR THRILLS AND SPILLS."
I'VE GOT ABOUT TWO HOURS BEFORE THEY START TO MISS ME. SUIT ON, STEALTH UP.
GET INTO THE CITY AND SOURCE SOME INFORMATION.
CROSSING FROM SANSARO INTO KHADYM **WON'T** BE EASY.
KHADYM'S A **ROGUE NATION.** I NEED **LOCAL** KNOWLEDGE...
...AND BACK IN MY **UNDERLIFE** DAYS, THE MAN IN THE KNOW HERE WAS **IVERSON.**
EX-CIA SPOOK TURNED DATA BROKER FOR THE **DARK WEB.**
LOOKS HUMAN, BUT HE **HASN'T** BEEN FOR ABOUT EIGHT YEARS.
MY VISOR CAN READ THE HEAT-BLEED COMING OFF HIS **BODY-MOD IMPLANTS** THROUGH THE WALL.
HOW DID YOU GET IN H--
SHHHHH

GOD, IVERSON. I THINK **WATCHING** YOU MIME A PLEA FOR YOUR LIFE IS WORSE THAN LETTING YOU **SCREAM.**

IT'S BEEN A LONG TIME.

SNAP

WH-WHAT DO YOU **WANT?** WHAT ARE YOU **DOING** HERE? I DIDN'T KNOW THE SILENCER WAS **ACTIVE** AGAIN!

D-DID LEVIATHAN SEND YOU TO **KILL** ME?

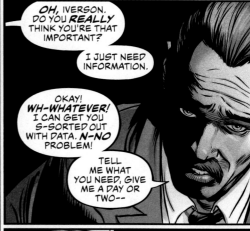

OH, IVERSON. DO YOU **REALLY** THINK YOU'RE THAT IMPORTANT?

I JUST NEED INFORMATION.

OKAY! **WH-WHATEVER!** I CAN GET YOU S-SORTED OUT WITH DATA. **N-NO** PROBLEM!

TELL ME WHAT YOU NEED, GIVE ME A DAY OR TWO--

UH-UH. FAST. **TIGHT CLOCK.**

WHY? WHAT'S SO URGENT? IS THERE SOMETHING I SHOULD--

NO.

I'M NOT GOING TO GIVE HIM ANYTHING...

...AND I'M **CERTAINLY** NOT GOING TO TELL HIM I NEED TO GET BACK TO MY FAMILY.

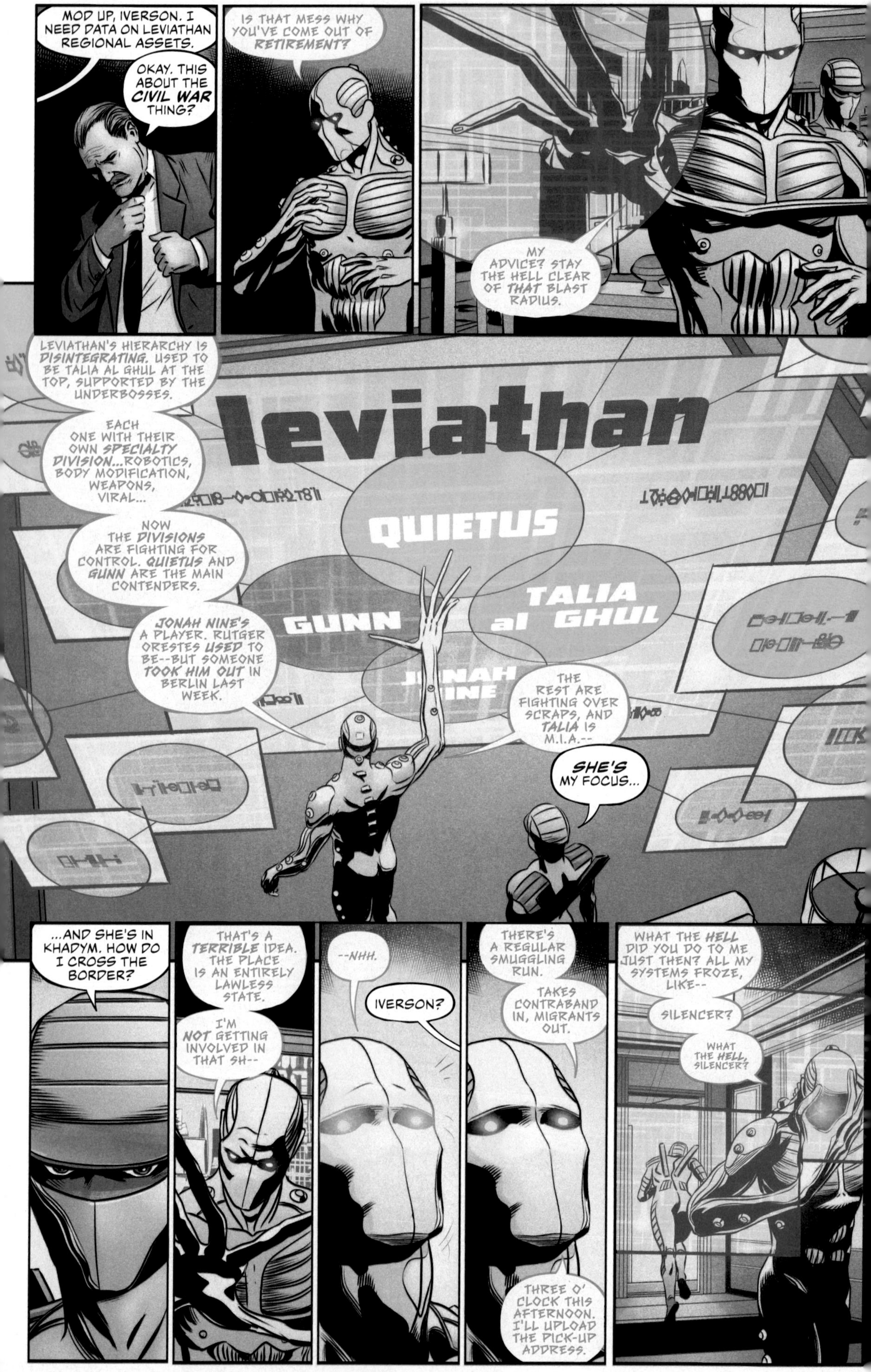
MOD UP, IVERSON. I NEED DATA ON LEVIATHAN REGIONAL ASSETS.
OKAY. THIS ABOUT THE CIVIL WAR THING?
IS THAT MESS WHY YOU'VE COME OUT OF RETIREMENT?
MY ADVICE? STAY THE HELL CLEAR OF THAT BLAST RADIUS.
LEVIATHAN'S HIERARCHY IS DISINTEGRATING. USED TO BE TALIA AL GHUL AT THE TOP, SUPPORTED BY THE UNDERBOSSES.
EACH ONE WITH THEIR OWN SPECIALTY DIVISION...ROBOTICS, BODY MODIFICATION, WEAPONS, VIRAL...
leviathan
QUIETUS
GUNN
TALIA al GHUL
NOW THE DIVISIONS ARE FIGHTING FOR CONTROL. QUIETUS AND GUNN ARE THE MAIN CONTENDERS.
JONAH NINE'S A PLAYER. RUTGER ORESTES USED TO BE--BUT SOMEONE TOOK HIM OUT IN BERLIN LAST WEEK.
THE REST ARE FIGHTING OVER SCRAPS, AND TALIA IS M.I.A.--
SHE'S MY FOCUS...
...AND SHE'S IN KHADYM. HOW DO I CROSS THE BORDER?
THAT'S A TERRIBLE IDEA. THE PLACE IS AN ENTIRELY LAWLESS STATE.
I'M NOT GETTING INVOLVED IN THAT SH--
--NHH.
IVERSON?
THERE'S A REGULAR SMUGGLING RUN.
TAKES CONTRABAND IN, MIGRANTS OUT.
THREE O' CLOCK THIS AFTERNOON. I'LL UPLOAD THE PICK-UP ADDRESS.
WHAT THE HELL DID YOU DO TO ME JUST THEN? ALL MY SYSTEMS FROZE, LIKE--
SILENCER?
WHAT THE HELL, SILENCER?

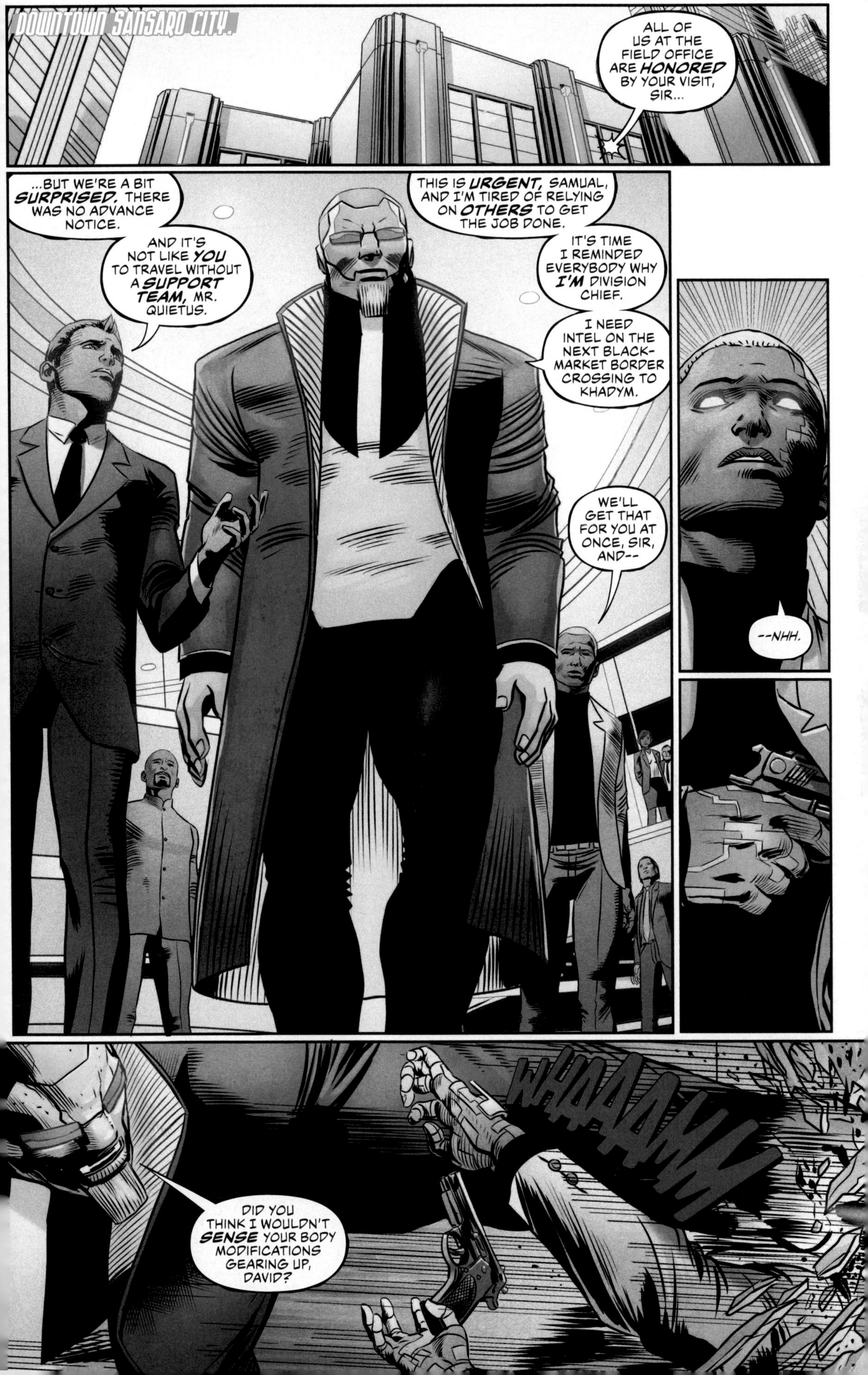
DOWNTOWN SANSARO CITY.
ALL OF US AT THE FIELD OFFICE ARE HONORED BY YOUR VISIT, SIR...
...BUT WE'RE A BIT SURPRISED. THERE WAS NO ADVANCE NOTICE.
AND IT'S NOT LIKE YOU TO TRAVEL WITHOUT A SUPPORT TEAM, MR. QUIETUS.
THIS IS URGENT, SAMUAL, AND I'M TIRED OF RELYING ON OTHERS TO GET THE JOB DONE.
IT'S TIME I REMINDED EVERYBODY WHY I'M DIVISION CHIEF.
I NEED INTEL ON THE NEXT BLACK-MARKET BORDER CROSSING TO KHADYM.
WE'LL GET THAT FOR YOU AT ONCE, SIR, AND--
--NHH.
WHAAAMM
DID YOU THINK I WOULDN'T SENSE YOUR BODY MODIFICATIONS GEARING UP, DAVID?

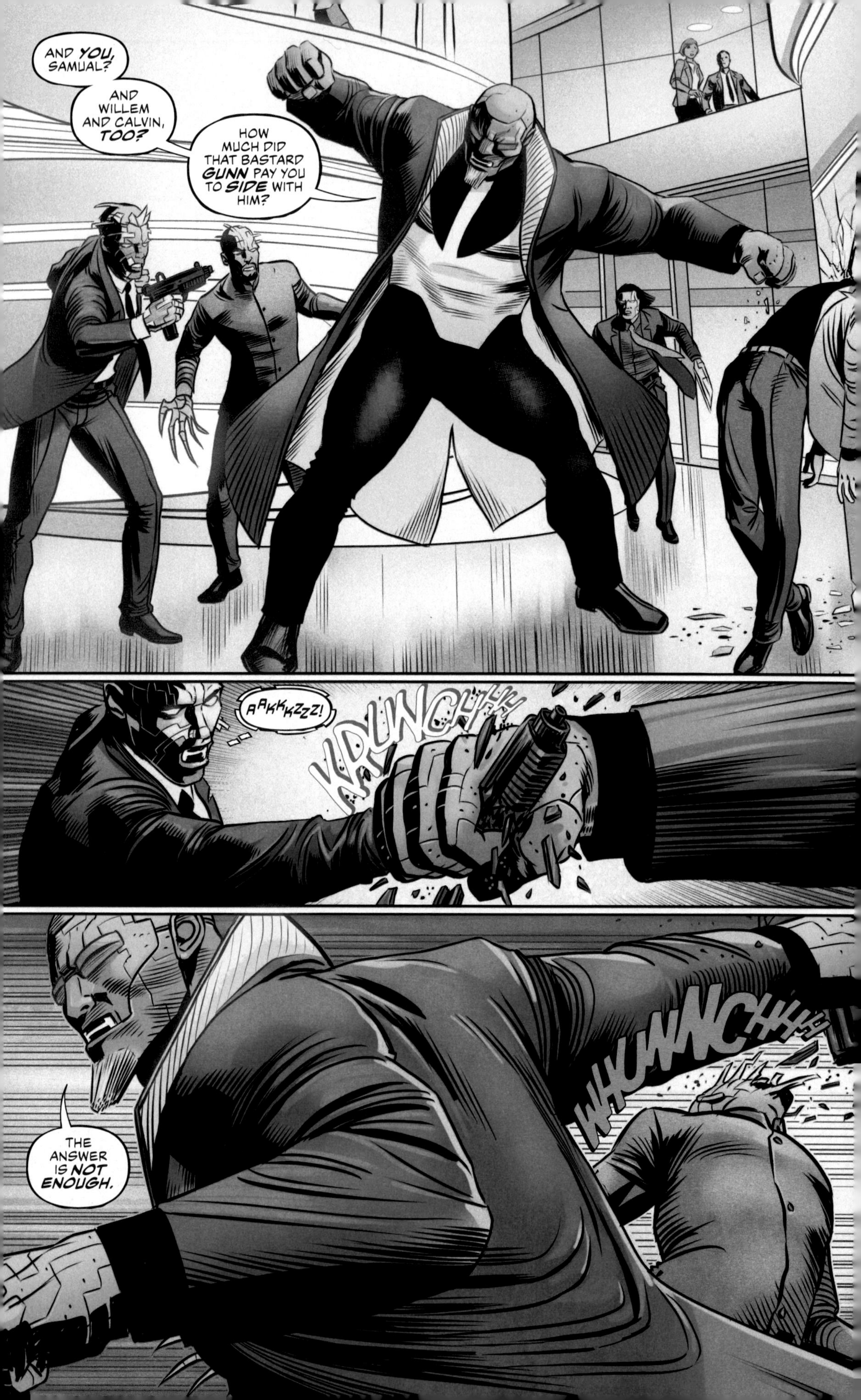
AND YOU, SAMUAL?
AND WILLEM AND CALVIN, TOO?
HOW MUCH DID THAT BASTARD GUNN PAY YOU TO SIDE WITH HIM?
AAKKKZZZ!
KRUNCHHH
WHUNNCHHH
THE ANSWER IS NOT ENOUGH.

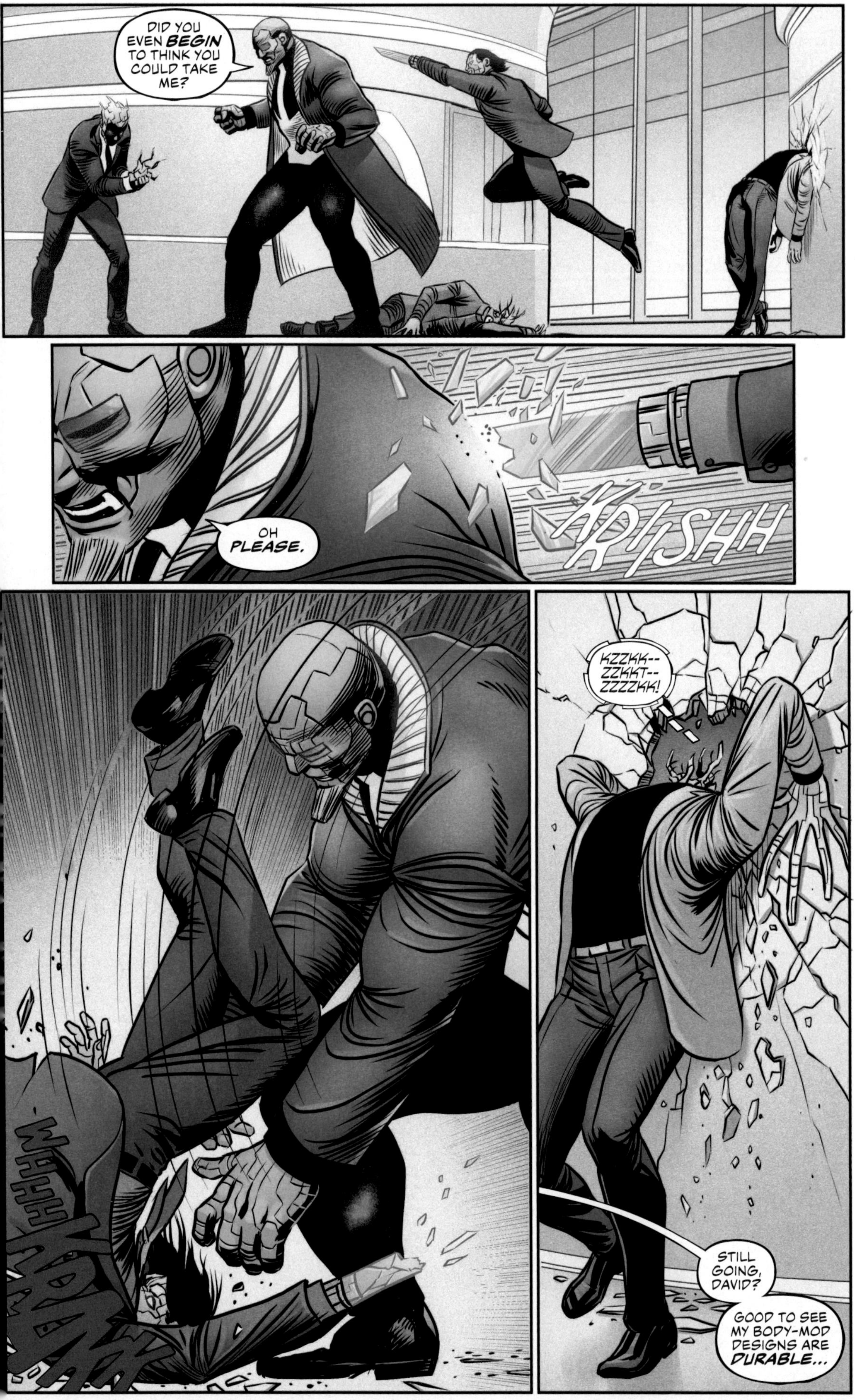
DID YOU EVEN BEGIN TO THINK YOU COULD TAKE ME?
OH PLEASE.
KRISHH
WHHH
KZZKK-- ZZKKT-- ZZZZKK!
STILL GOING, DAVID?
GOOD TO SEE MY BODY-MOD DESIGNS ARE DURABLE...

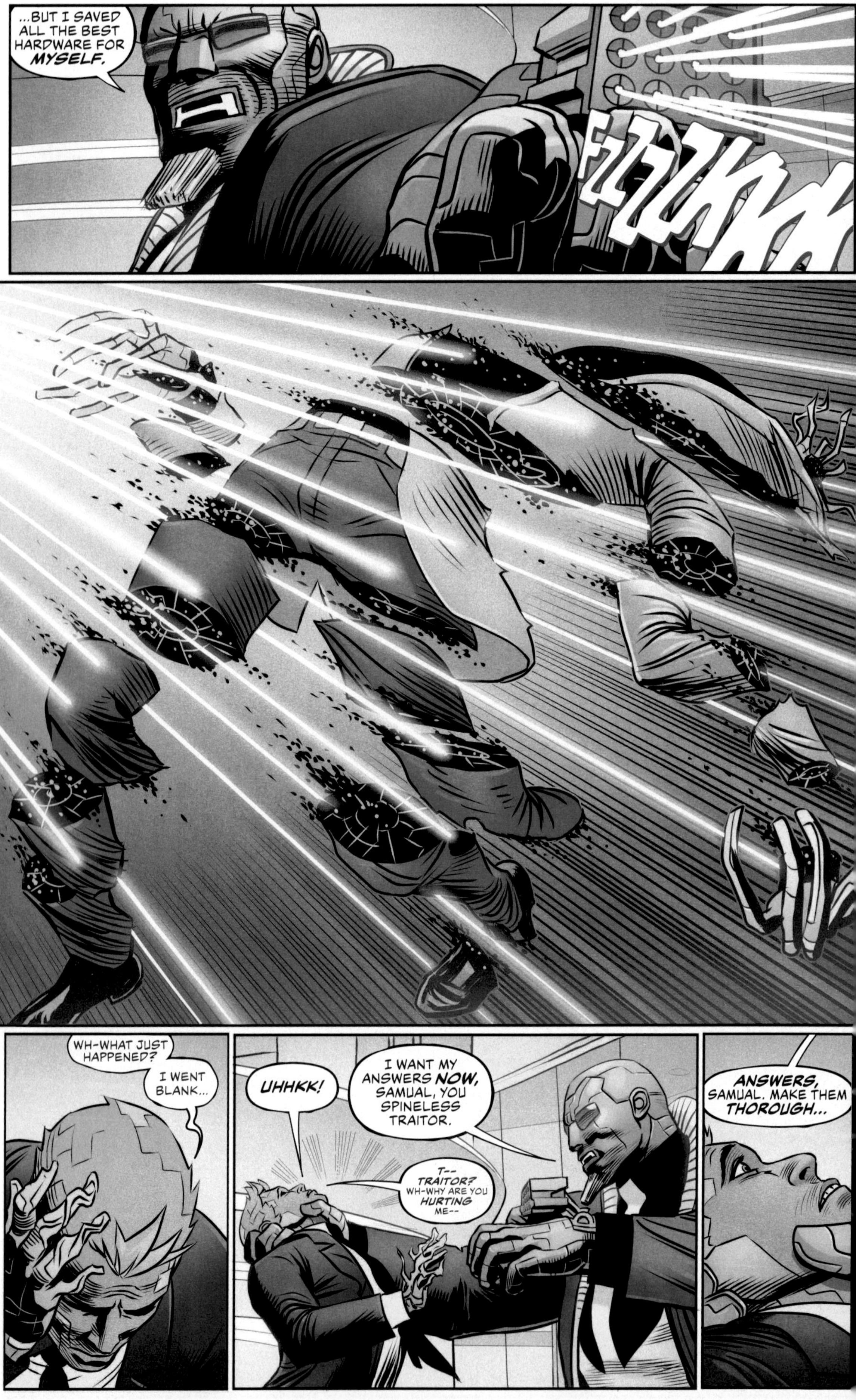
...BUT I SAVED ALL THE BEST HARDWARE FOR MYSELF.
FZZZKKK
WH-WHAT JUST HAPPENED?
I WENT BLANK...
UHHKK!
I WANT MY ANSWERS NOW, SAMUAL, YOU SPINELESS TRAITOR.
T-- TRAITOR? WH-WHY ARE YOU HURTING ME--
ANSWERS, SAMUAL. MAKE THEM THOROUGH...

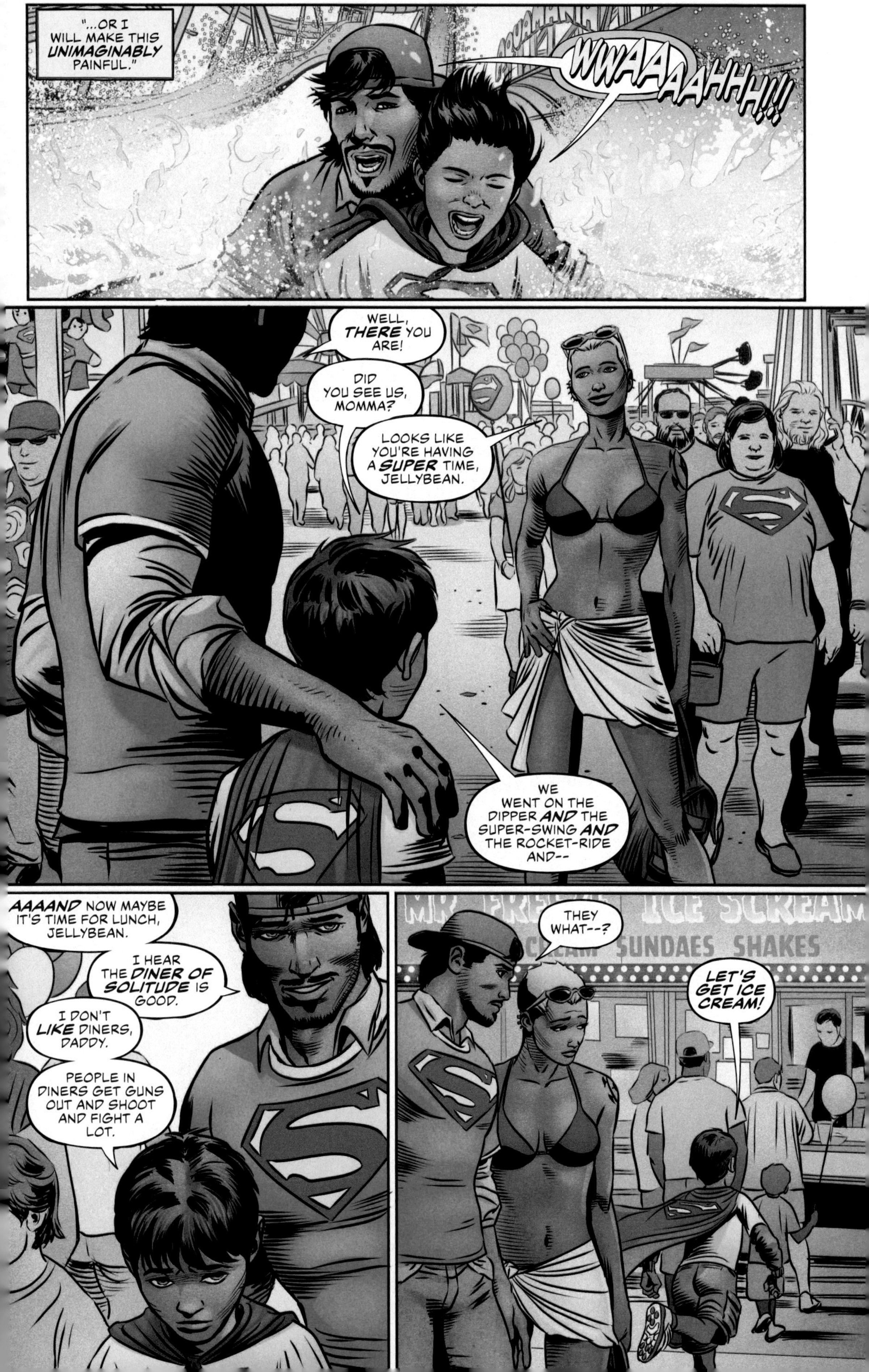
"...OR I WILL MAKE THIS UNIMAGINABLY PAINFUL."
WWAAAAAHHH!!!
WELL, THERE YOU ARE!
DID YOU SEE US, MOMMA?
LOOKS LIKE YOU'RE HAVING A SUPER TIME, JELLYBEAN.
WE WENT ON THE DIPPER AND THE SUPER-SWING AND THE ROCKET-RIDE AND--
AAAAND NOW MAYBE IT'S TIME FOR LUNCH, JELLYBEAN.
I HEAR THE DINER OF SOLITUDE IS GOOD.
I DON'T LIKE DINERS, DADDY.
PEOPLE IN DINERS GET GUNS OUT AND SHOOT AND FIGHT A LOT.
SUNDAES SHAKES
THEY WHAT--?
LET'S GET ICE CREAM!

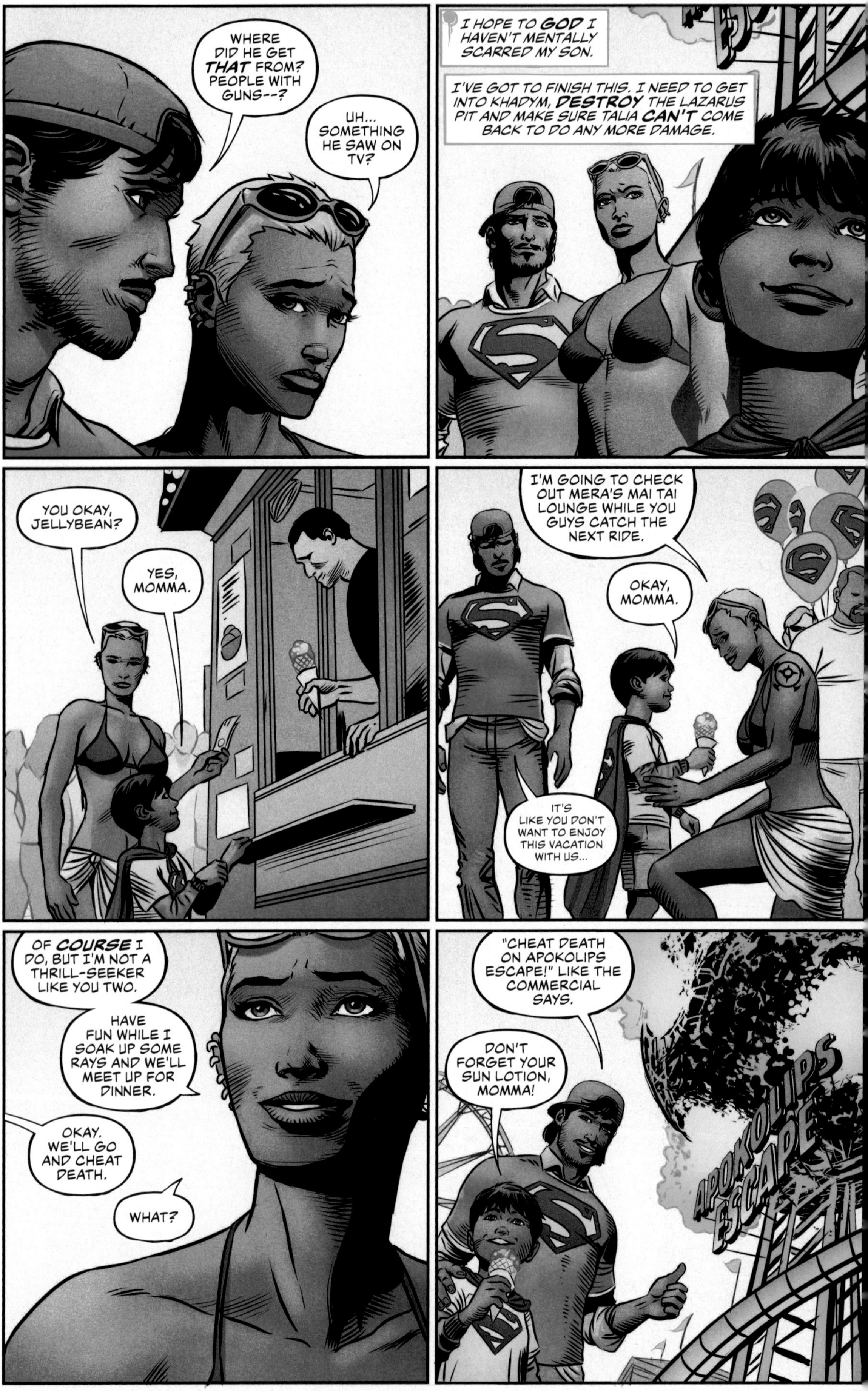
WHERE DID HE GET THAT FROM? PEOPLE WITH GUNS--?
UH... SOMETHING HE SAW ON TV?
I HOPE TO GOD I HAVEN'T MENTALLY SCARRED MY SON.
I'VE GOT TO FINISH THIS. I NEED TO GET INTO KHADYM, DESTROY THE LAZARUS PIT AND MAKE SURE TALIA CAN'T COME BACK TO DO ANY MORE DAMAGE.
YOU OKAY, JELLYBEAN?
YES, MOMMA.
I'M GOING TO CHECK OUT MERA'S MAI TAI LOUNGE WHILE YOU GUYS CATCH THE NEXT RIDE.
OKAY, MOMMA.
IT'S LIKE YOU DON'T WANT TO ENJOY THIS VACATION WITH US...
OF COURSE I DO, BUT I'M NOT A THRILL-SEEKER LIKE YOU TWO.
HAVE FUN WHILE I SOAK UP SOME RAYS AND WE'LL MEET UP FOR DINNER.
OKAY. WE'LL GO AND CHEAT DEATH.
WHAT?
"CHEAT DEATH ON APOKOLIPS ESCAPE!" LIKE THE COMMERCIAL SAYS.
DON'T FORGET YOUR SUN LOTION, MOMMA!
APOKOLIPS ESCAPE

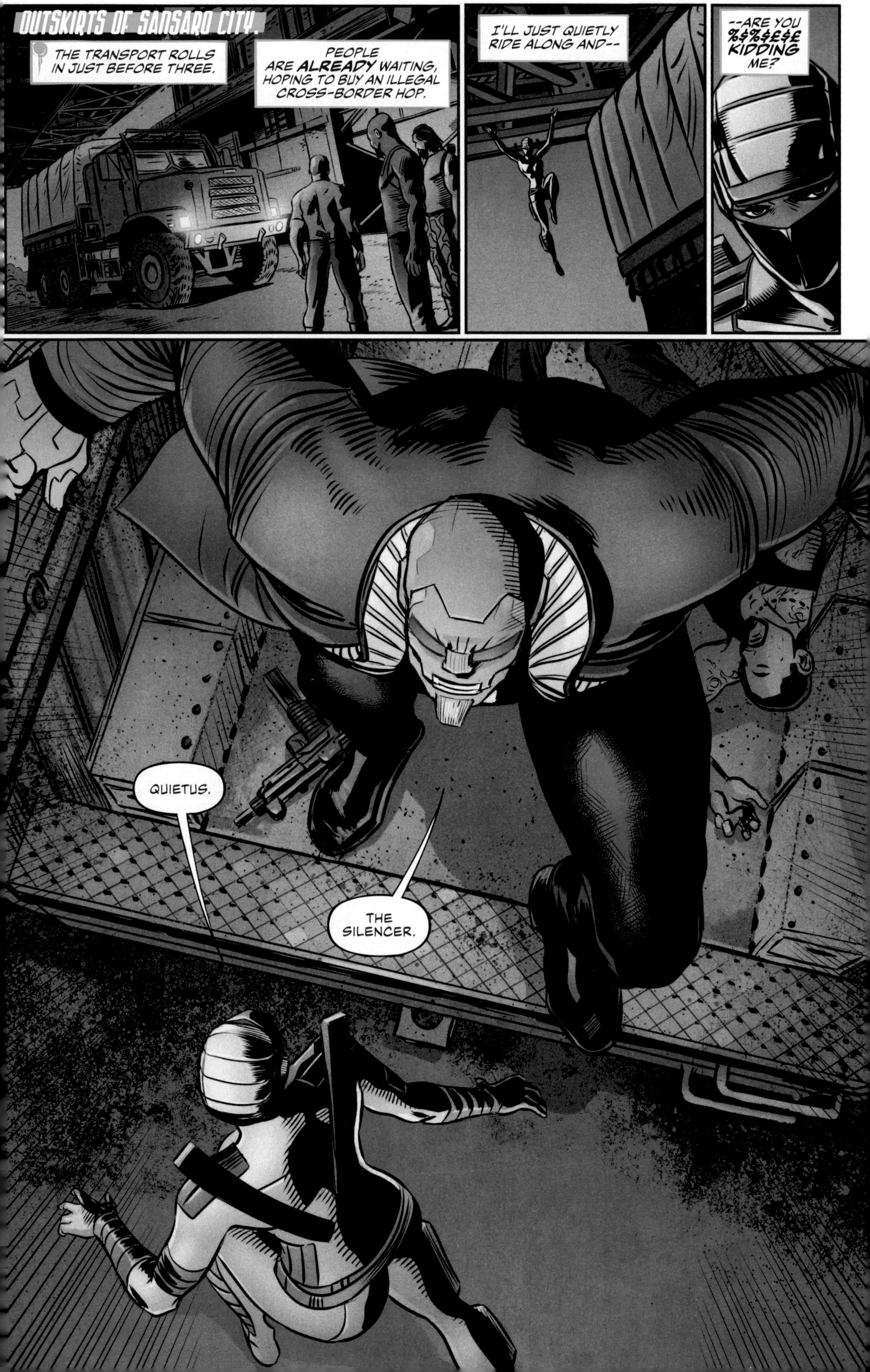
OUTSKIRTS OF SANSARO CITY.
THE TRANSPORT ROLLS IN JUST BEFORE THREE.
PEOPLE ARE **ALREADY** WAITING, HOPING TO BUY AN ILLEGAL CROSS-BORDER HOP.
I'LL JUST QUIETLY RIDE ALONG AND--
--ARE YOU **%$%$£$£ KIDDING** ME?
QUIETUS.
THE SILENCER.

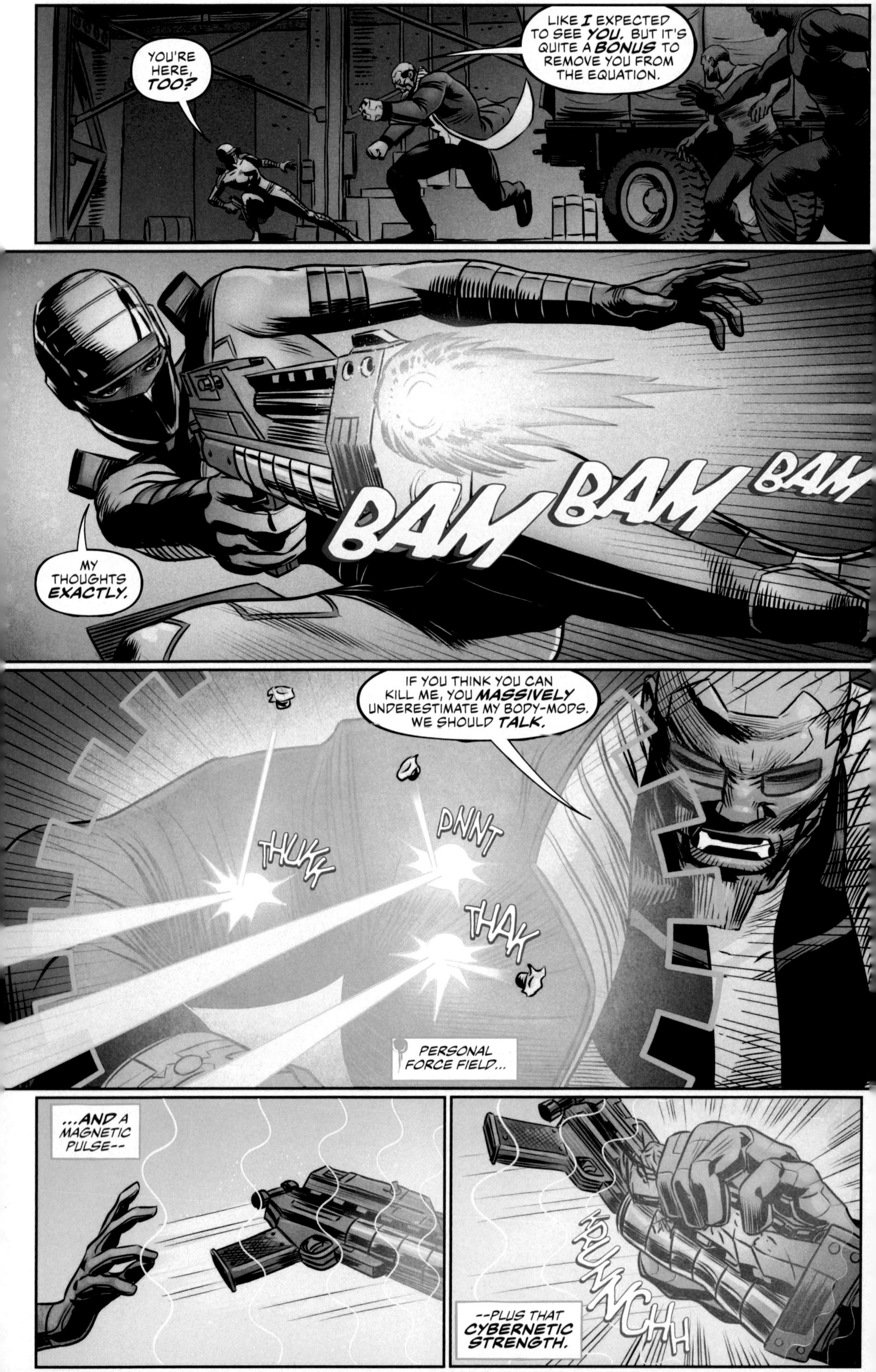
YOU'RE HERE, TOO?
LIKE I EXPECTED TO SEE YOU. BUT IT'S QUITE A BONUS TO REMOVE YOU FROM THE EQUATION.
MY THOUGHTS EXACTLY.
BAM BAM BAM
IF YOU THINK YOU CAN KILL ME, YOU MASSIVELY UNDERESTIMATE MY BODY-MODS. WE SHOULD TALK.
THUKK
PNNT
THAK
PERSONAL FORCE FIELD...
...AND A MAGNETIC PULSE--
KRUNCHH
--PLUS THAT CYBERNETIC STRENGTH.

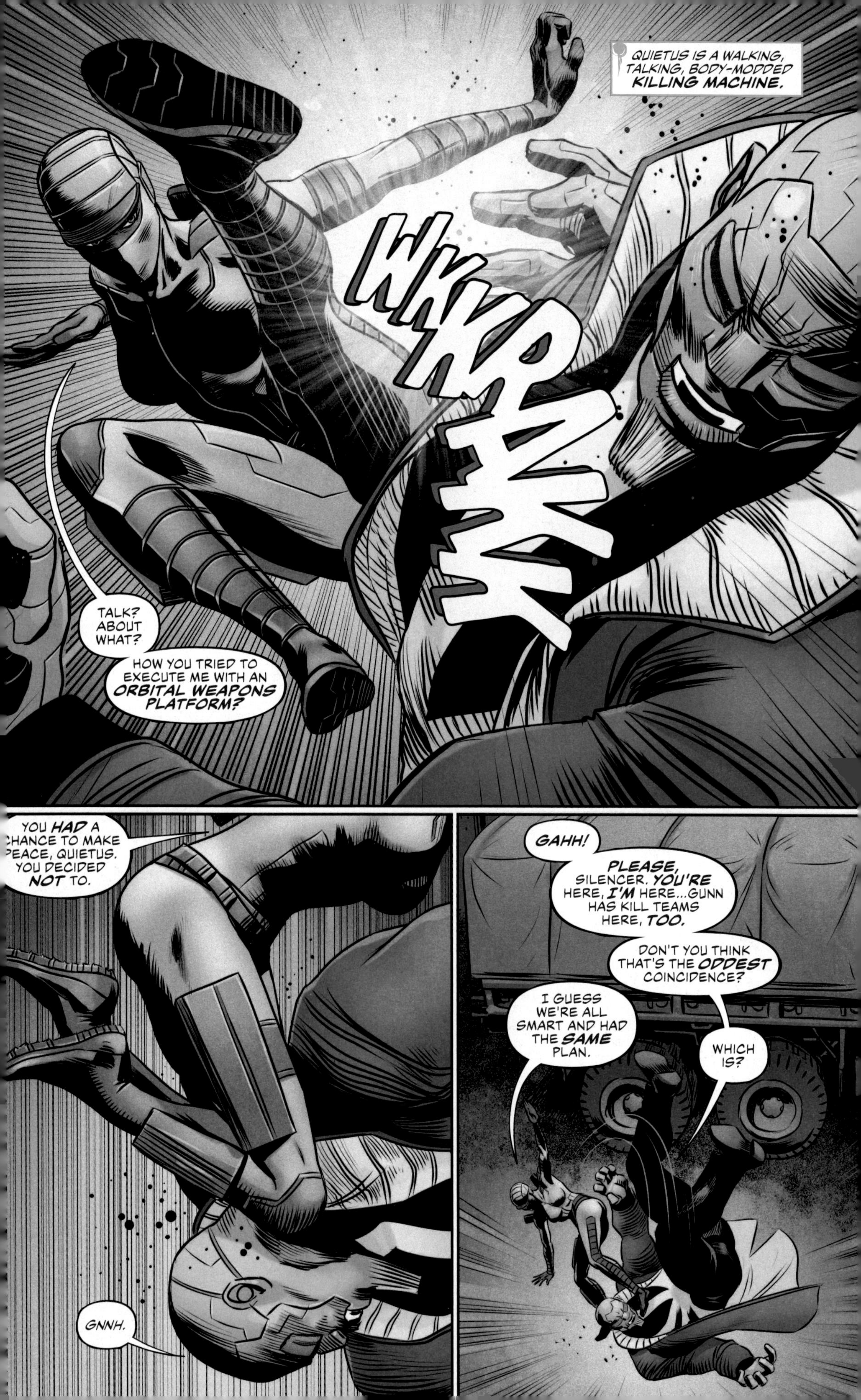
QUIETUS IS A WALKING, TALKING, BODY-MODDED KILLING MACHINE.
WKKRAKK
TALK? ABOUT WHAT?
HOW YOU TRIED TO EXECUTE ME WITH AN ORBITAL WEAPONS PLATFORM?
YOU HAD A CHANCE TO MAKE PEACE, QUIETUS. YOU DECIDED NOT TO.
GNNH.
GAHH!
PLEASE, SILENCER. YOU'RE HERE, I'M HERE...GUNN HAS KILL TEAMS HERE, TOO.
DON'T YOU THINK THAT'S THE ODDEST COINCIDENCE?
I GUESS WE'RE ALL SMART AND HAD THE SAME PLAN.
WHICH IS?

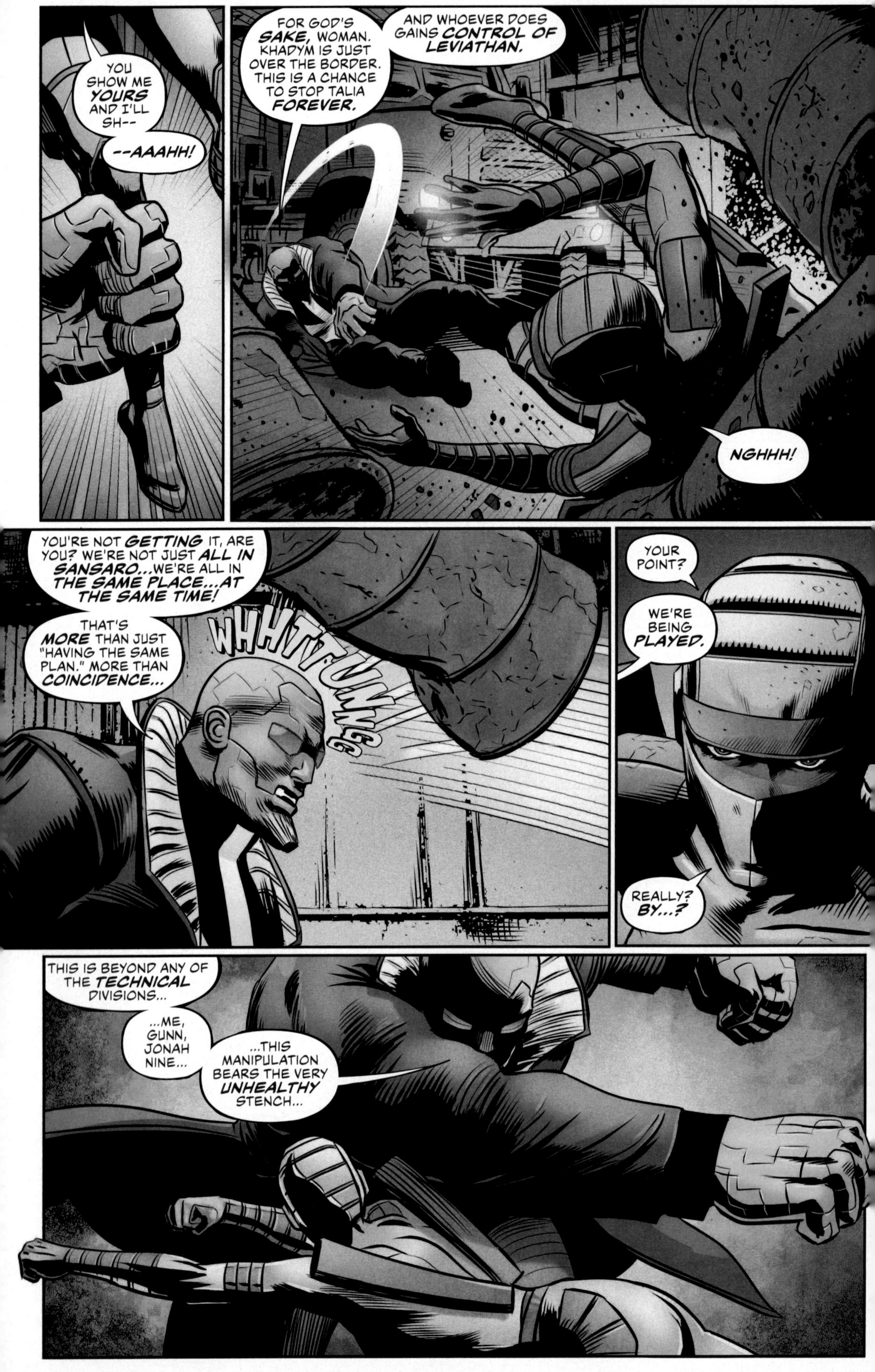
YOU SHOW ME YOURS AND I'LL SH--
--AAAHH!
FOR GOD'S SAKE, WOMAN. KHADYM IS JUST OVER THE BORDER. THIS IS A CHANCE TO STOP TALIA FOREVER.
AND WHOEVER DOES GAINS CONTROL OF LEVIATHAN.
NGHHH!
YOU'RE NOT GETTING IT, ARE YOU? WE'RE NOT JUST ALL IN SANSARO...WE'RE ALL IN THE SAME PLACE...AT THE SAME TIME!
THAT'S MORE THAN JUST "HAVING THE SAME PLAN." MORE THAN COINCIDENCE...
WHHTTUNNG
YOUR POINT?
WE'RE BEING PLAYED.
REALLY? BY...?
THIS IS BEYOND ANY OF THE TECHNICAL DIVISIONS...
...ME, GUNN, JONAH NINE...
...THIS MANIPULATION BEARS THE VERY UNHEALTHY STENCH...

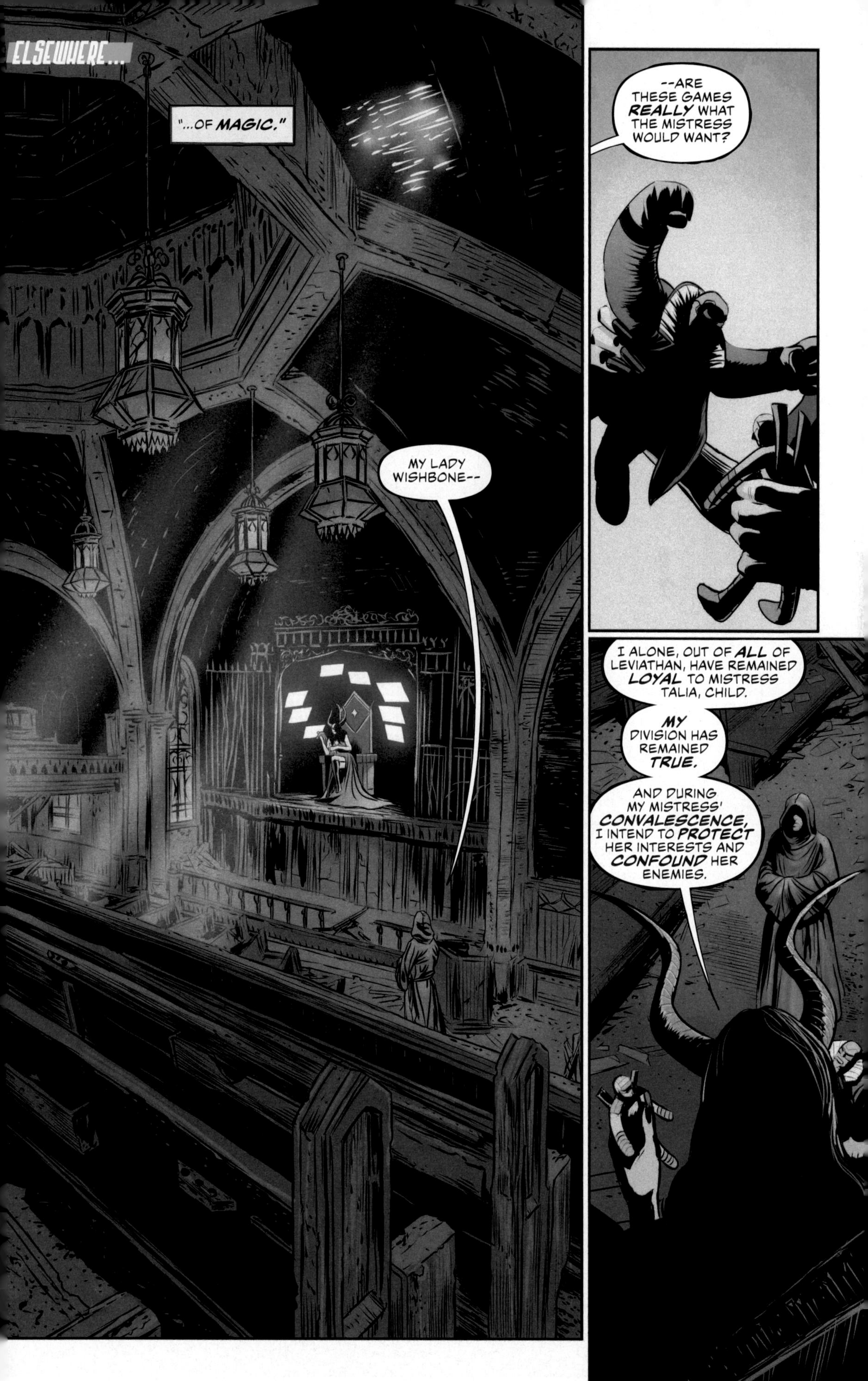
ELSEWHERE...
"...OF MAGIC."
MY LADY WISHBONE--
--ARE THESE GAMES REALLY WHAT THE MISTRESS WOULD WANT?
I ALONE, OUT OF ALL OF LEVIATHAN, HAVE REMAINED LOYAL TO MISTRESS TALIA, CHILD.
MY DIVISION HAS REMAINED TRUE.
AND DURING MY MISTRESS' CONVALESCENCE, I INTEND TO PROTECT HER INTERESTS AND CONFOUND HER ENEMIES.

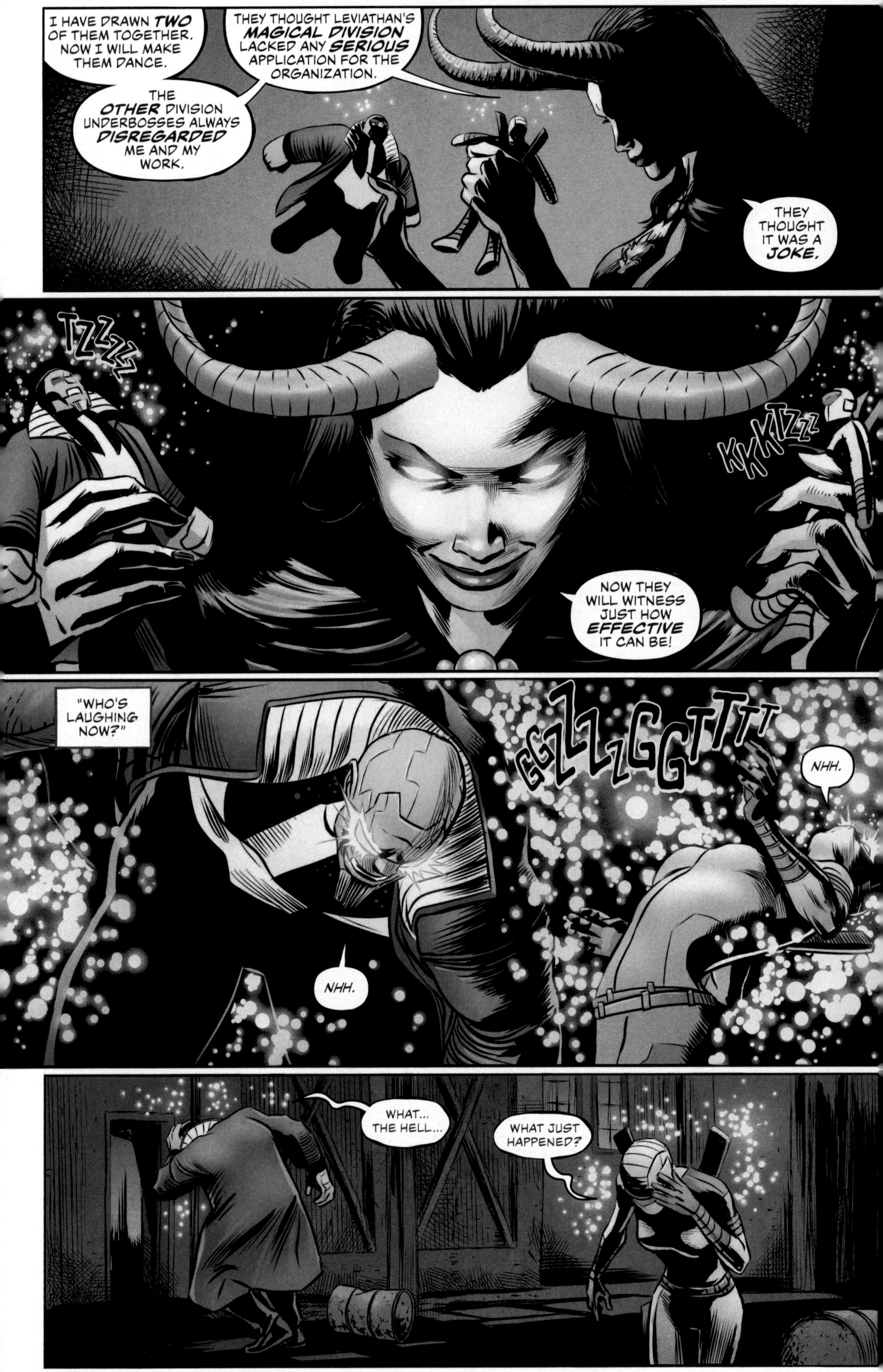
I HAVE DRAWN TWO OF THEM TOGETHER. NOW I WILL MAKE THEM DANCE.
THE OTHER DIVISION UNDERBOSSES ALWAYS DISREGARDED ME AND MY WORK.
THEY THOUGHT LEVIATHAN'S MAGICAL DIVISION LACKED ANY SERIOUS APPLICATION FOR THE ORGANIZATION.
THEY THOUGHT IT WAS A JOKE.
TZZZZZ
KKKTZZZ
NOW THEY WILL WITNESS JUST HOW EFFECTIVE IT CAN BE!
"WHO'S LAUGHING NOW?"
GGZZZZGGTTTT
NHH.
NHH.
WHAT... THE HELL...
WHAT JUST HAPPENED?

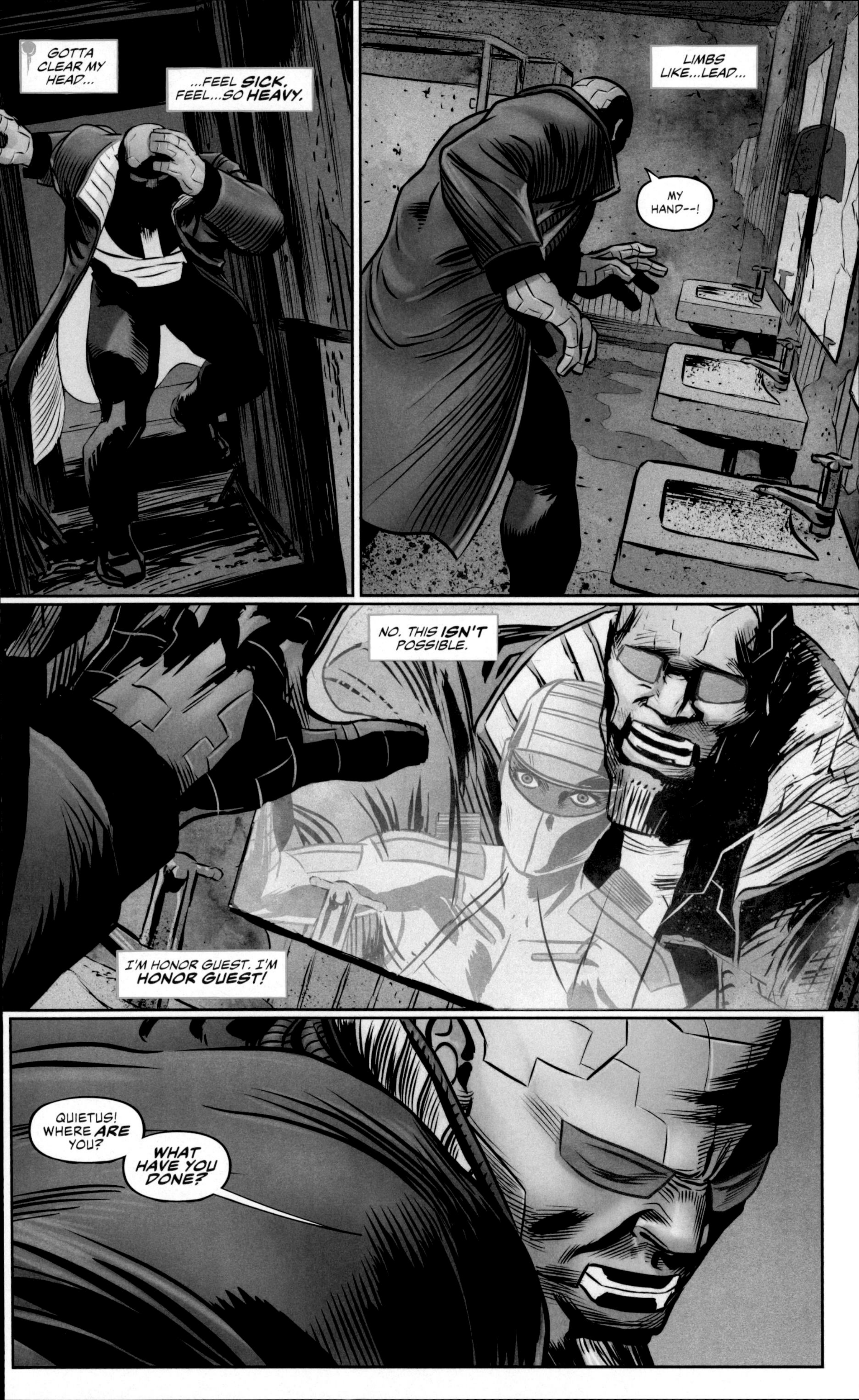
GOTTA CLEAR MY HEAD...
...FEEL SICK. FEEL...SO HEAVY.
LIMBS LIKE...LEAD...
MY HAND--!
NO. THIS ISN'T POSSIBLE.
I'M HONOR GUEST. I'M HONOR GUEST!
QUIETUS! WHERE ARE YOU?
WHAT HAVE YOU DONE?

"QUIETUS!"

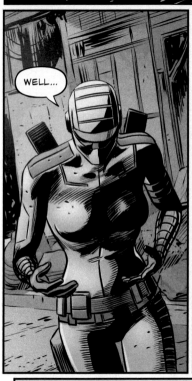

WELL...

...THIS IS DIFFERENT.

NOW LET'S FIND OUT WHO THE SILENCER REALLY IS...

ACTION LAND

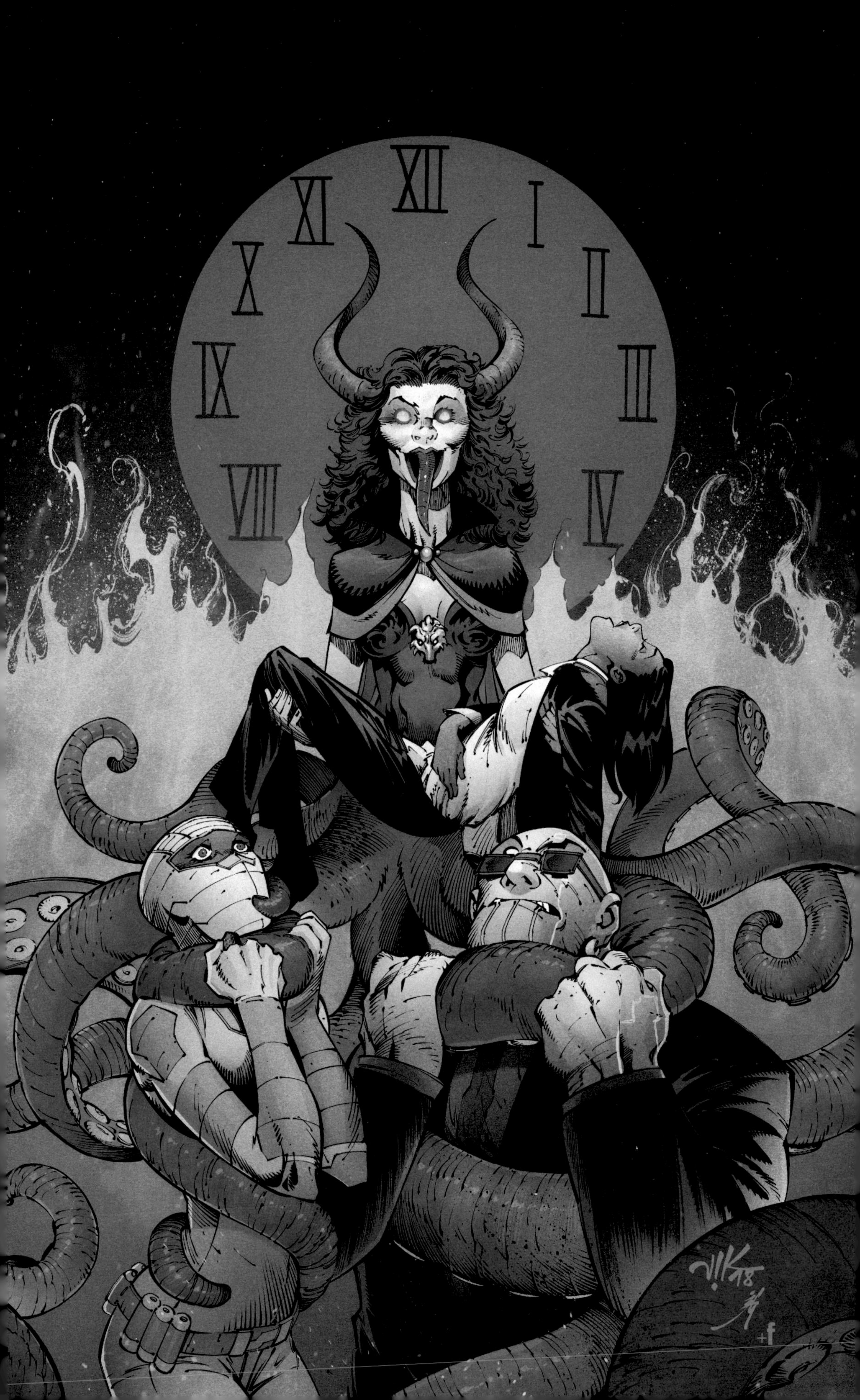

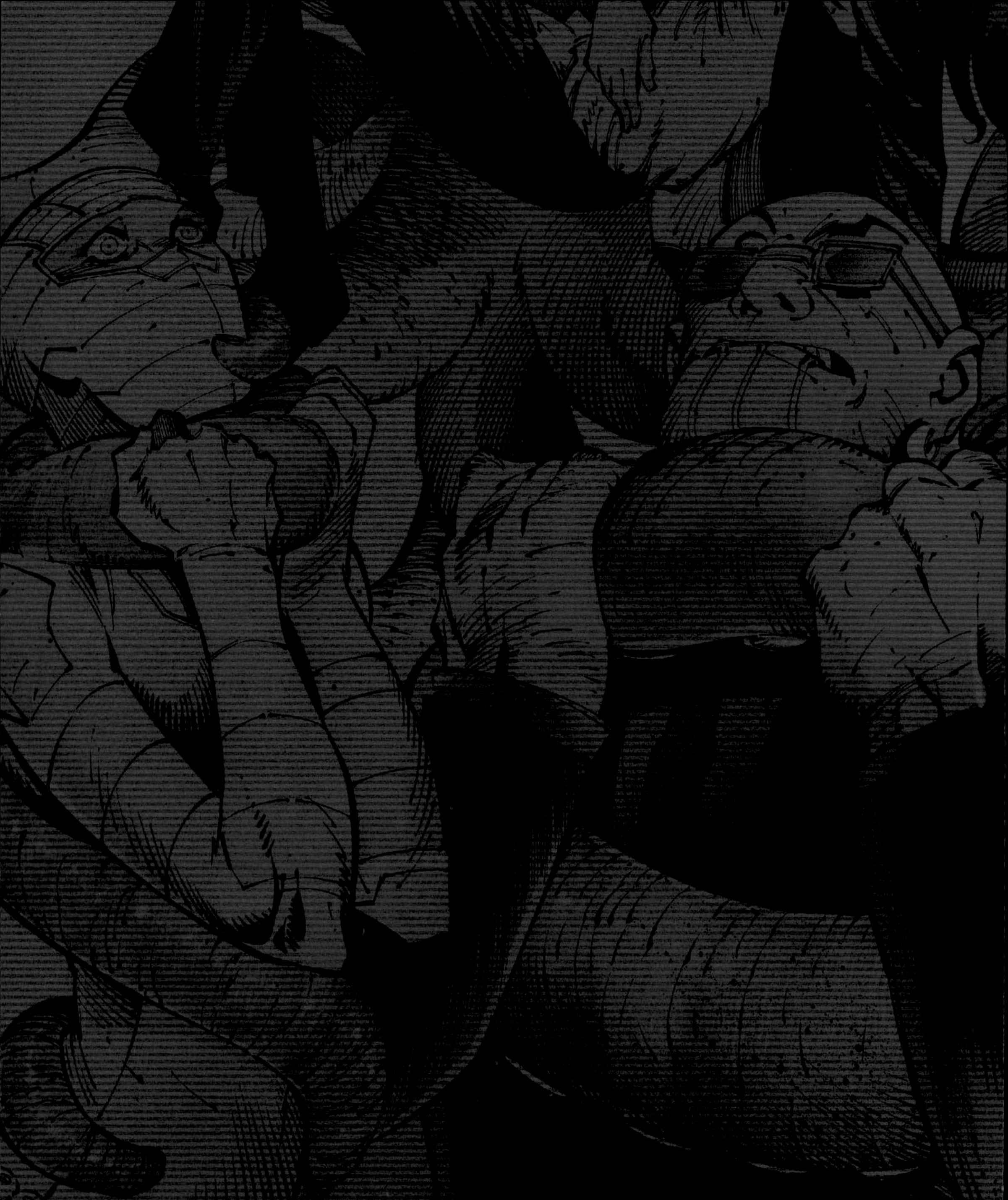

THE SILENCER
#9

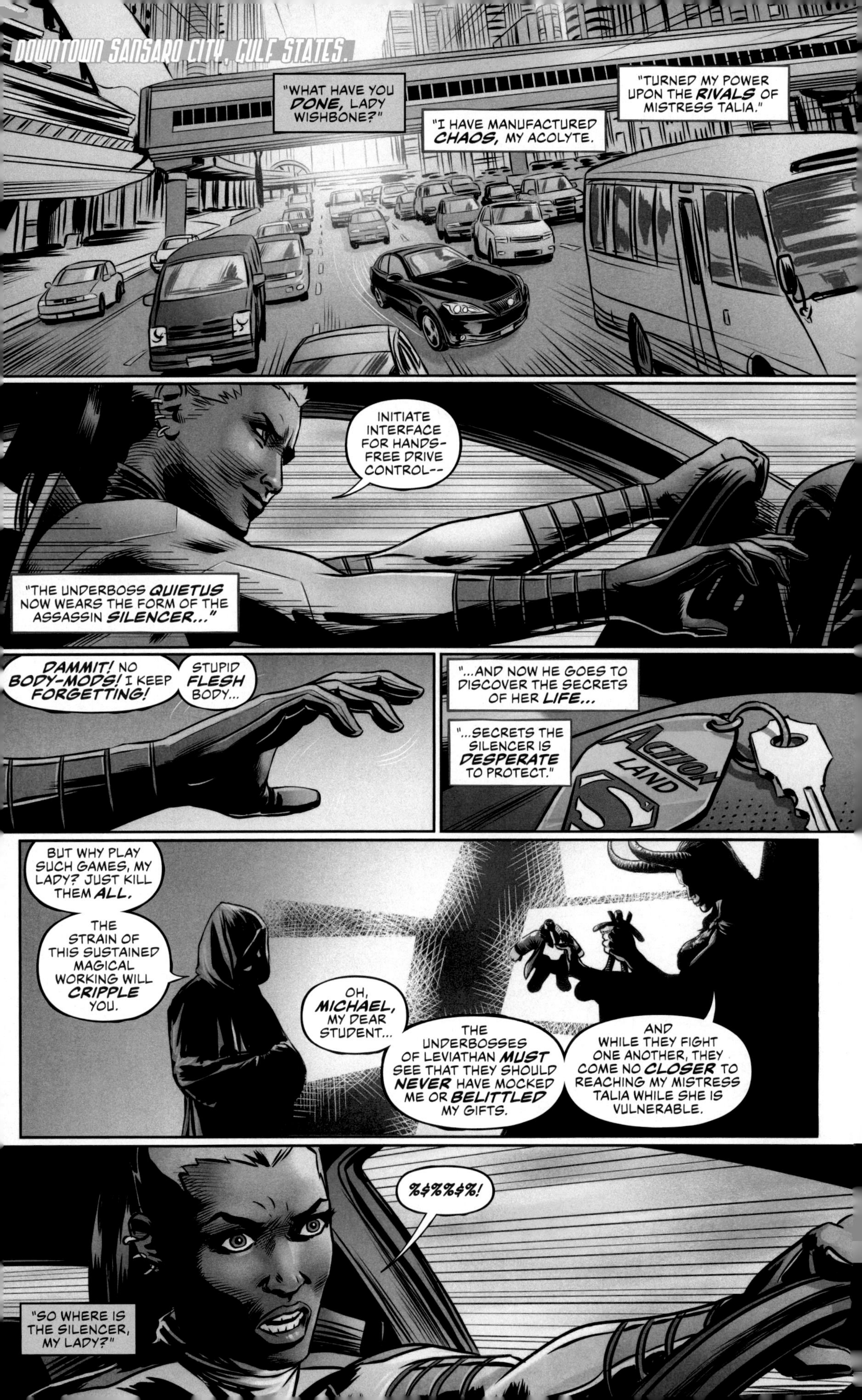
DOWNTOWN SANSARO CITY, GULF STATES.
"WHAT HAVE YOU DONE, LADY WISHBONE?"
"I HAVE MANUFACTURED CHAOS, MY ACOLYTE.
"TURNED MY POWER UPON THE RIVALS OF MISTRESS TALIA."
INITIATE INTERFACE FOR HANDS-FREE DRIVE CONTROL--
"THE UNDERBOSS QUIETUS NOW WEARS THE FORM OF THE ASSASSIN SILENCER..."
DAMMIT! NO BODY-MODS! I KEEP FORGETTING!
STUPID FLESH BODY...
"...AND NOW HE GOES TO DISCOVER THE SECRETS OF HER LIFE...
"...SECRETS THE SILENCER IS DESPERATE TO PROTECT."
ACTION LAND
BUT WHY PLAY SUCH GAMES, MY LADY? JUST KILL THEM ALL.
THE STRAIN OF THIS SUSTAINED MAGICAL WORKING WILL CRIPPLE YOU.
OH, MICHAEL, MY DEAR STUDENT...
THE UNDERBOSSES OF LEVIATHAN MUST SEE THAT THEY SHOULD NEVER HAVE MOCKED ME OR BELITTLED MY GIFTS.
AND WHILE THEY FIGHT ONE ANOTHER, THEY COME NO CLOSER TO REACHING MY MISTRESS TALIA WHILE SHE IS VULNERABLE.
%$%%$%!
"SO WHERE IS THE SILENCER, MY LADY?"

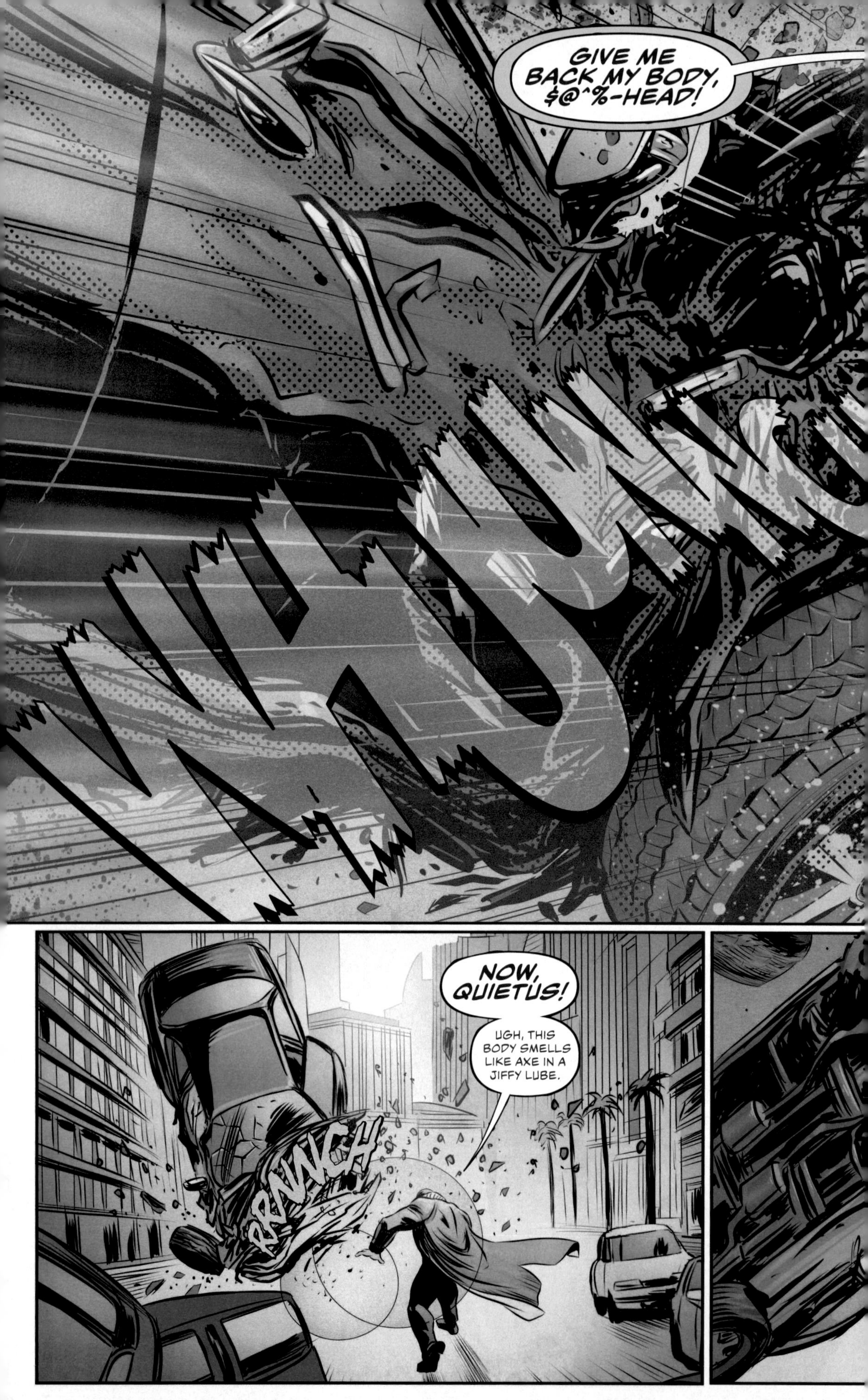
GIVE ME BACK MY BODY, $@^%-HEAD!
NOW, QUIETUS!
UGH, THIS BODY SMELLS LIKE AXE IN A JIFFY LUBE.

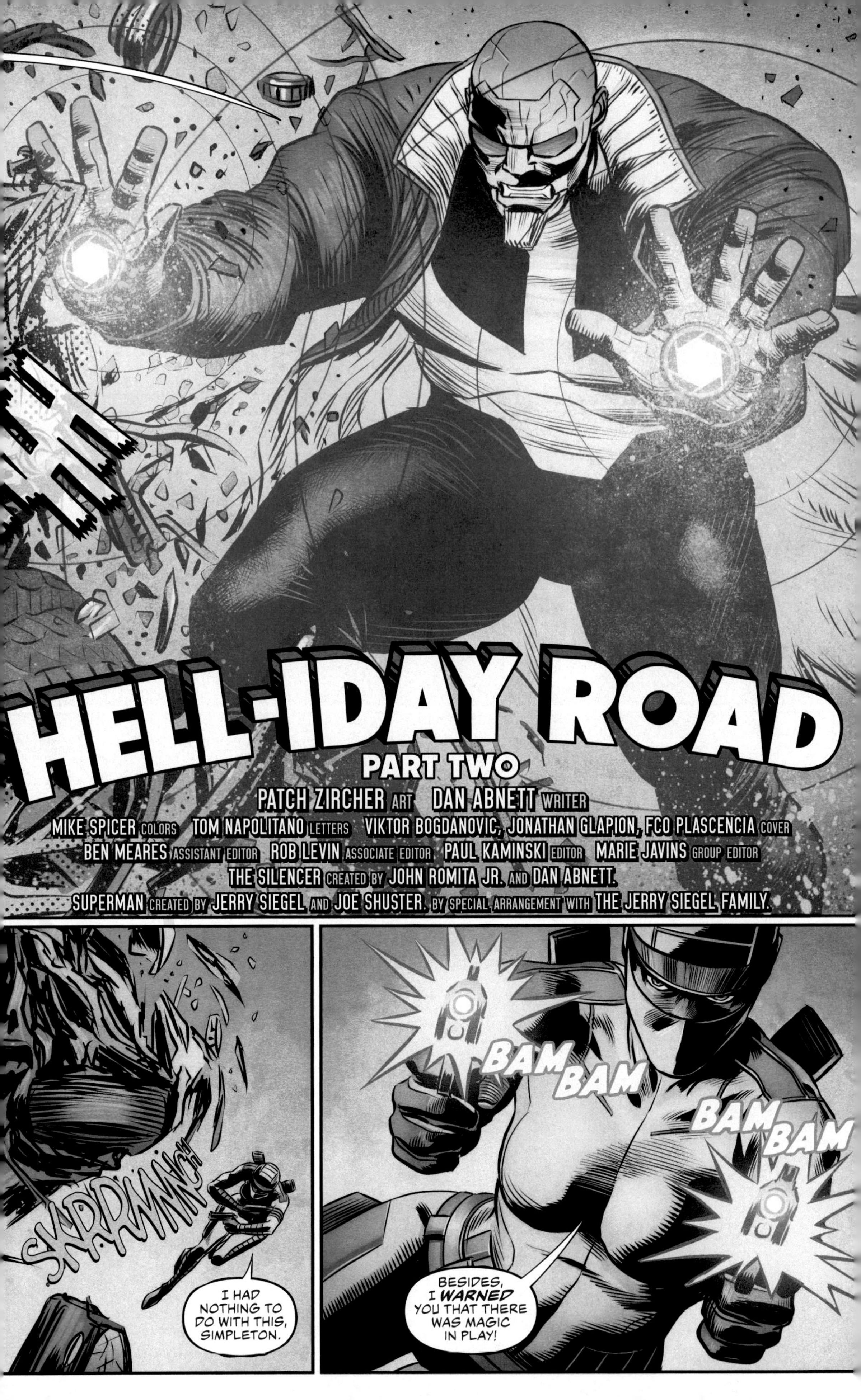
HELL-IDAY ROAD
PART TWO
PATCH ZIRCHER ART DAN ABNETT WRITER
MIKE SPICER COLORS TOM NAPOLITANO LETTERS VIKTOR BOGDANOVIC, JONATHAN GLAPION, FCO PLASCENCIA COVER
BEN MEARES ASSISTANT EDITOR ROB LEVIN ASSOCIATE EDITOR PAUL KAMINSKI EDITOR MARIE JAVINS GROUP EDITOR
THE SILENCER CREATED BY JOHN ROMITA JR. AND DAN ABNETT.
SUPERMAN CREATED BY JERRY SIEGEL AND JOE SHUSTER. BY SPECIAL ARRANGEMENT WITH THE JERRY SIEGEL FAMILY.
SKRRWNNCH!
I HAD NOTHING TO DO WITH THIS, SIMPLETON.
BAM BAM
BAM BAM
BESIDES, I WARNED YOU THAT THERE WAS MAGIC IN PLAY!

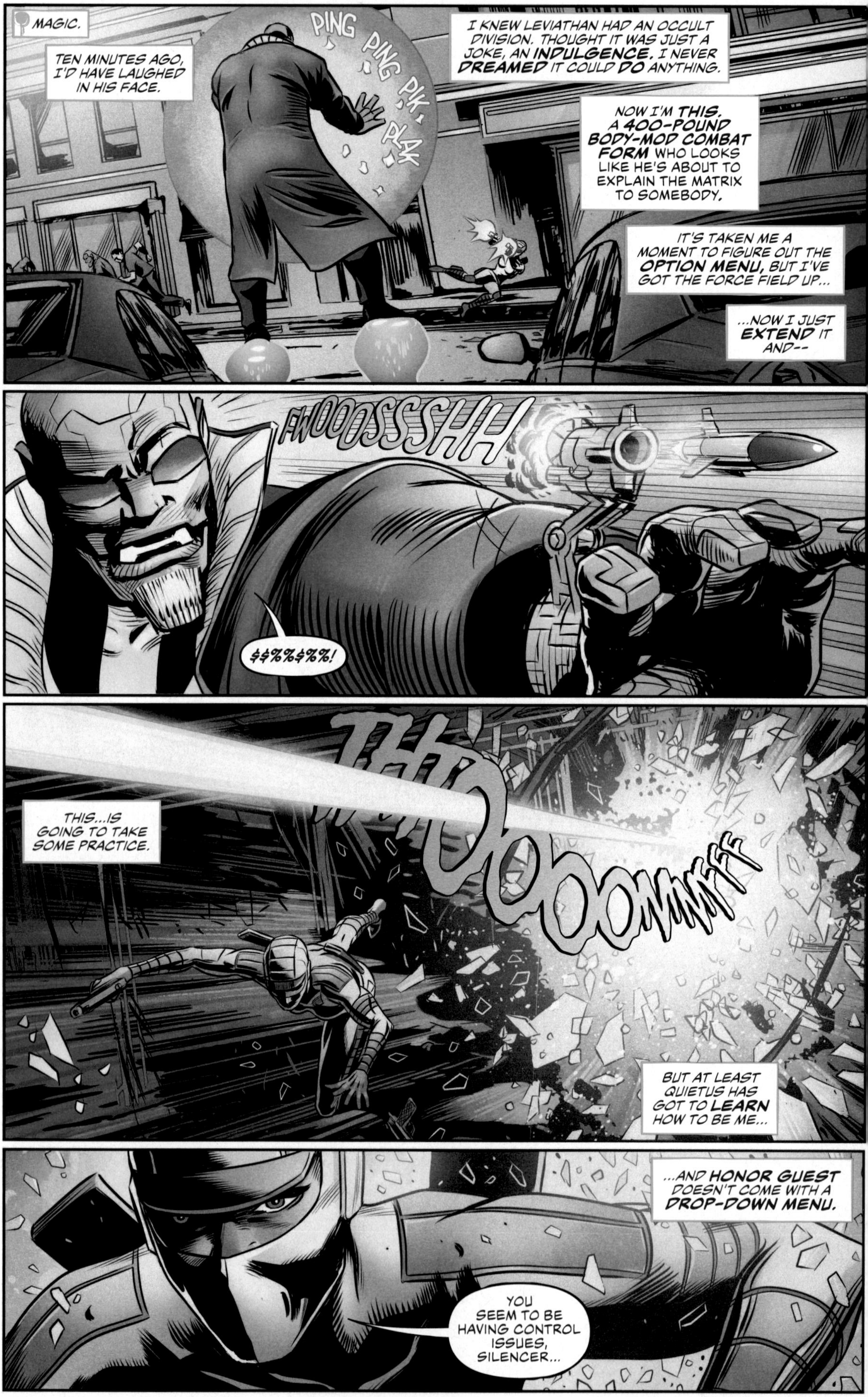
MAGIC.
TEN MINUTES AGO, I'D HAVE LAUGHED IN HIS FACE.
PING PING PIK PLAK
I KNEW LEVIATHAN HAD AN OCCULT DIVISION. THOUGHT IT WAS JUST A JOKE, AN INDULGENCE. I NEVER DREAMED IT COULD DO ANYTHING.
NOW I'M THIS. A 400-POUND BODY-MOD COMBAT FORM WHO LOOKS LIKE HE'S ABOUT TO EXPLAIN THE MATRIX TO SOMEBODY.
IT'S TAKEN ME A MOMENT TO FIGURE OUT THE OPTION MENU, BUT I'VE GOT THE FORCE FIELD UP...
...NOW I JUST EXTEND IT AND--
FWOOOSSSSHH
$$%%$%%!
THOOOOOOMFF
THIS...IS GOING TO TAKE SOME PRACTICE.
BUT AT LEAST QUIETUS HAS GOT TO LEARN HOW TO BE ME...
...AND HONOR GUEST DOESN'T COME WITH A DROP-DOWN MENU.
YOU SEEM TO BE HAVING CONTROL ISSUES, SILENCER...

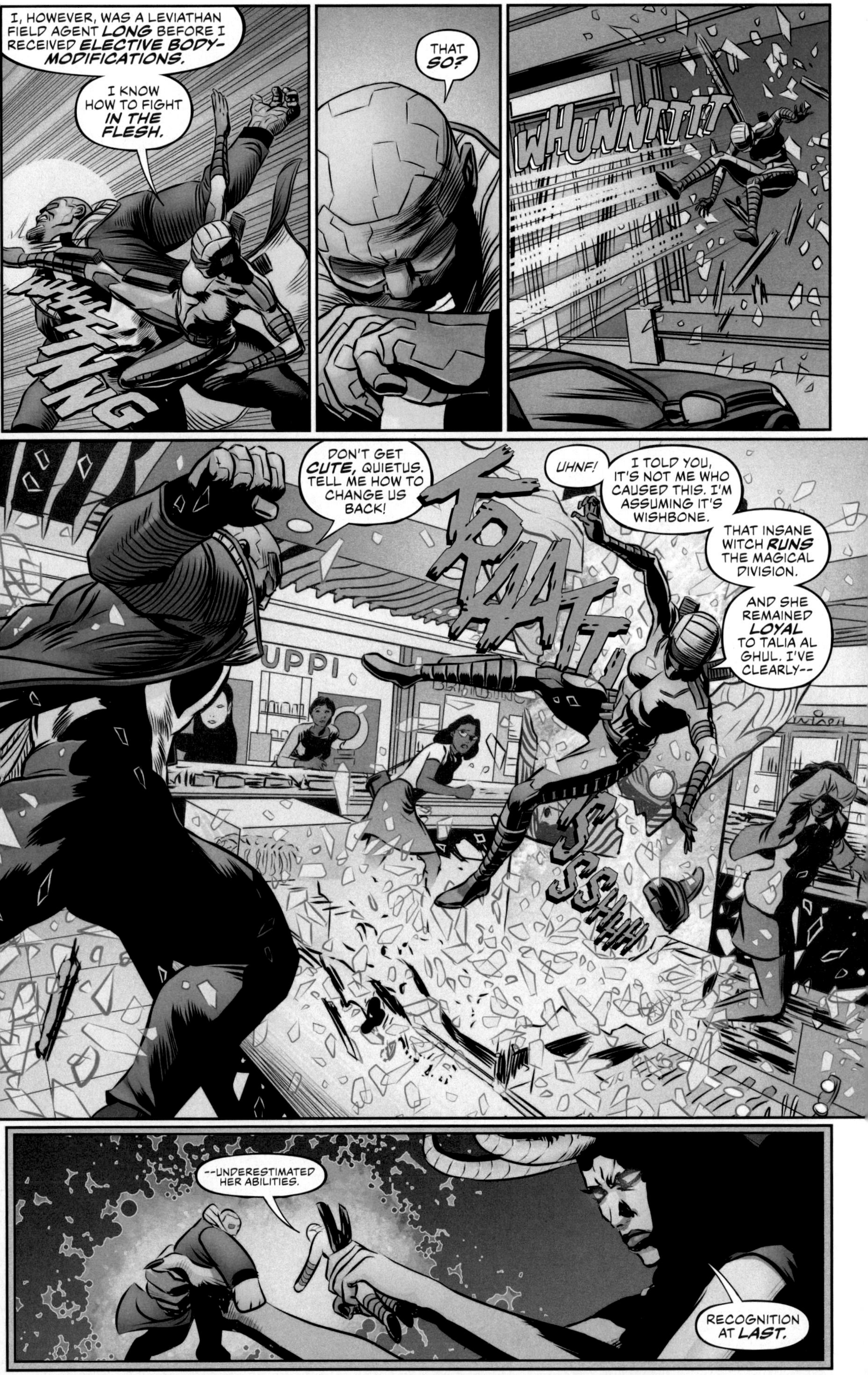
I, HOWEVER, WAS A LEVIATHAN FIELD AGENT LONG BEFORE I RECEIVED ELECTIVE BODY-MODIFICATIONS.
I KNOW HOW TO FIGHT IN THE FLESH.
THAT SO?
DON'T GET CUTE, QUIETUS. TELL ME HOW TO CHANGE US BACK!
UHNF!
I TOLD YOU, IT'S NOT ME WHO CAUSED THIS. I'M ASSUMING IT'S WISHBONE.
THAT INSANE WITCH RUNS THE MAGICAL DIVISION.
AND SHE REMAINED LOYAL TO TALIA AL GHUL. I'VE CLEARLY--
--UNDERESTIMATED HER ABILITIES.
RECOGNITION AT LAST.

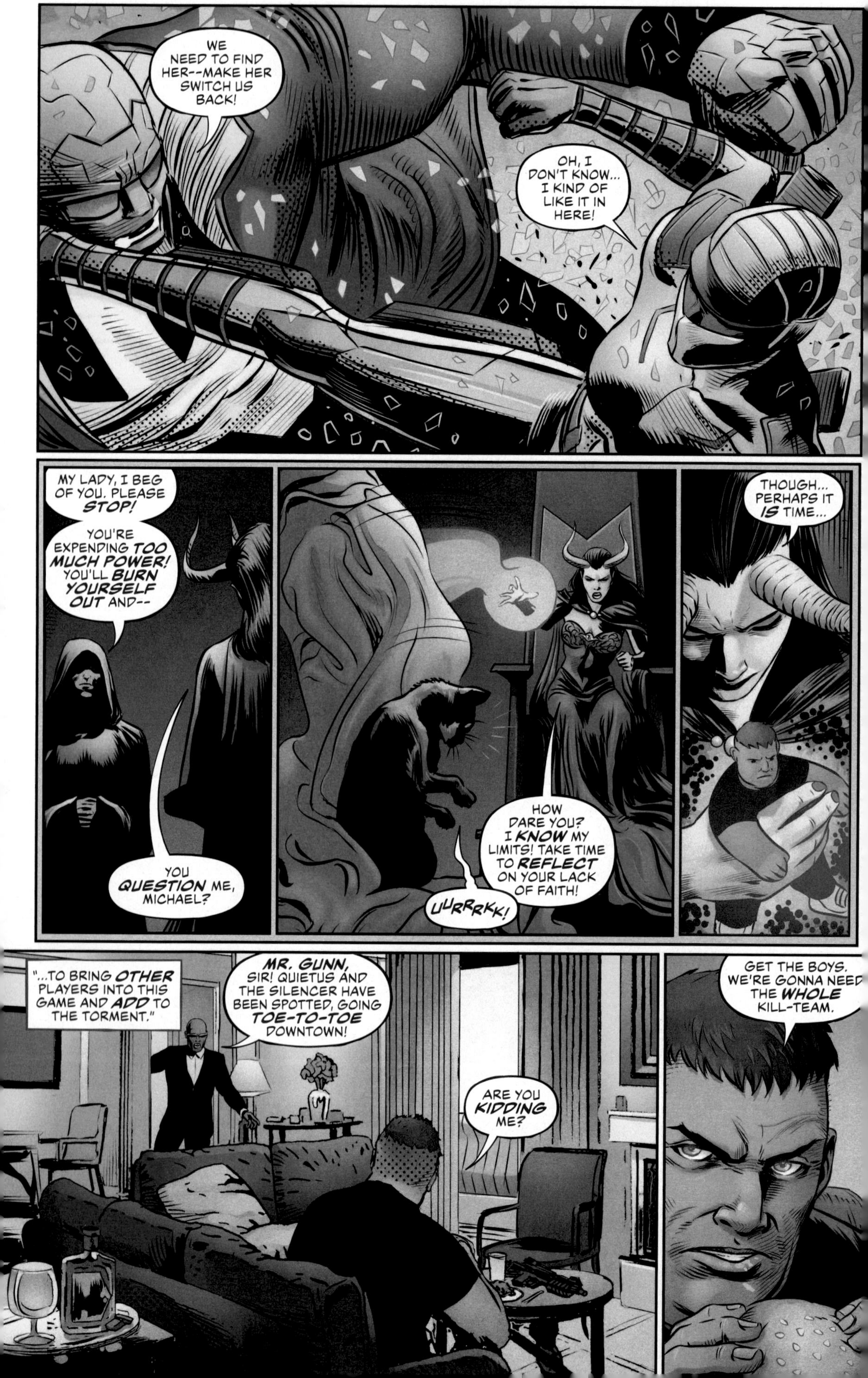
WE NEED TO FIND HER--MAKE HER SWITCH US BACK!
OH, I DON'T KNOW... I KIND OF LIKE IT IN HERE!
MY LADY, I BEG OF YOU. PLEASE STOP!
YOU'RE EXPENDING TOO MUCH POWER! YOU'LL BURN YOURSELF OUT AND--
YOU QUESTION ME, MICHAEL?
HOW DARE YOU? I KNOW MY LIMITS! TAKE TIME TO REFLECT ON YOUR LACK OF FAITH!
UURRRKK!
THOUGH... PERHAPS IT IS TIME...
"...TO BRING OTHER PLAYERS INTO THIS GAME AND ADD TO THE TORMENT."
MR. GUNN, SIR! QUIETUS AND THE SILENCER HAVE BEEN SPOTTED, GOING TOE-TO-TOE DOWNTOWN!
ARE YOU KIDDING ME?
GET THE BOYS. WE'RE GONNA NEED THE WHOLE KILL-TEAM.

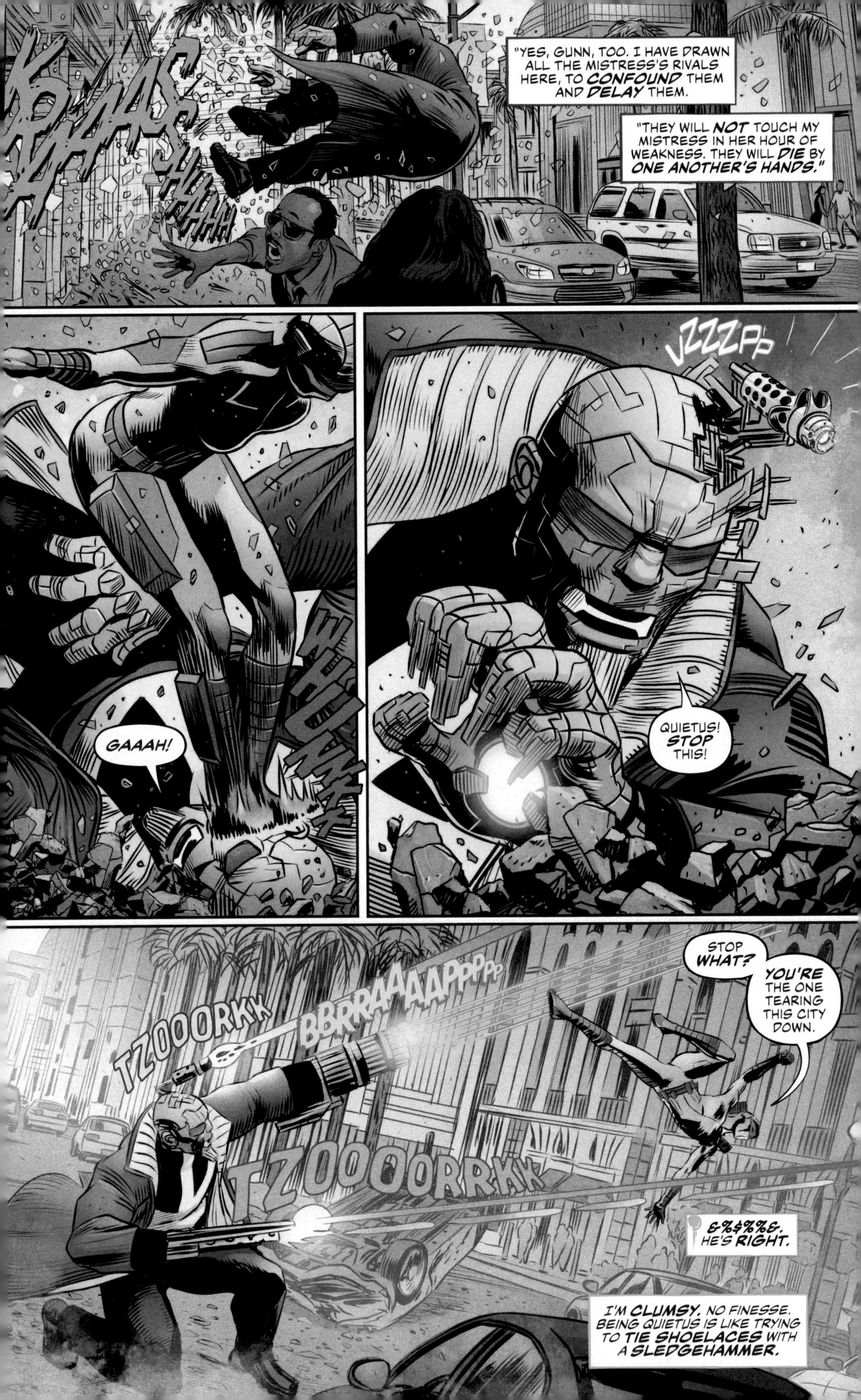
"YES, GUNN, TOO. I HAVE DRAWN ALL THE MISTRESS'S RIVALS HERE, TO CONFOUND THEM AND DELAY THEM.
"THEY WILL NOT TOUCH MY MISTRESS IN HER HOUR OF WEAKNESS. THEY WILL DIE BY ONE ANOTHER'S HANDS."
GAAAH!
QUIETUS! STOP THIS!
STOP WHAT? YOU'RE THE ONE TEARING THIS CITY DOWN.
TZOOORKK
BBRRAAAAPPPP
TZOOOOORRKK
&%$%%&. HE'S RIGHT.
I'M CLUMSY. NO FINESSE. BEING QUIETUS IS LIKE TRYING TO TIE SHOELACES WITH A SLEDGEHAMMER.

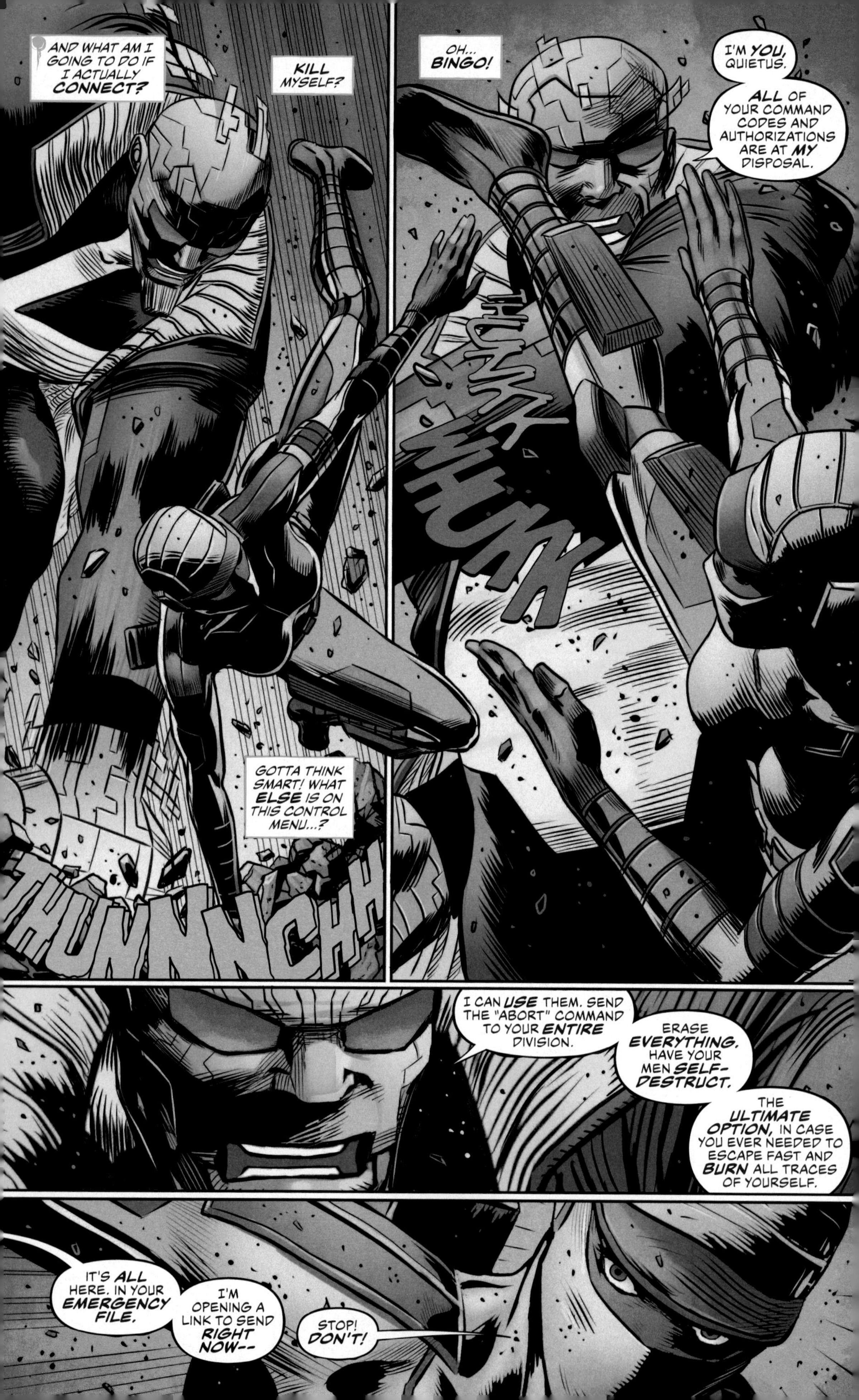

AND WHAT AM I GOING TO DO IF I ACTUALLY CONNECT?
KILL MYSELF?
GOTTA THINK SMART! WHAT ELSE IS ON THIS CONTROL MENU...?
THUNNCH!
OH... BINGO!
I'M YOU, QUIETUS.
ALL OF YOUR COMMAND CODES AND AUTHORIZATIONS ARE AT MY DISPOSAL.
THUNK
WHUNK
I CAN USE THEM. SEND THE "ABORT" COMMAND TO YOUR ENTIRE DIVISION.
ERASE EVERYTHING. HAVE YOUR MEN SELF-DESTRUCT.
THE ULTIMATE OPTION, IN CASE YOU EVER NEEDED TO ESCAPE FAST AND BURN ALL TRACES OF YOURSELF.
IT'S ALL HERE. IN YOUR EMERGENCY FILE.
I'M OPENING A LINK TO SEND RIGHT NOW--
STOP! DON'T!

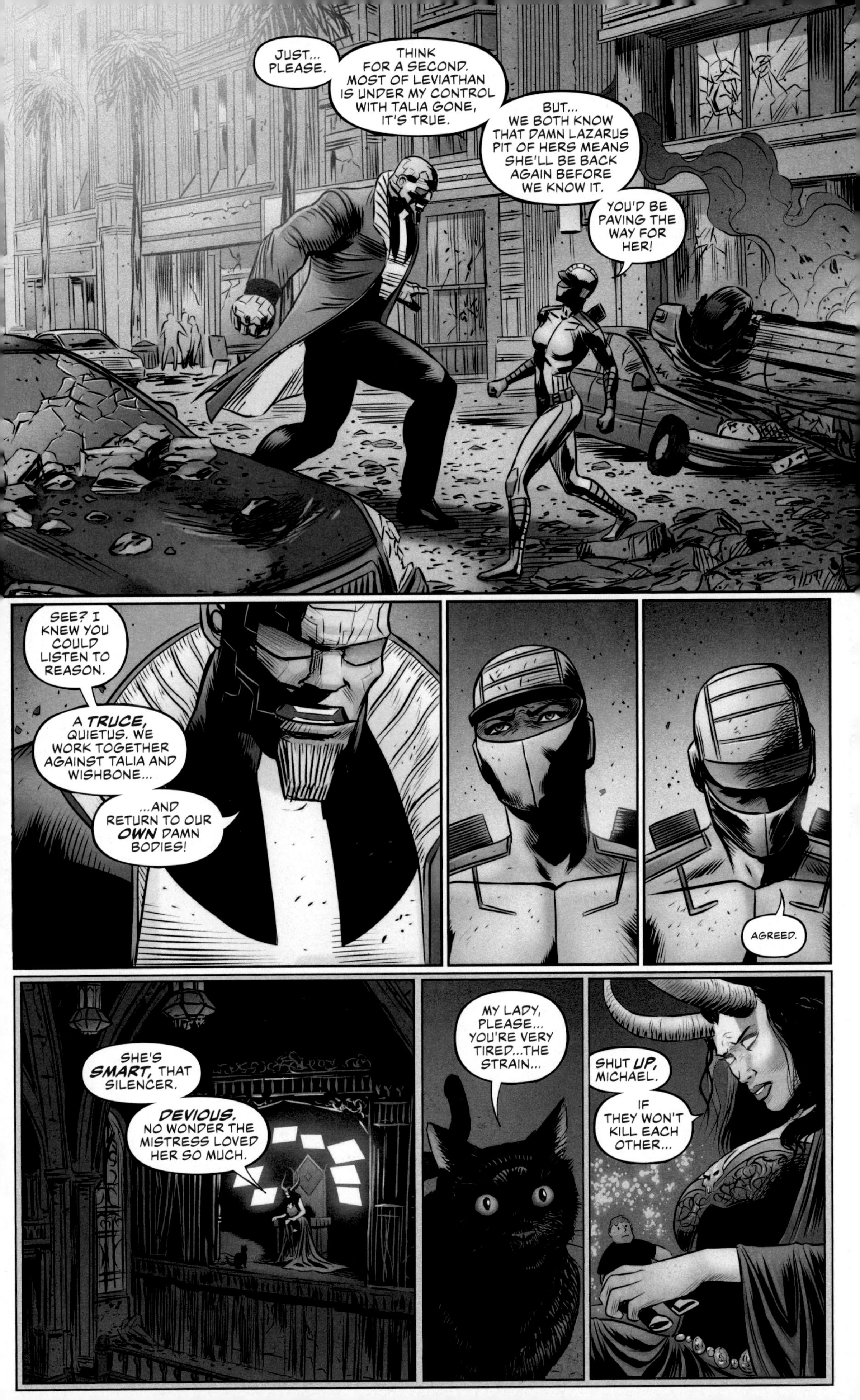
JUST... PLEASE.
THINK FOR A SECOND. MOST OF LEVIATHAN IS UNDER MY CONTROL WITH TALIA GONE, IT'S TRUE.
BUT... WE BOTH KNOW THAT DAMN LAZARUS PIT OF HERS MEANS SHE'LL BE BACK AGAIN BEFORE WE KNOW IT.
YOU'D BE PAVING THE WAY FOR HER!
SEE? I KNEW YOU COULD LISTEN TO REASON.
A **TRUCE,** QUIETUS. WE WORK TOGETHER AGAINST TALIA AND WISHBONE...
...AND RETURN TO OUR ***OWN*** DAMN BODIES!
AGREED.
SHE'S **SMART,** THAT SILENCER.
DEVIOUS. NO WONDER THE MISTRESS LOVED HER SO MUCH.
MY LADY, PLEASE... YOU'RE VERY TIRED...THE STRAIN...
SHUT ***UP,*** MICHAEL.
IF THEY WON'T KILL EACH OTHER...

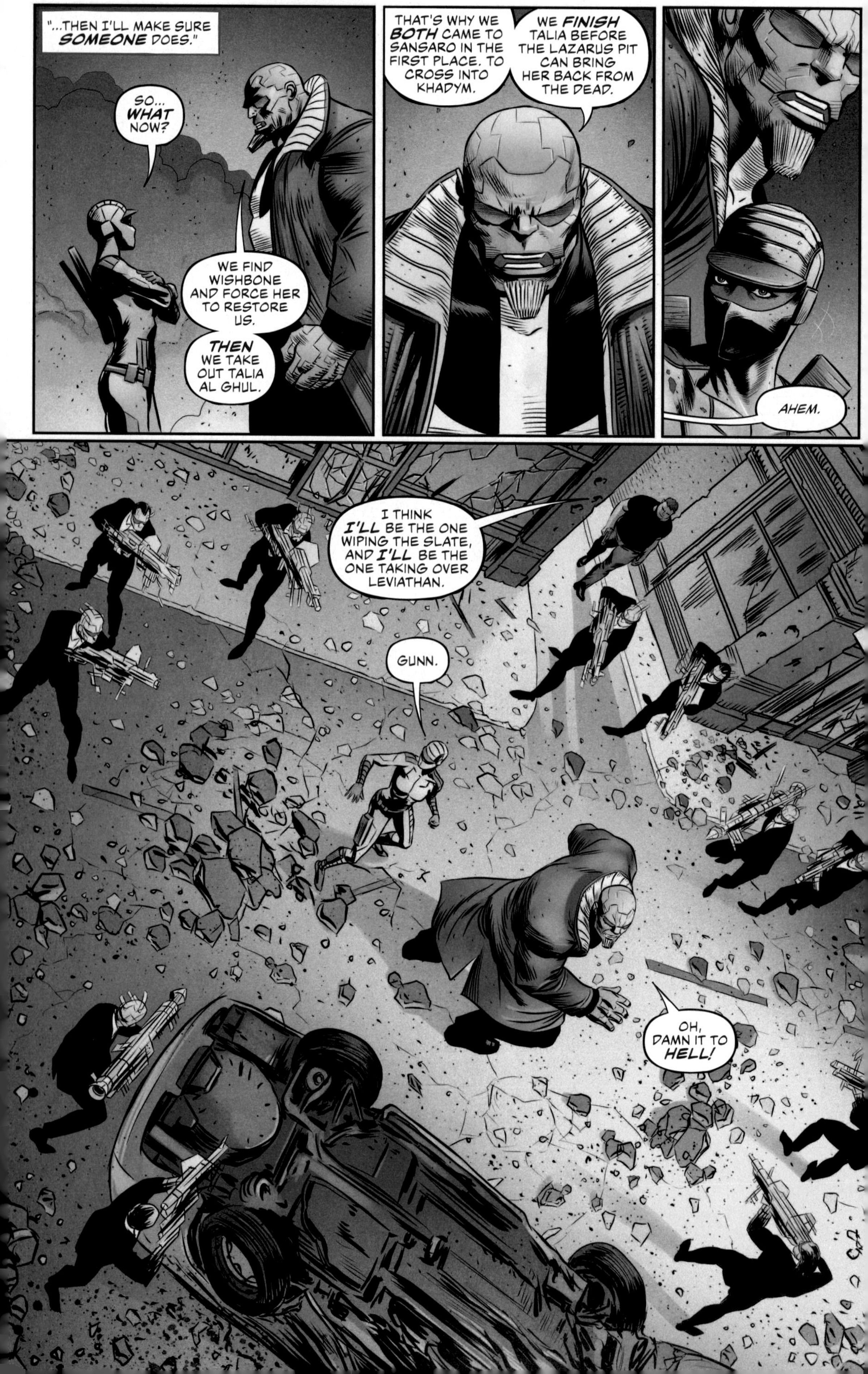
"...THEN I'LL MAKE SURE SOMEONE DOES."
SO... WHAT NOW?
WE FIND WISHBONE AND FORCE HER TO RESTORE US.
THEN WE TAKE OUT TALIA AL GHUL.
THAT'S WHY WE BOTH CAME TO SANSARO IN THE FIRST PLACE. TO CROSS INTO KHADYM.
WE FINISH TALIA BEFORE THE LAZARUS PIT CAN BRING HER BACK FROM THE DEAD.
AHEM.
I THINK I'LL BE THE ONE WIPING THE SLATE, AND I'LL BE THE ONE TAKING OVER LEVIATHAN.
GUNN.
OH, DAMN IT TO HELL!

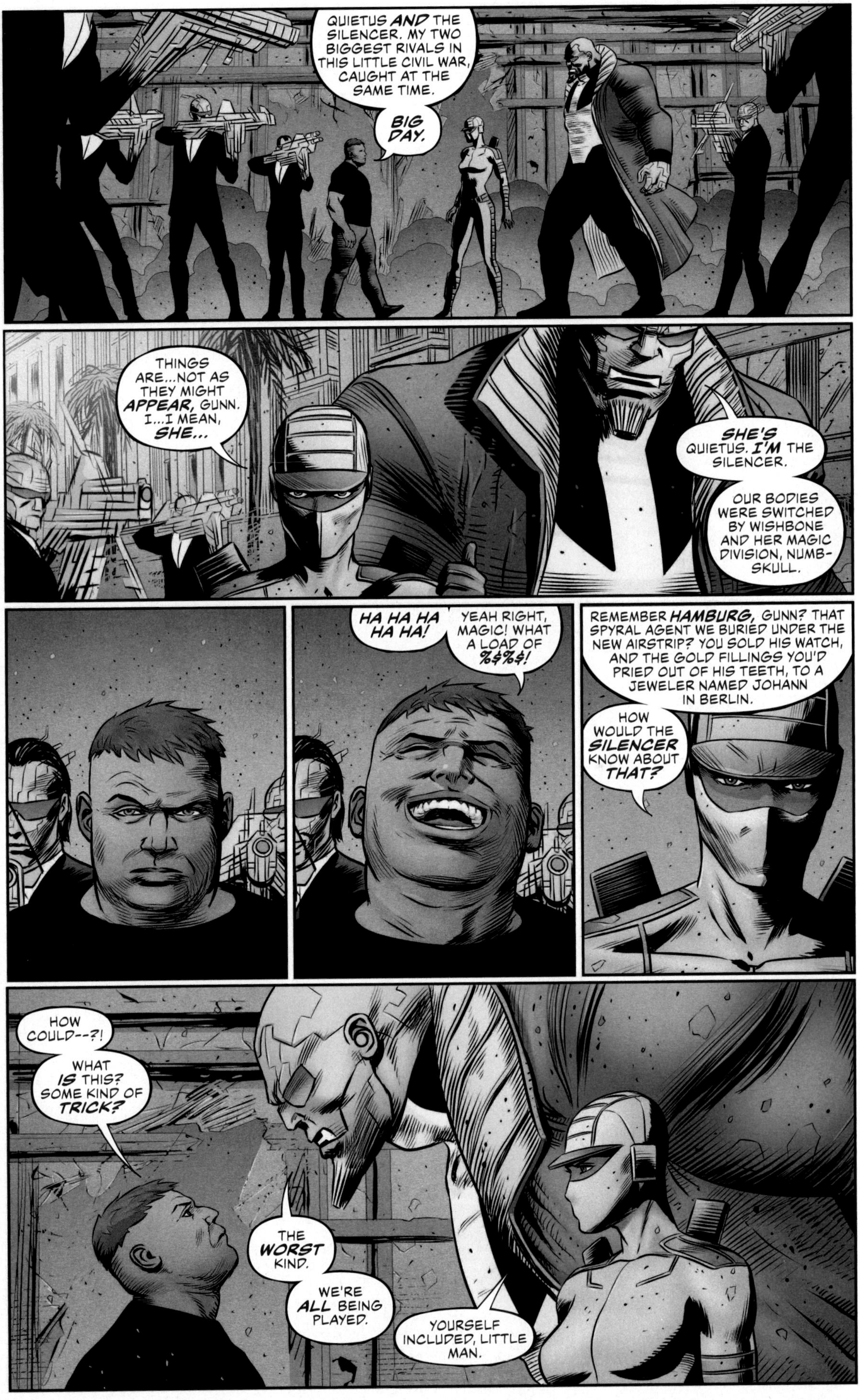
QUIETUS AND THE SILENCER. MY TWO BIGGEST RIVALS IN THIS LITTLE CIVIL WAR, CAUGHT AT THE SAME TIME.
BIG DAY.
THINGS ARE...NOT AS THEY MIGHT APPEAR, GUNN. I...I MEAN, SHE...
SHE'S QUIETUS. I'M THE SILENCER.
OUR BODIES WERE SWITCHED BY WISHBONE AND HER MAGIC DIVISION, NUMB-SKULL.
HA HA HA HA HA!
YEAH RIGHT, MAGIC! WHAT A LOAD OF %$%$!
REMEMBER HAMBURG, GUNN? THAT SPYRAL AGENT WE BURIED UNDER THE NEW AIRSTRIP? YOU SOLD HIS WATCH, AND THE GOLD FILLINGS YOU'D PRIED OUT OF HIS TEETH, TO A JEWELER NAMED JOHANN IN BERLIN.
HOW WOULD THE SILENCER KNOW ABOUT THAT?
HOW COULD--?!
WHAT IS THIS? SOME KIND OF TRICK?
THE WORST KIND.
WE'RE ALL BEING PLAYED.
YOURSELF INCLUDED, LITTLE MAN.

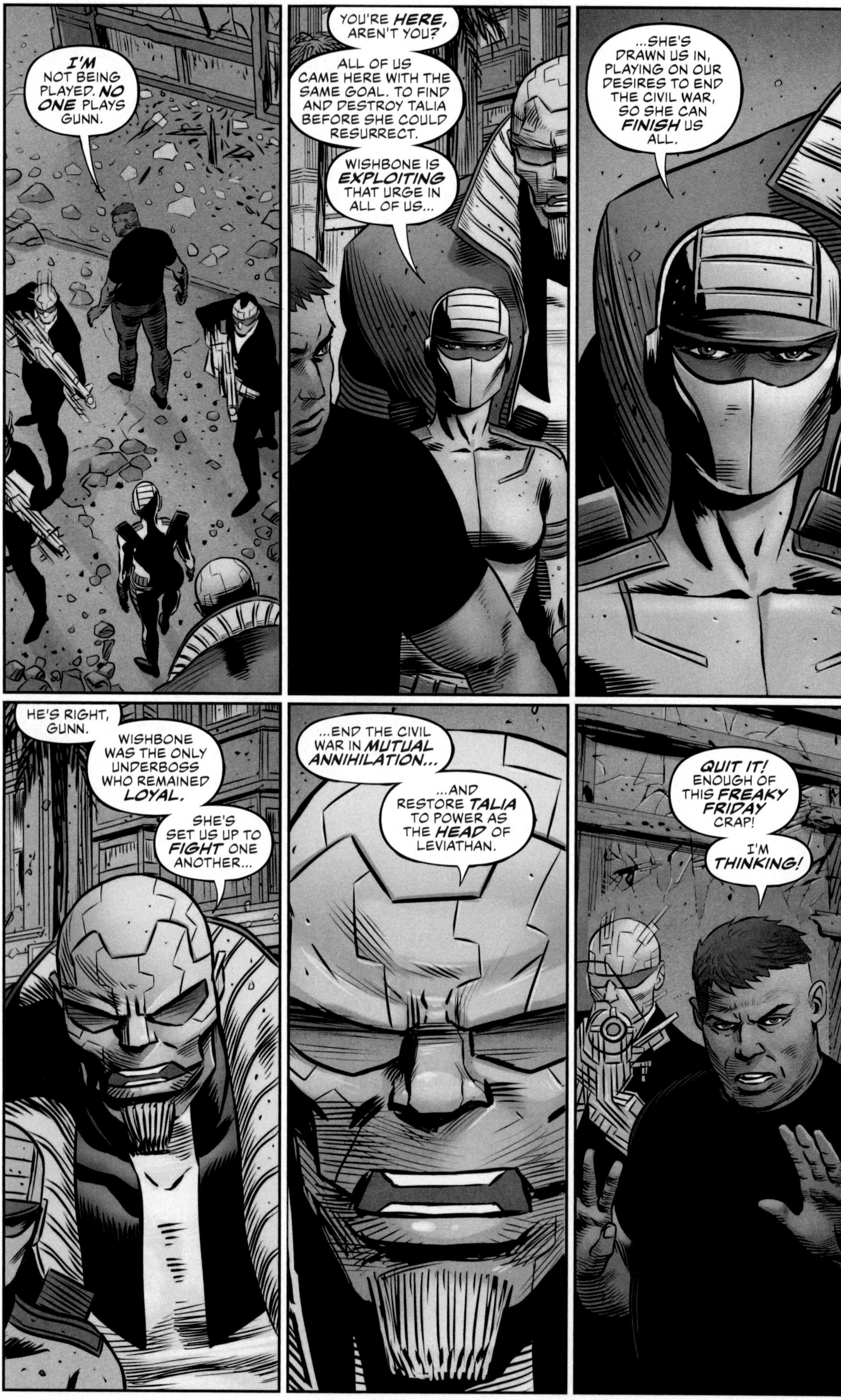
I'M NOT BEING PLAYED. NO ONE PLAYS GUNN.
YOU'RE HERE, AREN'T YOU?
ALL OF US CAME HERE WITH THE SAME GOAL. TO FIND AND DESTROY TALIA BEFORE SHE COULD RESURRECT.
WISHBONE IS EXPLOITING THAT URGE IN ALL OF US...
...SHE'S DRAWN US IN, PLAYING ON OUR DESIRES TO END THE CIVIL WAR, SO SHE CAN FINISH US ALL.
HE'S RIGHT, GUNN.
WISHBONE WAS THE ONLY UNDERBOSS WHO REMAINED LOYAL.
SHE'S SET US UP TO FIGHT ONE ANOTHER...
...END THE CIVIL WAR IN MUTUAL ANNIHILATION...
...AND RESTORE TALIA TO POWER AS THE HEAD OF LEVIATHAN.
QUIT IT! ENOUGH OF THIS FREAKY FRIDAY CRAP!
I'M THINKING!

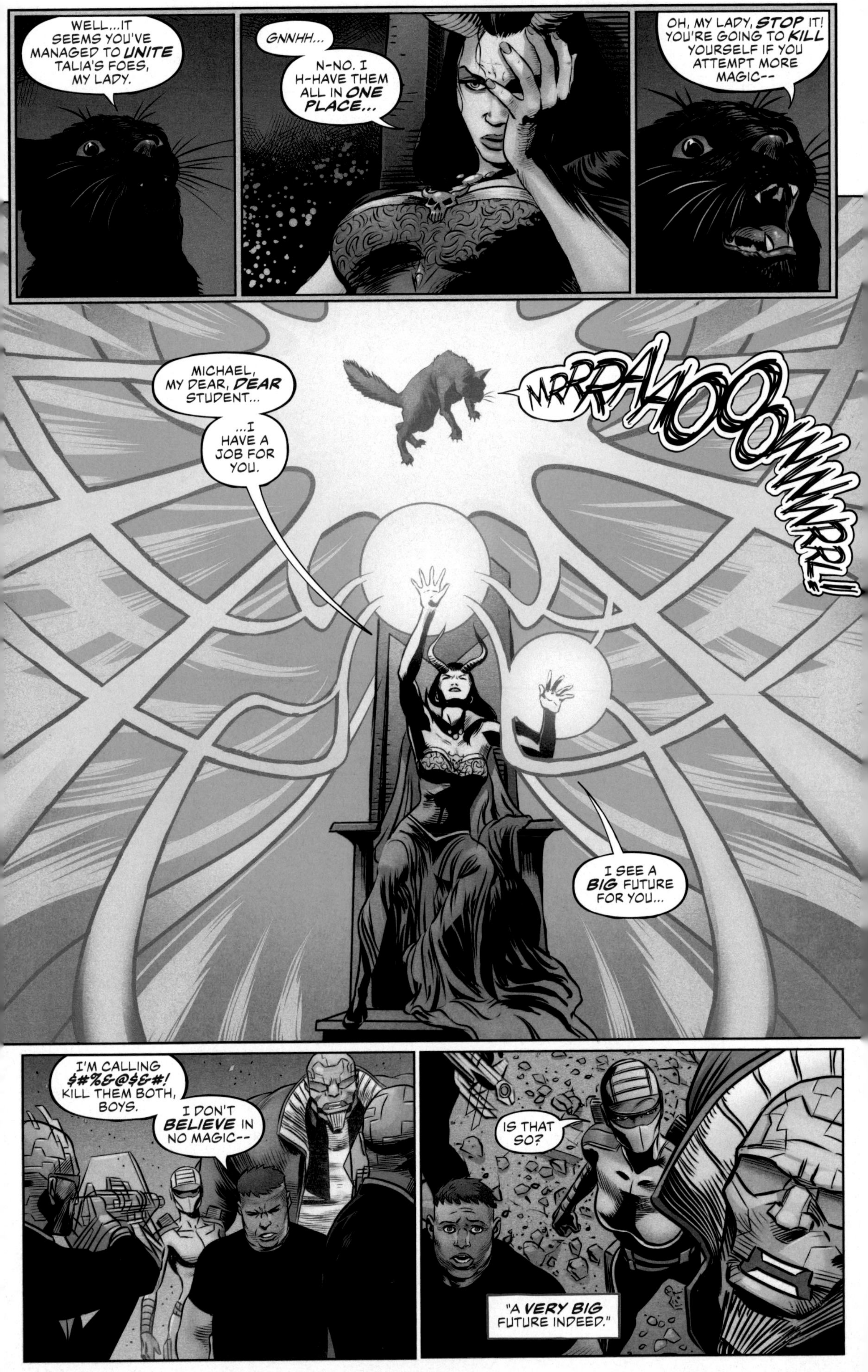
WELL...IT SEEMS YOU'VE MANAGED TO UNITE TALIA'S FOES, MY LADY.
GNNHH...
N-NO. I H-HAVE THEM ALL IN ONE PLACE...
OH, MY LADY, STOP IT! YOU'RE GOING TO KILL YOURSELF IF YOU ATTEMPT MORE MAGIC--
MICHAEL, MY DEAR, DEAR STUDENT...
...I HAVE A JOB FOR YOU.
MRRRRAHOOOWWRRL!!
I SEE A BIG FUTURE FOR YOU...
I'M CALLING $#%&@$&#! KILL THEM BOTH, BOYS.
I DON'T BELIEVE IN NO MAGIC--
IS THAT SO?
"A VERY BIG FUTURE INDEED."

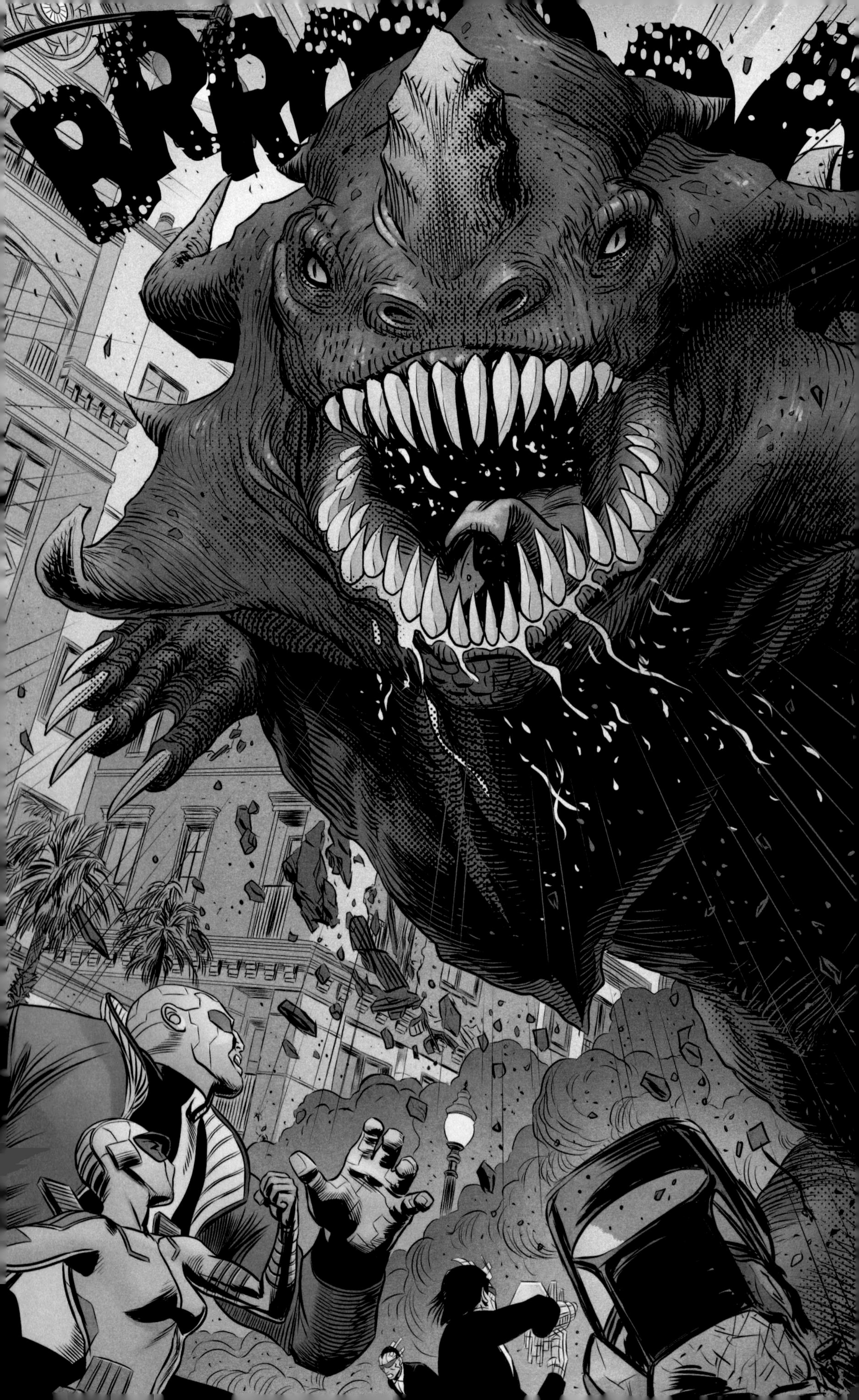
BRR

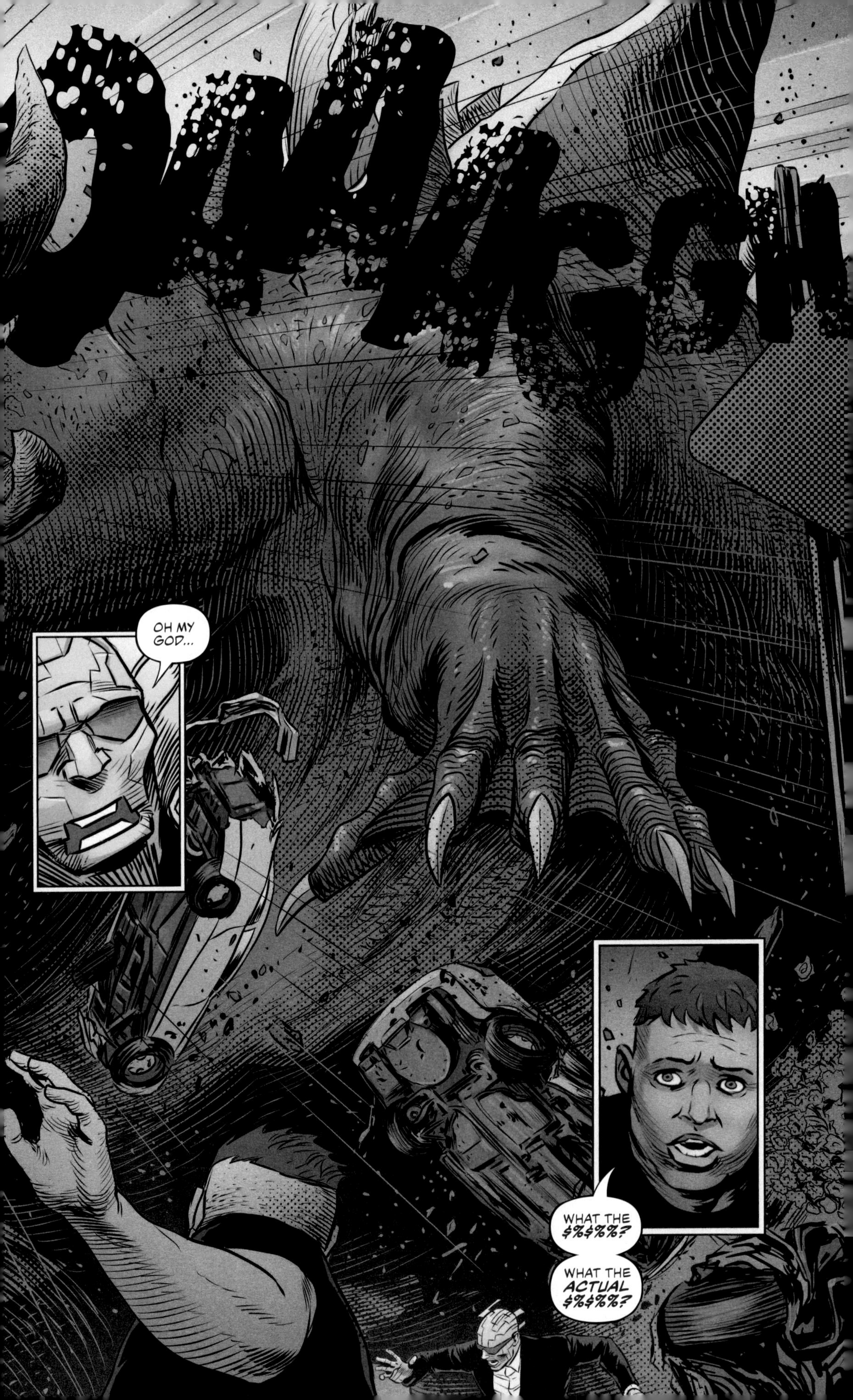

OH MY GOD...
WHAT THE $%$%%?
WHAT THE ACTUAL $%$%%?

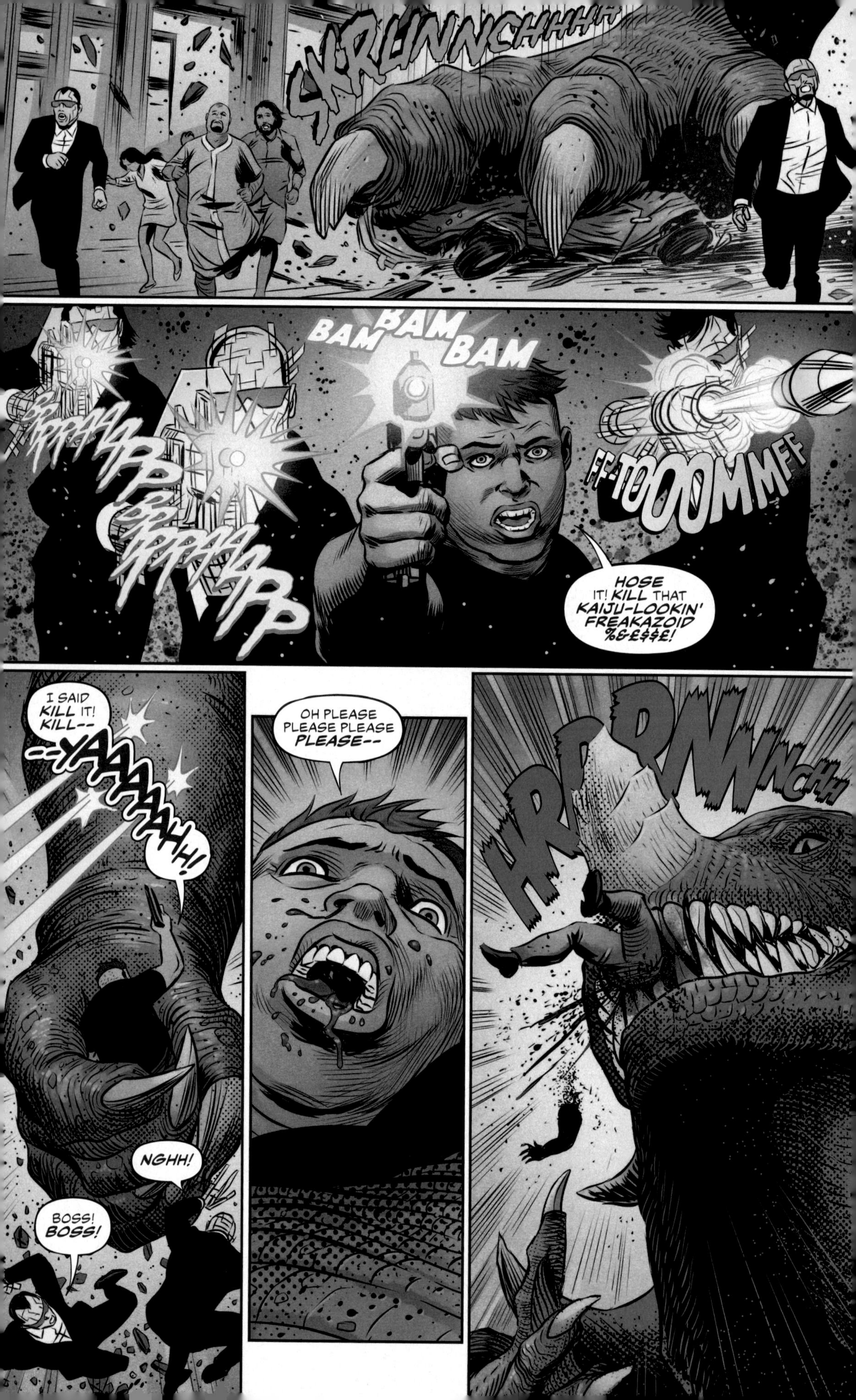
SKRUNNCHHHH
BAM BAM BAM BAM
FF-TOOOOMMFF
HOSE IT! KILL THAT KAIJU-LOOKIN' FREAKAZOID %&£$$£!
I SAID KILL IT! KILL--
--YAAAAAHH!
NGHH!
BOSS! BOSS!
OH PLEASE PLEASE PLEASE PLEASE--
HRRDNNNCHH

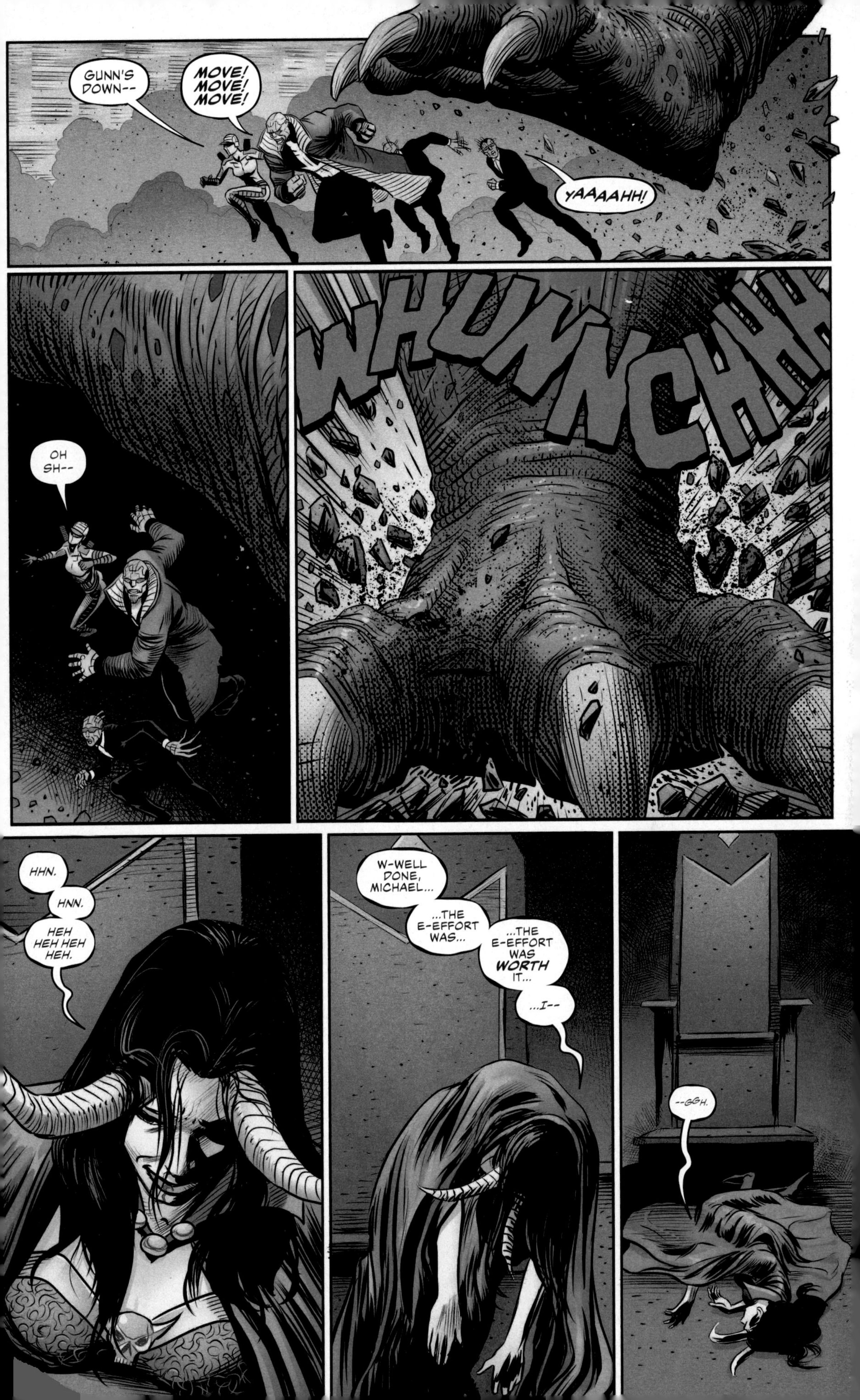
GUNN'S DOWN--
MOVE! MOVE! MOVE!
YAAAAHH!
OH SH--
WHUNNCHH
HHN.
HNN.
HEH HEH HEH HEH.
W-WELL DONE, MICHAEL...
...THE E-EFFORT WAS...
...THE E-EFFORT WAS WORTH IT...
...I--
--GGH.

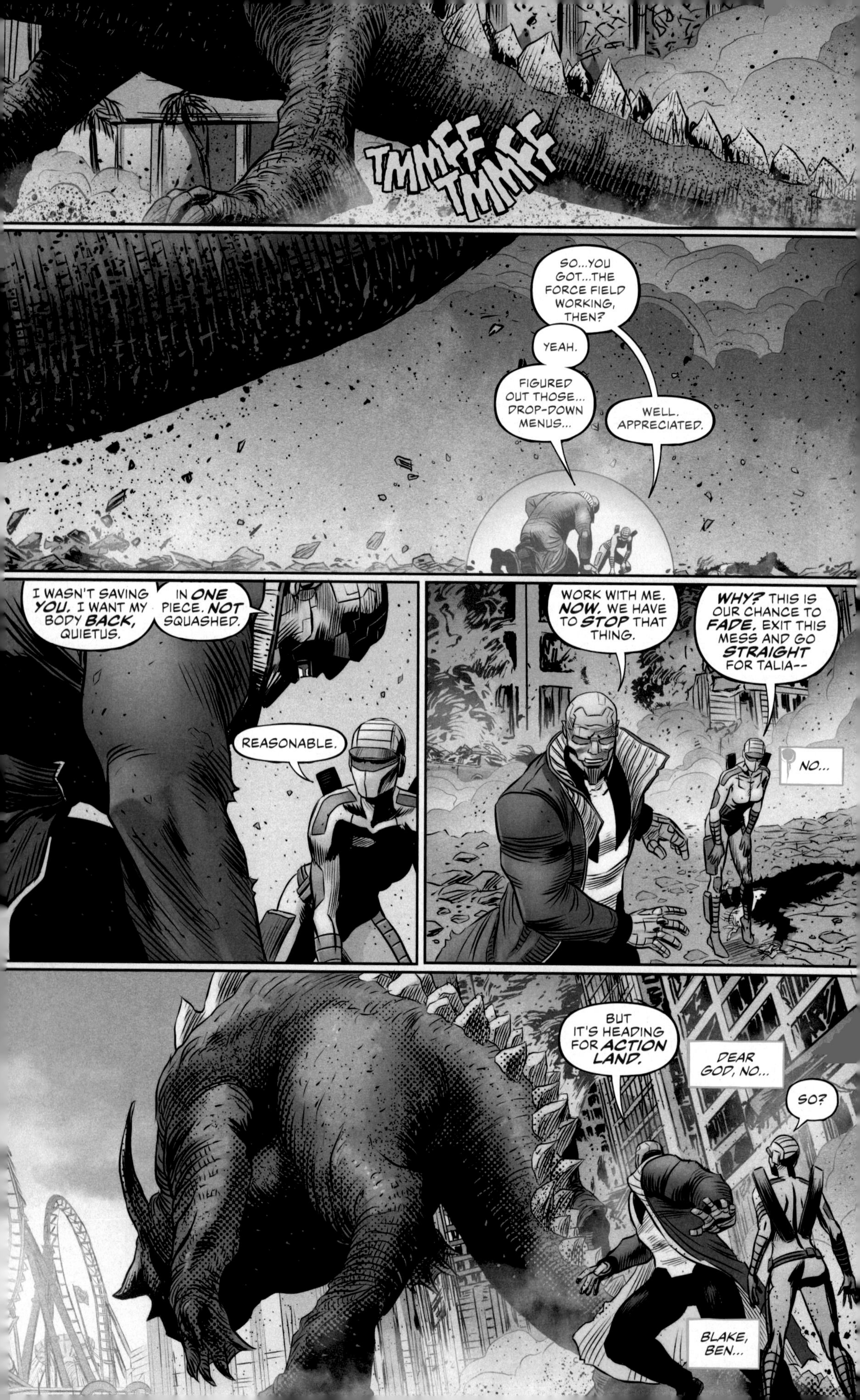
TMMFF TMMFF
SO...YOU GOT...THE FORCE FIELD WORKING, THEN?
YEAH.
FIGURED OUT THOSE... DROP-DOWN MENUS...
WELL. APPRECIATED.
I WASN'T SAVING YOU. I WANT MY BODY BACK, QUIETUS.
IN ONE PIECE. NOT SQUASHED.
REASONABLE.
WORK WITH ME. NOW. WE HAVE TO STOP THAT THING.
WHY? THIS IS OUR CHANCE TO FADE. EXIT THIS MESS AND GO STRAIGHT FOR TALIA--
NO...
BUT IT'S HEADING FOR ACTION LAND.
DEAR GOD, NO...
SO?
BLAKE, BEN...

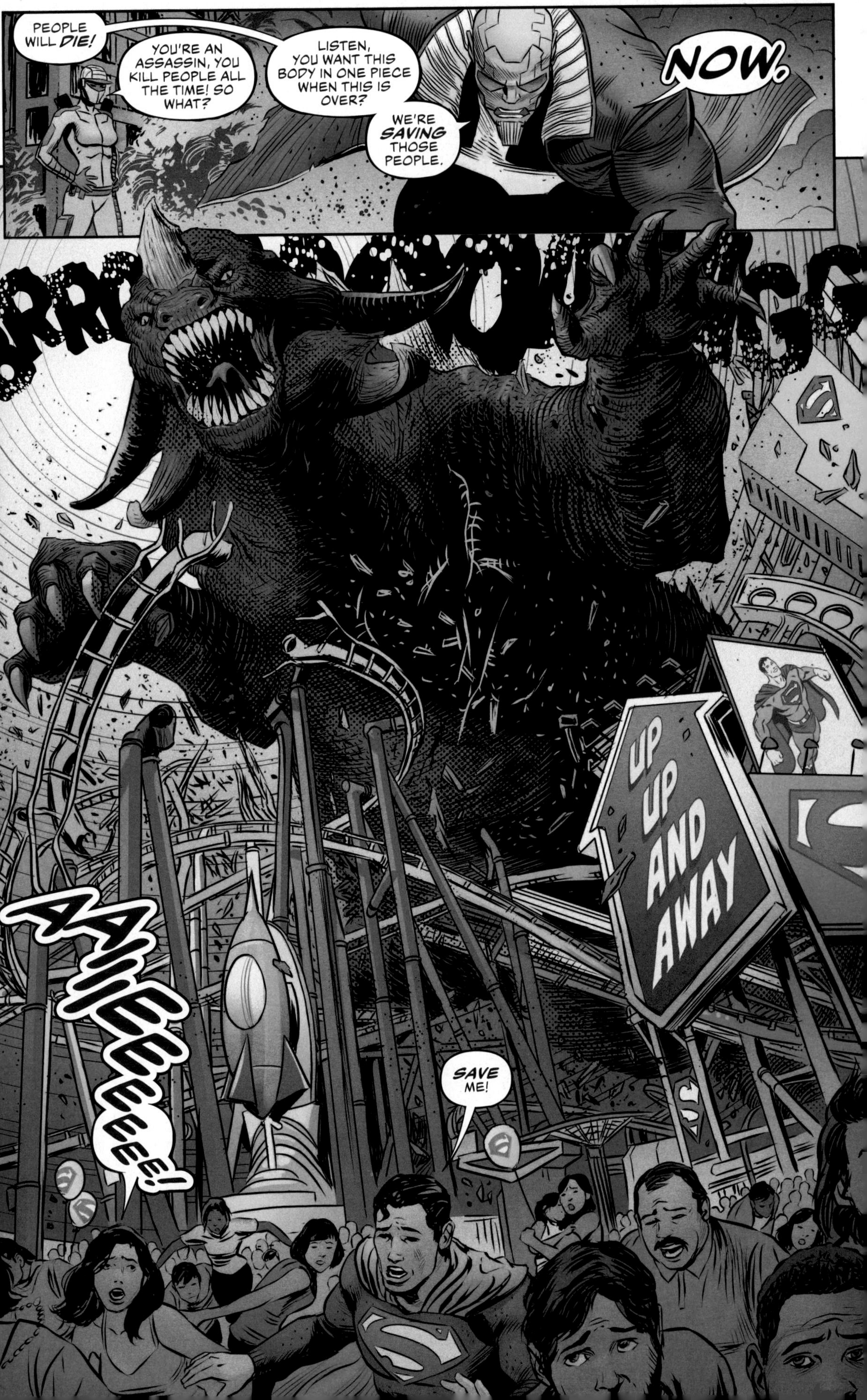
PEOPLE WILL *DIE!*
YOU'RE AN ASSASSIN, YOU KILL PEOPLE ALL THE TIME! SO WHAT?
LISTEN, YOU WANT THIS BODY IN ONE PIECE WHEN THIS IS OVER?
WE'RE *SAVING* THOSE PEOPLE.
NOW.
UP UP AND AWAY
SAVE ME!

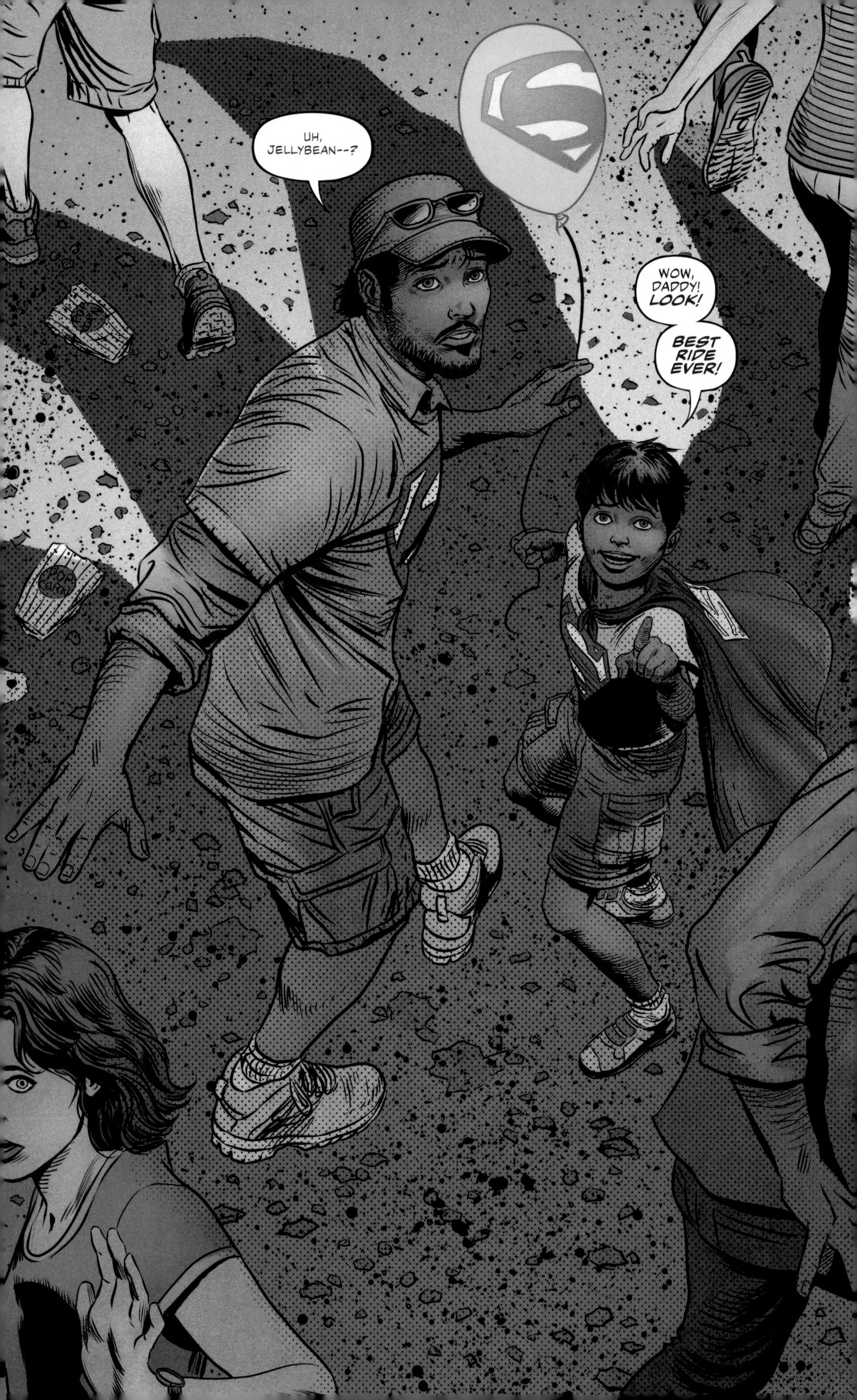
UH, JELLYBEAN--?
WOW, DADDY! LOOK!
BEST RIDE EVER!

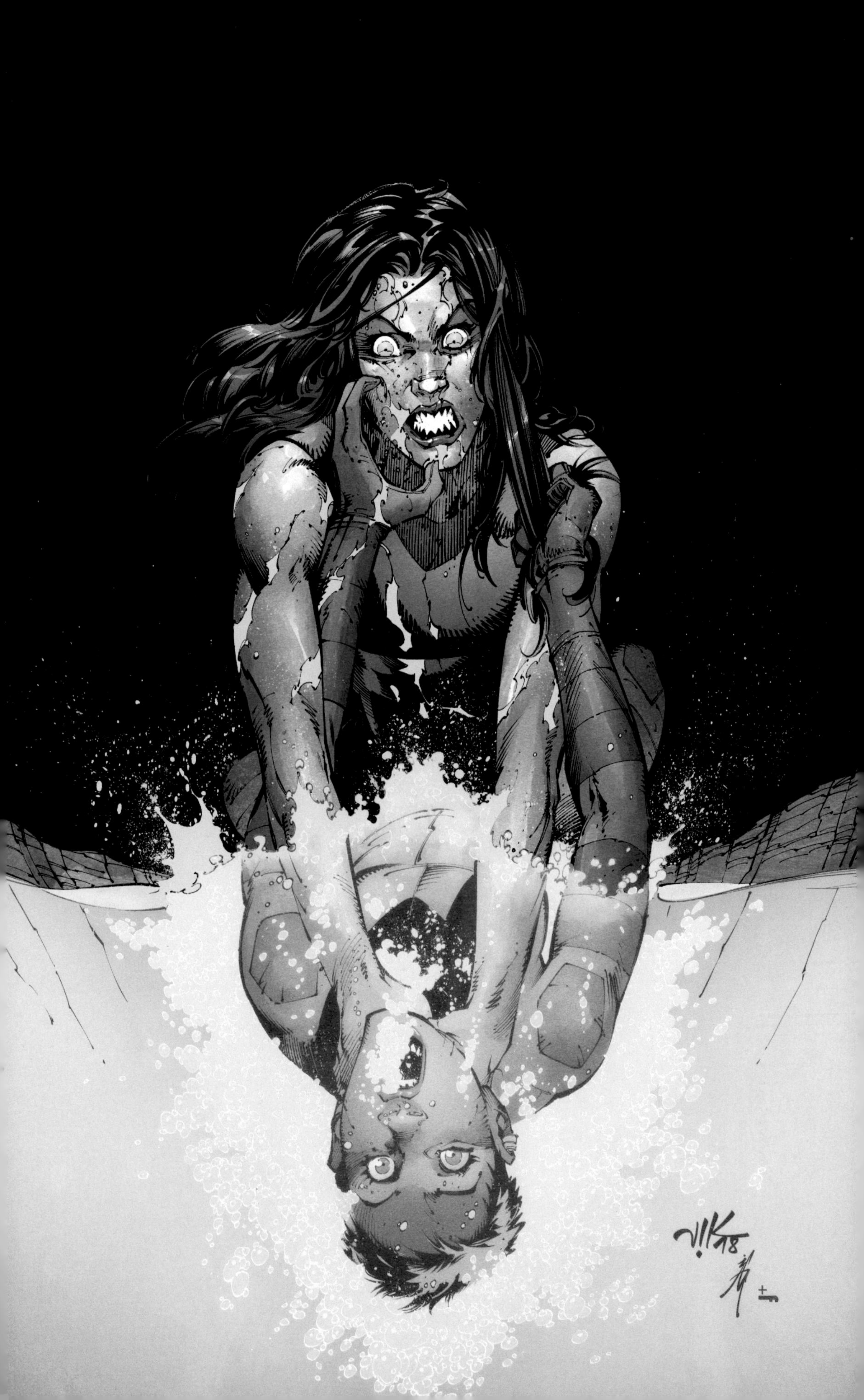

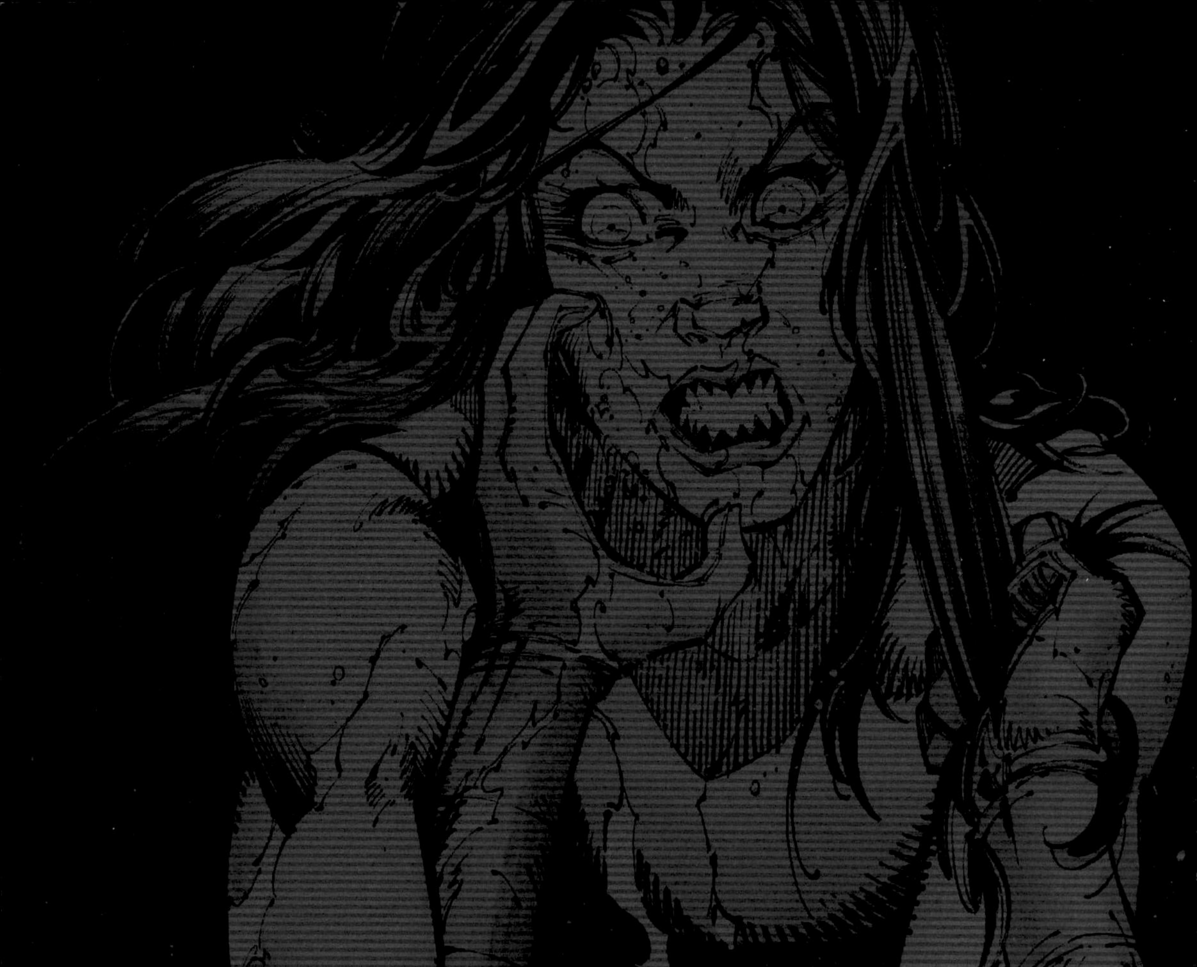

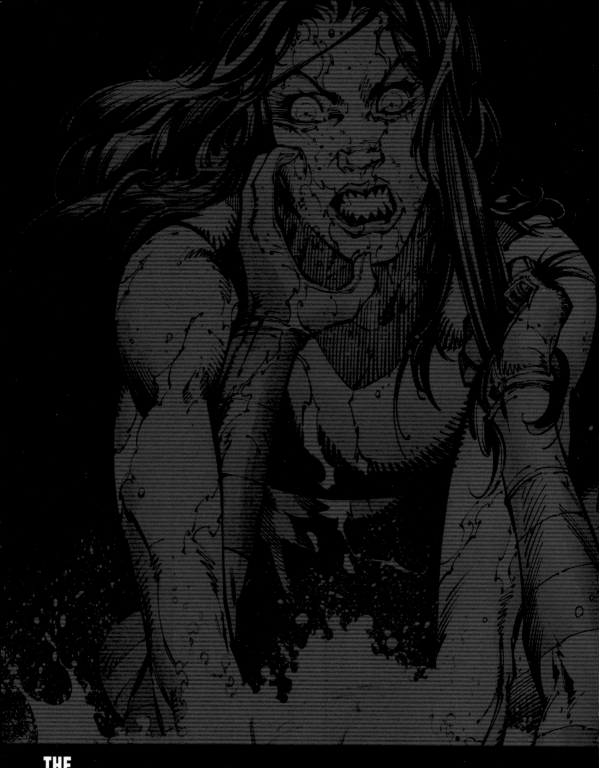

THE SILENCER #10

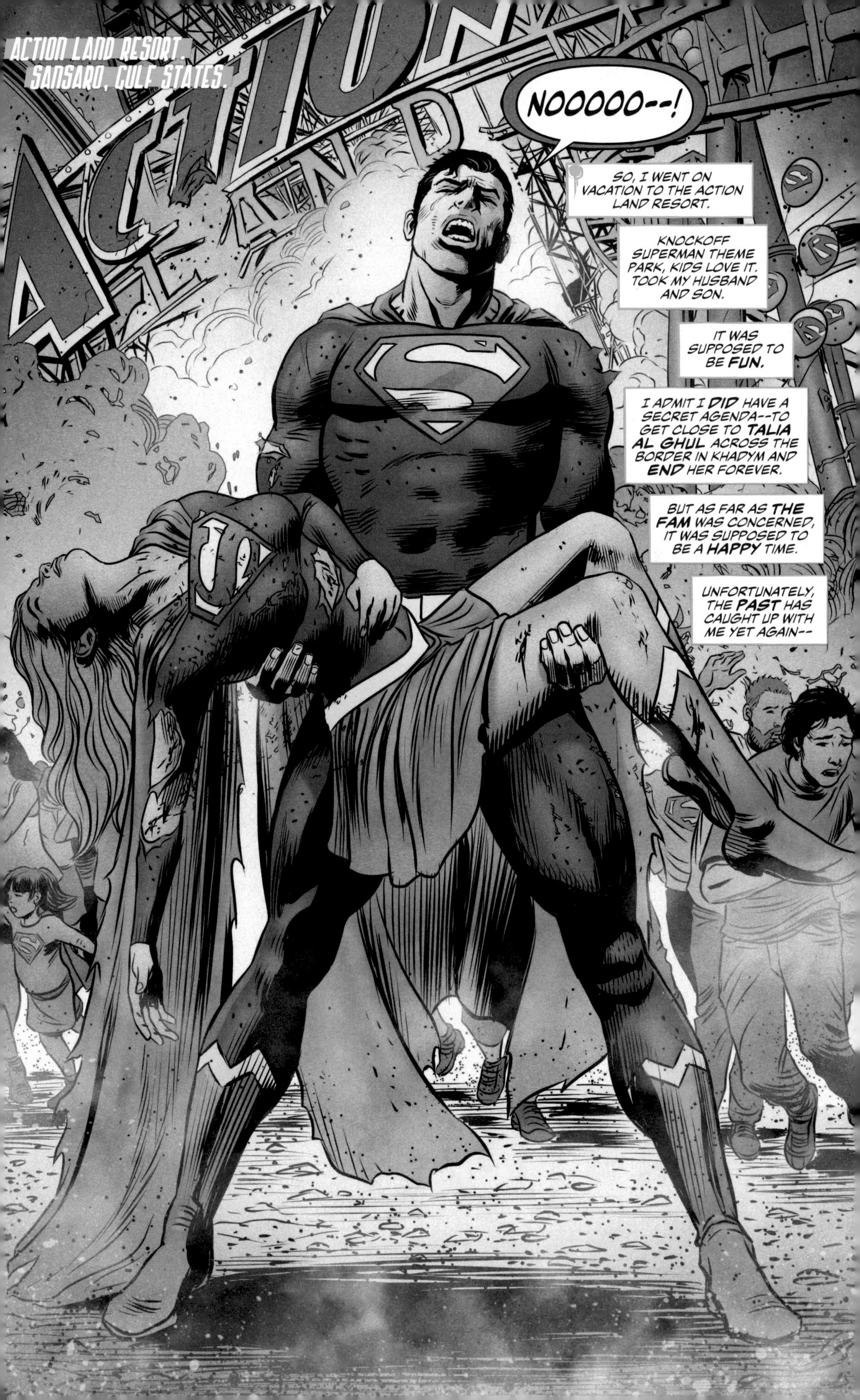
ACTION LAND RESORT. SANSARO, GULF STATES.
NOOOOO--!
SO, I WENT ON VACATION TO THE ACTION LAND RESORT.
KNOCKOFF SUPERMAN THEME PARK, KIDS LOVE IT. TOOK MY HUSBAND AND SON.
IT WAS SUPPOSED TO BE FUN.
I ADMIT I DID HAVE A SECRET AGENDA--TO GET CLOSE TO TALIA AL GHUL ACROSS THE BORDER IN KHADYM AND END HER FOREVER.
BUT AS FAR AS THE FAM WAS CONCERNED, IT WAS SUPPOSED TO BE A HAPPY TIME.
UNFORTUNATELY, THE PAST HAS CAUGHT UP WITH ME YET AGAIN--

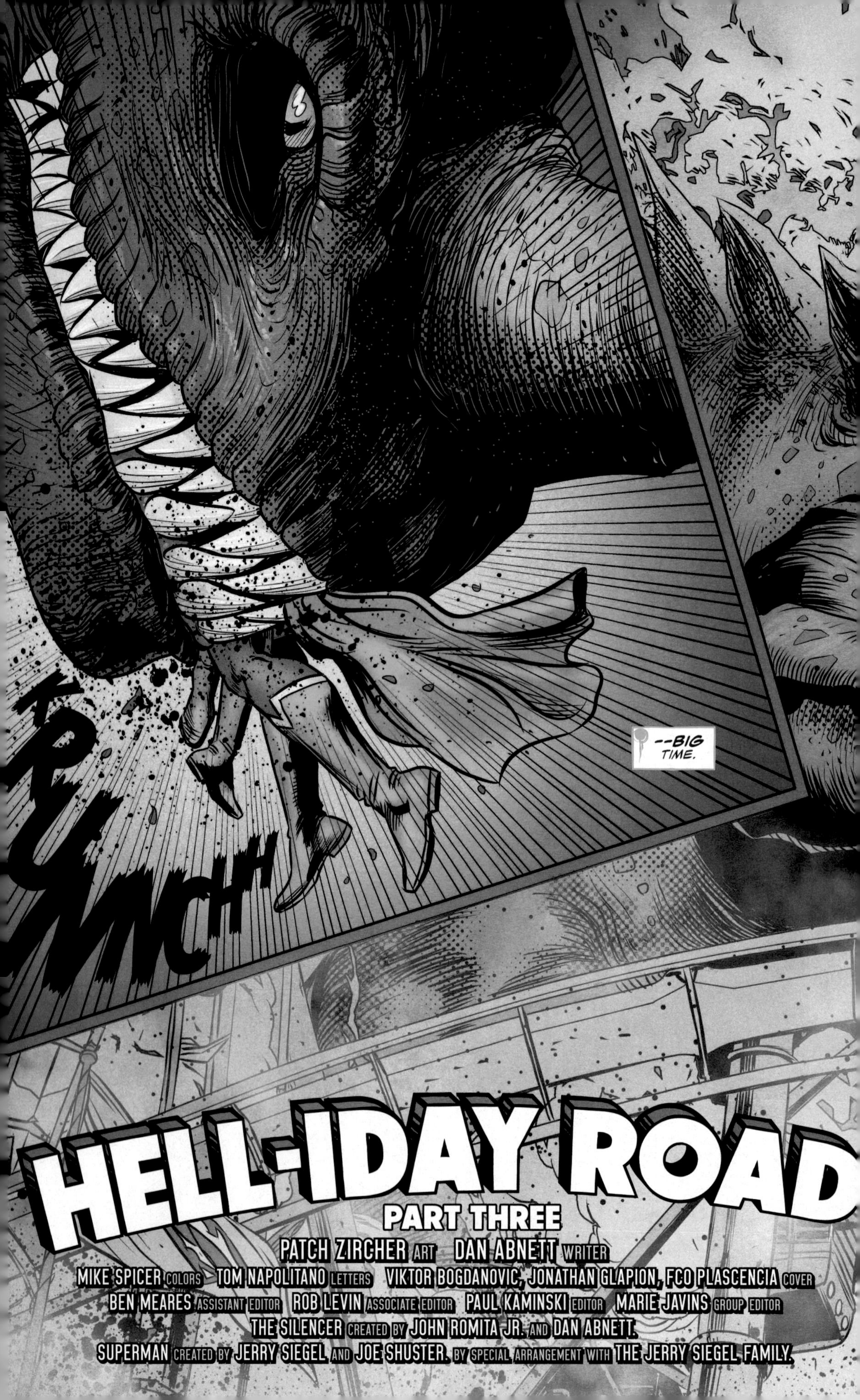
KRUNCH
--BIG TIME.

HELL-IDAY ROAD

PART THREE

PATCH ZIRCHER ART DAN ABNETT WRITER
MIKE SPICER COLORS TOM NAPOLITANO LETTERS VIKTOR BOGDANOVIC, JONATHAN GLAPION, FCO PLASCENCIA COVER
BEN MEARES ASSISTANT EDITOR ROB LEVIN ASSOCIATE EDITOR PAUL KAMINSKI EDITOR MARIE JAVINS GROUP EDITOR

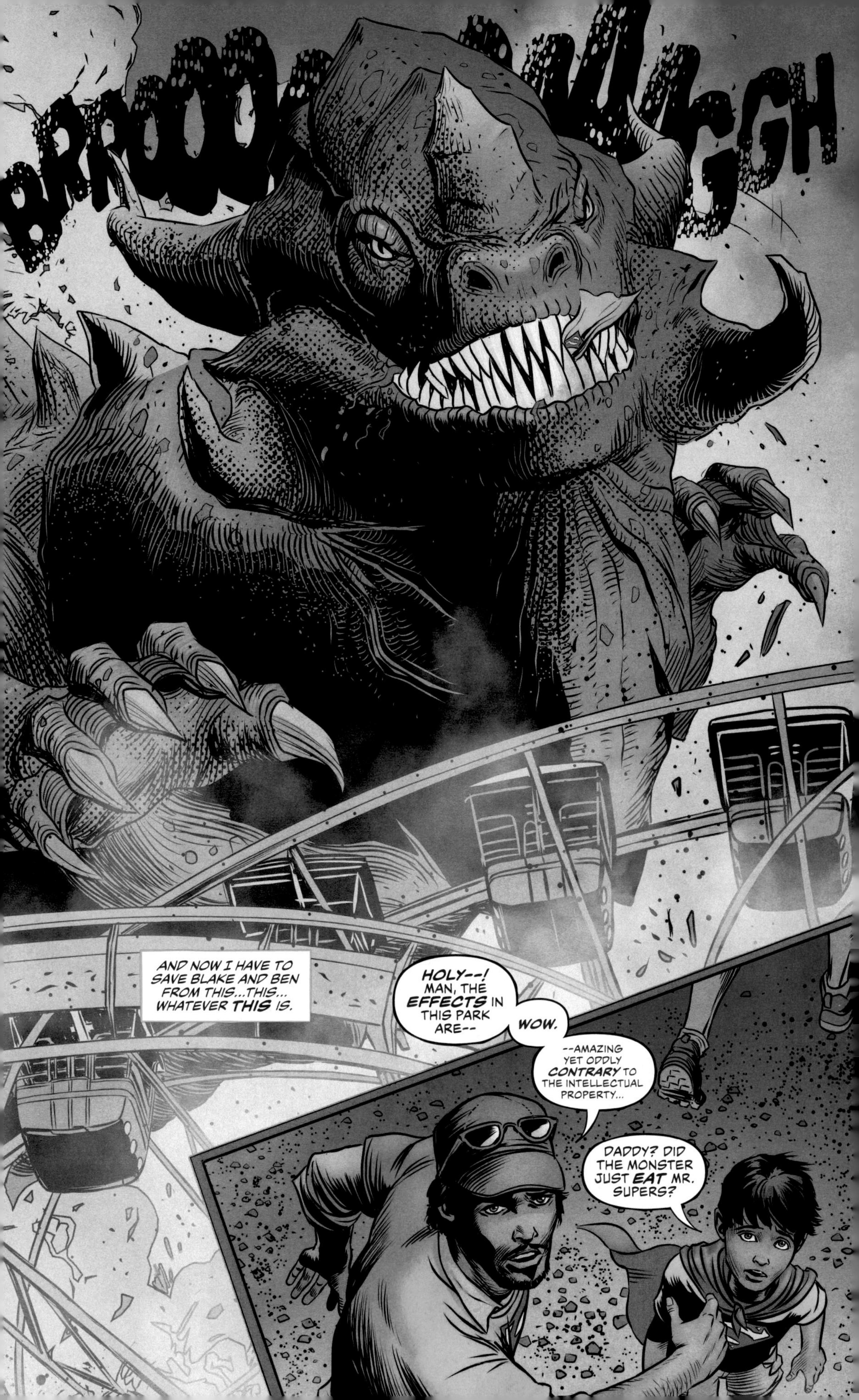
BRROOO...MUUGH
AND NOW I HAVE TO SAVE BLAKE AND BEN FROM THIS...THIS... WHATEVER THIS IS.
HOLY--! MAN, THE EFFECTS IN THIS PARK ARE--
WOW.
--AMAZING YET ODDLY CONTRARY TO THE INTELLECTUAL PROPERTY...
DADDY? DID THE MONSTER JUST EAT MR. SUPERS?

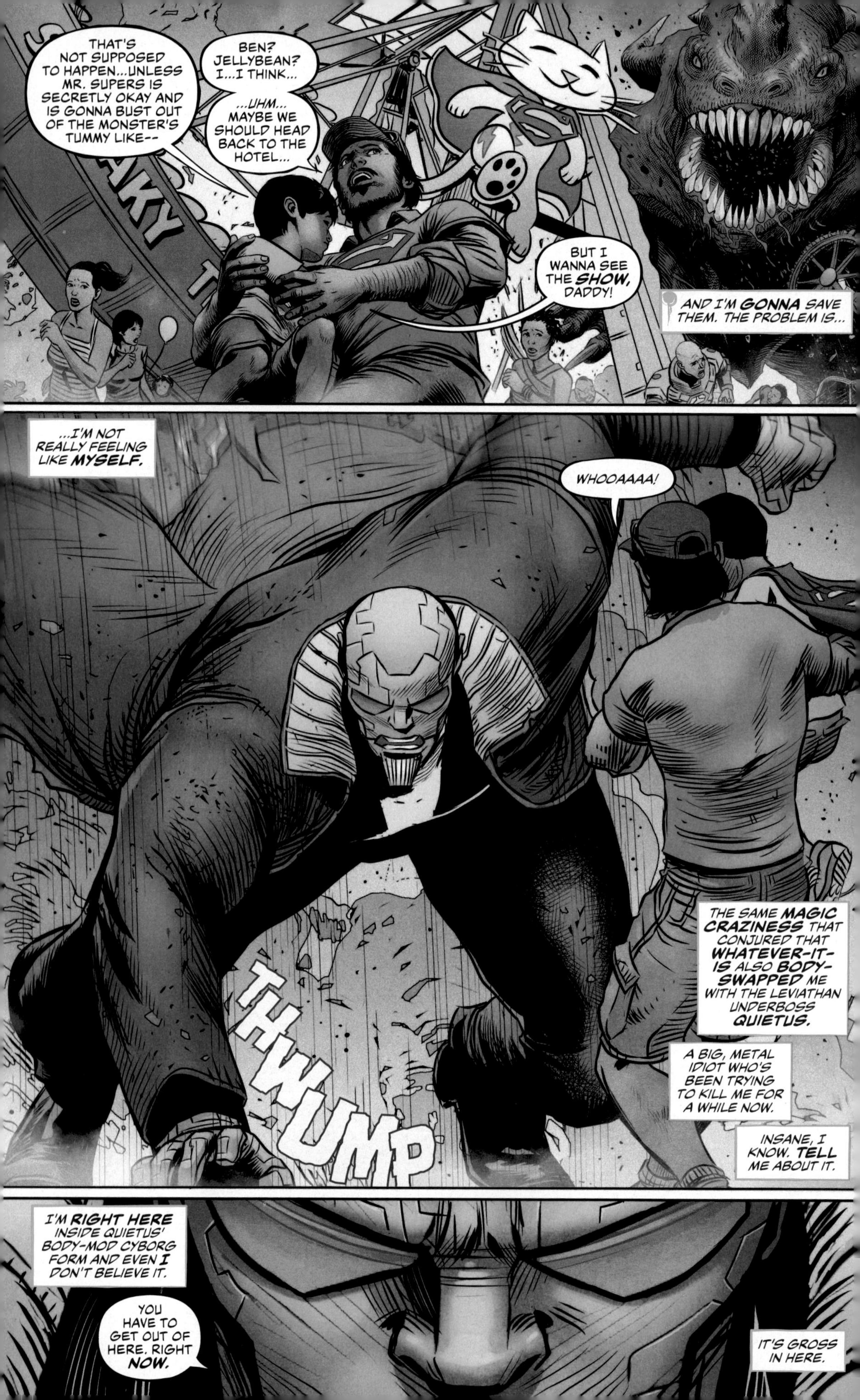

THAT'S NOT SUPPOSED TO HAPPEN...UNLESS MR. SUPERS IS SECRETLY OKAY AND IS GONNA BUST OUT OF THE MONSTER'S TUMMY LIKE--
BEN? JELLYBEAN? I...I THINK...
...UHM... MAYBE WE SHOULD HEAD BACK TO THE HOTEL...
BUT I WANNA SEE THE SHOW, DADDY!
AND I'M GONNA SAVE THEM. THE PROBLEM IS...
...I'M NOT REALLY FEELING LIKE MYSELF.
WHOOAAAA!
THE SAME MAGIC CRAZINESS THAT CONJURED THAT WHATEVER-IT-IS ALSO BODY-SWAPPED ME WITH THE LEVIATHAN UNDERBOSS QUIETUS.
A BIG, METAL IDIOT WHO'S BEEN TRYING TO KILL ME FOR A WHILE NOW.
INSANE, I KNOW. TELL ME ABOUT IT.
THWUMP
I'M RIGHT HERE INSIDE QUIETUS' BODY-MOD CYBORG FORM AND EVEN I DON'T BELIEVE IT.
YOU HAVE TO GET OUT OF HERE. RIGHT NOW.
IT'S GROSS IN HERE.

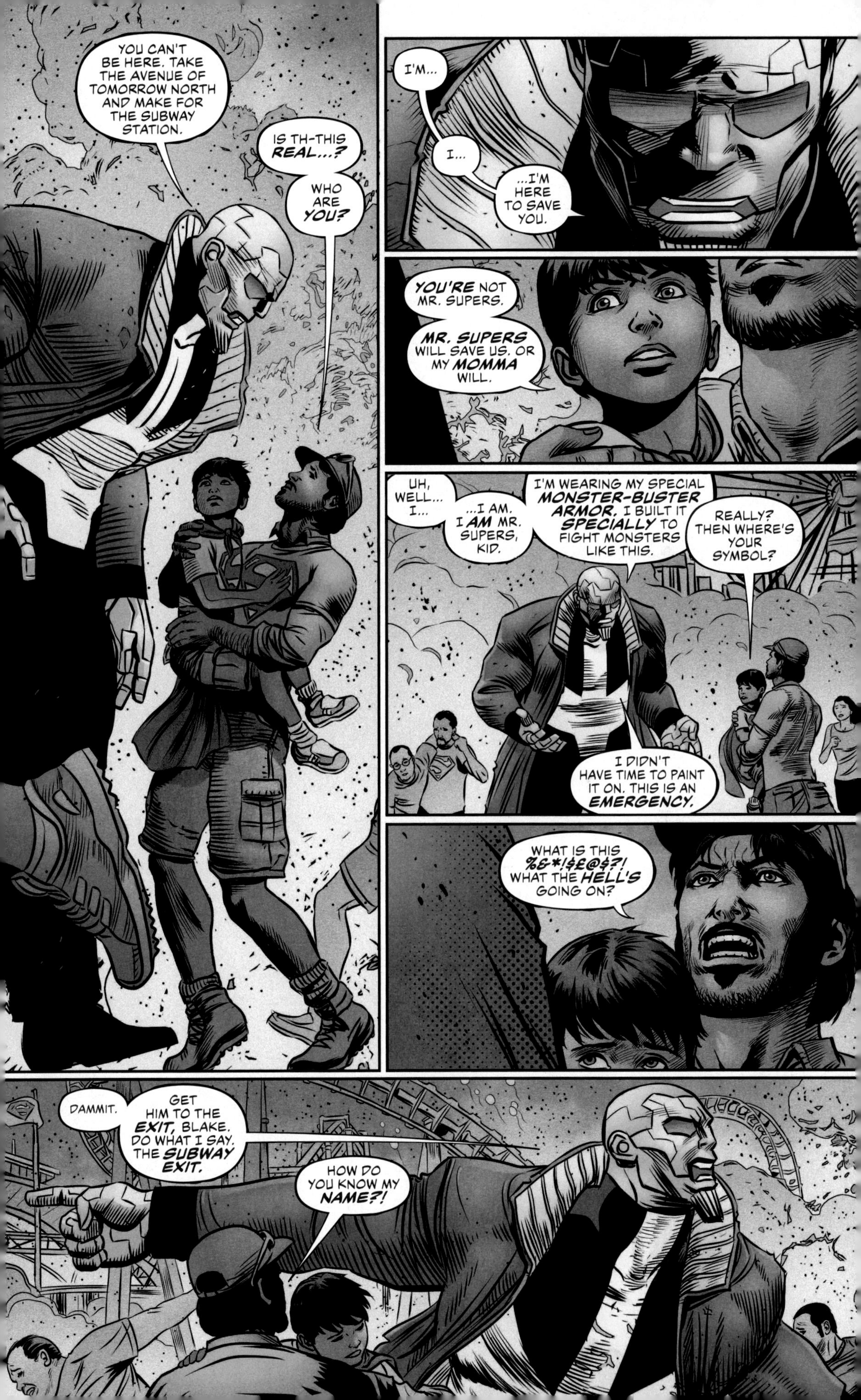
YOU CAN'T BE HERE. TAKE THE AVENUE OF TOMORROW NORTH AND MAKE FOR THE SUBWAY STATION.
IS TH-THIS REAL...?
WHO ARE YOU?
I'M...
I...
...I'M HERE TO SAVE YOU.
YOU'RE NOT MR. SUPERS.
MR. SUPERS WILL SAVE US. OR MY MOMMA WILL.
UH, WELL... I...
...I AM. I AM MR. SUPERS, KID.
I'M WEARING MY SPECIAL MONSTER-BUSTER ARMOR. I BUILT IT SPECIALLY TO FIGHT MONSTERS LIKE THIS.
REALLY? THEN WHERE'S YOUR SYMBOL?
I DIDN'T HAVE TIME TO PAINT IT ON. THIS IS AN EMERGENCY.
WHAT IS THIS %&*!$£@$?! WHAT THE HELL'S GOING ON?
DAMMIT.
GET HIM TO THE EXIT, BLAKE. DO WHAT I SAY. THE SUBWAY EXIT.
HOW DO YOU KNOW MY NAME?!

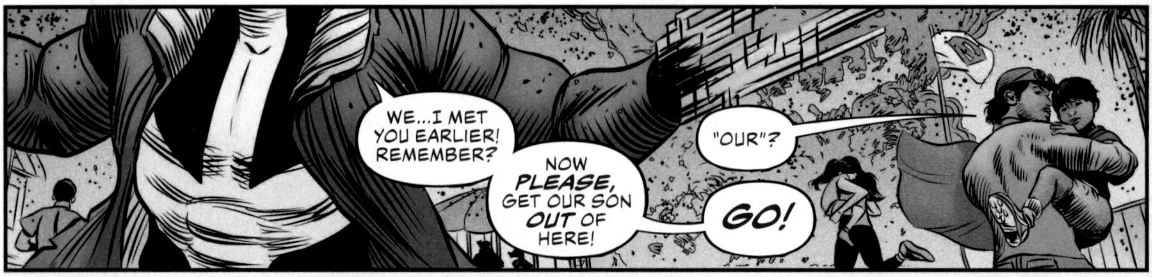
WE...I MET YOU EARLIER! REMEMBER?
NOW PLEASE, GET OUR SON OUT OF HERE!
"OUR"?
GO!

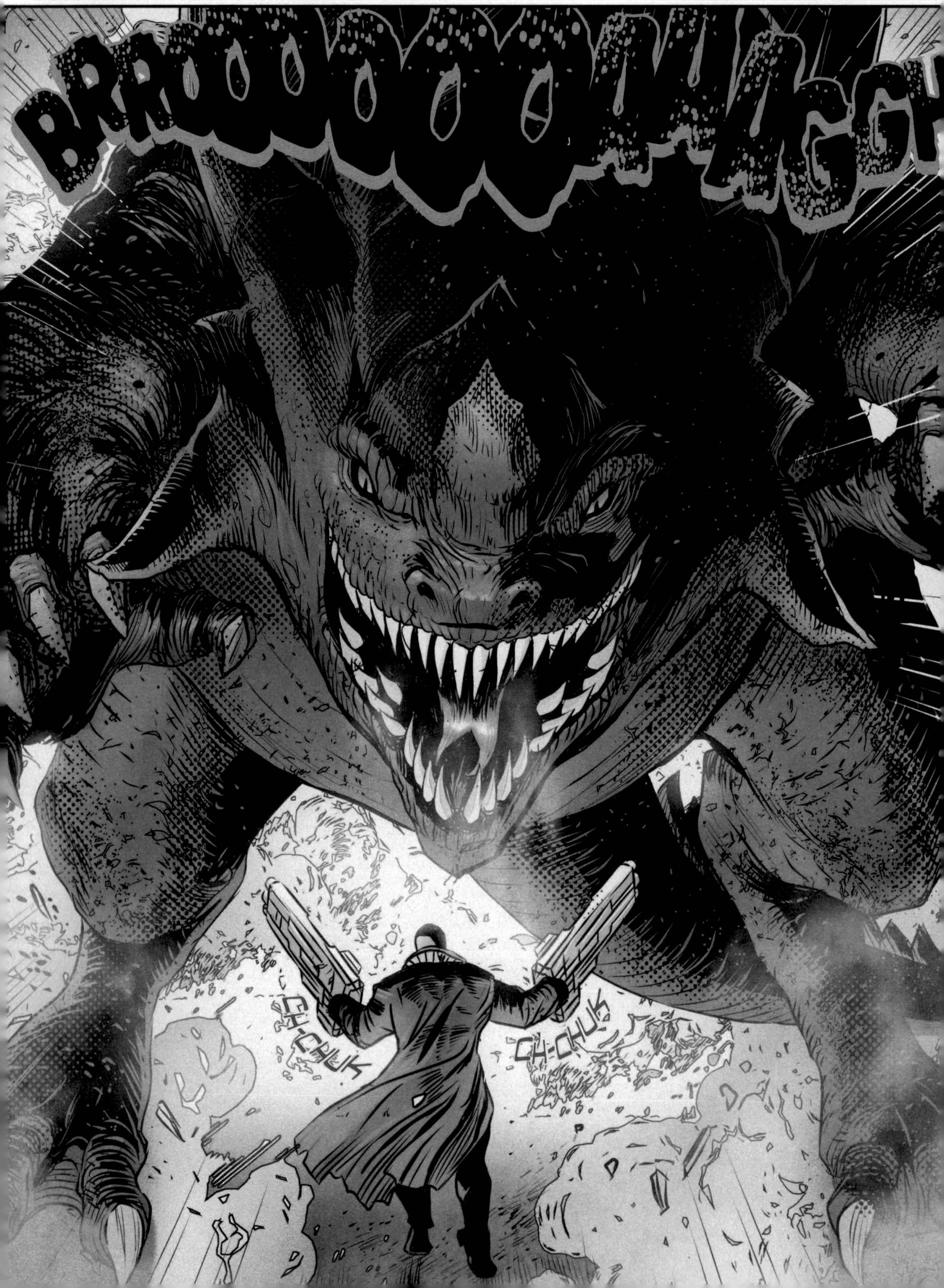
BRROOOOOMMGH
CH-CHUK
CH-CHUK

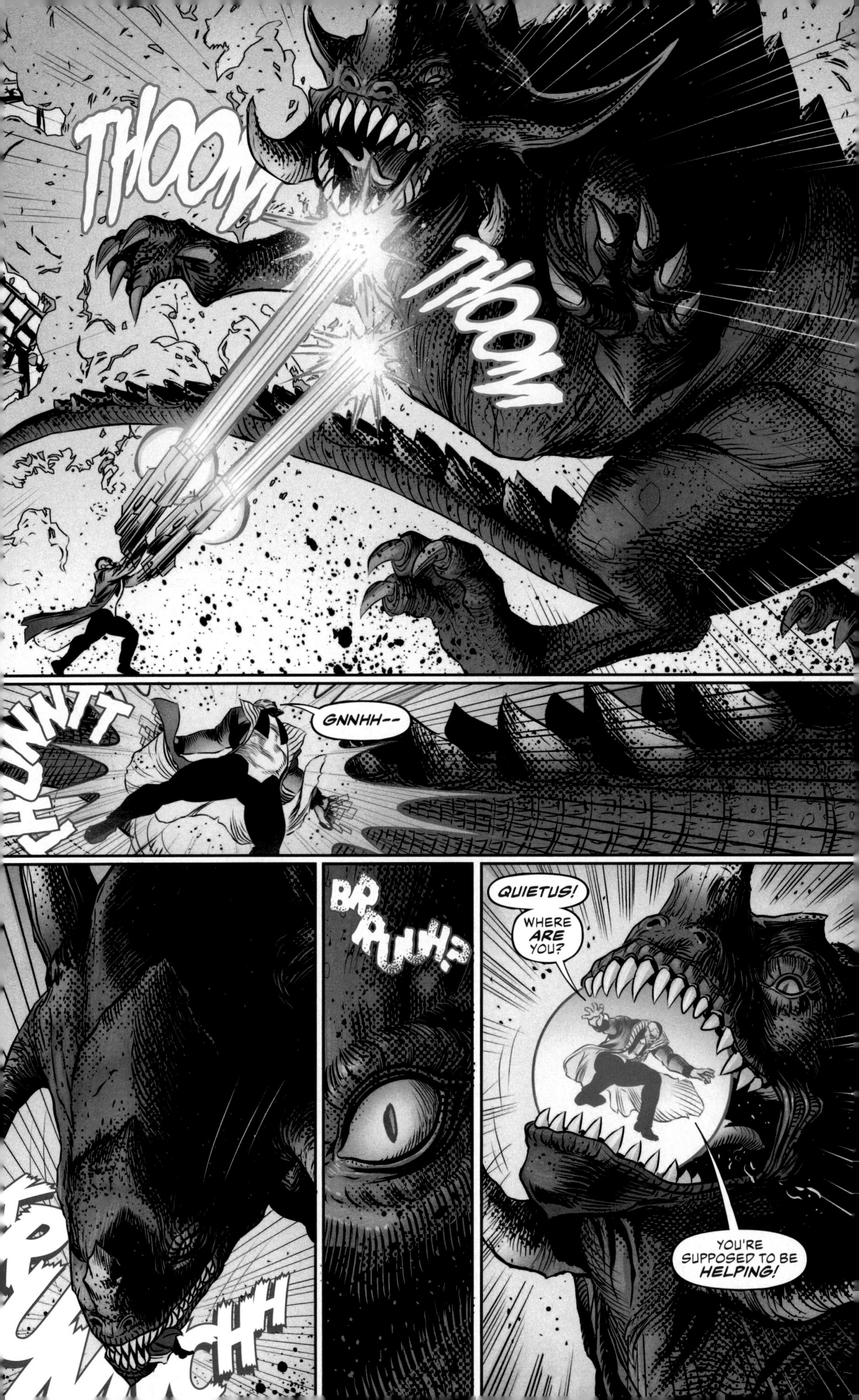
THOOM
THOOM
GNNHH--
BRRUH?
QUIETUS!
WHERE ARE YOU?
YOU'RE SUPPOSED TO BE HELPING!

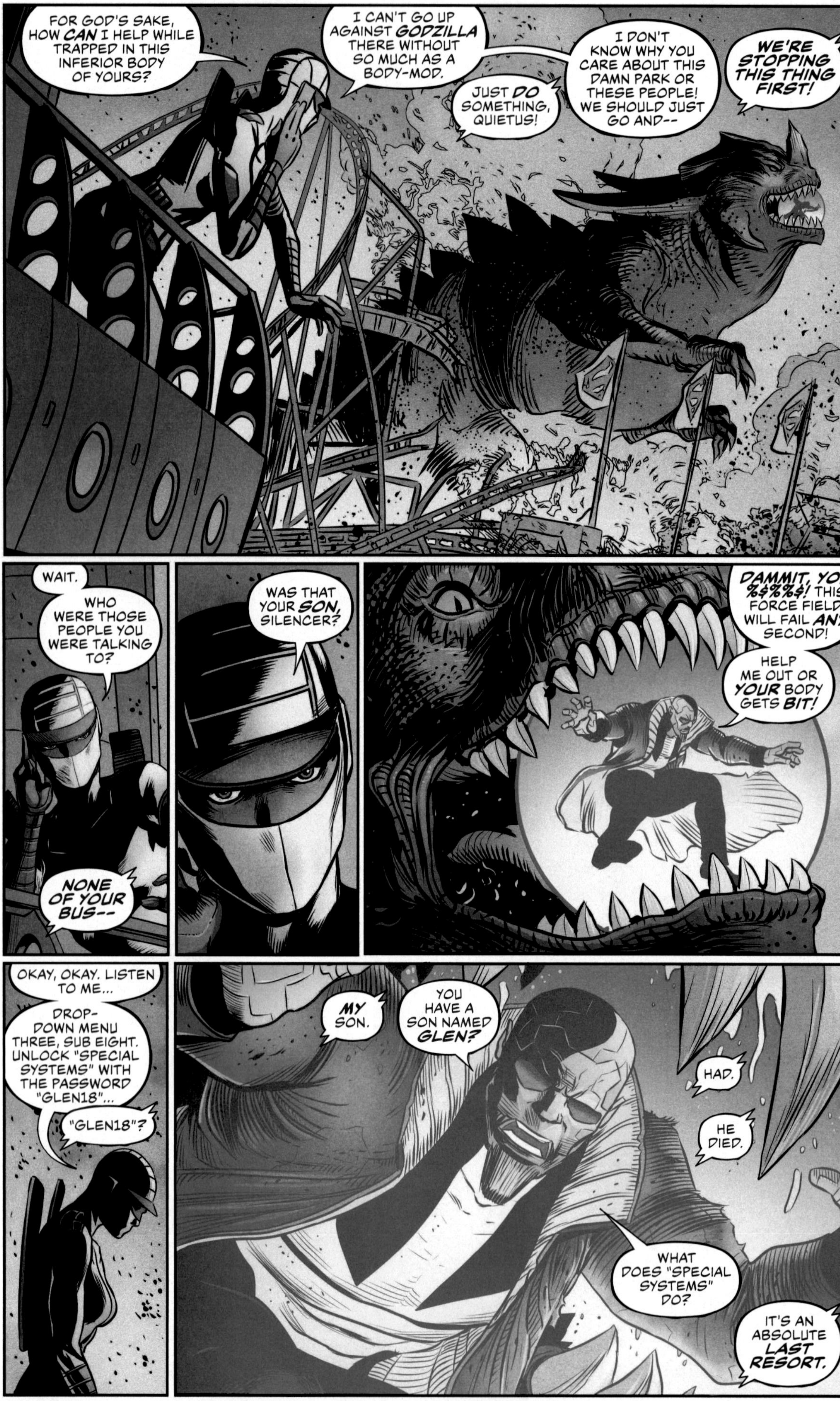
FOR GOD'S SAKE, HOW CAN I HELP WHILE TRAPPED IN THIS INFERIOR BODY OF YOURS?
I CAN'T GO UP AGAINST GODZILLA THERE WITHOUT SO MUCH AS A BODY-MOD.
JUST DO SOMETHING, QUIETUS!
I DON'T KNOW WHY YOU CARE ABOUT THIS DAMN PARK OR THESE PEOPLE! WE SHOULD JUST GO AND--
WE'RE STOPPING THIS THING FIRST!
WAIT.
WHO WERE THOSE PEOPLE YOU WERE TALKING TO?
NONE OF YOUR BUS--
WAS THAT YOUR SON, SILENCER?
DAMMIT, YOU %$%$! THIS FORCE FIELD WILL FAIL ANY SECOND!
HELP ME OUT OR YOUR BODY GETS BIT!
OKAY, OKAY. LISTEN TO ME...
DROP-DOWN MENU THREE, SUB EIGHT. UNLOCK "SPECIAL SYSTEMS" WITH THE PASSWORD "GLEN18"...
"GLEN18"?
MY SON.
YOU HAVE A SON NAMED GLEN?
HAD.
HE DIED.
WHAT DOES "SPECIAL SYSTEMS" DO?
IT'S AN ABSOLUTE LAST RESORT.

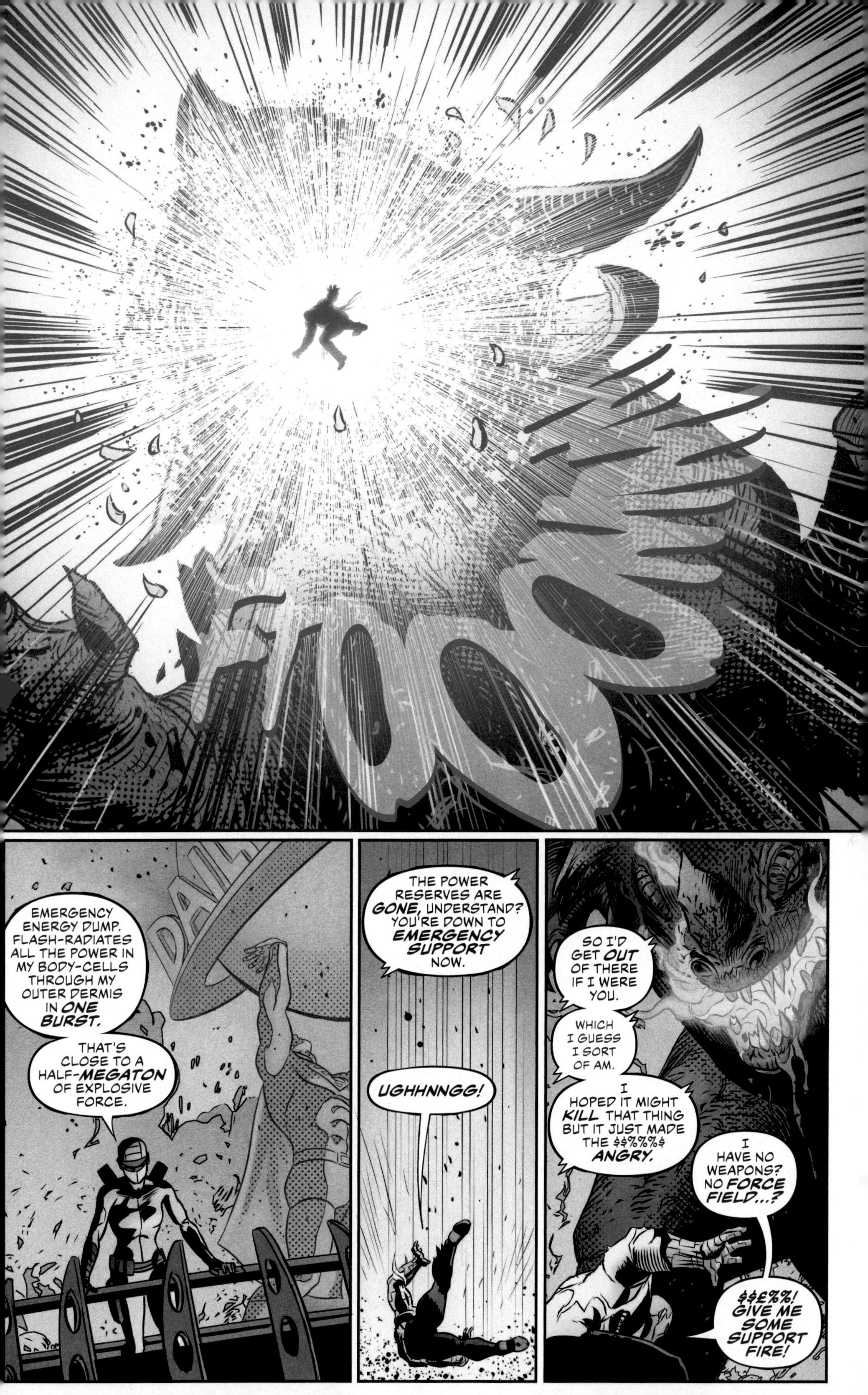
FOOOM
EMERGENCY ENERGY DUMP. FLASH-RADIATES ALL THE POWER IN MY BODY-CELLS THROUGH MY OUTER DERMIS IN ONE BURST.
THAT'S CLOSE TO A HALF-MEGATON OF EXPLOSIVE FORCE.
THE POWER RESERVES ARE GONE, UNDERSTAND? YOU'RE DOWN TO EMERGENCY SUPPORT NOW.
UGHHNNGG!
SO I'D GET OUT OF THERE IF I WERE YOU.
WHICH I GUESS I SORT OF AM.
I HOPED IT MIGHT KILL THAT THING BUT IT JUST MADE THE $$%%%$ ANGRY.
I HAVE NO WEAPONS? NO FORCE FIELD...?
$$£%%! GIVE ME SOME SUPPORT FIRE!

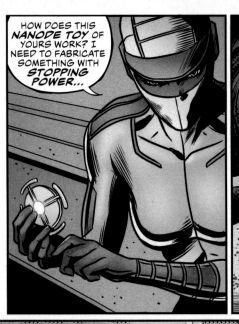

HOW DOES THIS **NANODE TOY** OF YOURS WORK? I NEED TO FABRICATE SOMETHING WITH **STOPPING POWER**...

CYCLE IT UP, THEN FEED IT **RAW MATERIALS!**

ANYTHING-- METAL, STONE, PLASTICS...

...THEN IT CAN **PRINT-WEAVE** SOMETHING FROM A STORED TEMPLATE!

METAL, YES?

YES! **ANYTHING!**

DO IT **FAST**, QUIETUS!

WORKING ON IT.

TIKA-TIKA-TIKA-TIKA-TIKA

WORK **FASTER!**

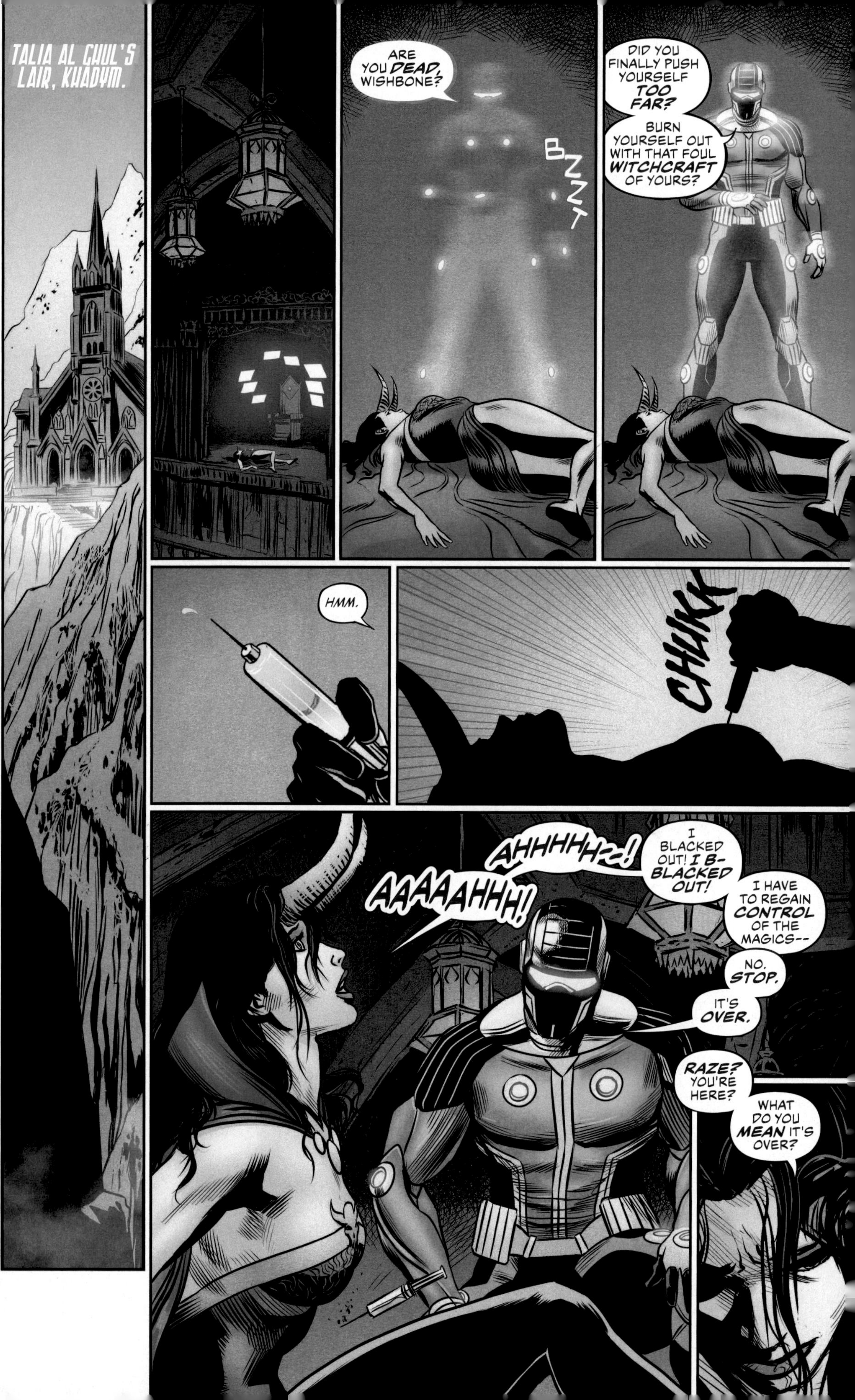
TALIA AL GHUL'S LAIR, KHADYM.
ARE YOU DEAD, WISHBONE?
BZZZT
DID YOU FINALLY PUSH YOURSELF TOO FAR?
BURN YOURSELF OUT WITH THAT FOUL WITCHCRAFT OF YOURS?
HMM.
CHUKK
AAAAAHHH!
AHHHHH--!
I BLACKED OUT! I B-BLACKED OUT!
I HAVE TO REGAIN CONTROL OF THE MAGICS--
NO. STOP.
IT'S OVER.
RAZE? YOU'RE HERE?
WHAT DO YOU MEAN IT'S OVER?

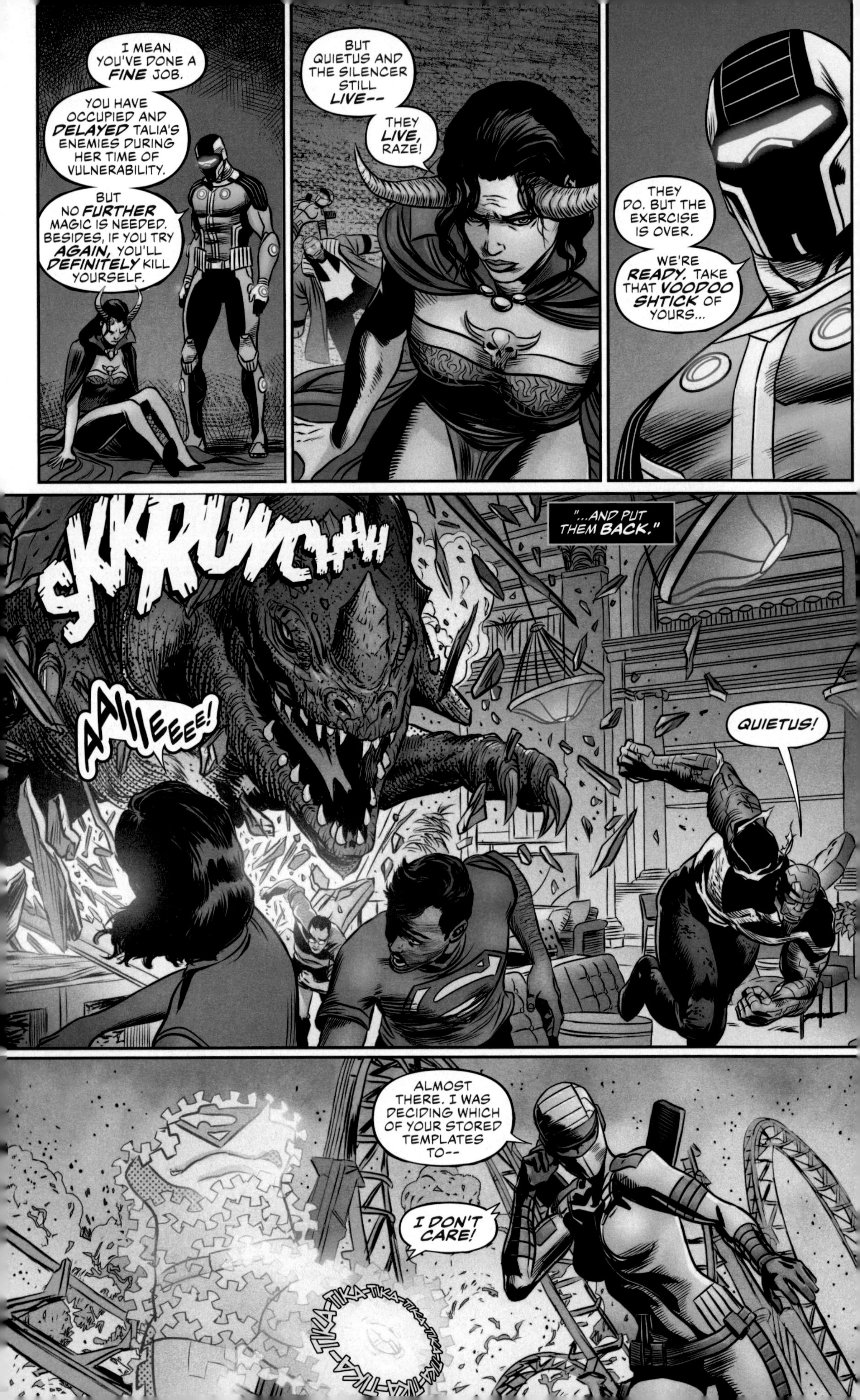
I MEAN YOU'VE DONE A FINE JOB.
YOU HAVE OCCUPIED AND DELAYED TALIA'S ENEMIES DURING HER TIME OF VULNERABILITY.
BUT NO FURTHER MAGIC IS NEEDED. BESIDES, IF YOU TRY AGAIN, YOU'LL DEFINITELY KILL YOURSELF.
BUT QUIETUS AND THE SILENCER STILL LIVE--
THEY LIVE, RAZE!
THEY DO. BUT THE EXERCISE IS OVER.
WE'RE READY. TAKE THAT VOODOO SHTICK OF YOURS...
"...AND PUT THEM BACK."
SKKRUNCHHH
AAIIIEEEEE!
QUIETUS!
ALMOST THERE. I WAS DECIDING WHICH OF YOUR STORED TEMPLATES TO--
I DON'T CARE!
TIKA-TIKA-TIKA-TIKA

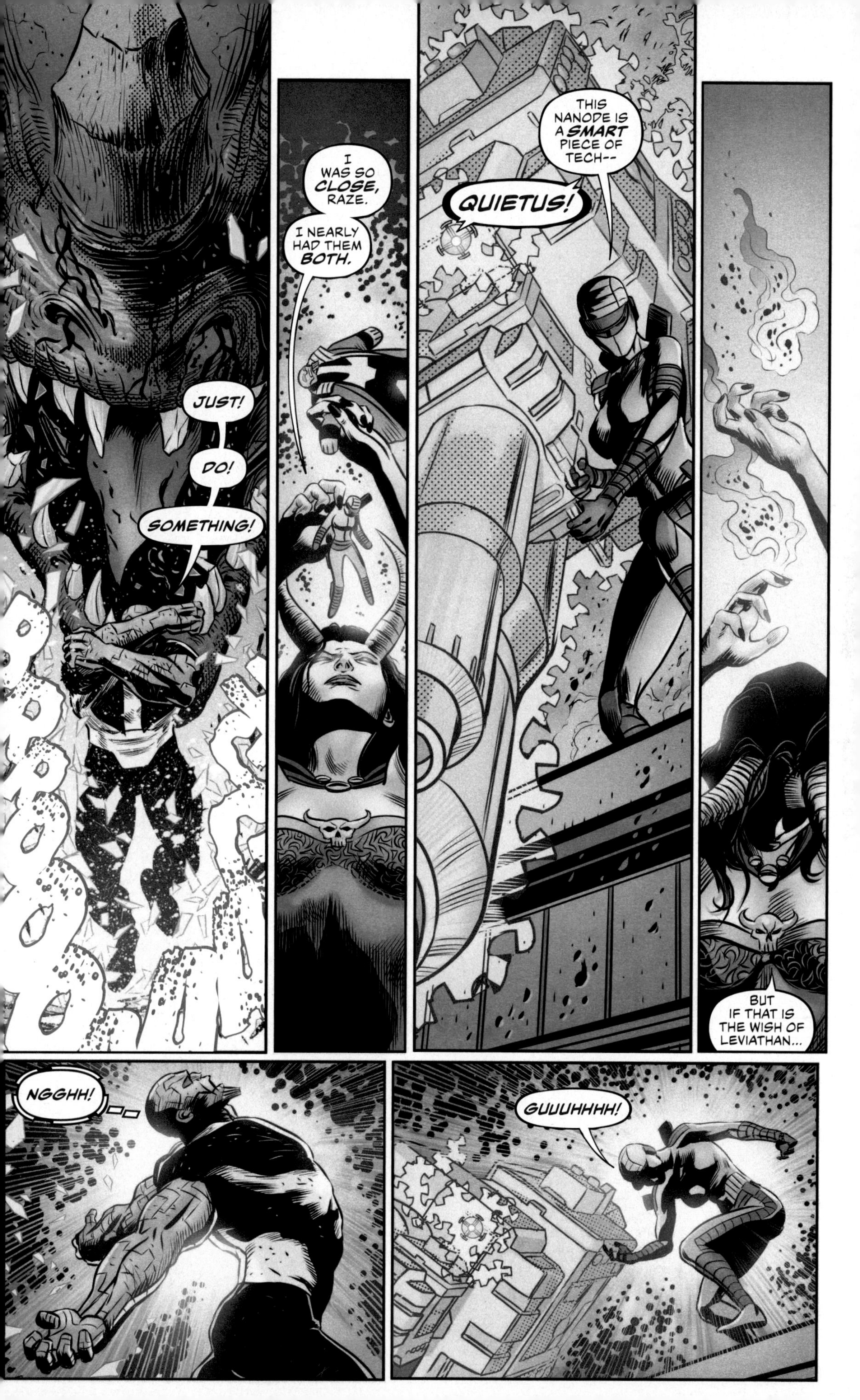
JUST!
DO!
SOMETHING!
I WAS SO CLOSE, RAZE.
I NEARLY HAD THEM BOTH.
THIS NANODE IS A SMART PIECE OF TECH--
QUIETUS!
BUT IF THAT IS THE WISH OF LEVIATHAN...
NGGHH!
GUUUHHHH!

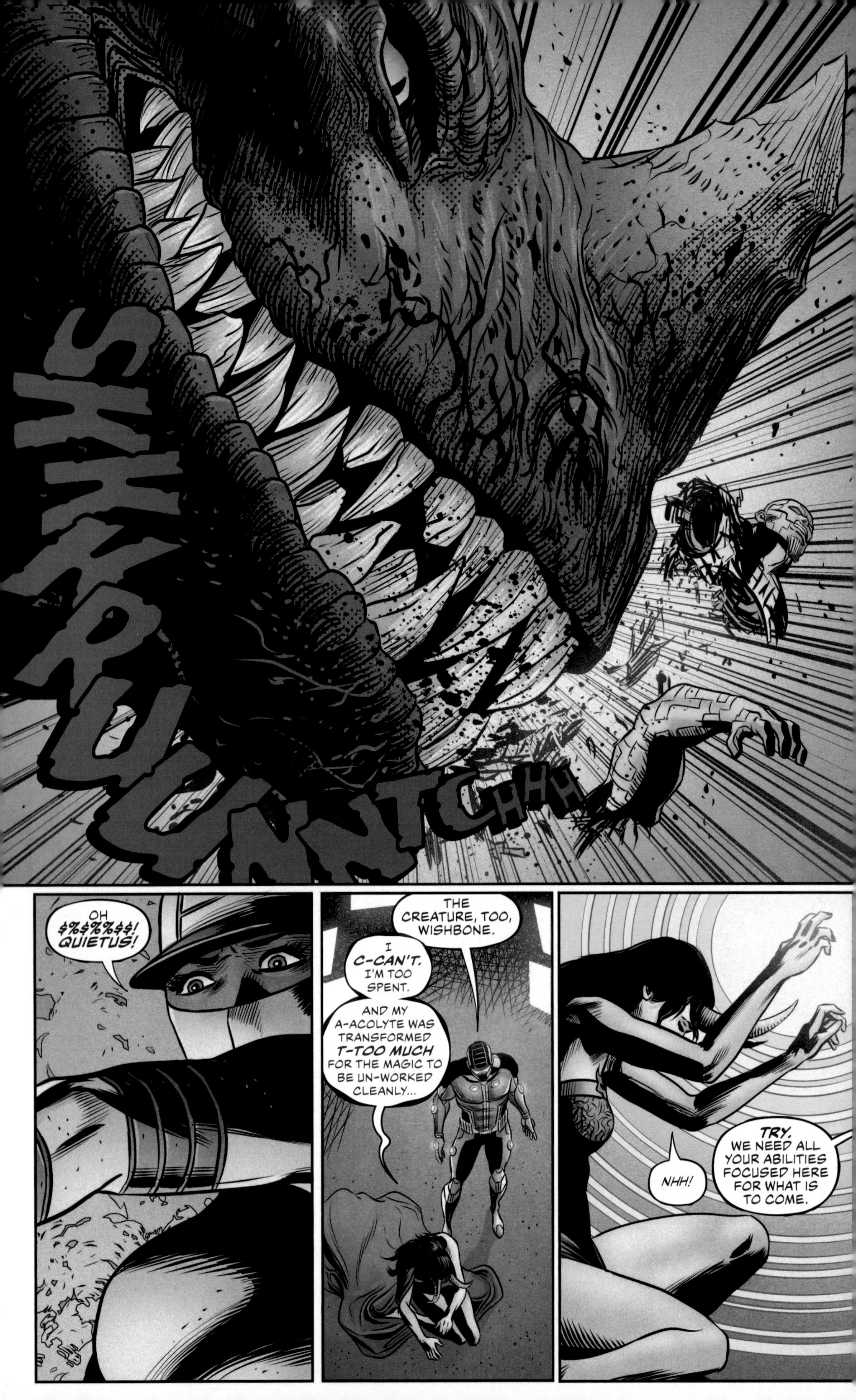
SHKRUNTCHH
OH $%$%%$$! QUIETUS!
THE CREATURE, TOO, WISHBONE.
I C-CAN'T. I'M TOO SPENT.
AND MY A-ACOLYTE WAS TRANSFORMED T-TOO MUCH FOR THE MAGIC TO BE UN-WORKED CLEANLY...
NHH!
TRY. WE NEED ALL YOUR ABILITIES FOCUSED HERE FOR WHAT IS TO COME.

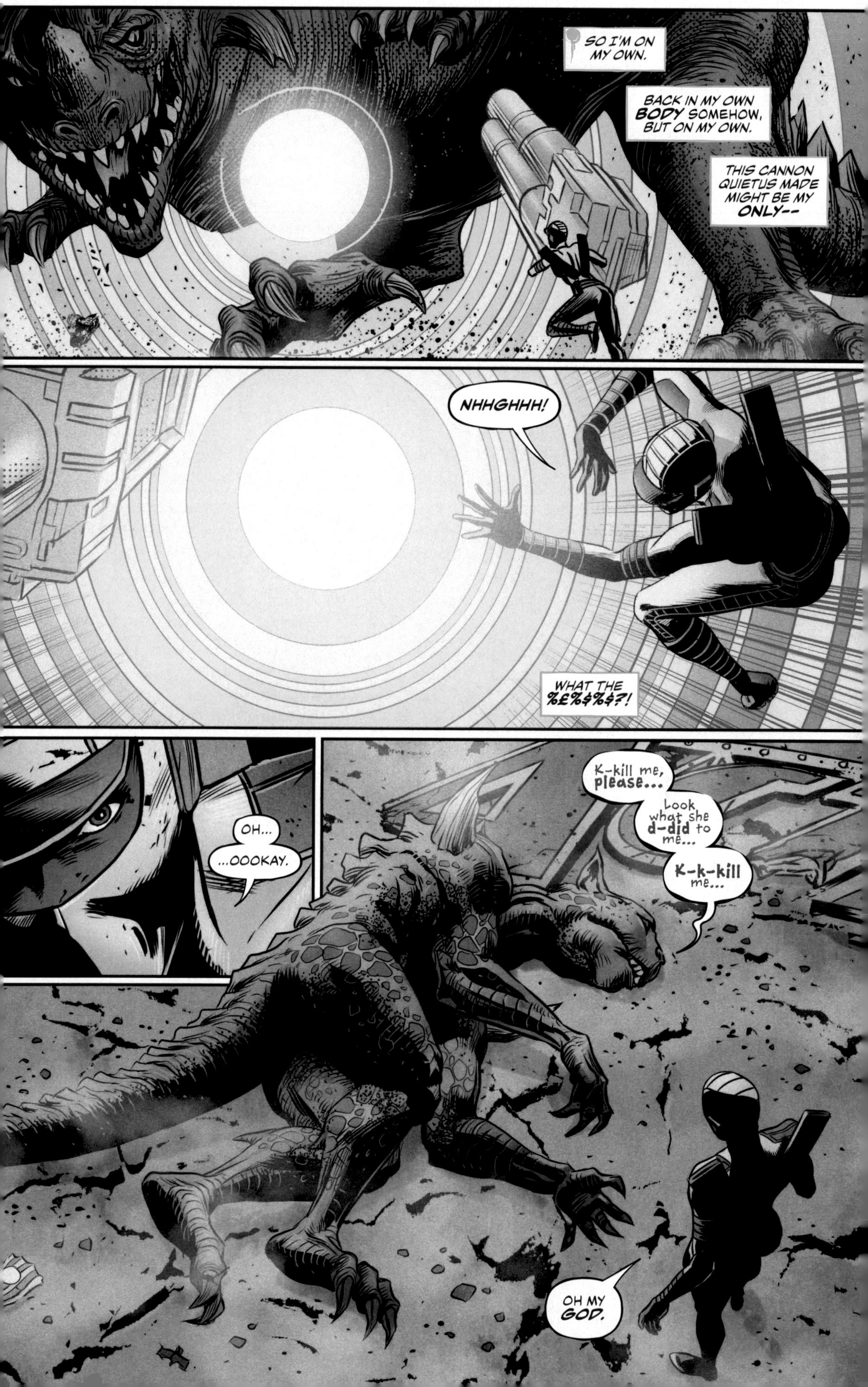
SO I'M ON MY OWN.
BACK IN MY OWN BODY SOMEHOW, BUT ON MY OWN.
THIS CANNON QUIETUS MADE MIGHT BE MY ONLY--
NHHGHHH!
WHAT THE %£%$%$?!
OH...
...OOOKAY.
K-kill me, please...
Look what she d-did to me...
K-k-kill me...
OH MY GOD.

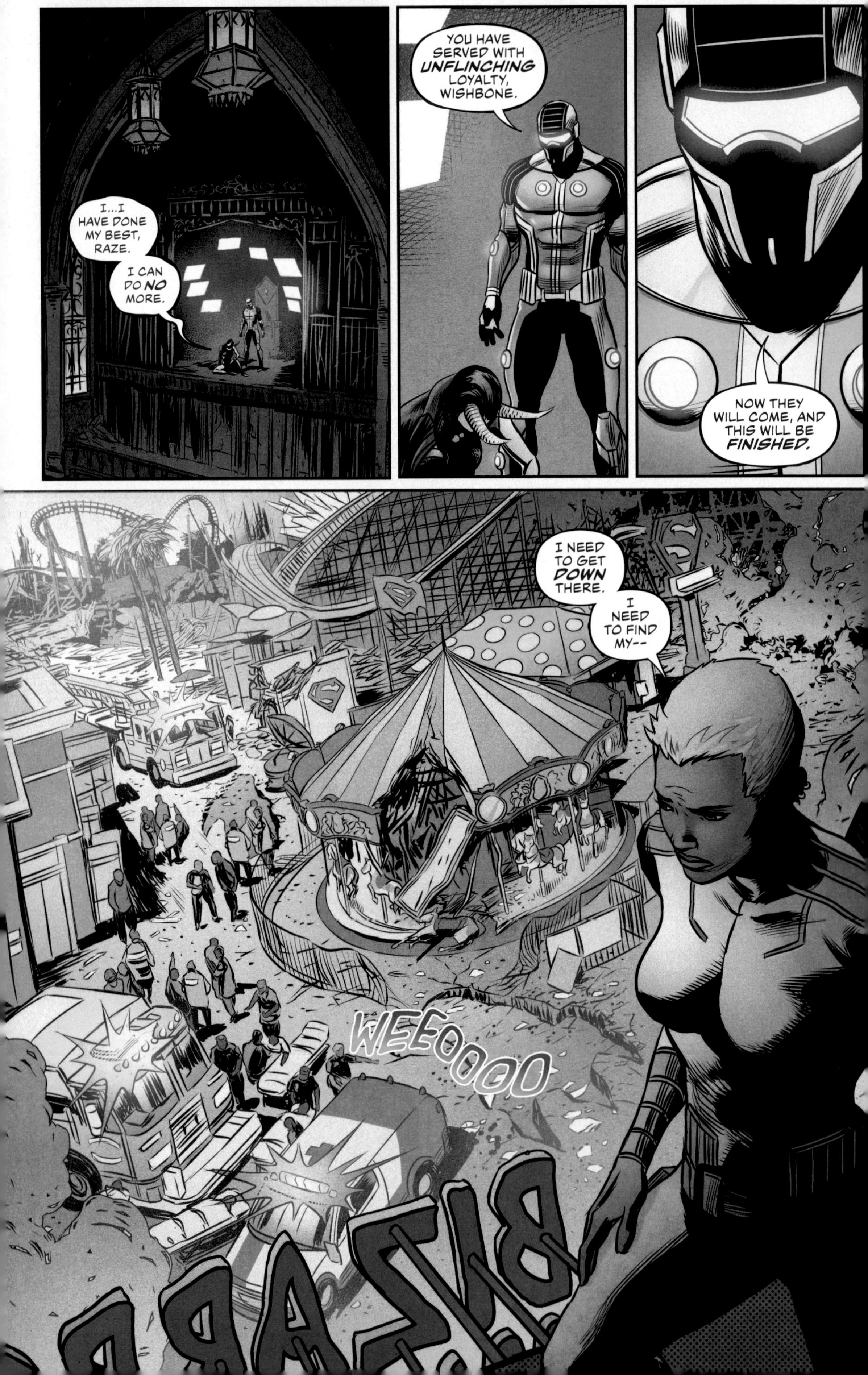

I...I HAVE DONE MY BEST, RAZE.
I CAN DO NO MORE.
YOU HAVE SERVED WITH UNFLINCHING LOYALTY, WISHBONE.
NOW THEY WILL COME, AND THIS WILL BE FINISHED.
I NEED TO GET DOWN THERE.
I NEED TO FIND MY--
WEEOOOO
BIZZAP

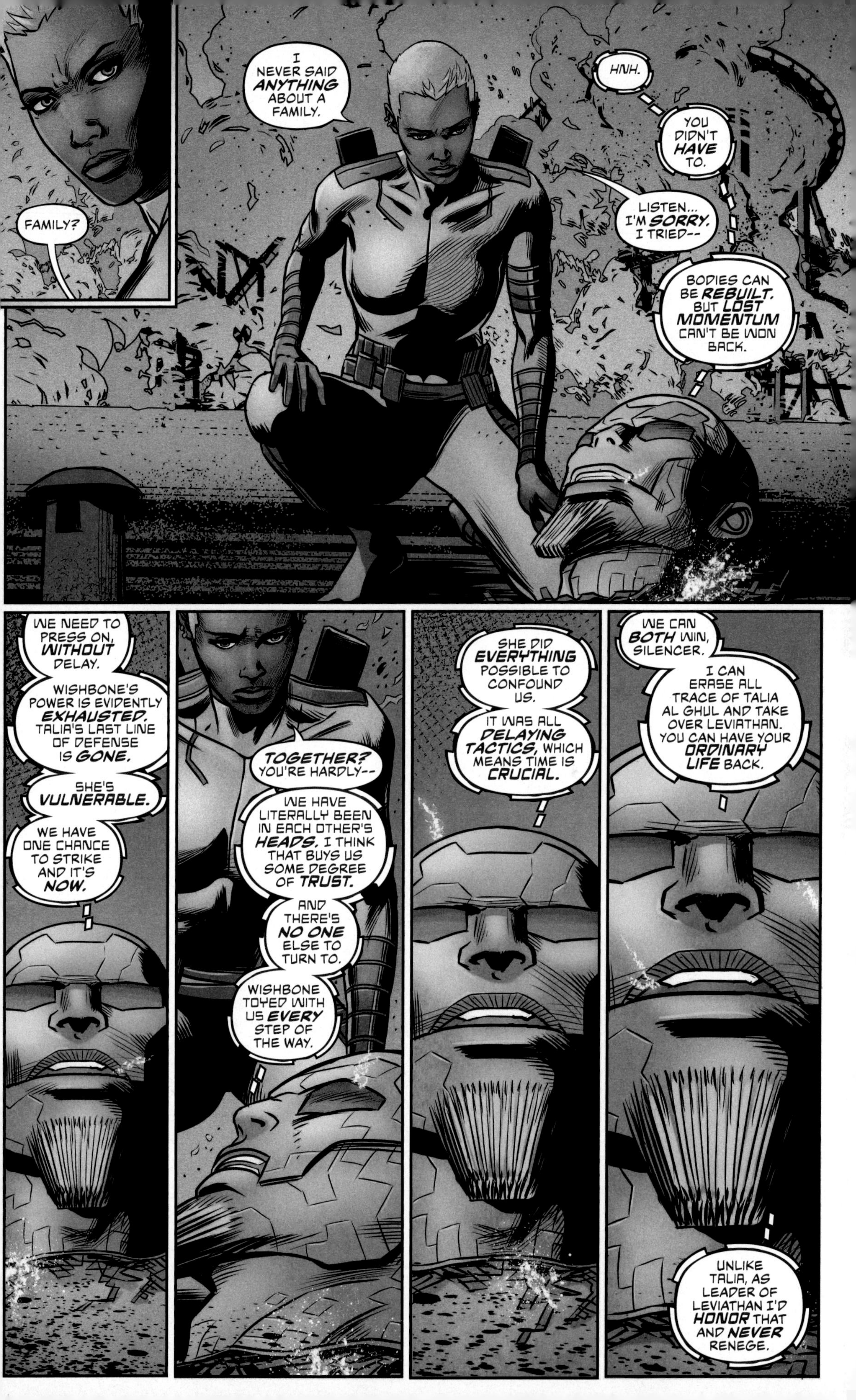
FAMILY?
I NEVER SAID ANYTHING ABOUT A FAMILY.
HNH.
YOU DIDN'T HAVE TO.
LISTEN... I'M SORRY. I TRIED--
BODIES CAN BE REBUILT, BUT LOST MOMENTUM CAN'T BE WON BACK.
WE NEED TO PRESS ON, WITHOUT DELAY.
WISHBONE'S POWER IS EVIDENTLY EXHAUSTED. TALIA'S LAST LINE OF DEFENSE IS GONE.
SHE'S VULNERABLE.
WE HAVE ONE CHANCE TO STRIKE AND IT'S NOW.
TOGETHER? YOU'RE HARDLY--
WE HAVE LITERALLY BEEN IN EACH OTHER'S HEADS. I THINK THAT BUYS US SOME DEGREE OF TRUST.
AND THERE'S NO ONE ELSE TO TURN TO.
WISHBONE TOYED WITH US EVERY STEP OF THE WAY.
SHE DID EVERYTHING POSSIBLE TO CONFOUND US.
IT WAS ALL DELAYING TACTICS, WHICH MEANS TIME IS CRUCIAL.
WE CAN BOTH WIN, SILENCER.
I CAN ERASE ALL TRACE OF TALIA AL GHUL AND TAKE OVER LEVIATHAN. YOU CAN HAVE YOUR ORDINARY LIFE BACK.
UNLIKE TALIA, AS LEADER OF LEVIATHAN I'D HONOR THAT AND NEVER RENEGE.

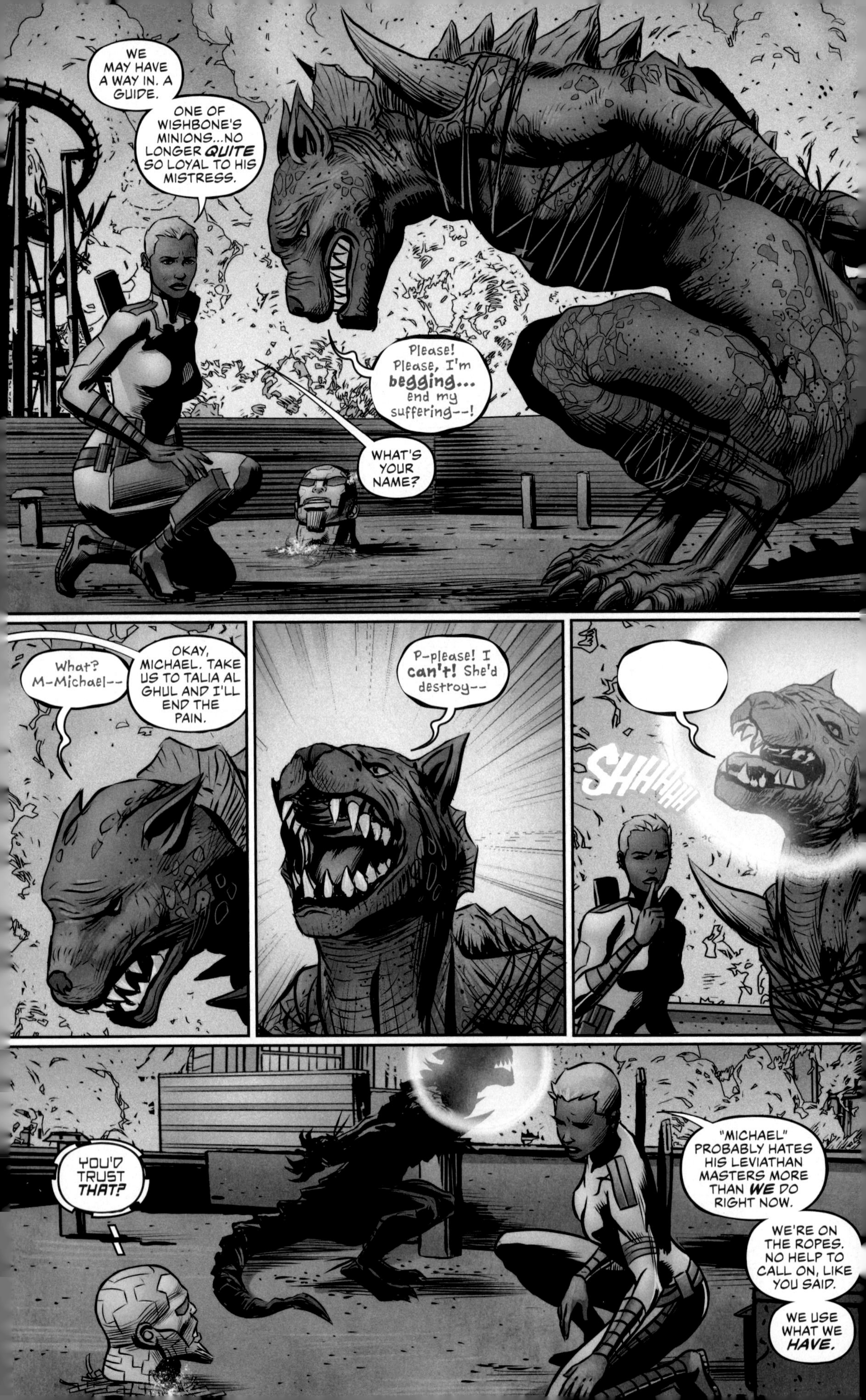

WE MAY HAVE A WAY IN. A GUIDE.
ONE OF WISHBONE'S MINIONS...NO LONGER QUITE SO LOYAL TO HIS MISTRESS.
Please! Please, I'm begging... end my suffering--!
WHAT'S YOUR NAME?
What? M-Michael--
OKAY, MICHAEL. TAKE US TO TALIA AL GHUL AND I'LL END THE PAIN.
P-please! I can't! She'd destroy--
SHHHHH
YOU'D TRUST THAT?
"MICHAEL" PROBABLY HATES HIS LEVIATHAN MASTERS MORE THAN WE DO RIGHT NOW.
WE'RE ON THE ROPES. NO HELP TO CALL ON, LIKE YOU SAID.
WE USE WHAT WE HAVE.

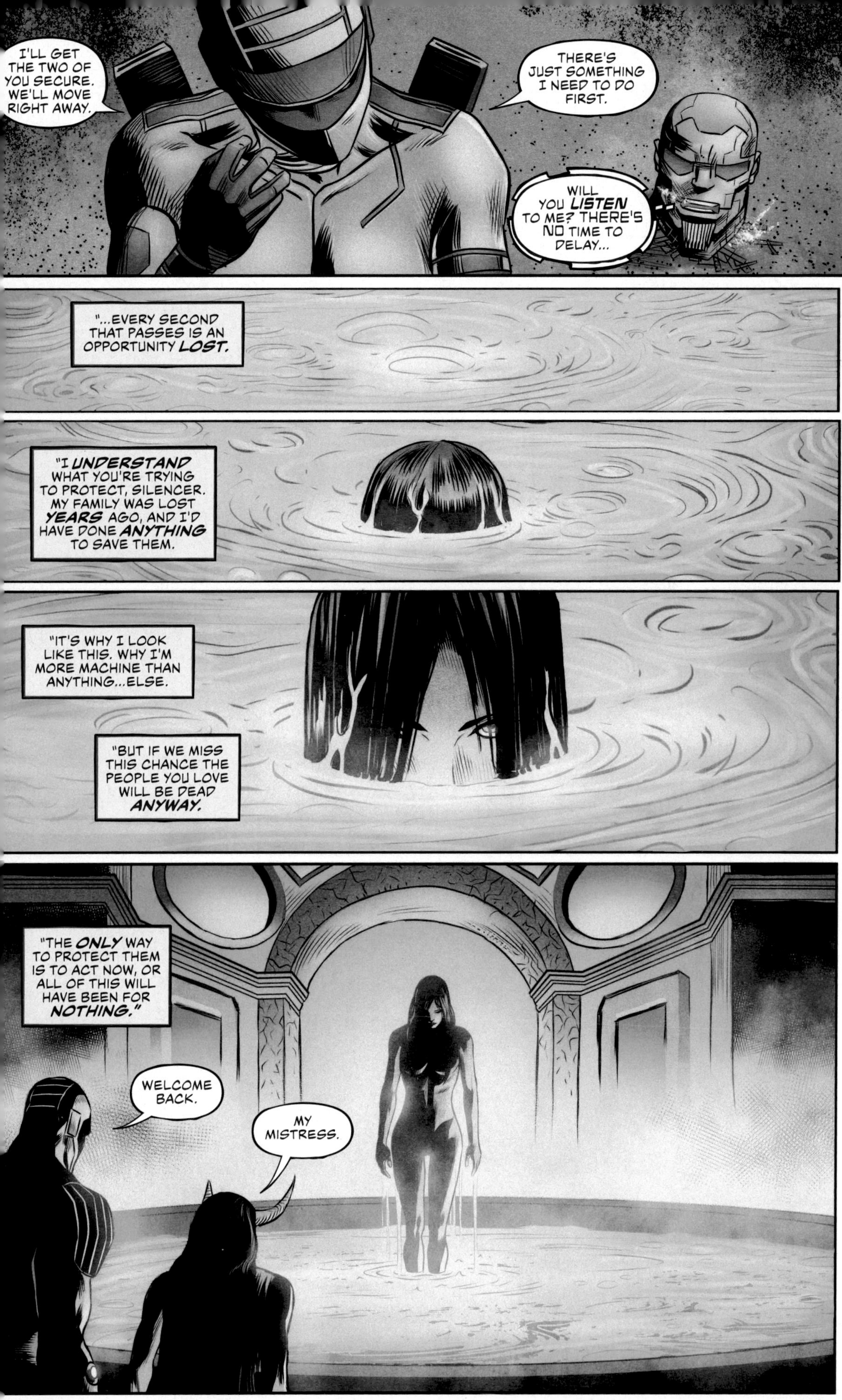
I'LL GET THE TWO OF YOU SECURE. WE'LL MOVE RIGHT AWAY.
THERE'S JUST SOMETHING I NEED TO DO FIRST.
WILL YOU LISTEN TO ME? THERE'S NO TIME TO DELAY...
"...EVERY SECOND THAT PASSES IS AN OPPORTUNITY LOST.
"I UNDERSTAND WHAT YOU'RE TRYING TO PROTECT, SILENCER. MY FAMILY WAS LOST YEARS AGO, AND I'D HAVE DONE ANYTHING TO SAVE THEM.
"IT'S WHY I LOOK LIKE THIS. WHY I'M MORE MACHINE THAN ANYTHING...ELSE.
"BUT IF WE MISS THIS CHANCE THE PEOPLE YOU LOVE WILL BE DEAD ANYWAY.
"THE ONLY WAY TO PROTECT THEM IS TO ACT NOW, OR ALL OF THIS WILL HAVE BEEN FOR NOTHING."
WELCOME BACK.
MY MISTRESS.

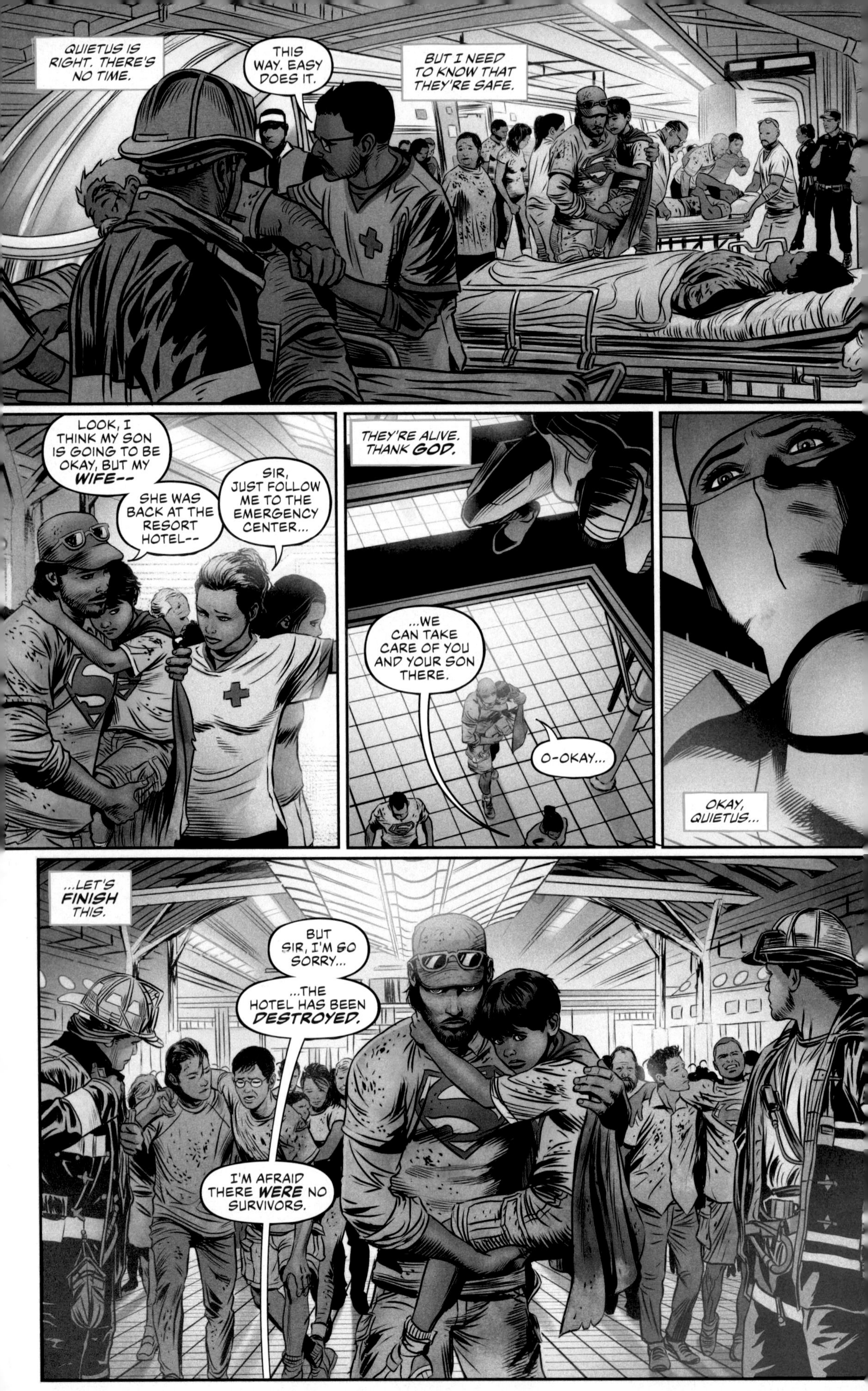
QUIETUS IS RIGHT. THERE'S NO TIME.
THIS WAY. EASY DOES IT.
BUT I NEED TO KNOW THAT THEY'RE SAFE.
LOOK, I THINK MY SON IS GOING TO BE OKAY, BUT MY WIFE--
SHE WAS BACK AT THE RESORT HOTEL--
SIR, JUST FOLLOW ME TO THE EMERGENCY CENTER...
THEY'RE ALIVE. THANK GOD.
...WE CAN TAKE CARE OF YOU AND YOUR SON THERE.
O-OKAY...
OKAY, QUIETUS...
...LET'S FINISH THIS.
BUT SIR, I'M SO SORRY...
...THE HOTEL HAS BEEN DESTROYED.
I'M AFRAID THERE WERE NO SURVIVORS.

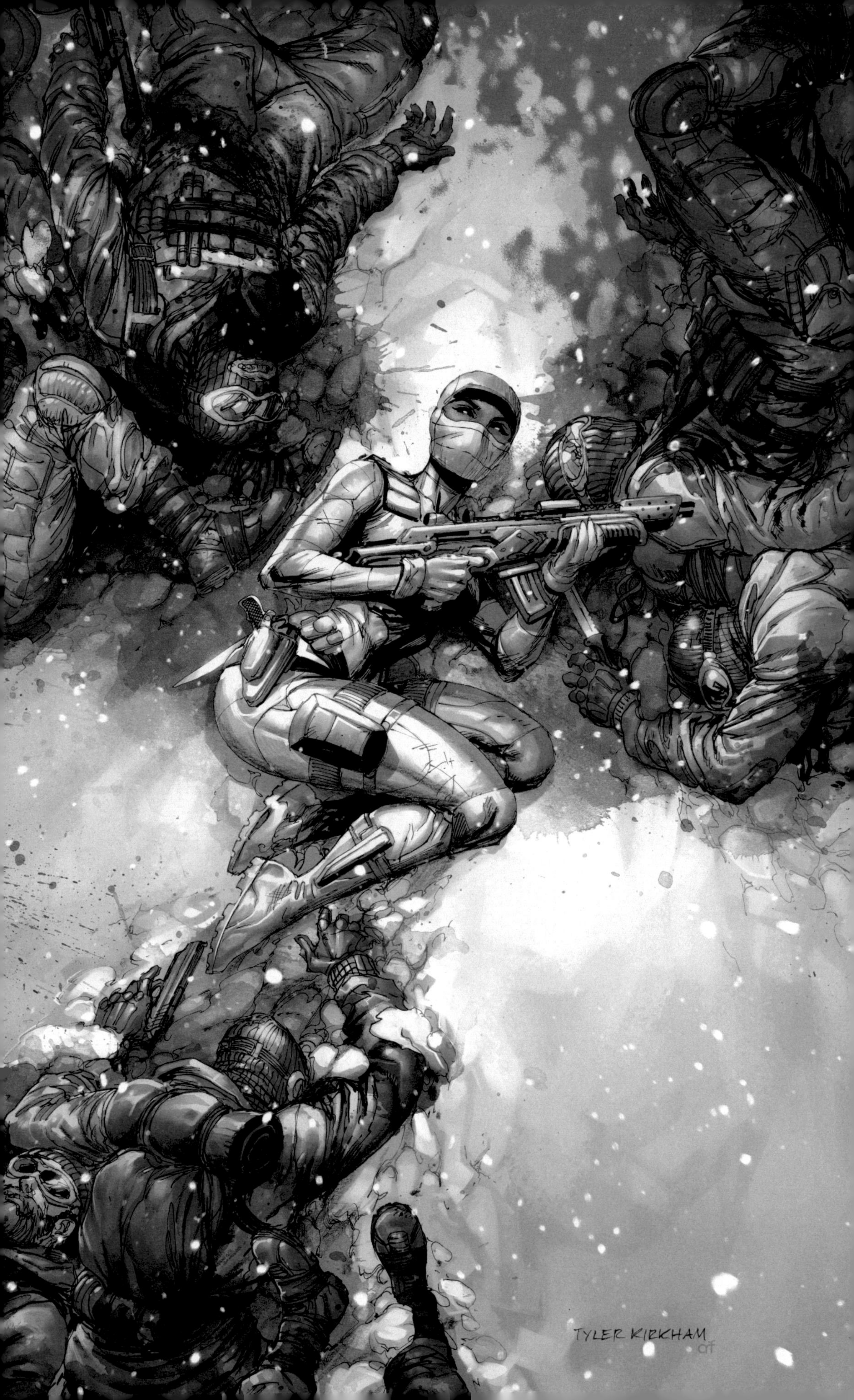
TYLER KIRKHAM

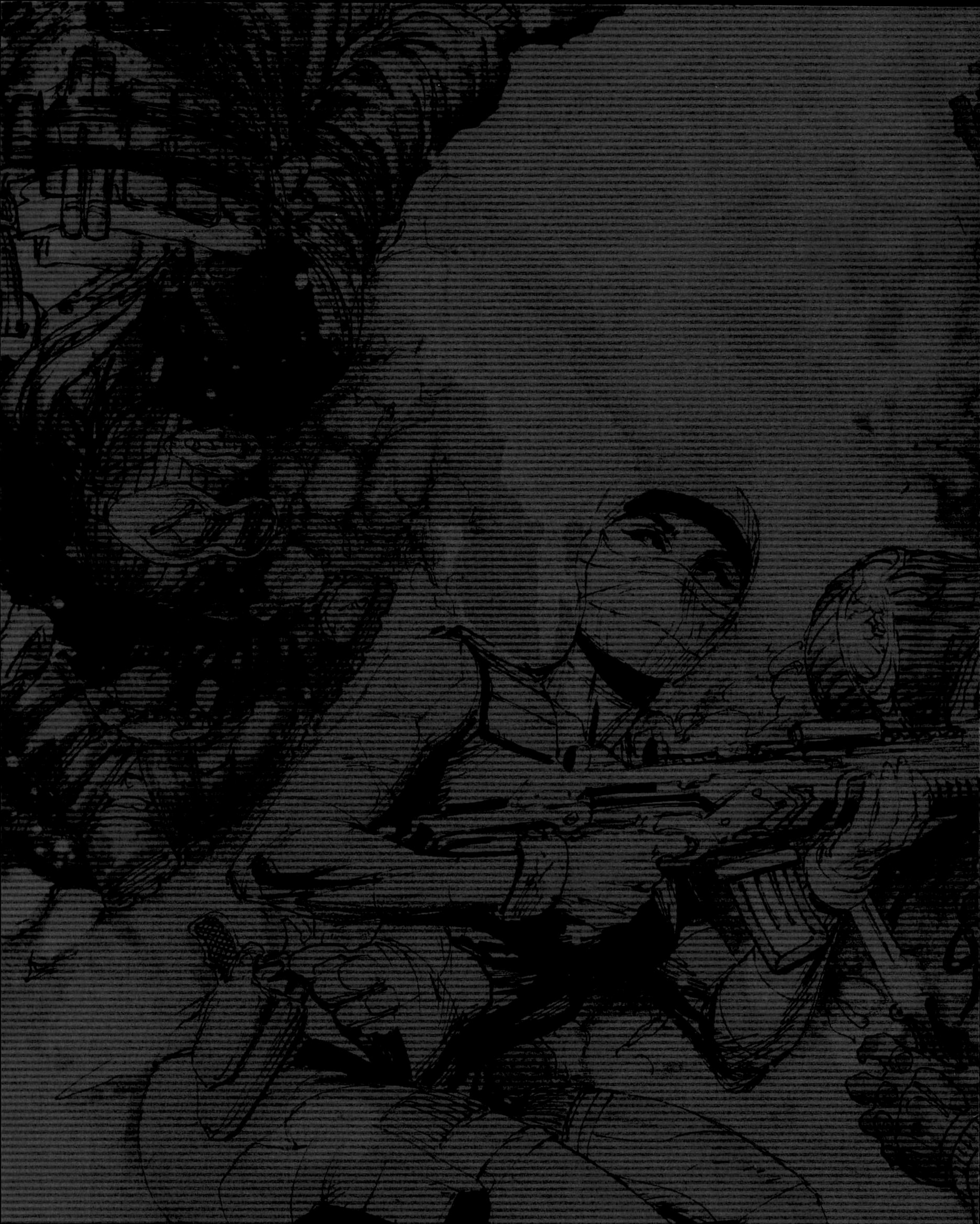

THE SILENCER

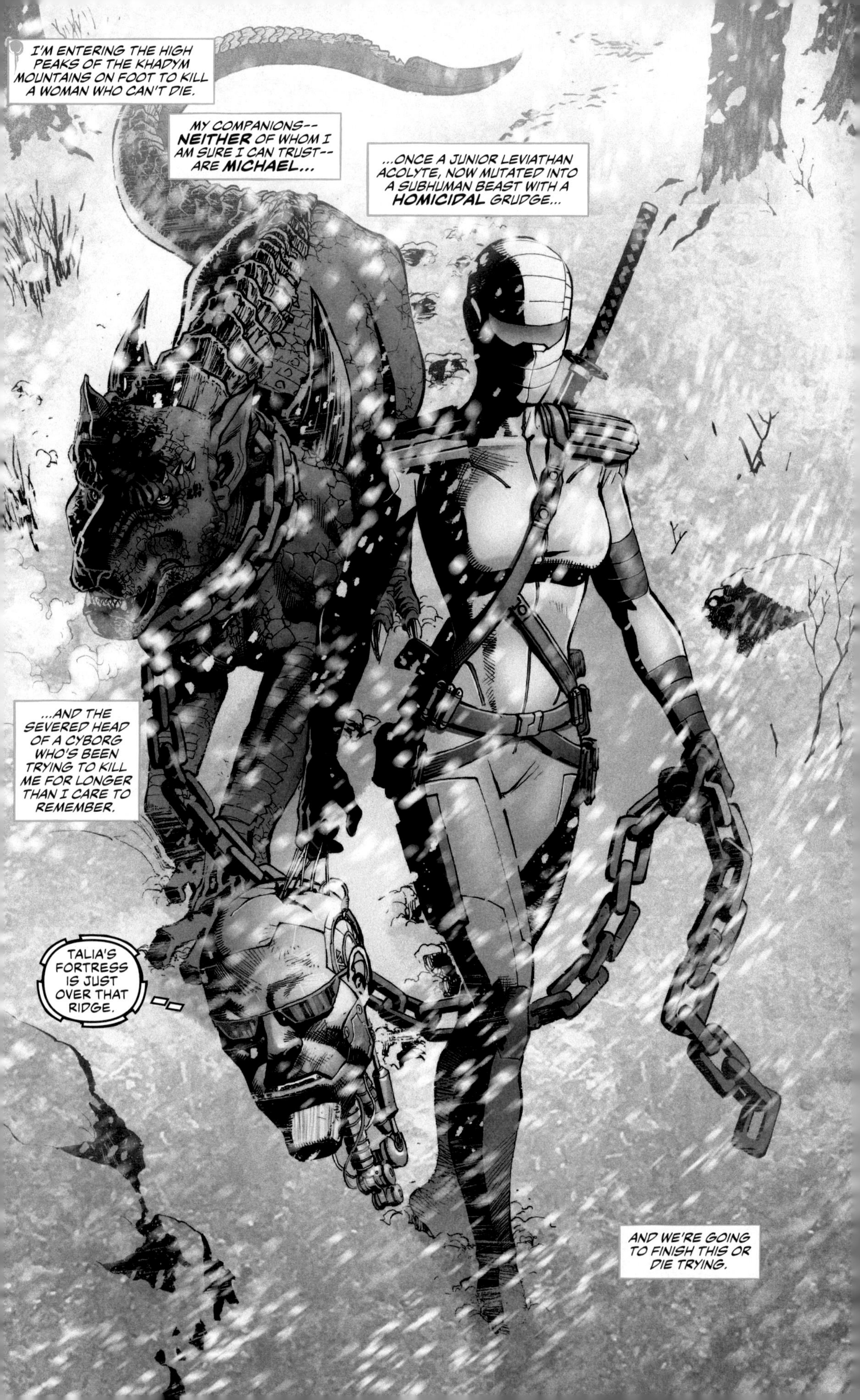
I'M ENTERING THE HIGH PEAKS OF THE KHADYM MOUNTAINS ON FOOT TO KILL A WOMAN WHO CAN'T DIE.
MY COMPANIONS-- NEITHER OF WHOM I AM SURE I CAN TRUST-- ARE MICHAEL...
...ONCE A JUNIOR LEVIATHAN ACOLYTE, NOW MUTATED INTO A SUBHUMAN BEAST WITH A HOMICIDAL GRUDGE...
...AND THE SEVERED HEAD OF A CYBORG WHO'S BEEN TRYING TO KILL ME FOR LONGER THAN I CARE TO REMEMBER.
TALIA'S FORTRESS IS JUST OVER THAT RIDGE.
AND WE'RE GOING TO FINISH THIS OR DIE TRYING.

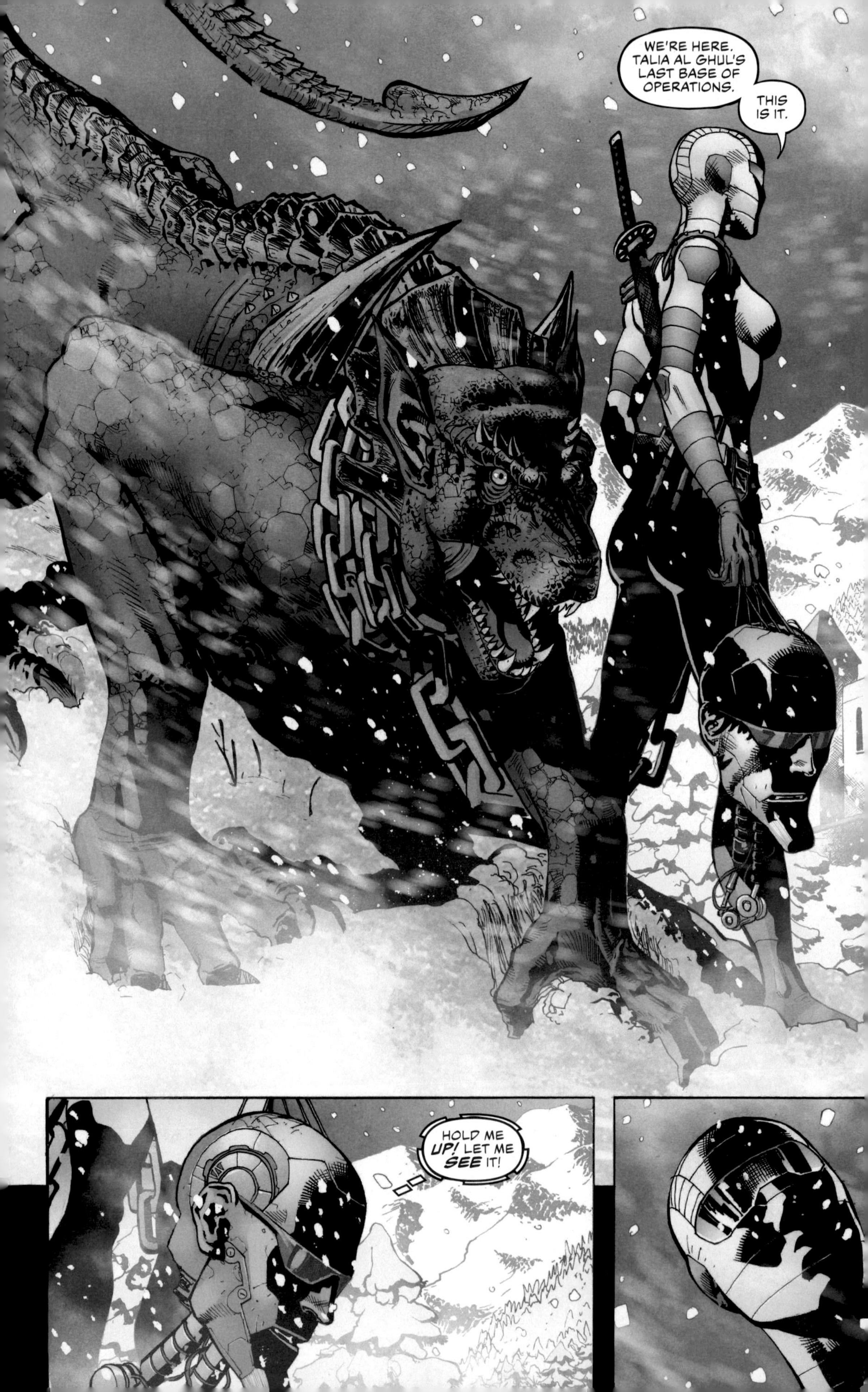
WE'RE HERE. TALIA AL GHUL'S LAST BASE OF OPERATIONS.
THIS IS IT.
HOLD ME UP! LET ME SEE IT!

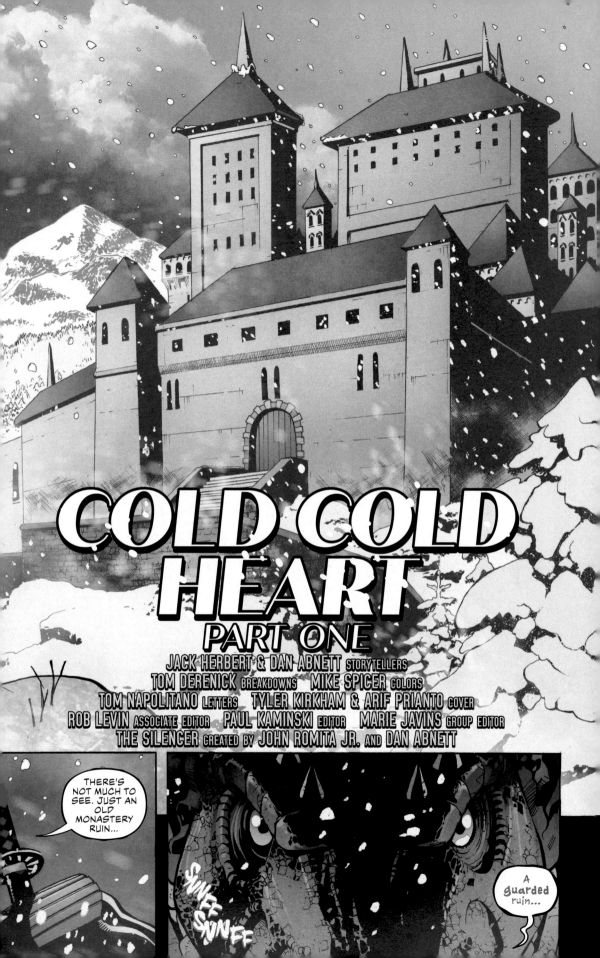

COLD COLD HEART
PART ONE

JACK HERBERT & DAN ABNETT STORYTELLERS
TOM DERENICK BREAKDOWNS   MIKE SPICER COLORS
TOM NAPOLITANO LETTERS   TYLER KIRKHAM & ARIF PRIANTO COVER
ROB LEVIN ASSOCIATE EDITOR   PAUL KAMINSKI EDITOR   MARIE JAVINS GROUP EDITOR
THE SILENCER CREATED BY JOHN ROMITA JR. AND DAN ABNETT

THERE'S NOT MUCH TO SEE. JUST AN OLD MONASTERY RUIN...

SNNFF SNNFF

A guarded ruin...

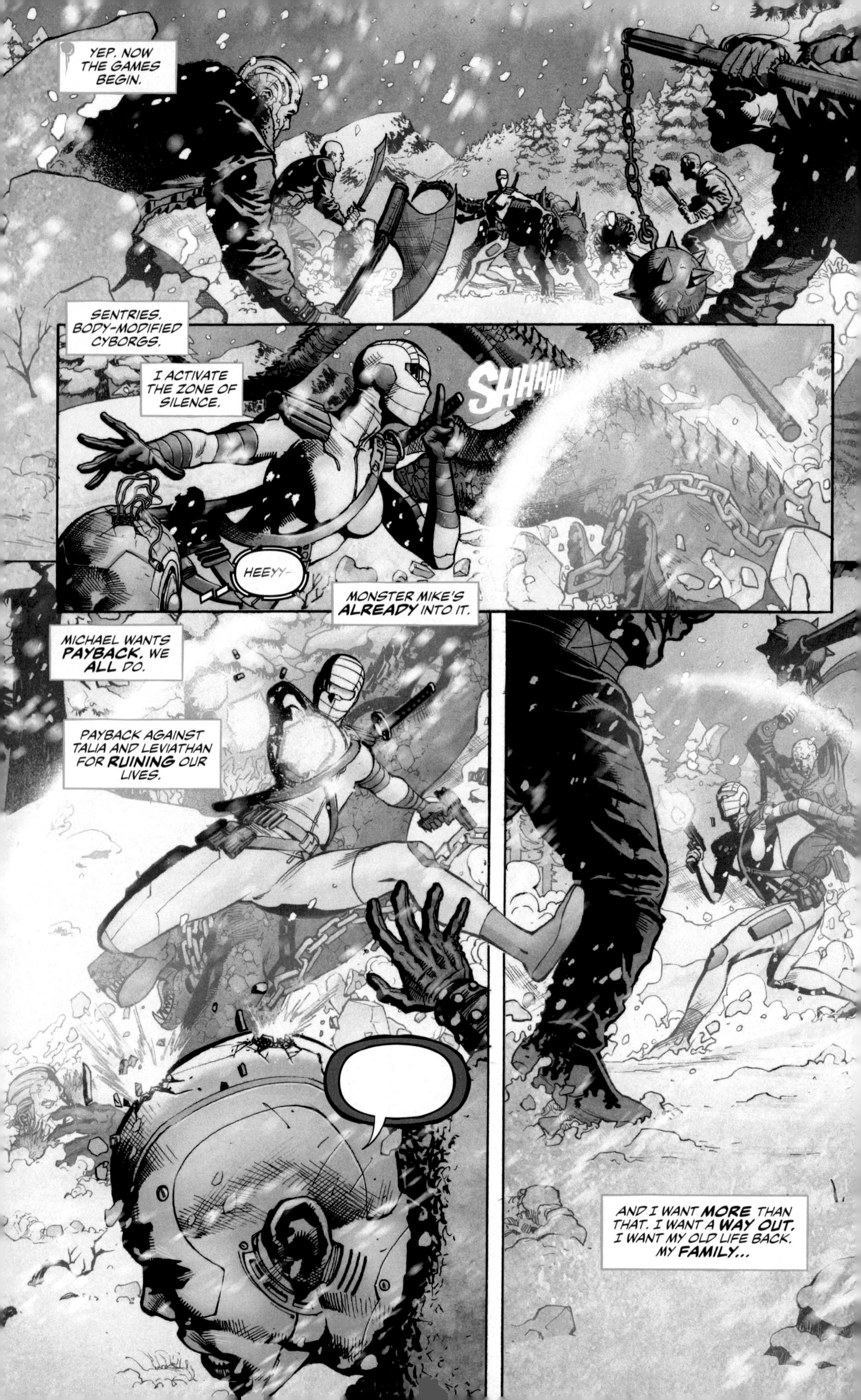
YEP. NOW THE GAMES BEGIN.
SENTRIES. BODY-MODIFIED CYBORGS.
I ACTIVATE THE ZONE OF SILENCE.
SHHHHH
HEEYY-
MONSTER MIKE'S ALREADY INTO IT.
MICHAEL WANTS PAYBACK. WE ALL DO.
PAYBACK AGAINST TALIA AND LEVIATHAN FOR RUINING OUR LIVES.
AND I WANT MORE THAN THAT. I WANT A WAY OUT. I WANT MY OLD LIFE BACK. MY FAMILY...

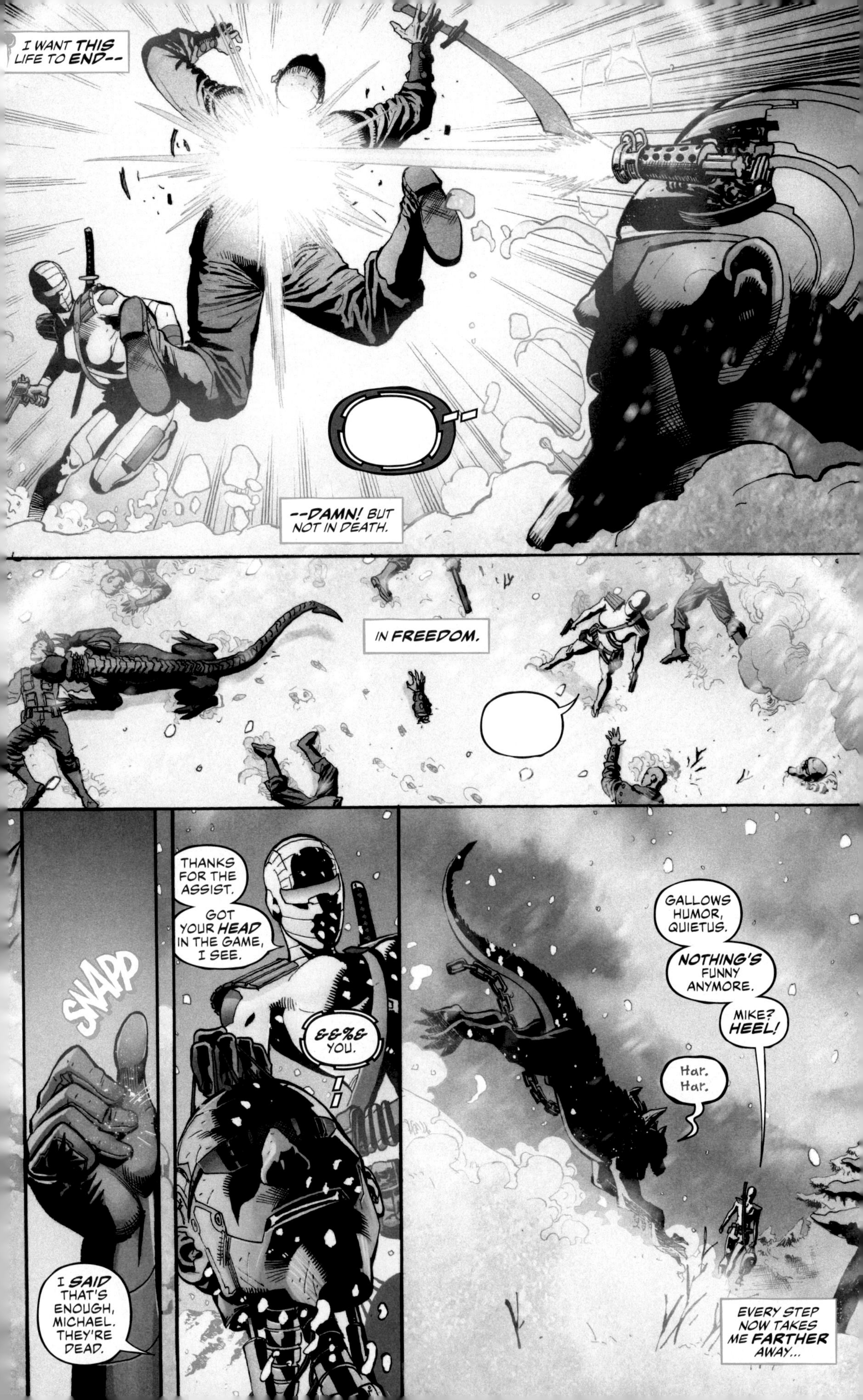
I WANT THIS LIFE TO END--
--DAMN! BUT NOT IN DEATH.
IN FREEDOM.
SNAPP
I SAID THAT'S ENOUGH, MICHAEL. THEY'RE DEAD.
THANKS FOR THE ASSIST.
GOT YOUR HEAD IN THE GAME, I SEE.
&&%& YOU.
GALLOWS HUMOR, QUIETUS.
NOTHING'S FUNNY ANYMORE.
MIKE? HEEL!
Har. Har.
EVERY STEP NOW TAKES ME FARTHER AWAY...

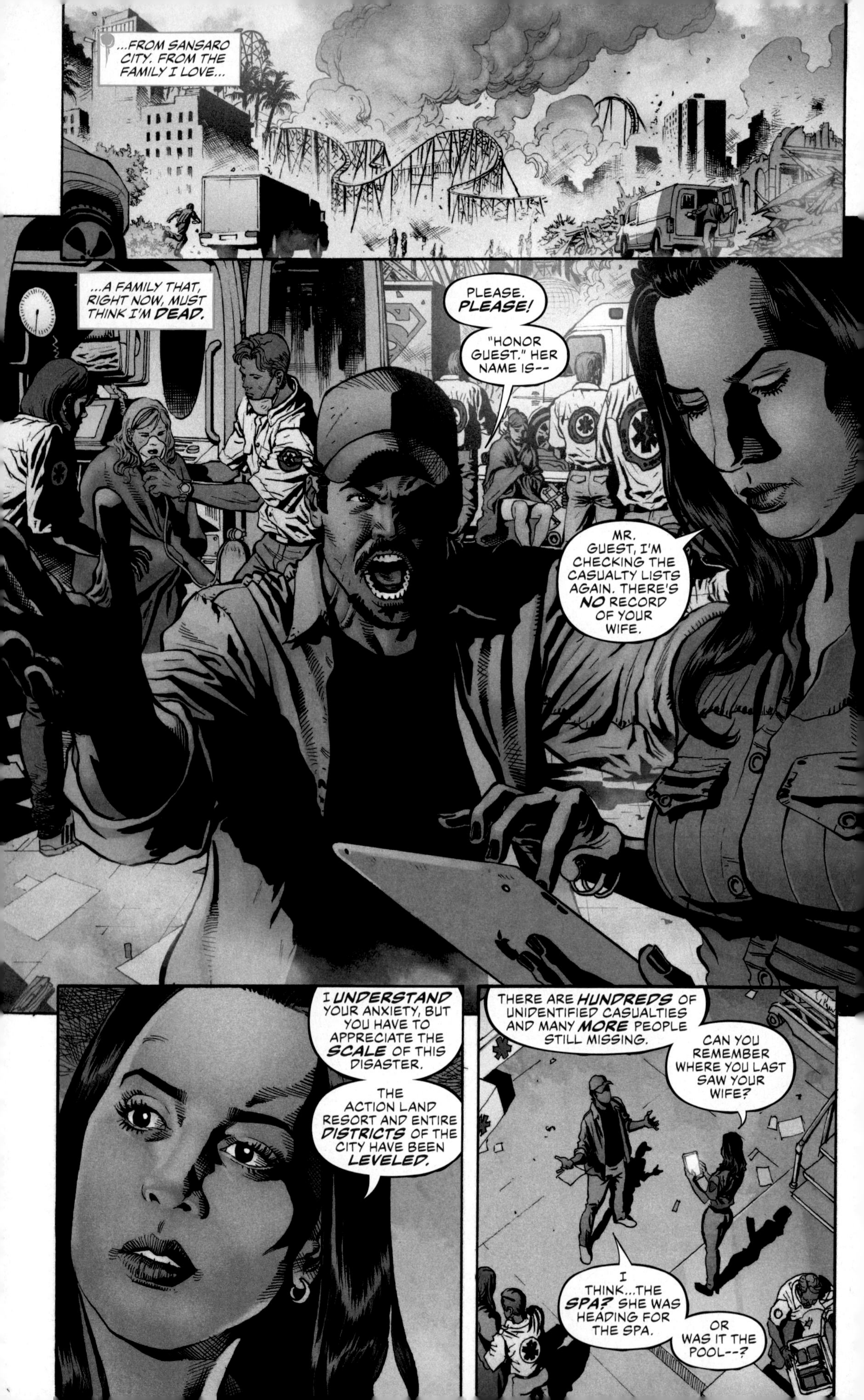

...FROM SANSARO CITY. FROM THE FAMILY I LOVE...
...A FAMILY THAT, RIGHT NOW, MUST THINK I'M DEAD.
PLEASE. PLEASE!
"HONOR GUEST." HER NAME IS--
MR. GUEST, I'M CHECKING THE CASUALTY LISTS AGAIN. THERE'S NO RECORD OF YOUR WIFE.
I UNDERSTAND YOUR ANXIETY, BUT YOU HAVE TO APPRECIATE THE SCALE OF THIS DISASTER.
THE ACTION LAND RESORT AND ENTIRE DISTRICTS OF THE CITY HAVE BEEN LEVELED.
THERE ARE HUNDREDS OF UNIDENTIFIED CASUALTIES AND MANY MORE PEOPLE STILL MISSING.
CAN YOU REMEMBER WHERE YOU LAST SAW YOUR WIFE?
I THINK...THE SPA? SHE WAS HEADING FOR THE SPA.
OR WAS IT THE POOL--?

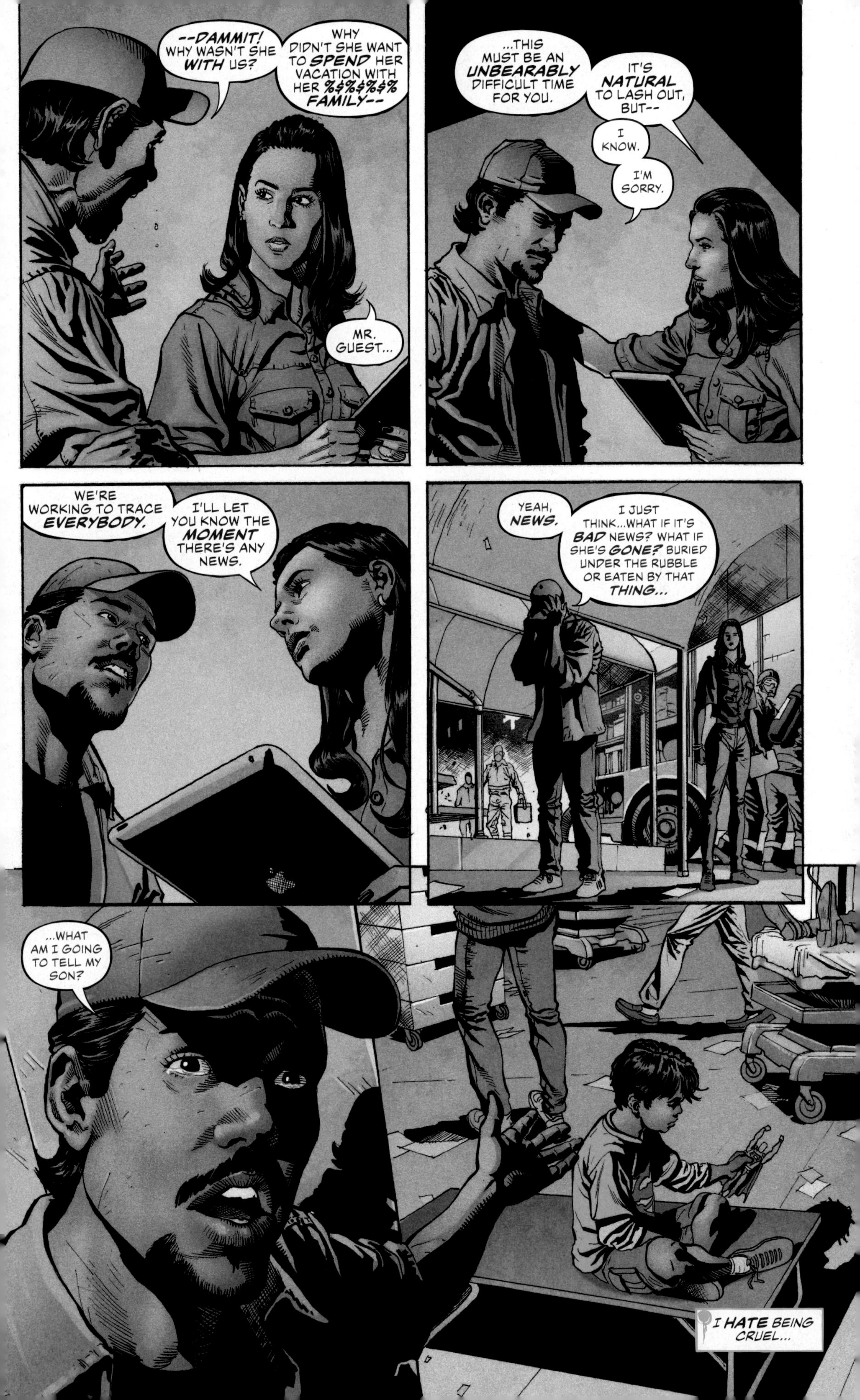
--DAMMIT! WHY WASN'T SHE WITH US?
WHY DIDN'T SHE WANT TO SPEND HER VACATION WITH HER %$%$%$% FAMILY--
MR. GUEST...
...THIS MUST BE AN UNBEARABLY DIFFICULT TIME FOR YOU.
IT'S NATURAL TO LASH OUT, BUT--
I KNOW.
I'M SORRY.
WE'RE WORKING TO TRACE EVERYBODY.
I'LL LET YOU KNOW THE MOMENT THERE'S ANY NEWS.
YEAH, NEWS.
I JUST THINK...WHAT IF IT'S BAD NEWS? WHAT IF SHE'S GONE? BURIED UNDER THE RUBBLE OR EATEN BY THAT THING...
...WHAT AM I GOING TO TELL MY SON?
I HATE BEING CRUEL...

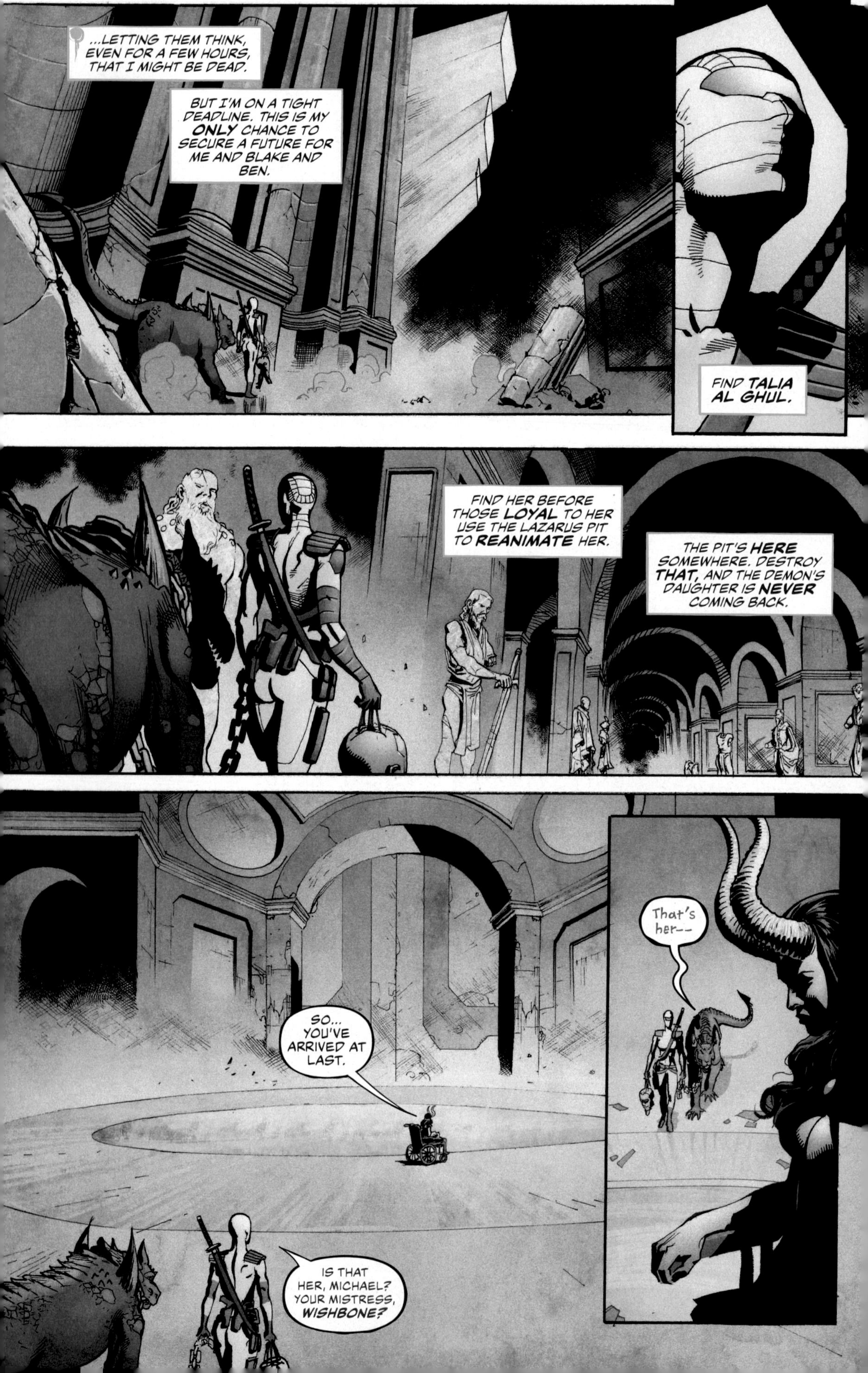
...LETTING THEM THINK, EVEN FOR A FEW HOURS, THAT I MIGHT BE DEAD.
BUT I'M ON A TIGHT DEADLINE. THIS IS MY ONLY CHANCE TO SECURE A FUTURE FOR ME AND BLAKE AND BEN.
FIND TALIA AL GHUL.
FIND HER BEFORE THOSE LOYAL TO HER USE THE LAZARUS PIT TO REANIMATE HER.
THE PIT'S HERE SOMEWHERE. DESTROY THAT, AND THE DEMON'S DAUGHTER IS NEVER COMING BACK.
SO... YOU'VE ARRIVED AT LAST.
IS THAT HER, MICHAEL? YOUR MISTRESS, WISHBONE?
That's her--

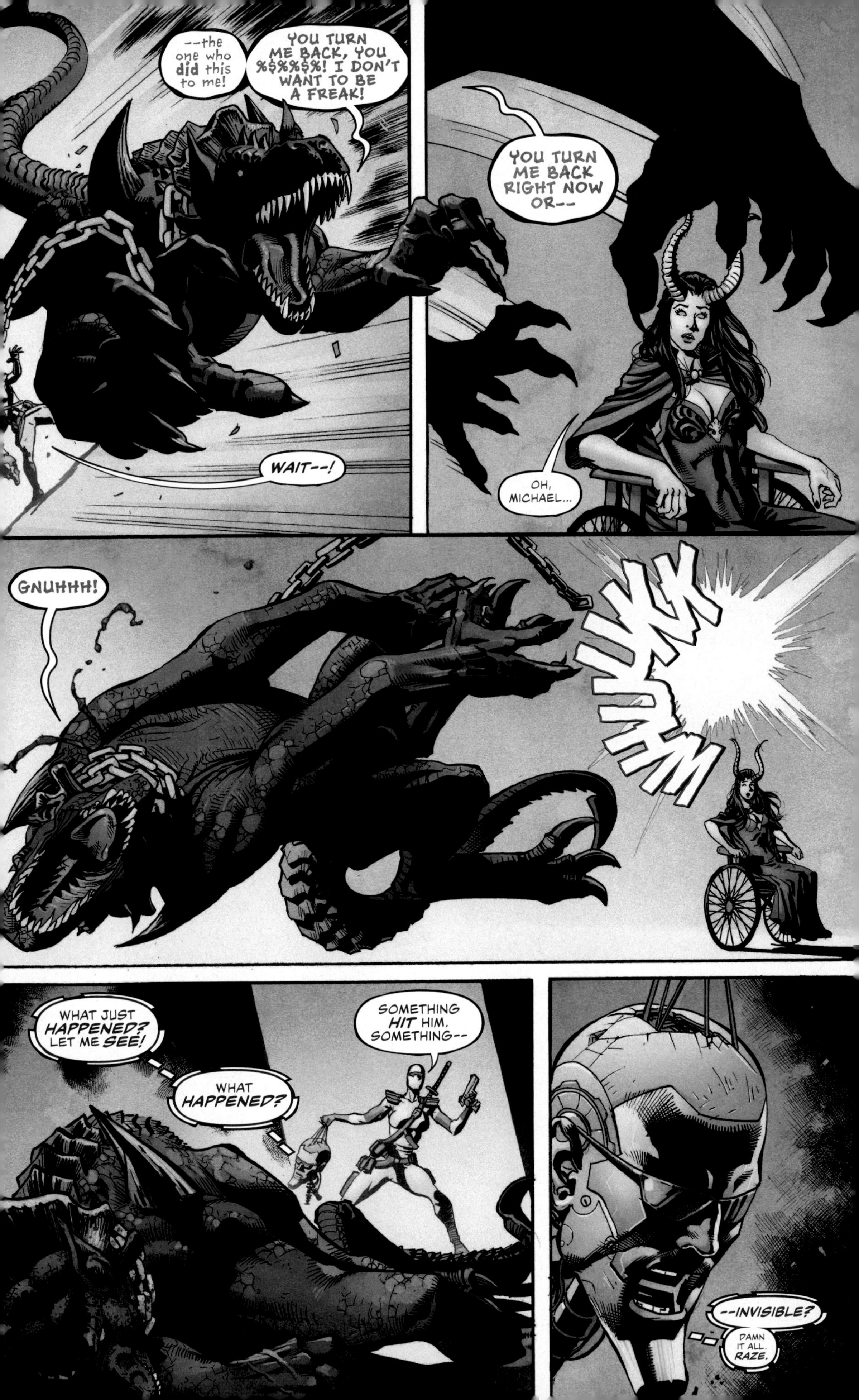
--the one who did this to me!
YOU TURN ME BACK, YOU %$%%$%! I DON'T WANT TO BE A FREAK!
WAIT--!
YOU TURN ME BACK RIGHT NOW OR--
OH, MICHAEL...
GNUHHH!
WHUMK
WHAT JUST HAPPENED? LET ME SEE!
WHAT HAPPENED?
SOMETHING HIT HIM. SOMETHING--
--INVISIBLE?
DAMN IT ALL. RAZE.

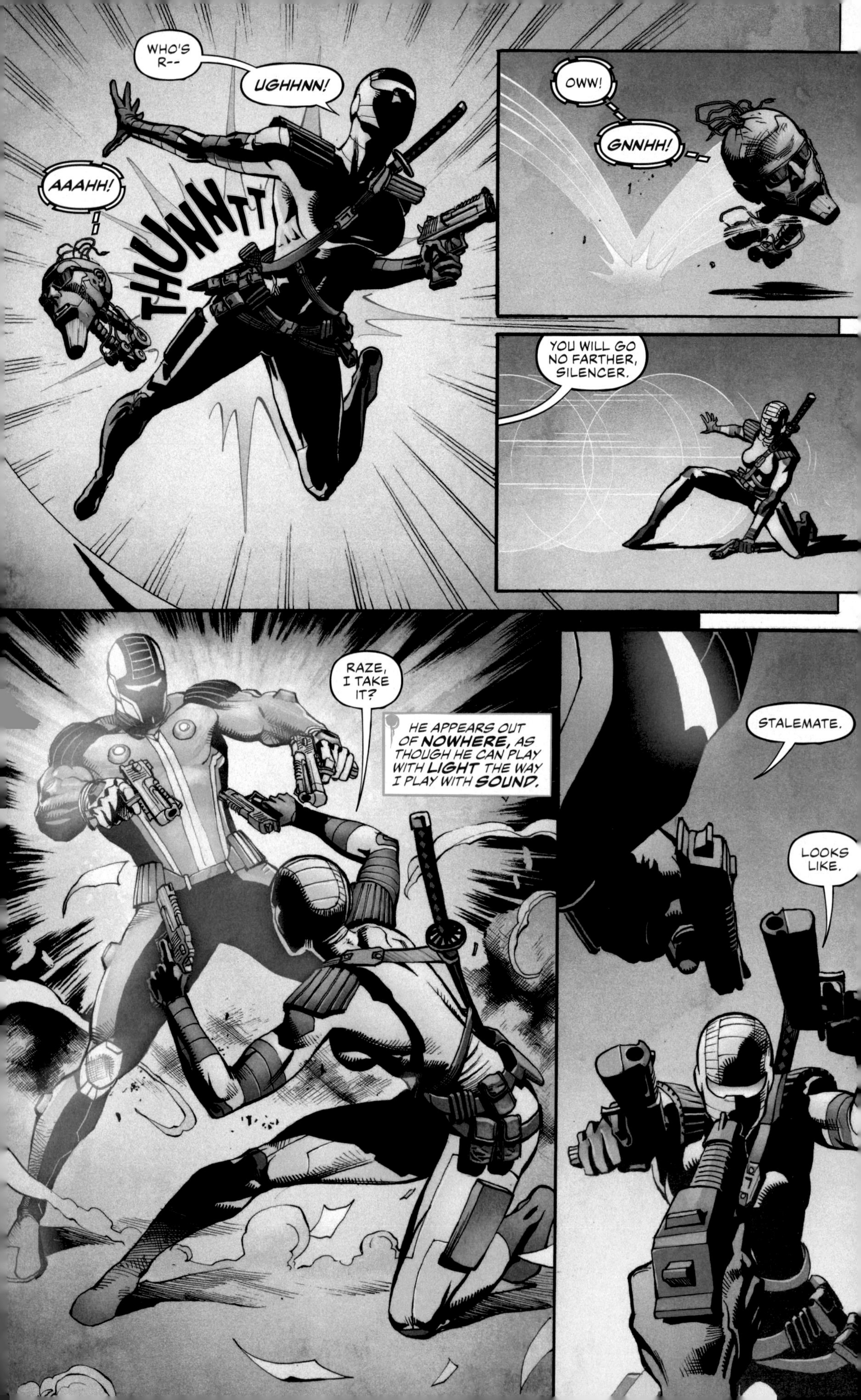

WHO'S R--
UGHHNN!
AAAHH!
THUNNTT
OWW!
GNNHH!
YOU WILL GO NO FARTHER, SILENCER.
RAZE, I TAKE IT?
HE APPEARS OUT OF NOWHERE, AS THOUGH HE CAN PLAY WITH LIGHT THE WAY I PLAY WITH SOUND.
STALEMATE.
LOOKS LIKE.

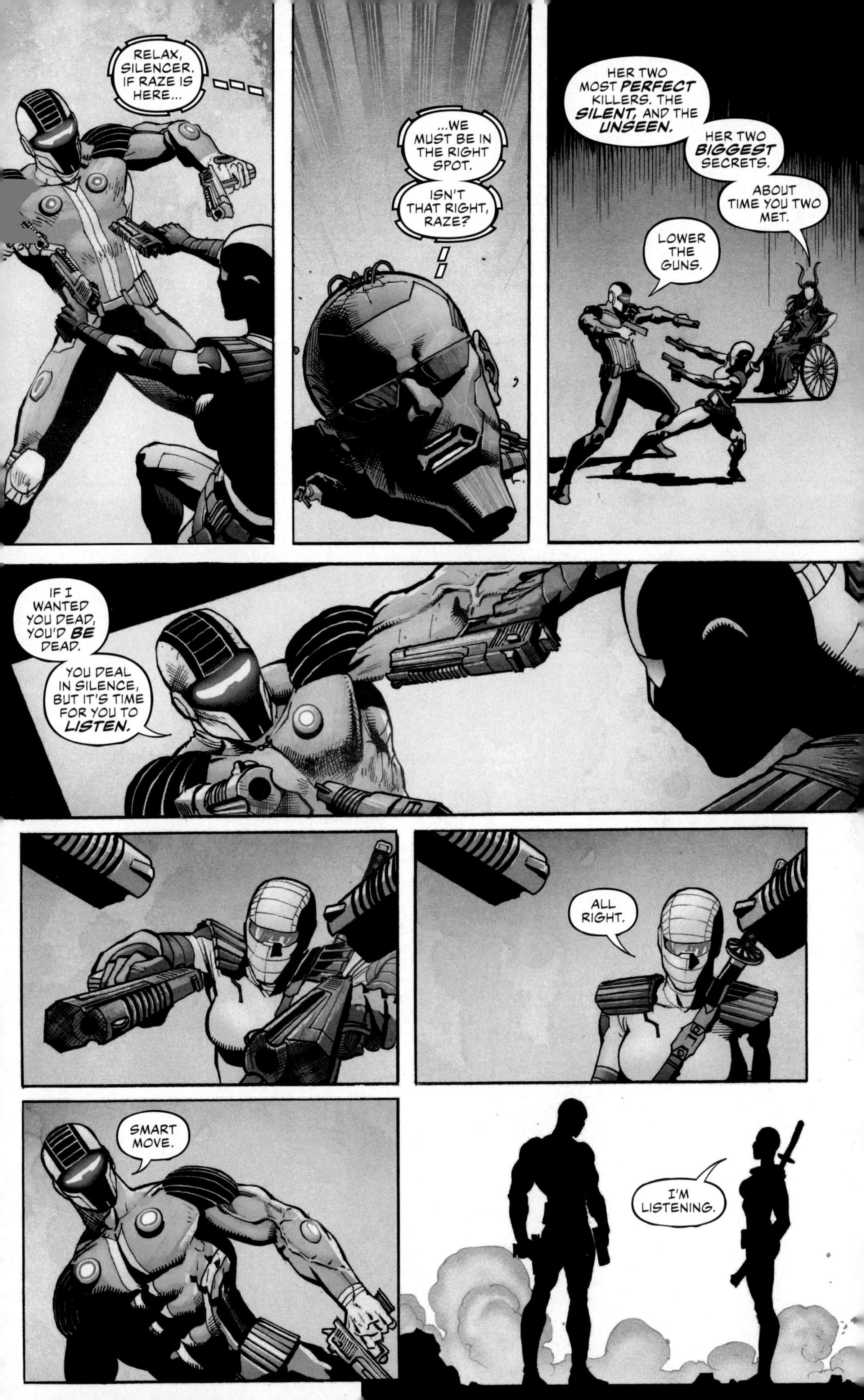
RELAX, SILENCER. IF RAZE IS HERE...
...WE MUST BE IN THE RIGHT SPOT.
ISN'T THAT RIGHT, RAZE?
HER TWO MOST PERFECT KILLERS. THE SILENT, AND THE UNSEEN.
HER TWO BIGGEST SECRETS.
ABOUT TIME YOU TWO MET.
LOWER THE GUNS.
IF I WANTED YOU DEAD, YOU'D BE DEAD.
YOU DEAL IN SILENCE, BUT IT'S TIME FOR YOU TO LISTEN.
ALL RIGHT.
SMART MOVE.
I'M LISTENING.

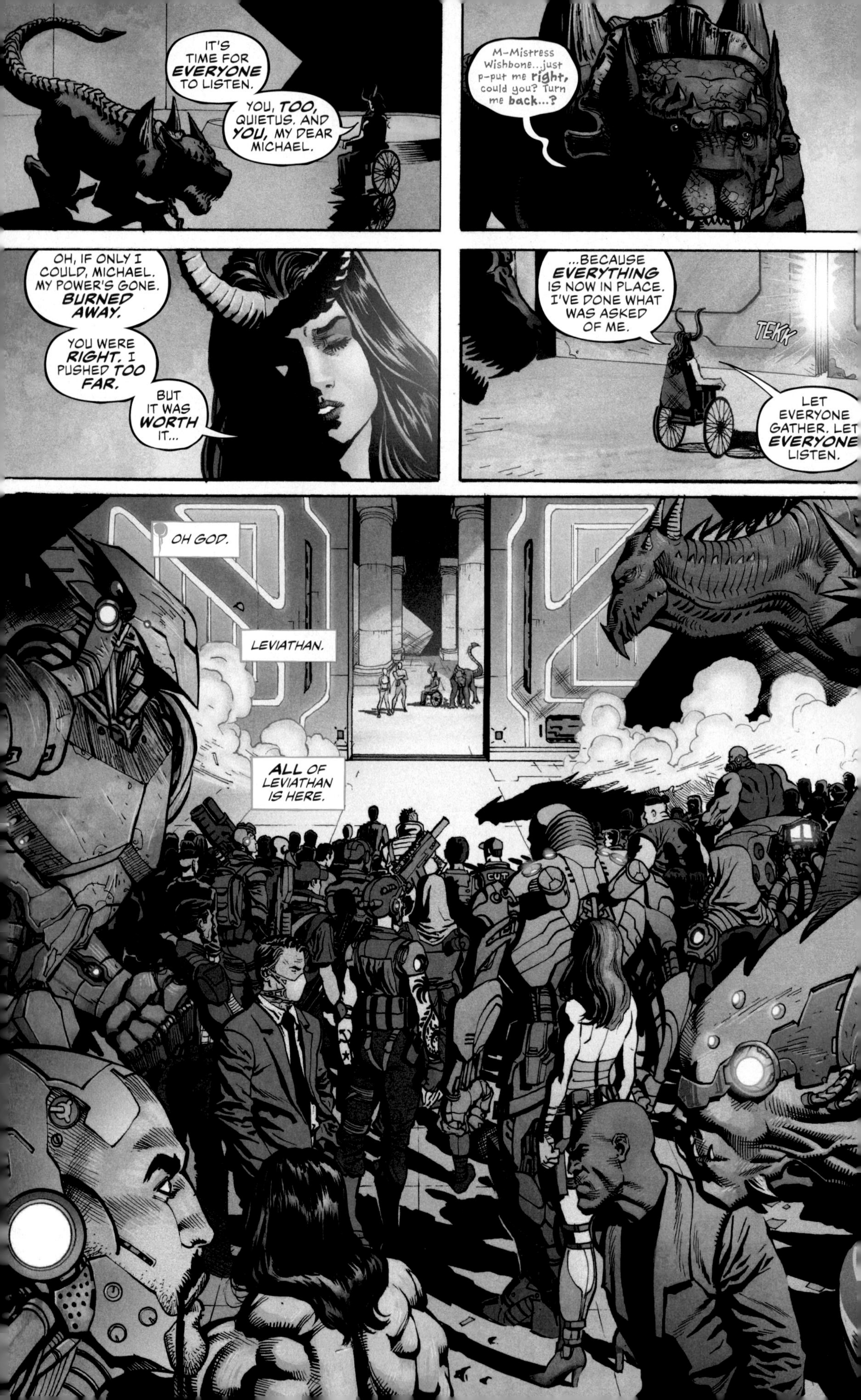

IT'S TIME FOR EVERYONE TO LISTEN.
YOU, TOO, QUIETUS. AND YOU, MY DEAR MICHAEL.
M-Mistress Wishbone...just p-put me right, could you? Turn me back...?
OH, IF ONLY I COULD, MICHAEL. MY POWER'S GONE. BURNED AWAY.
YOU WERE RIGHT. I PUSHED TOO FAR.
BUT IT WAS WORTH IT...
...BECAUSE EVERYTHING IS NOW IN PLACE. I'VE DONE WHAT WAS ASKED OF ME.
TEKK
LET EVERYONE GATHER. LET EVERYONE LISTEN.
OH GOD.
LEVIATHAN.
ALL OF LEVIATHAN IS HERE.

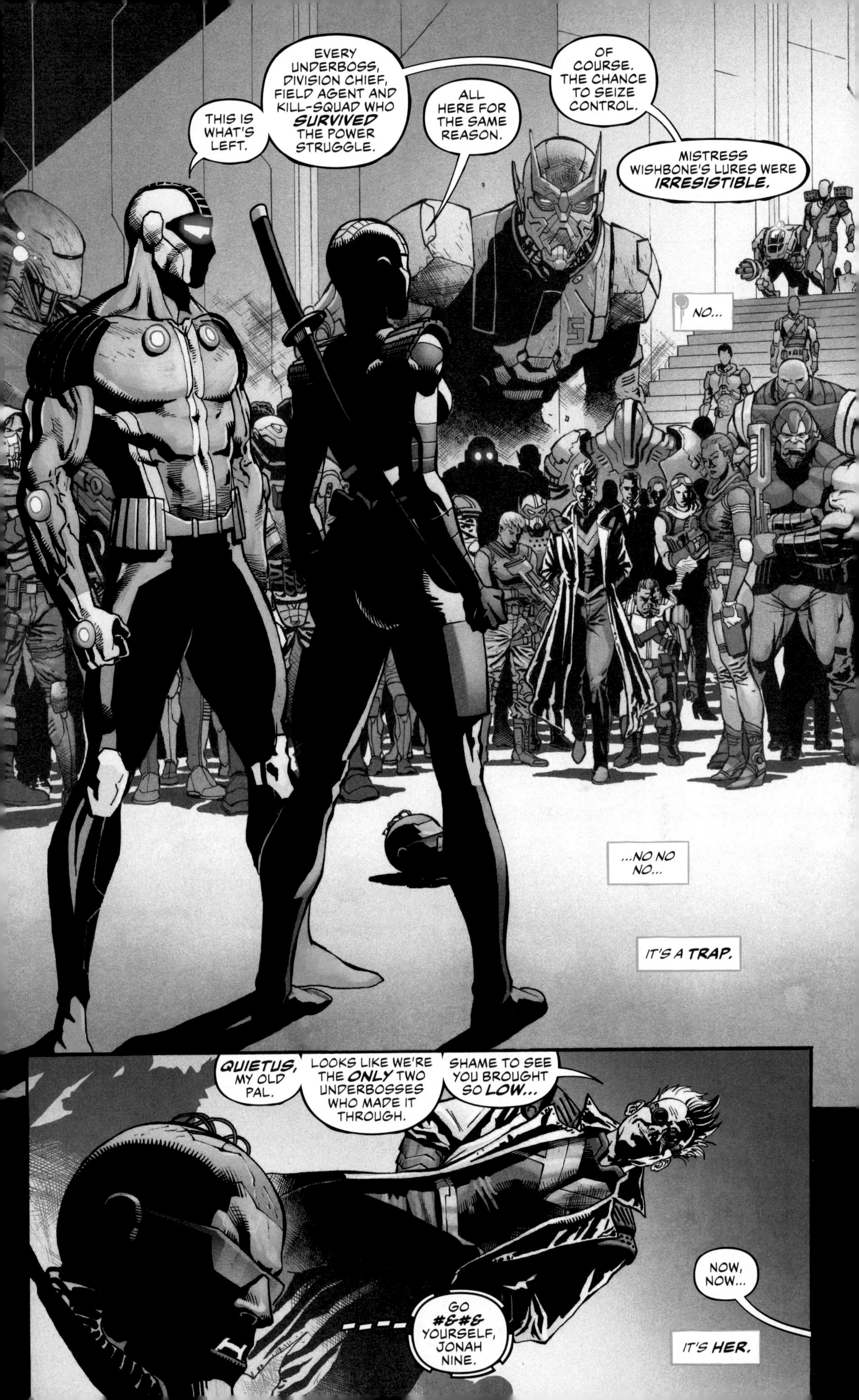
THIS IS WHAT'S LEFT.
EVERY UNDERBOSS, DIVISION CHIEF, FIELD AGENT AND KILL-SQUAD WHO SURVIVED THE POWER STRUGGLE.
ALL HERE FOR THE SAME REASON.
OF COURSE. THE CHANCE TO SEIZE CONTROL.
MISTRESS WISHBONE'S LURES WERE IRRESISTIBLE.
NO...
...NO NO NO...
IT'S A TRAP.
QUIETUS, MY OLD PAL.
LOOKS LIKE WE'RE THE ONLY TWO UNDERBOSSES WHO MADE IT THROUGH.
SHAME TO SEE YOU BROUGHT SO LOW...
GO #&#& YOURSELF, JONAH NINE.
NOW, NOW...
IT'S HER.

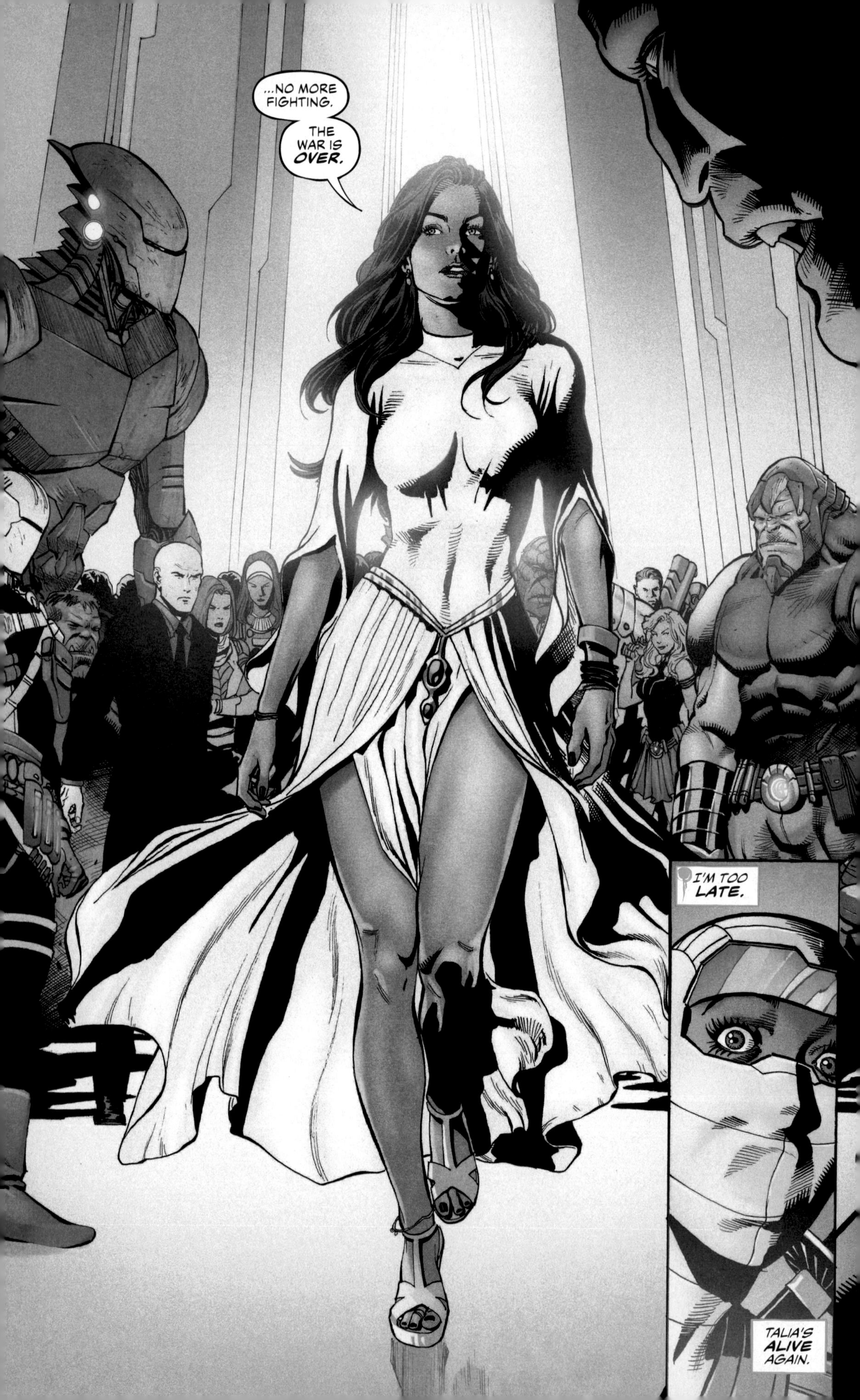
...NO MORE FIGHTING.
THE WAR IS OVER.
I'M TOO LATE.
TALIA'S ALIVE AGAIN.

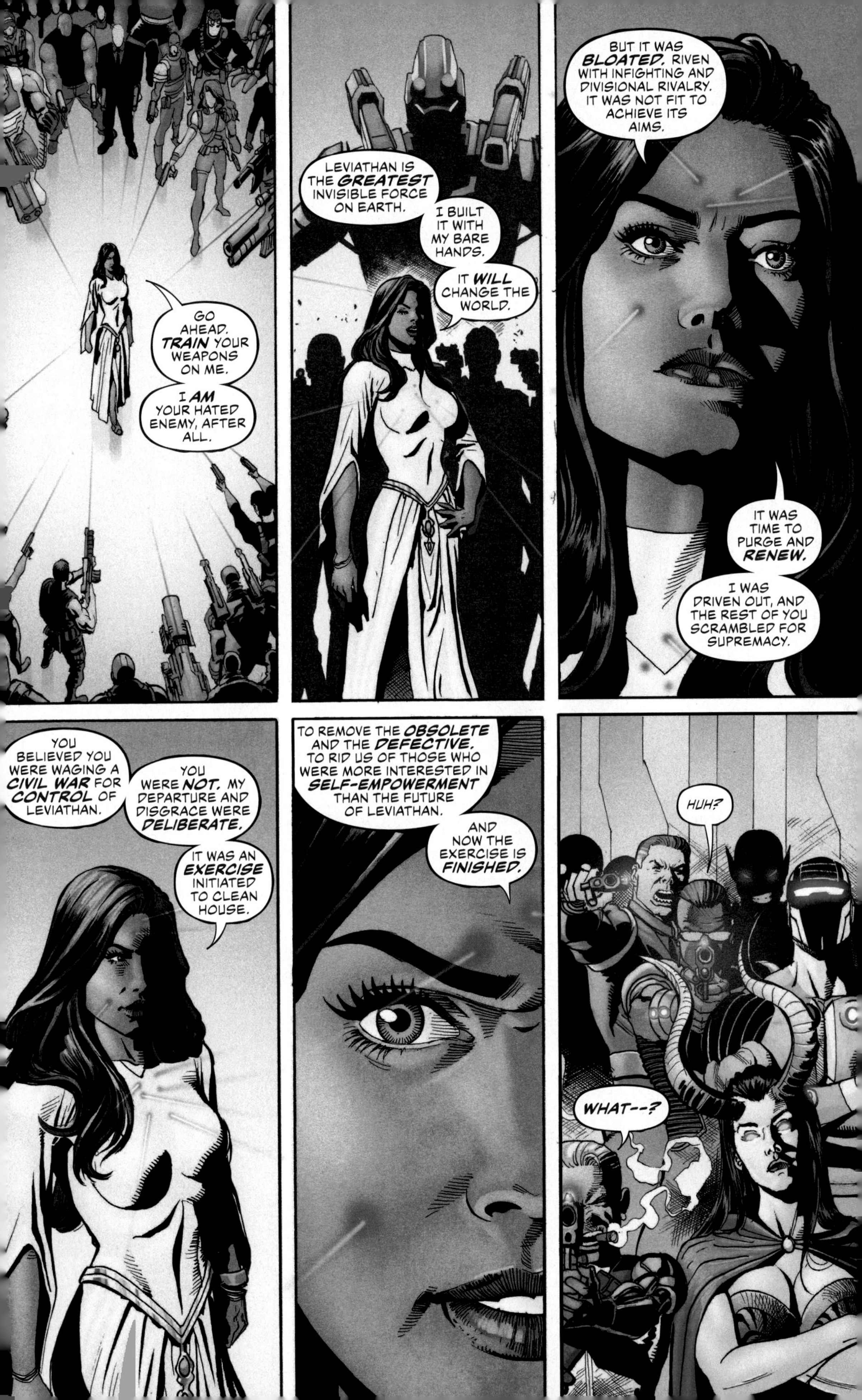
GO AHEAD. TRAIN YOUR WEAPONS ON ME.
I AM YOUR HATED ENEMY, AFTER ALL.
LEVIATHAN IS THE GREATEST INVISIBLE FORCE ON EARTH.
I BUILT IT WITH MY BARE HANDS.
IT WILL CHANGE THE WORLD.
BUT IT WAS BLOATED. RIVEN WITH INFIGHTING AND DIVISIONAL RIVALRY. IT WAS NOT FIT TO ACHIEVE ITS AIMS.
IT WAS TIME TO PURGE AND RENEW.
I WAS DRIVEN OUT, AND THE REST OF YOU SCRAMBLED FOR SUPREMACY.
YOU BELIEVED YOU WERE WAGING A CIVIL WAR FOR CONTROL OF LEVIATHAN.
YOU WERE NOT. MY DEPARTURE AND DISGRACE WERE DELIBERATE.
IT WAS AN EXERCISE INITIATED TO CLEAN HOUSE.
TO REMOVE THE OBSOLETE AND THE DEFECTIVE, TO RID US OF THOSE WHO WERE MORE INTERESTED IN SELF-EMPOWERMENT THAN THE FUTURE OF LEVIATHAN.
AND NOW THE EXERCISE IS FINISHED.
HUH?
WHAT--?

I ENGINEERED THE INTERNECINE CONFLICT TO *DISINFECT* OUR ORGANIZATION.

SOME OPERATIVES HAVE PASSED, AND SOME HAVE *FAILED.*

THOSE WHO HAVE COME HERE TODAY EITHER PASSED BECAUSE THEY REMAINED *LOYAL...*

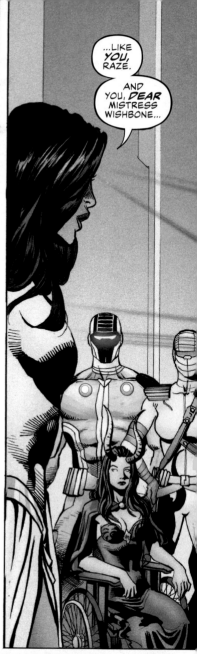

...LIKE *YOU,* RAZE.

AND YOU, *DEAR* MISTRESS WISHBONE...

...OR BECAUSE THEY FOUGHT TO TAKE CONTROL AND *STABILIZE* LEVIATHAN...

...LIKE *YOU,* JONAH NINE.

MA'AM.

OR THE *RELENTLESS* QUIETUS.

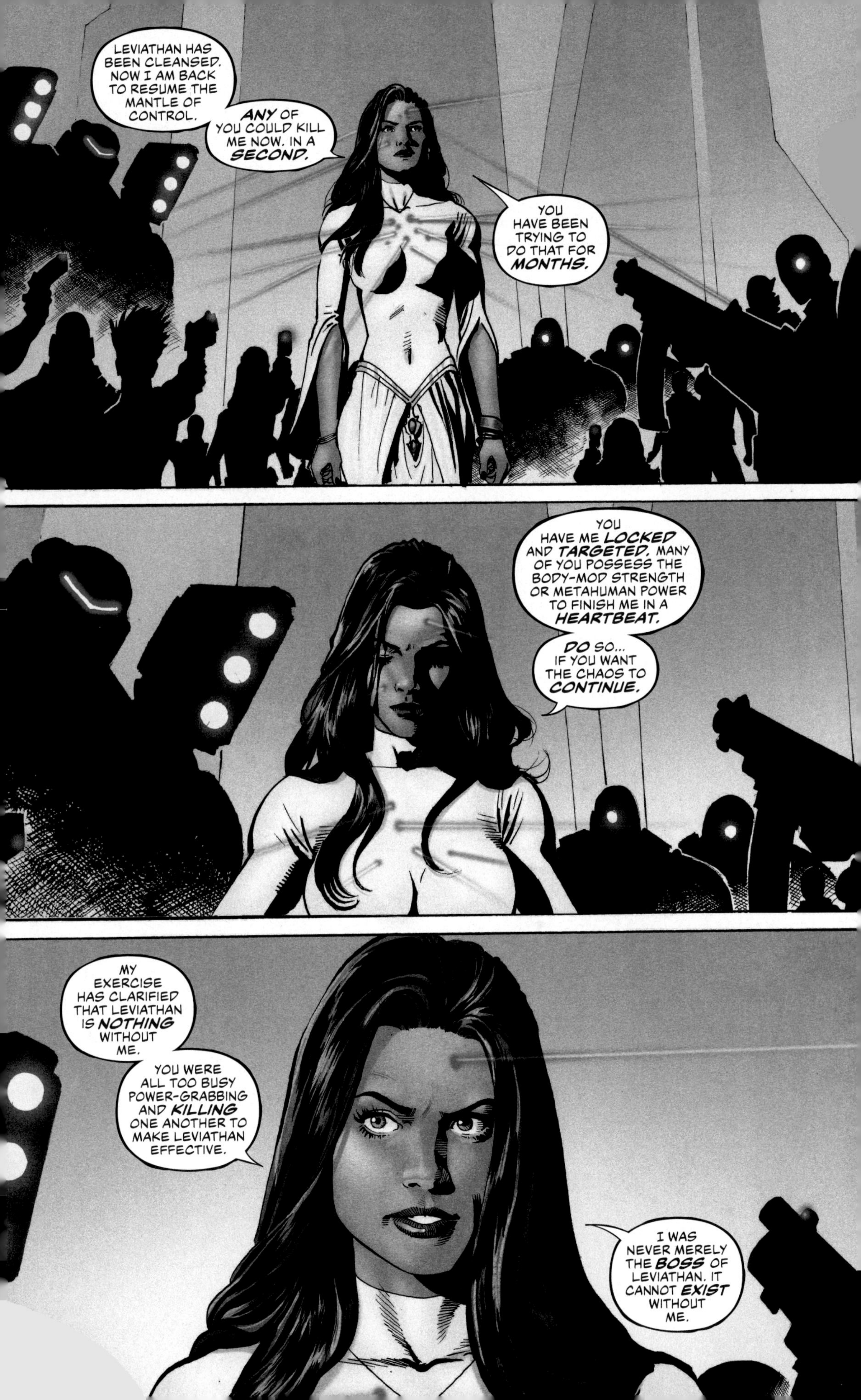

LEVIATHAN HAS BEEN CLEANSED. NOW I AM BACK TO RESUME THE MANTLE OF CONTROL.
ANY OF YOU COULD KILL ME NOW. IN A SECOND.
YOU HAVE BEEN TRYING TO DO THAT FOR MONTHS.
YOU HAVE ME LOCKED AND TARGETED. MANY OF YOU POSSESS THE BODY-MOD STRENGTH OR METAHUMAN POWER TO FINISH ME IN A HEARTBEAT.
DO SO... IF YOU WANT THE CHAOS TO CONTINUE.
MY EXERCISE HAS CLARIFIED THAT LEVIATHAN IS NOTHING WITHOUT ME.
YOU WERE ALL TOO BUSY POWER-GRABBING AND KILLING ONE ANOTHER TO MAKE LEVIATHAN EFFECTIVE.
I WAS NEVER MERELY THE BOSS OF LEVIATHAN. IT CANNOT EXIST WITHOUT ME.

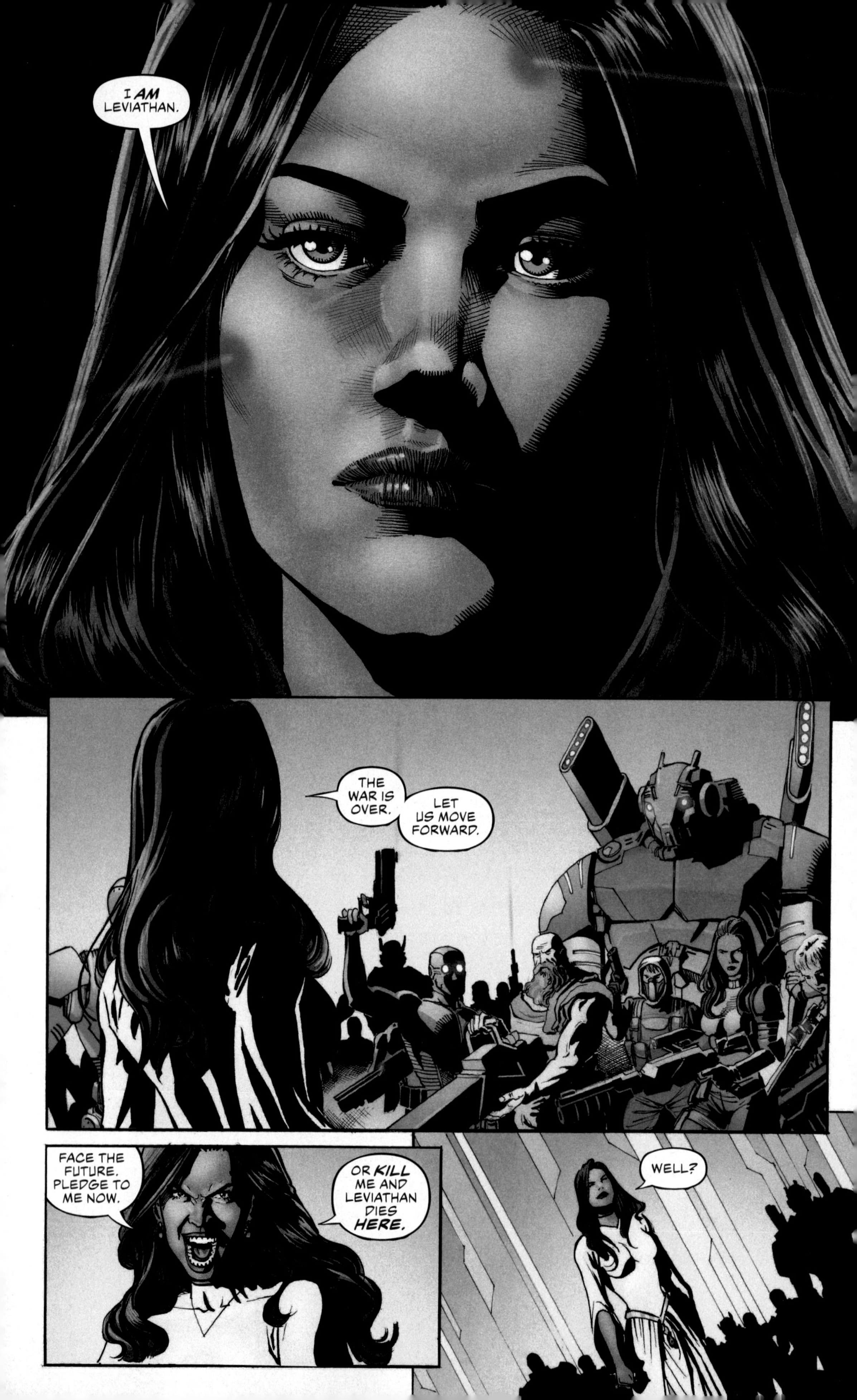
I AM LEVIATHAN.
THE WAR IS OVER.
LET US MOVE FORWARD.
FACE THE FUTURE. PLEDGE TO ME NOW.
OR KILL ME AND LEVIATHAN DIES HERE.
WELL?

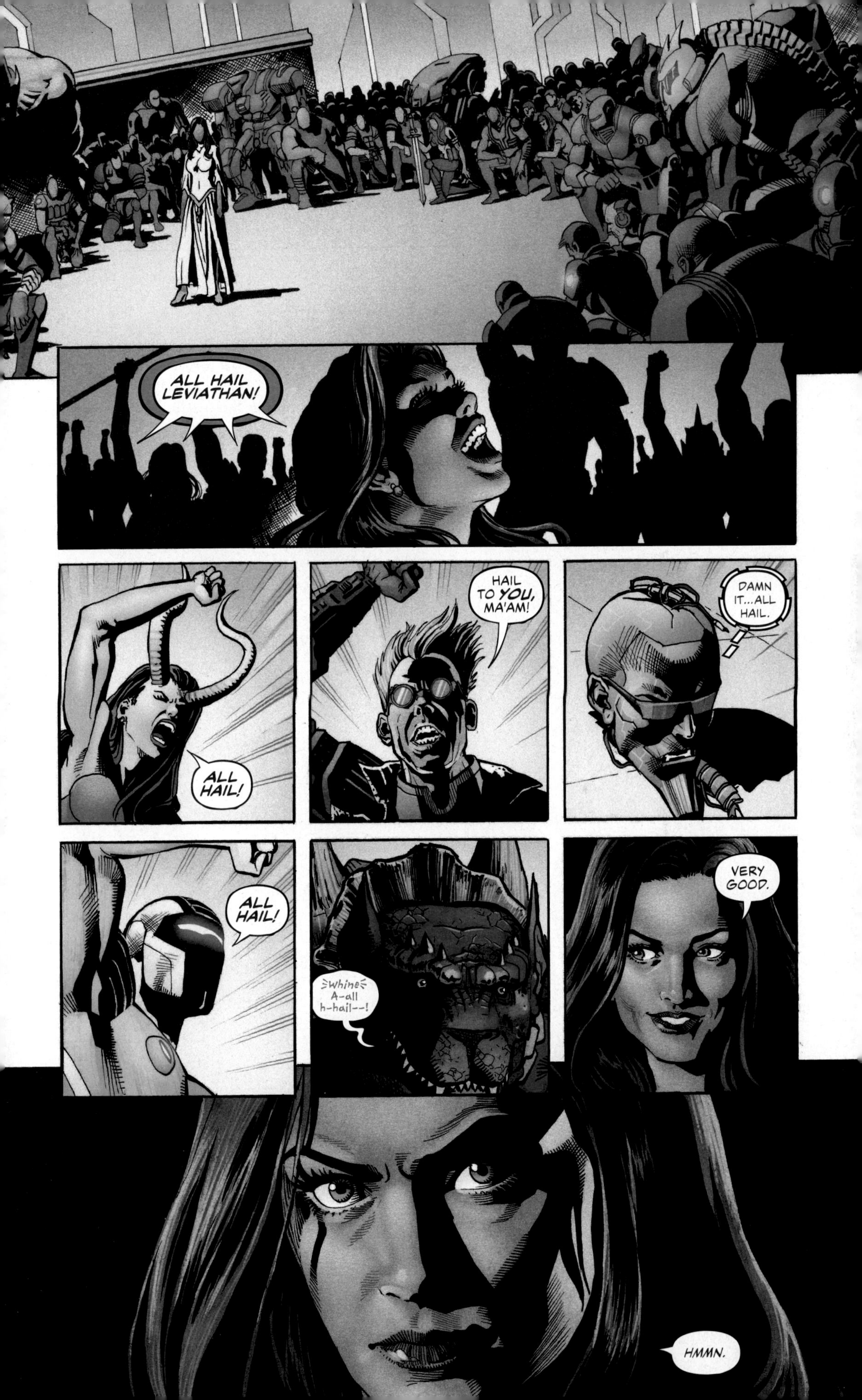
ALL HAIL LEVIATHAN!
ALL HAIL!
HAIL TO YOU, MA'AM!
DAMN IT...ALL HAIL.
ALL HAIL!
≶whine≶ A-all h-hail--!
VERY GOOD.
HMMN.

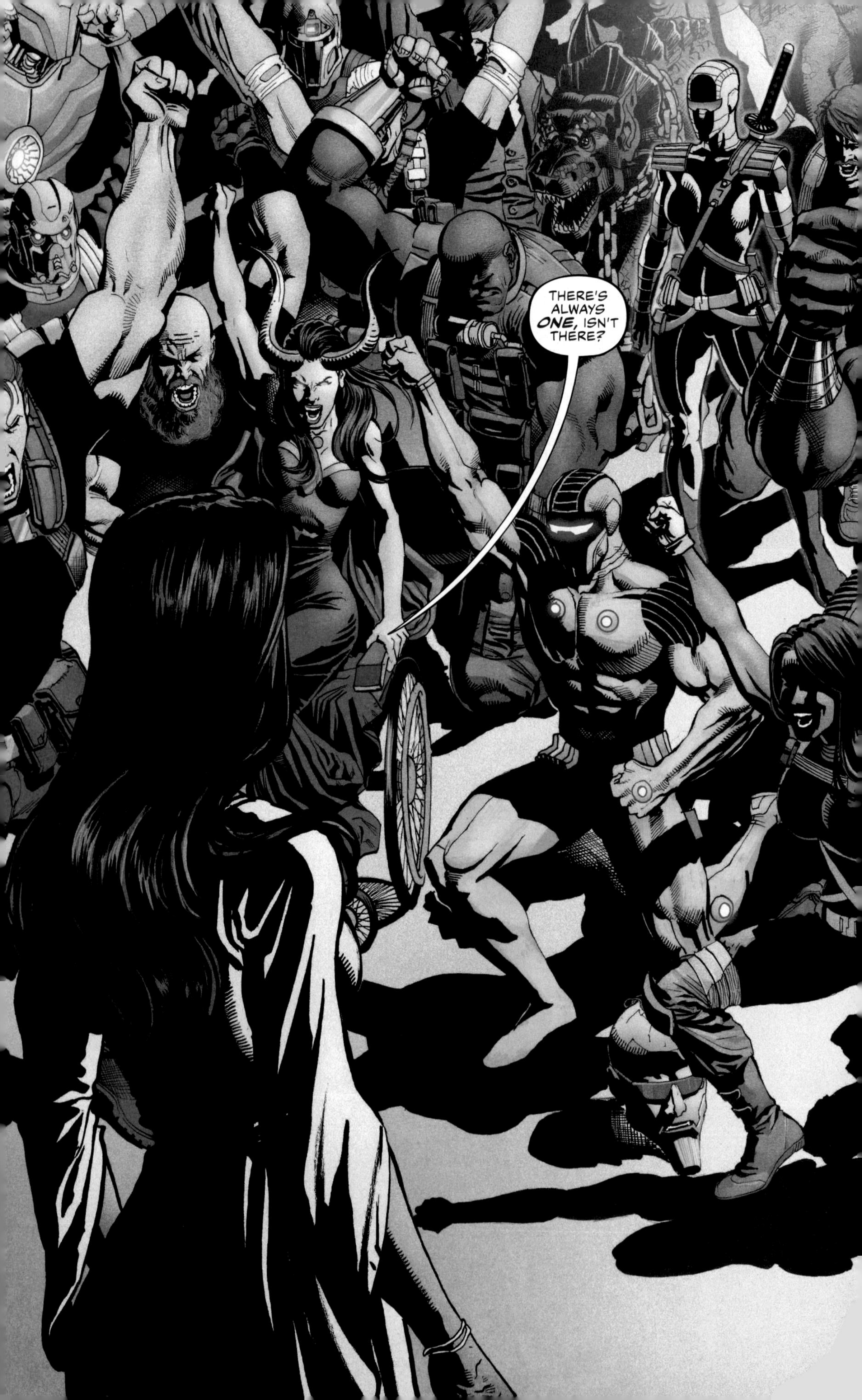
THERE'S ALWAYS ONE, ISN'T THERE?

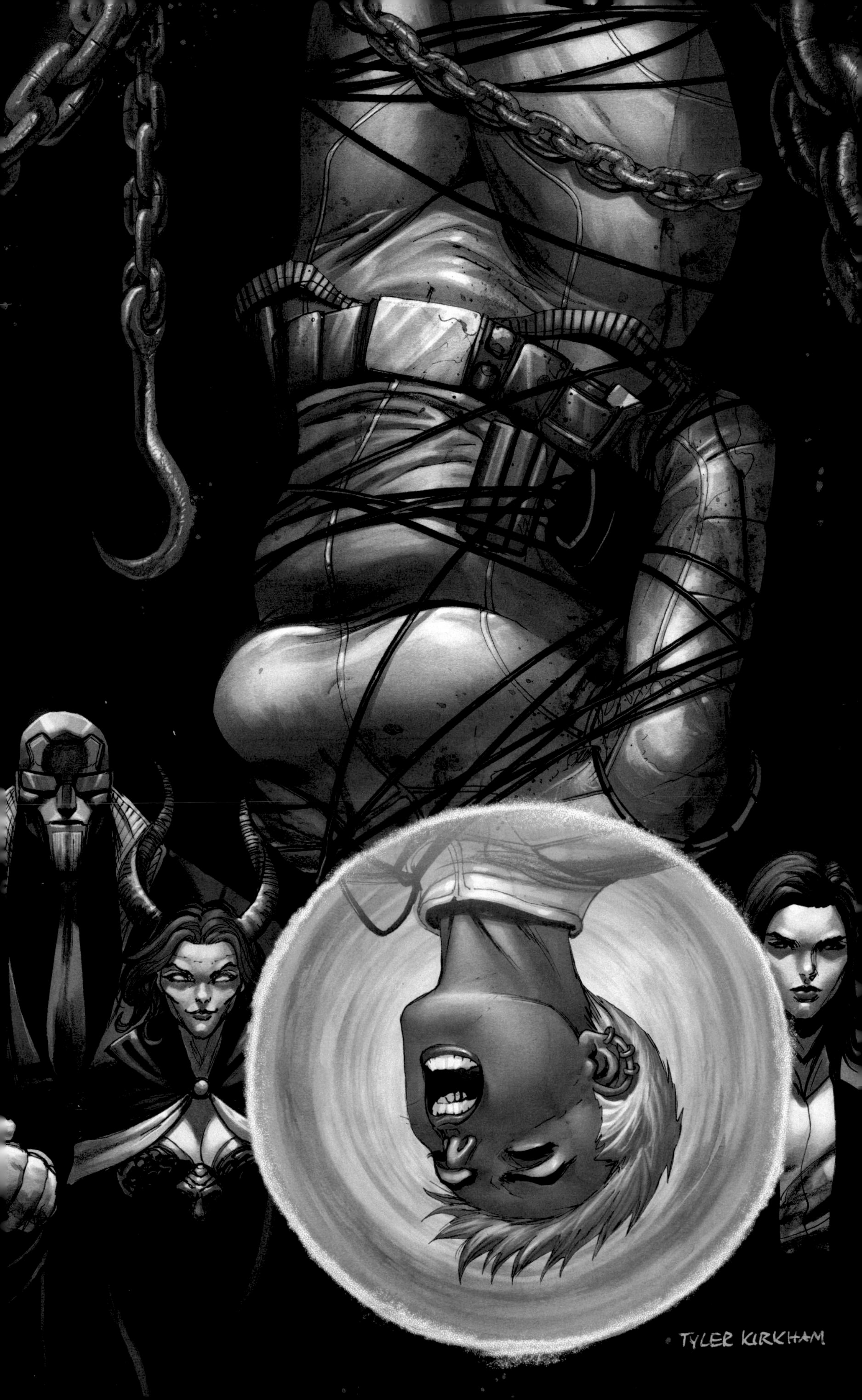
TYLER KIRKHAM

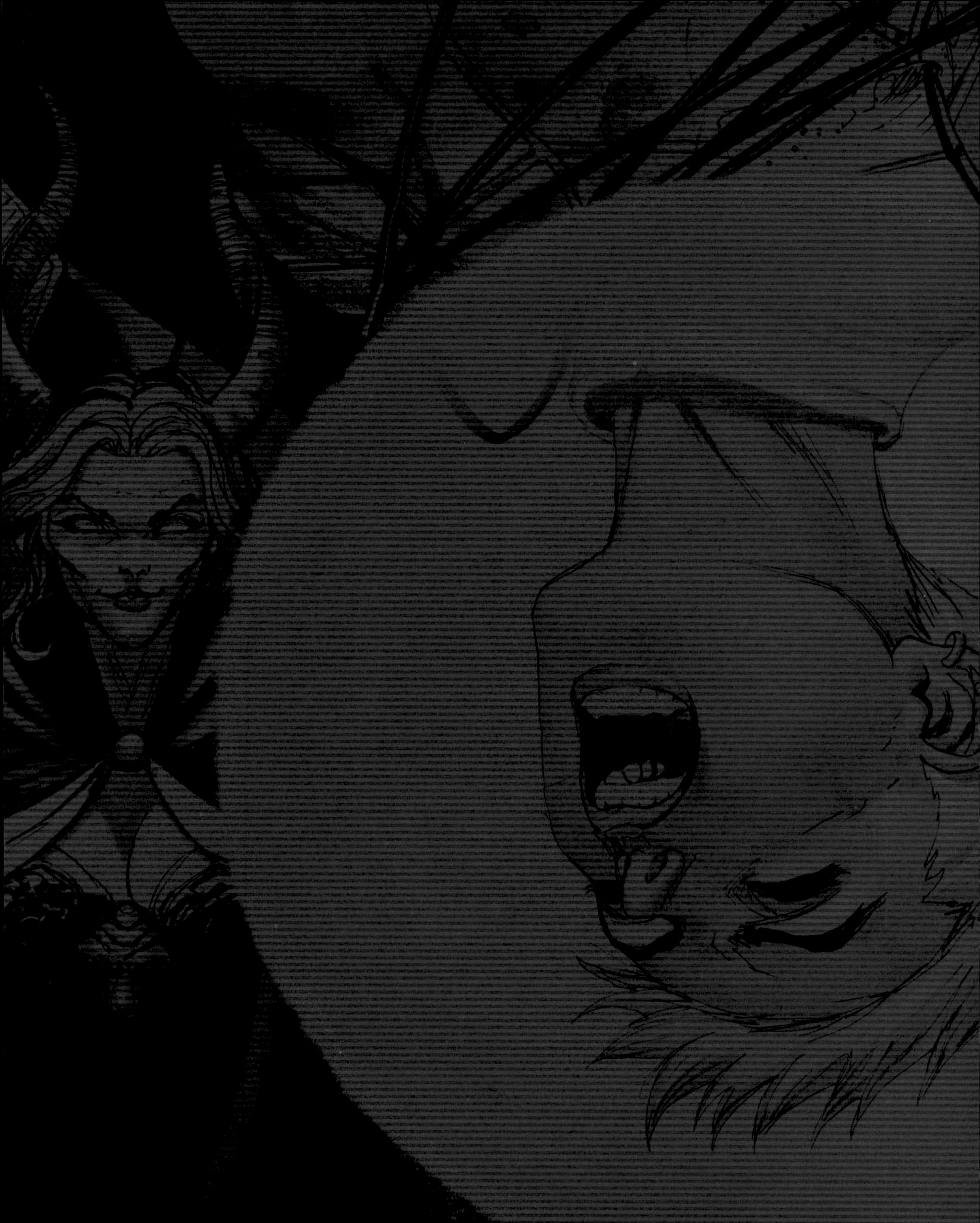

THE SILENCER

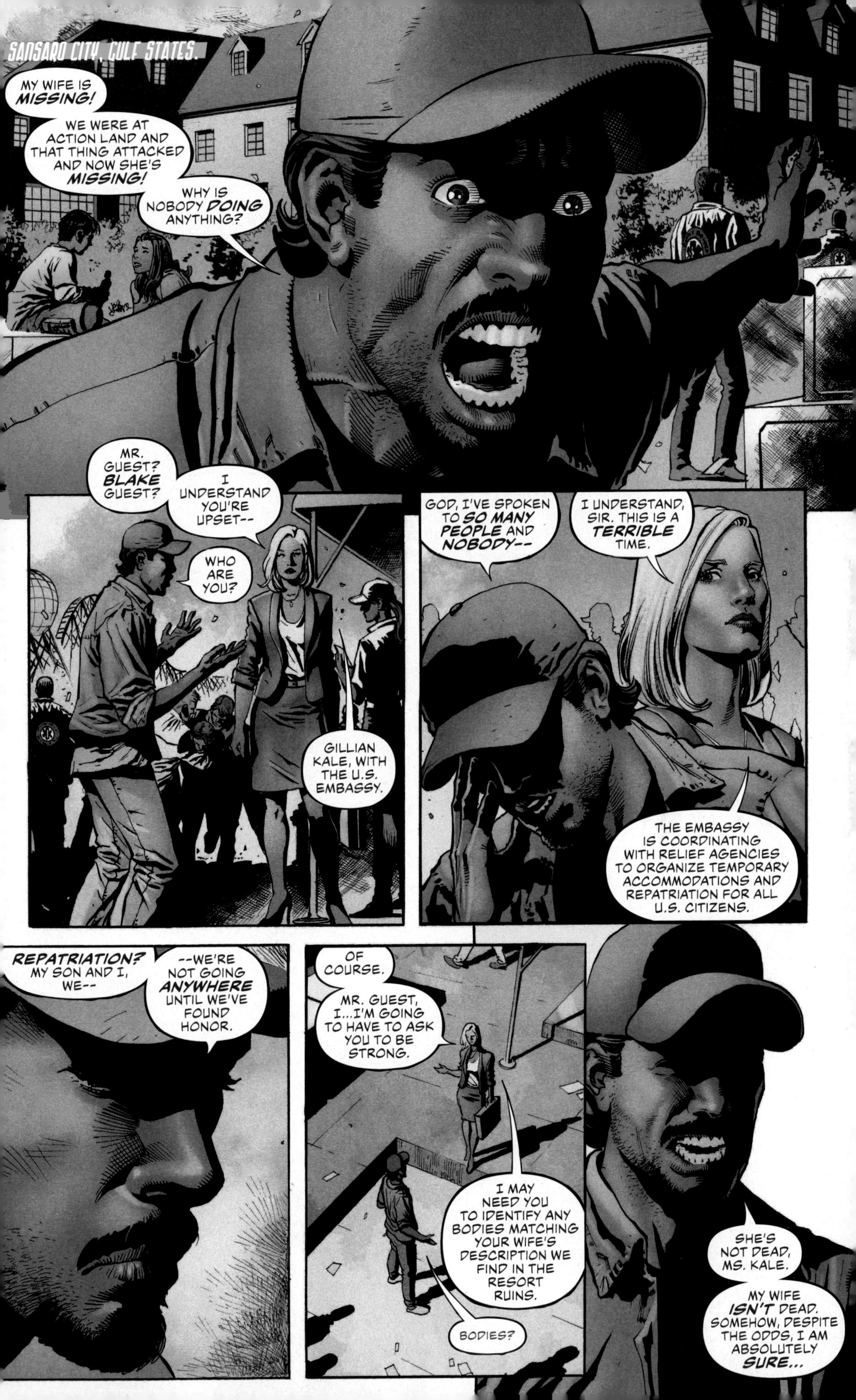
SANSARO CITY, GULF STATES.
MY WIFE IS MISSING!
WE WERE AT ACTION LAND AND THAT THING ATTACKED AND NOW SHE'S MISSING!
WHY IS NOBODY DOING ANYTHING?
MR. GUEST? BLAKE GUEST?
I UNDERSTAND YOU'RE UPSET--
WHO ARE YOU?
GILLIAN KALE, WITH THE U.S. EMBASSY.
GOD, I'VE SPOKEN TO SO MANY PEOPLE AND NOBODY--
I UNDERSTAND, SIR. THIS IS A TERRIBLE TIME.
THE EMBASSY IS COORDINATING WITH RELIEF AGENCIES TO ORGANIZE TEMPORARY ACCOMMODATIONS AND REPATRIATION FOR ALL U.S. CITIZENS.
REPATRIATION? MY SON AND I, WE--
--WE'RE NOT GOING ANYWHERE UNTIL WE'VE FOUND HONOR.
OF COURSE.
MR. GUEST, I...I'M GOING TO HAVE TO ASK YOU TO BE STRONG.
I MAY NEED YOU TO IDENTIFY ANY BODIES MATCHING YOUR WIFE'S DESCRIPTION WE FIND IN THE RESORT RUINS.
BODIES?
SHE'S NOT DEAD, MS. KALE.
MY WIFE ISN'T DEAD. SOMEHOW, DESPITE THE ODDS, I AM ABSOLUTELY SURE...

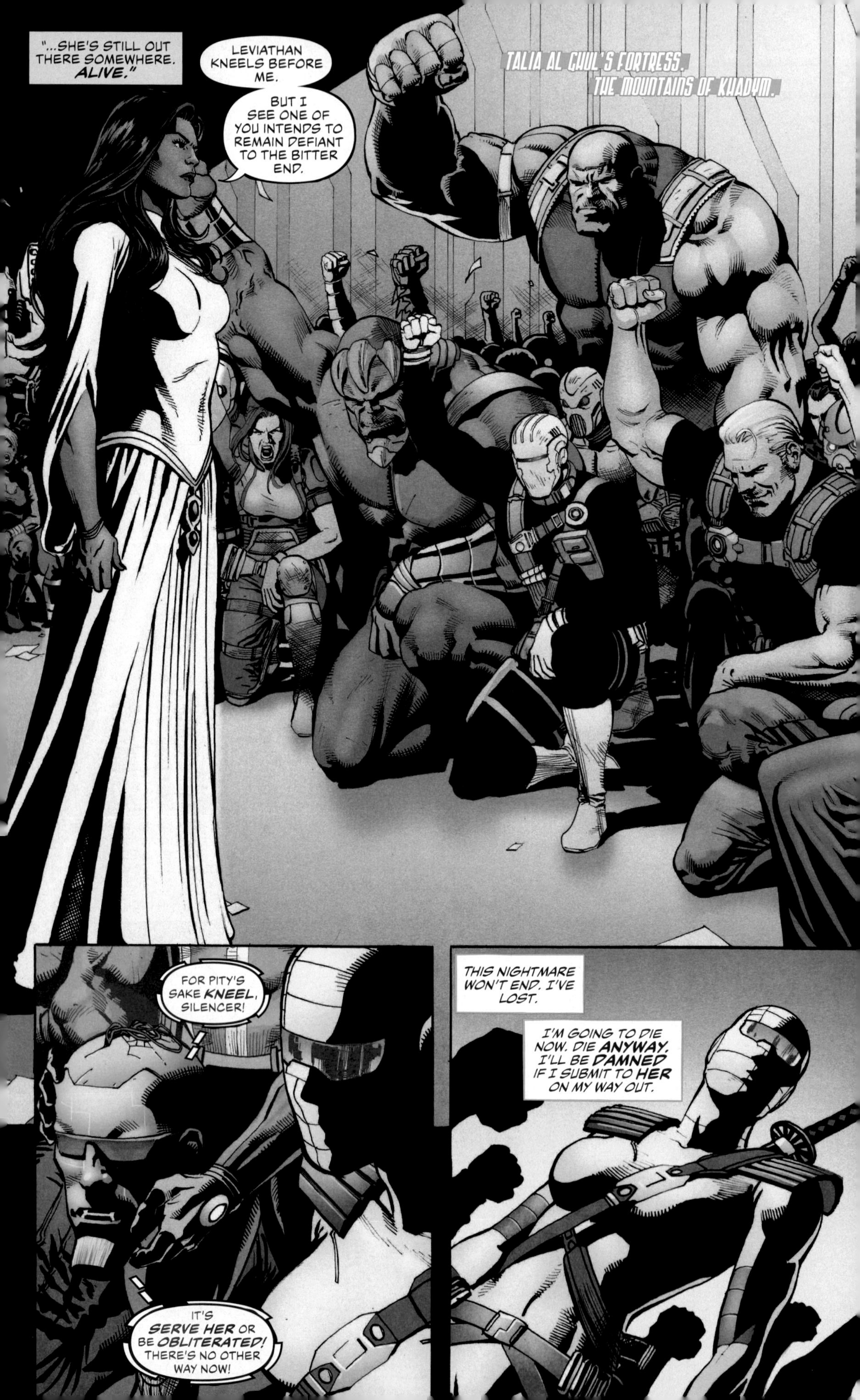
"...SHE'S STILL OUT THERE SOMEWHERE. ALIVE."
LEVIATHAN KNEELS BEFORE ME.
BUT I SEE ONE OF YOU INTENDS TO REMAIN DEFIANT TO THE BITTER END.
TALIA AL GHUL'S FORTRESS.
THE MOUNTAINS OF KHADYM.
FOR PITY'S SAKE KNEEL, SILENCER!
IT'S SERVE HER OR BE OBLITERATED! THERE'S NO OTHER WAY NOW!
THIS NIGHTMARE WON'T END. I'VE LOST.
I'M GOING TO DIE NOW. DIE ANYWAY. I'LL BE DAMNED IF I SUBMIT TO HER ON MY WAY OUT.

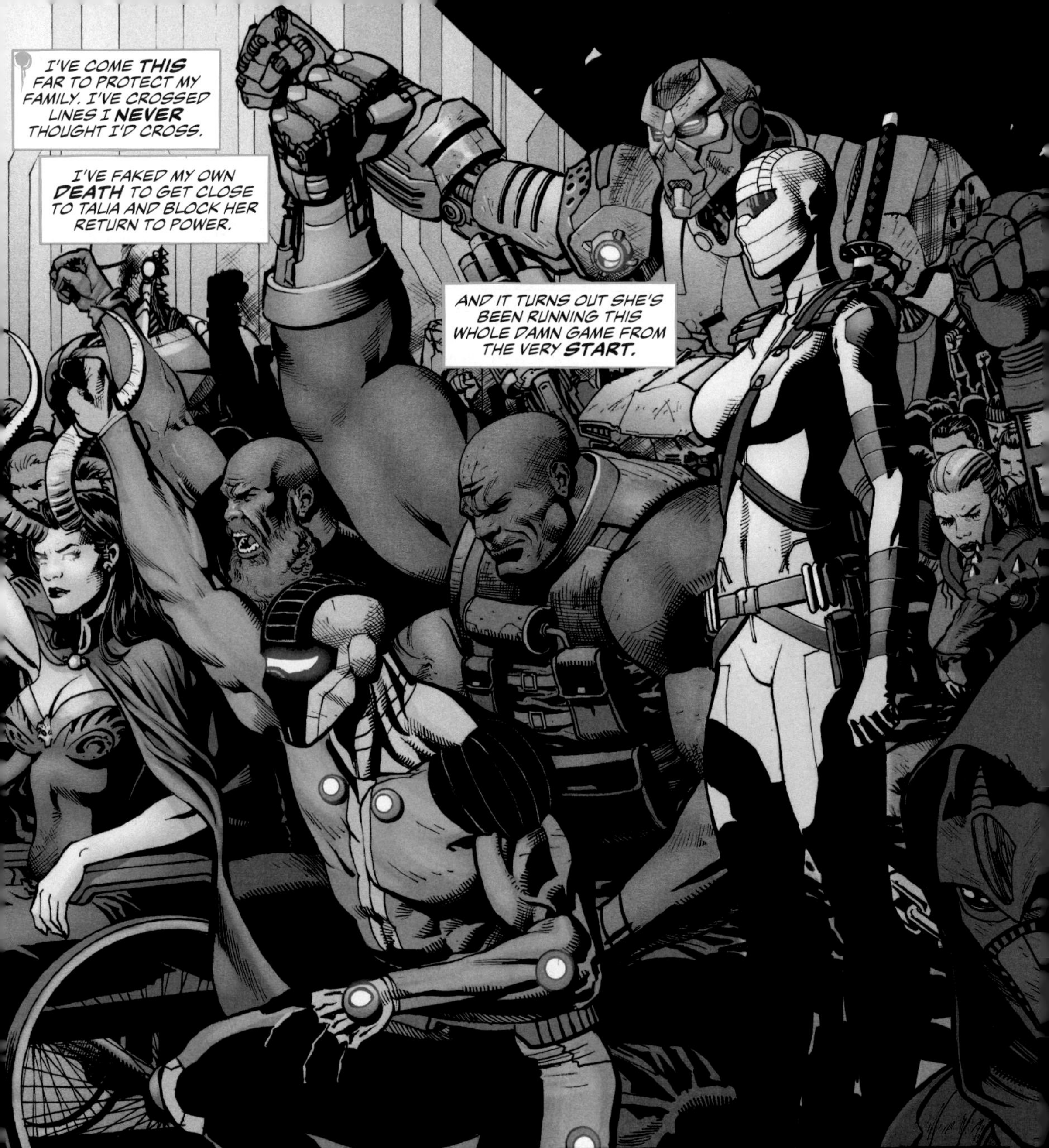
I'VE COME THIS FAR TO PROTECT MY FAMILY. I'VE CROSSED LINES I NEVER THOUGHT I'D CROSS.
I'VE FAKED MY OWN DEATH TO GET CLOSE TO TALIA AND BLOCK HER RETURN TO POWER.
AND IT TURNS OUT SHE'S BEEN RUNNING THIS WHOLE DAMN GAME FROM THE VERY START.

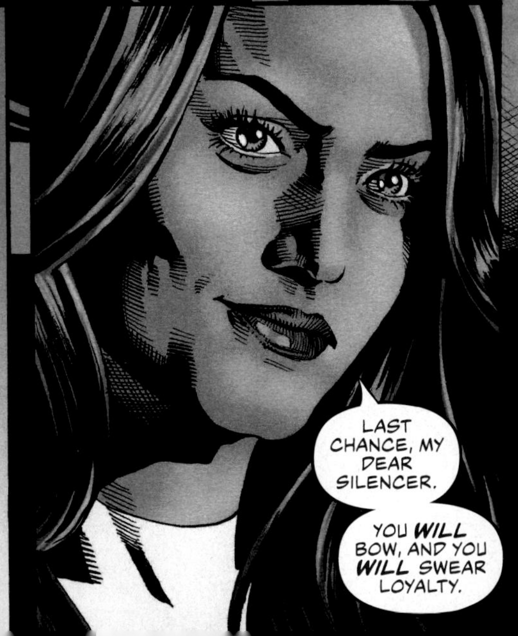
LAST CHANCE, MY DEAR SILENCER.
YOU WILL BOW, AND YOU WILL SWEAR LOYALTY.

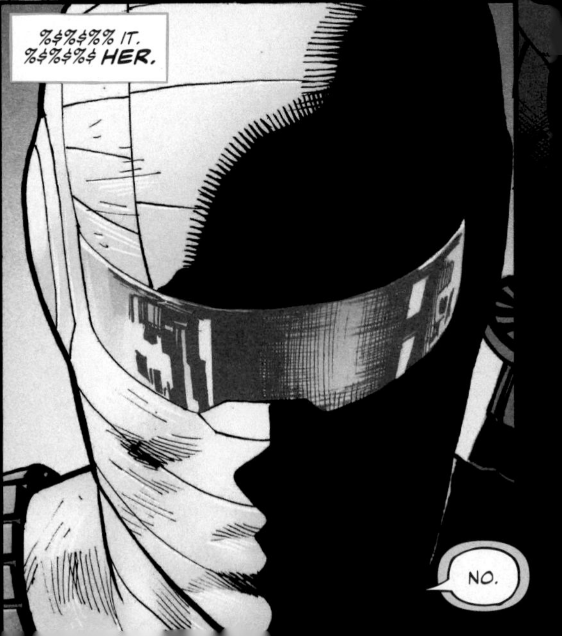
%$%$% IT. %$%$%$ HER.
NO.

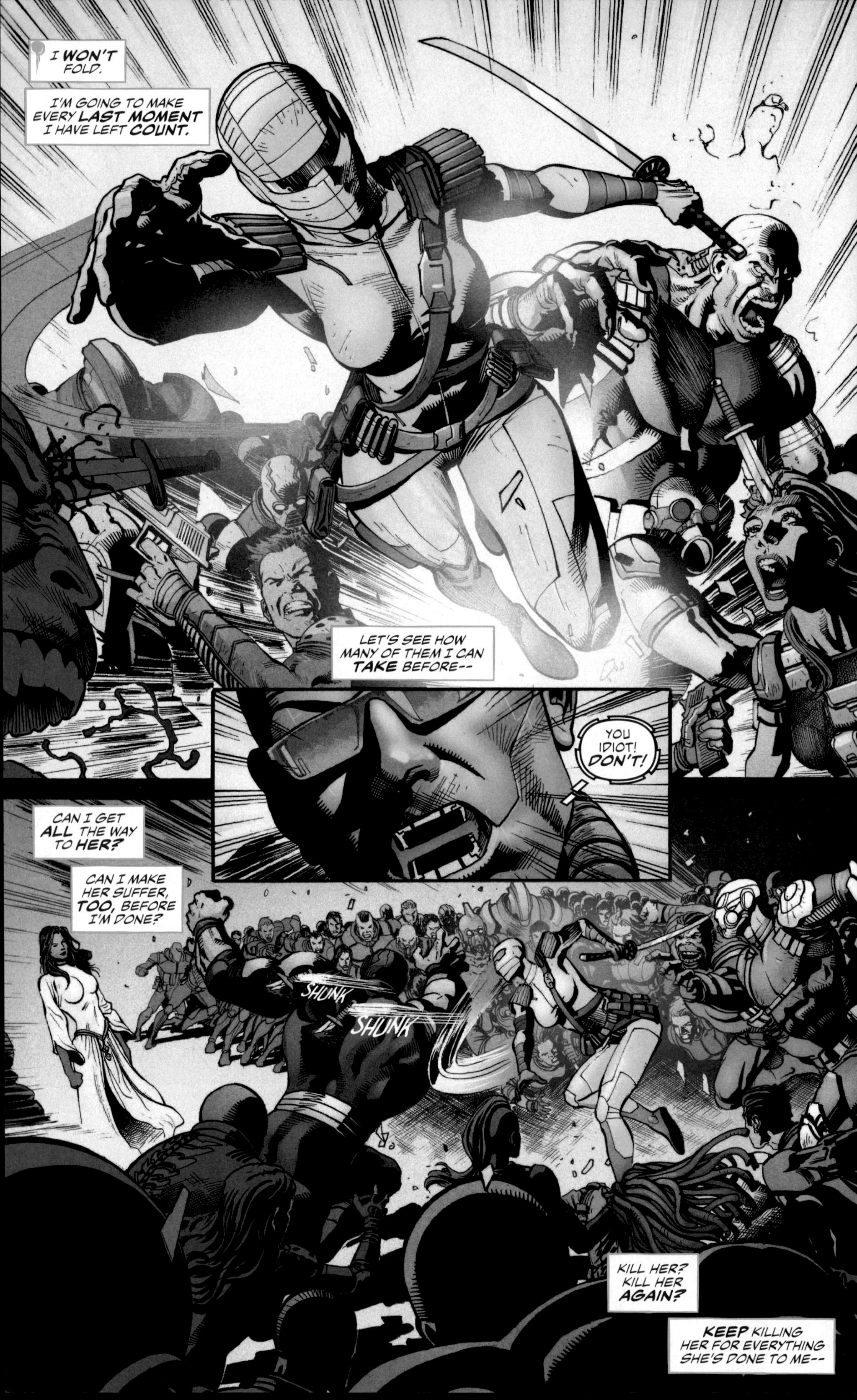

I WON'T FOLD.
I'M GOING TO MAKE EVERY LAST MOMENT I HAVE LEFT COUNT.
LET'S SEE HOW MANY OF THEM I CAN TAKE BEFORE--
YOU IDIOT! DON'T!
CAN I GET ALL THE WAY TO HER?
CAN I MAKE HER SUFFER, TOO, BEFORE I'M DONE?
SHUNK
SHUNK
KILL HER? KILL HER AGAIN?
KEEP KILLING HER FOR EVERYTHING SHE'S DONE TO ME--

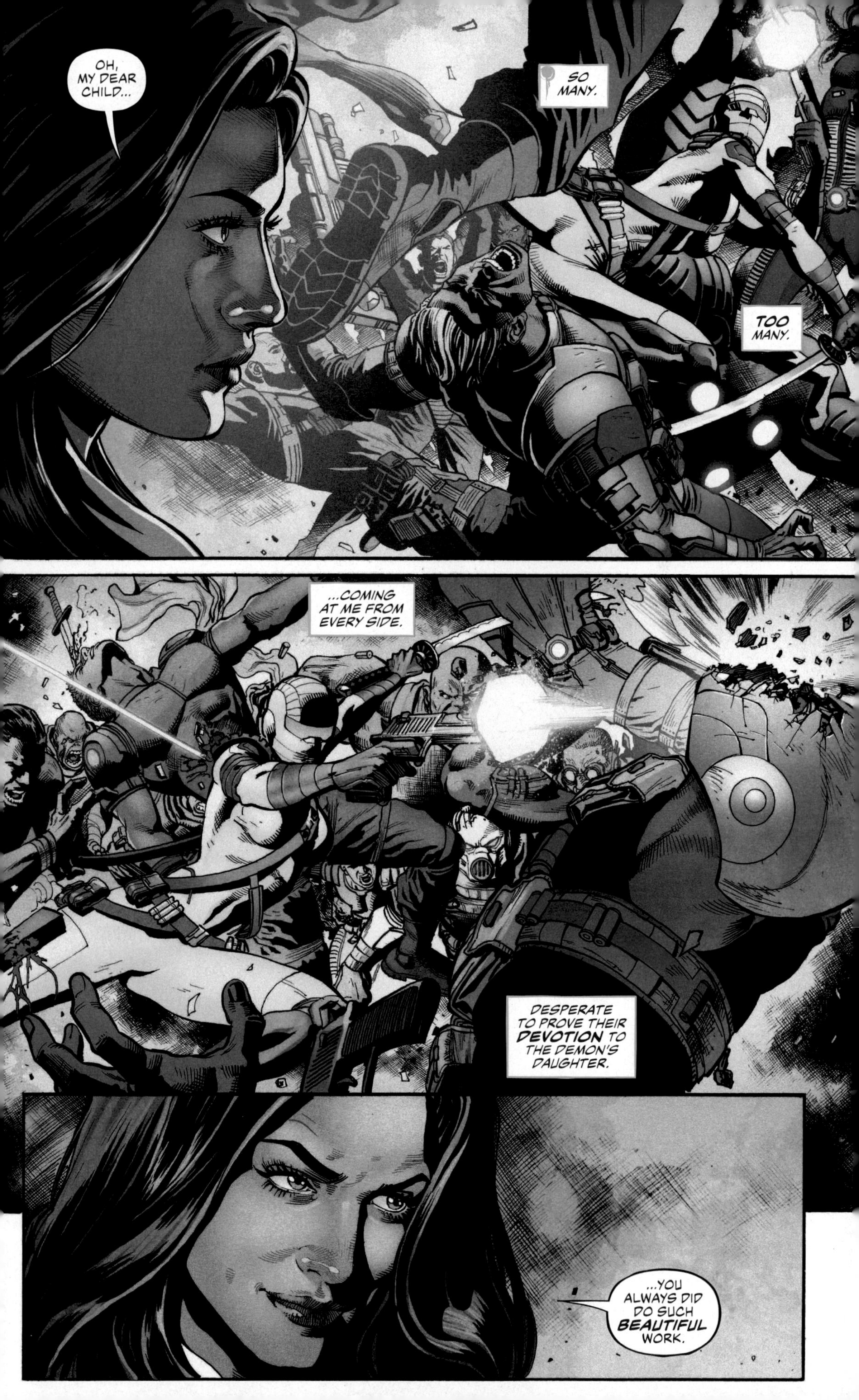
OH, MY DEAR CHILD...
SO MANY.
TOO MANY.
...COMING AT ME FROM EVERY SIDE.
DESPERATE TO PROVE THEIR DEVOTION TO THE DEMON'S DAUGHTER.
...YOU ALWAYS DID DO SUCH BEAUTIFUL WORK.

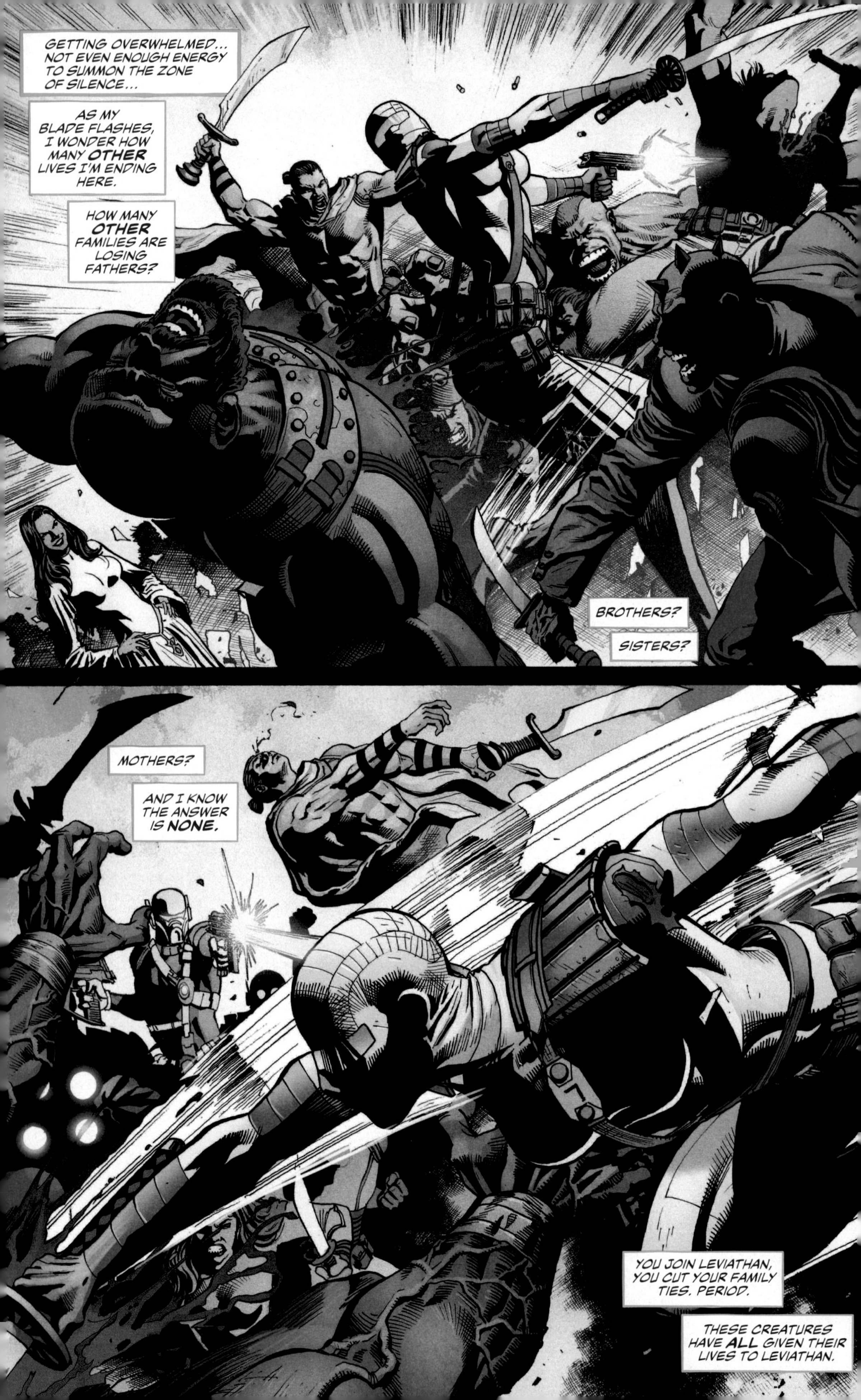
GETTING OVERWHELMED... NOT EVEN ENOUGH ENERGY TO SUMMON THE ZONE OF SILENCE...
AS MY BLADE FLASHES, I WONDER HOW MANY OTHER LIVES I'M ENDING HERE.
HOW MANY OTHER FAMILIES ARE LOSING FATHERS?
BROTHERS?
SISTERS?
MOTHERS?
AND I KNOW THE ANSWER IS NONE.
YOU JOIN LEVIATHAN, YOU CUT YOUR FAMILY TIES. PERIOD.
THESE CREATURES HAVE ALL GIVEN THEIR LIVES TO LEVIATHAN.

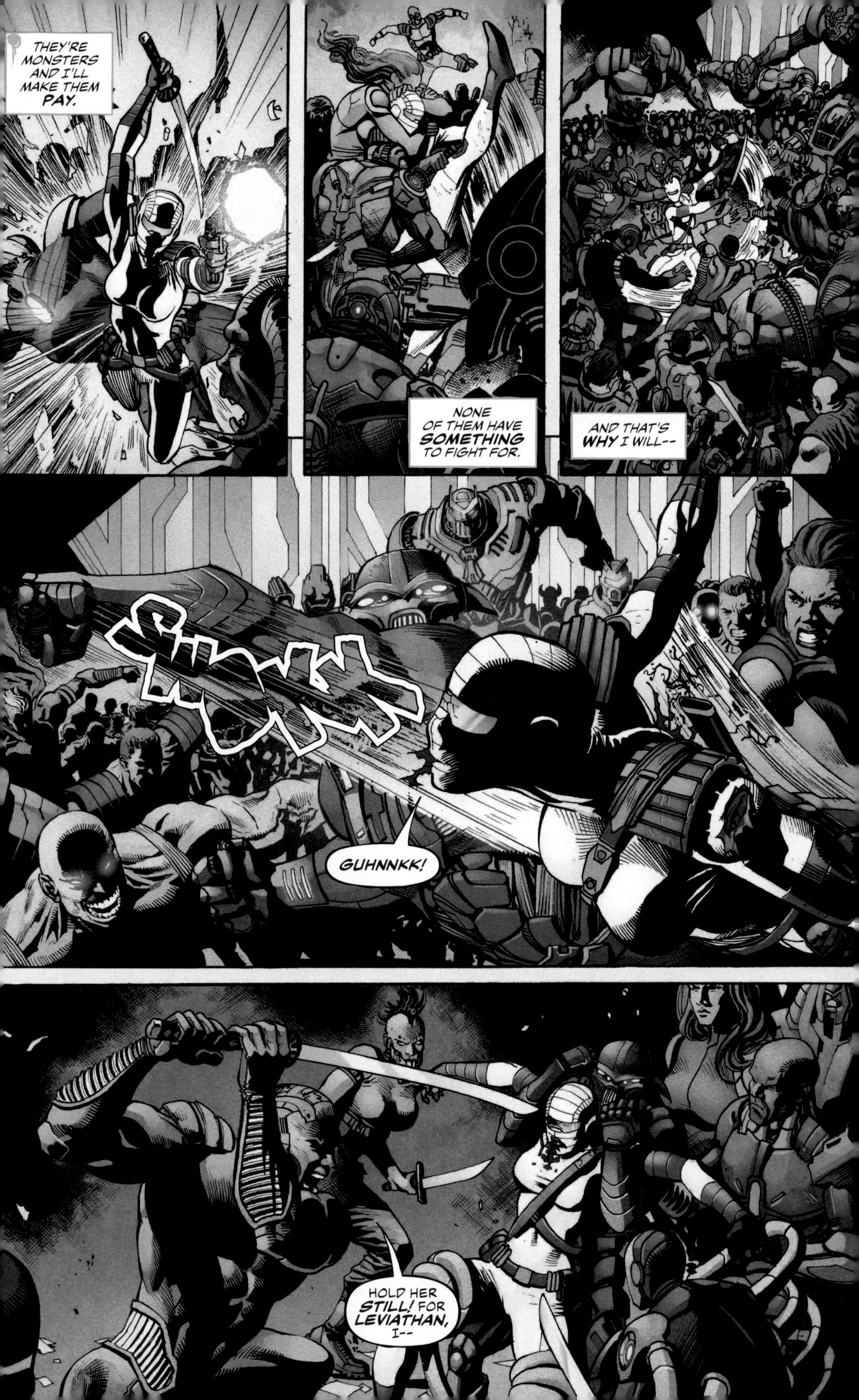
THEY'RE MONSTERS AND I'LL MAKE THEM PAY.
NONE OF THEM HAVE SOMETHING TO FIGHT FOR.
AND THAT'S WHY I WILL--
GUHNNKK!
HOLD HER STILL! FOR LEVIATHAN, I--

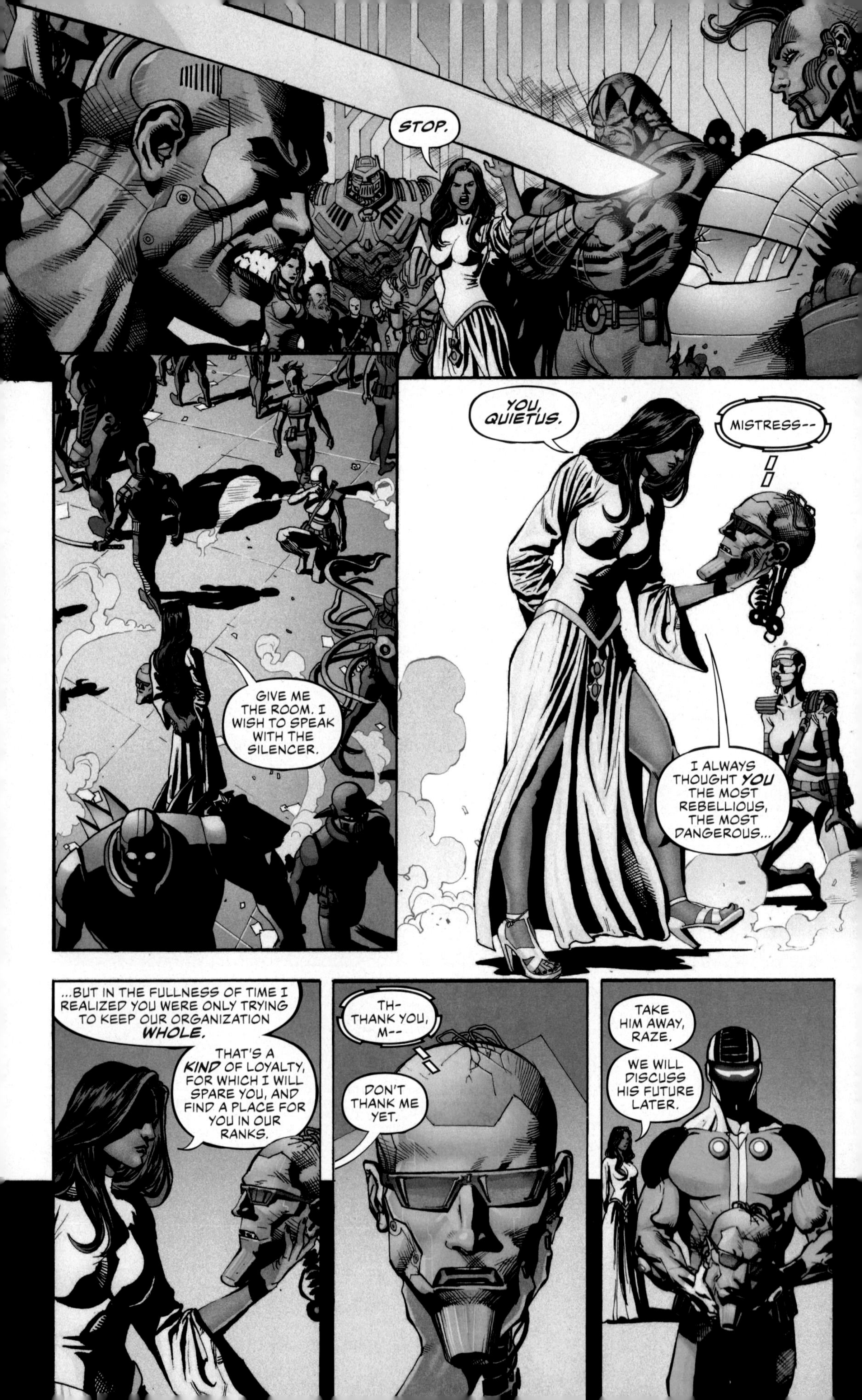
STOP.
GIVE ME THE ROOM. I WISH TO SPEAK WITH THE SILENCER.
YOU, QUIETUS.
MISTRESS--
I ALWAYS THOUGHT YOU THE MOST REBELLIOUS, THE MOST DANGEROUS...
...BUT IN THE FULLNESS OF TIME I REALIZED YOU WERE ONLY TRYING TO KEEP OUR ORGANIZATION WHOLE.
THAT'S A KIND OF LOYALTY, FOR WHICH I WILL SPARE YOU, AND FIND A PLACE FOR YOU IN OUR RANKS.
TH-THANK YOU, M--
DON'T THANK ME YET.
TAKE HIM AWAY, RAZE.
WE WILL DISCUSS HIS FUTURE LATER.

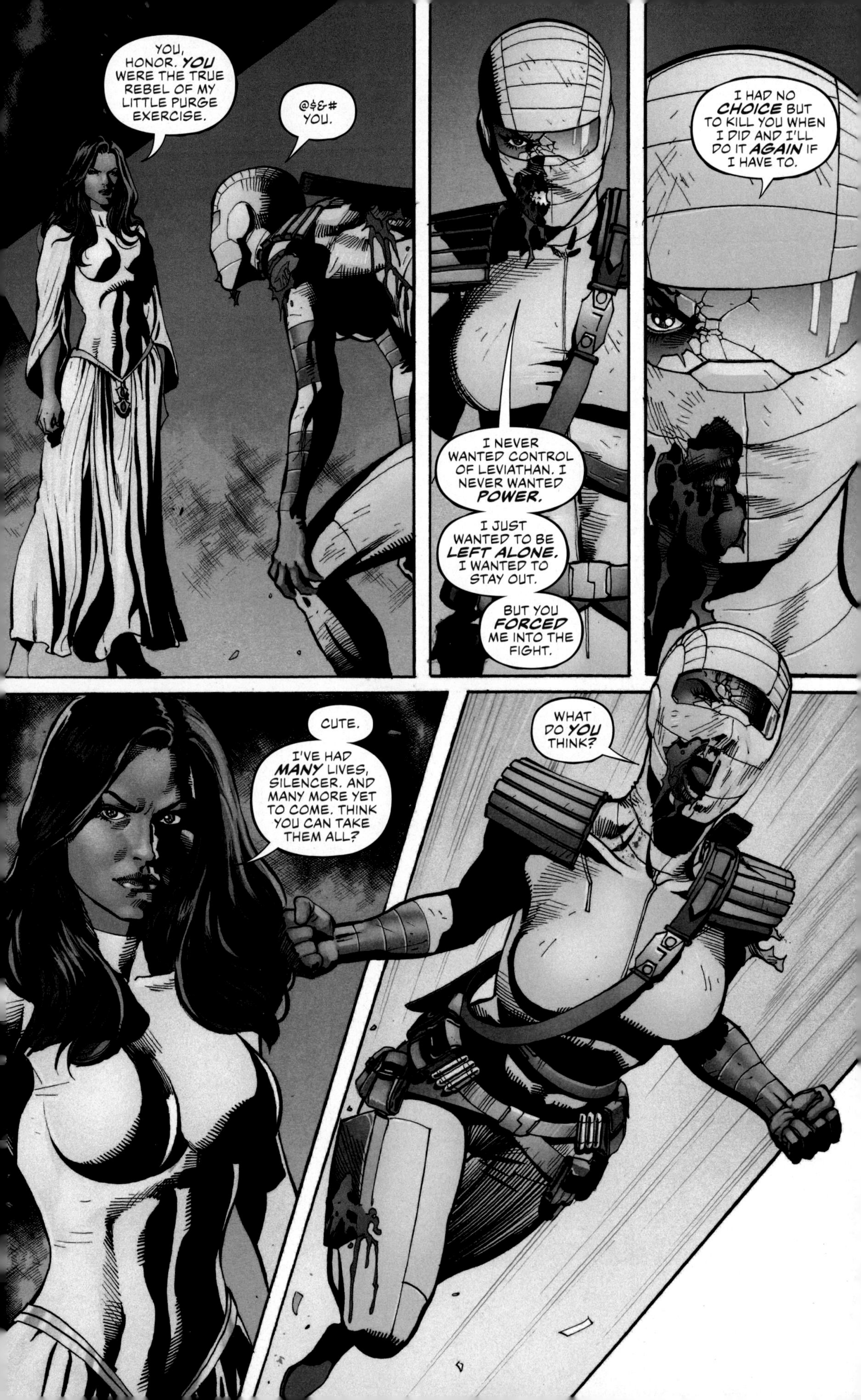
YOU, HONOR. YOU WERE THE TRUE REBEL OF MY LITTLE PURGE EXERCISE.
@$&# YOU.
I NEVER WANTED CONTROL OF LEVIATHAN. I NEVER WANTED POWER.
I JUST WANTED TO BE LEFT ALONE. I WANTED TO STAY OUT.
BUT YOU FORCED ME INTO THE FIGHT.
I HAD NO CHOICE BUT TO KILL YOU WHEN I DID AND I'LL DO IT AGAIN IF I HAVE TO.
CUTE.
I'VE HAD MANY LIVES, SILENCER. AND MANY MORE YET TO COME. THINK YOU CAN TAKE THEM ALL?
WHAT DO YOU THINK?

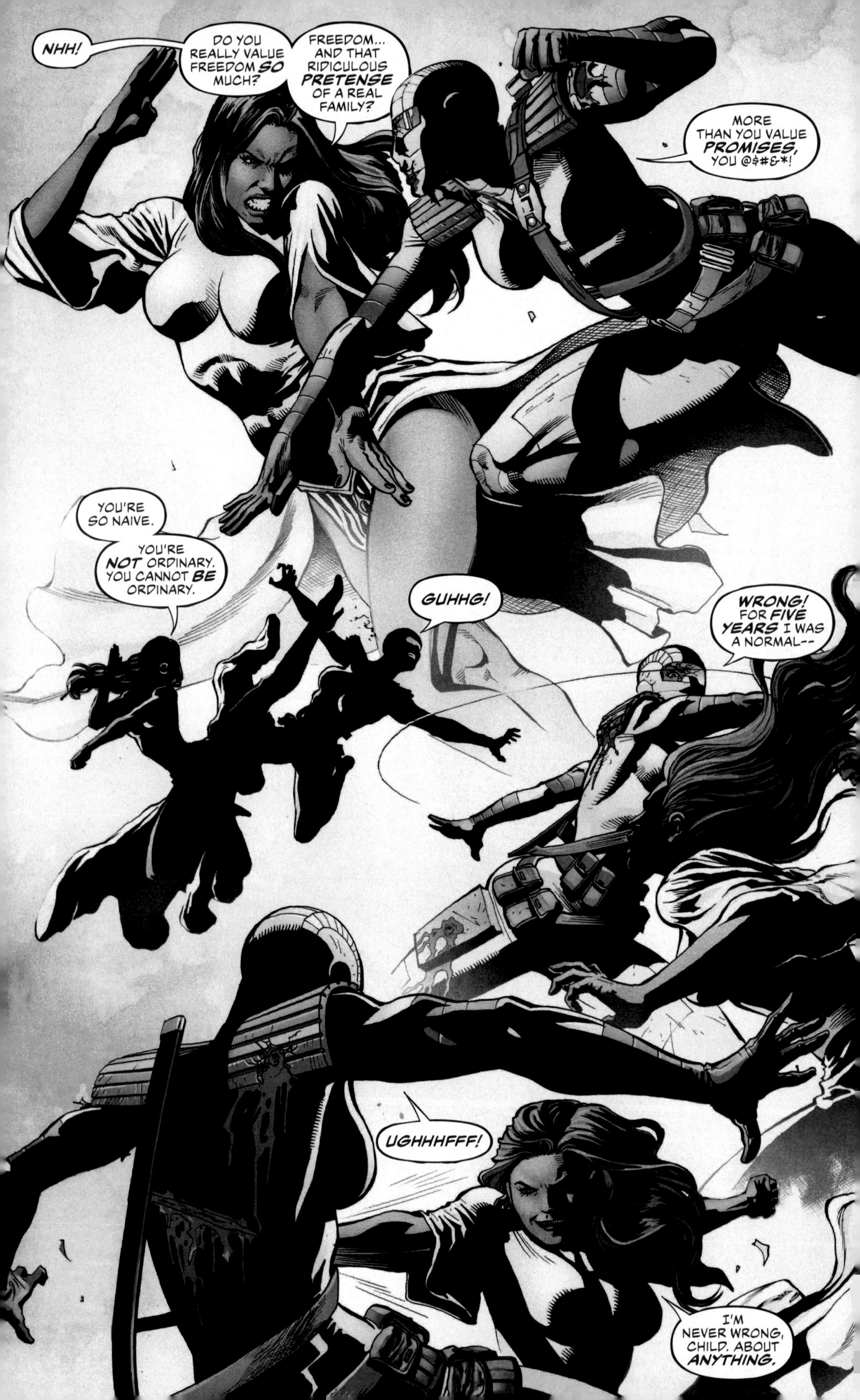
NHH!
DO YOU REALLY VALUE FREEDOM SO MUCH?
FREEDOM... AND THAT RIDICULOUS PRETENSE OF A REAL FAMILY?
MORE THAN YOU VALUE PROMISES, YOU @$#&*!
YOU'RE SO NAIVE.
YOU'RE NOT ORDINARY. YOU CANNOT BE ORDINARY.
GUHHG!
WRONG! FOR FIVE YEARS I WAS A NORMAL--
UGHHHFFF!
I'M NEVER WRONG, CHILD. ABOUT ANYTHING.

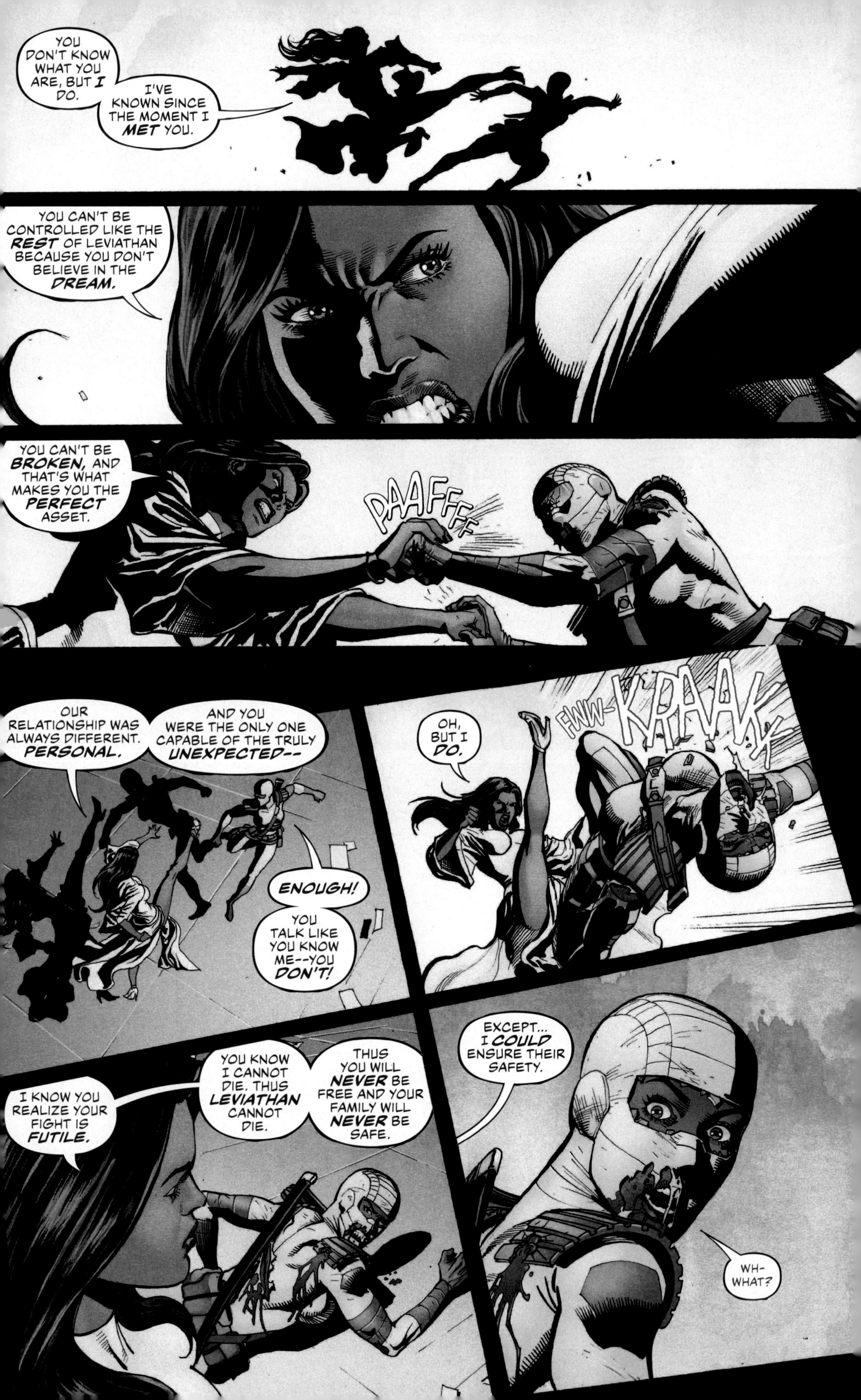
YOU DON'T KNOW WHAT YOU ARE, BUT I DO.
I'VE KNOWN SINCE THE MOMENT I MET YOU.
YOU CAN'T BE CONTROLLED LIKE THE REST OF LEVIATHAN BECAUSE YOU DON'T BELIEVE IN THE DREAM.
YOU CAN'T BE BROKEN, AND THAT'S WHAT MAKES YOU THE PERFECT ASSET.
PAAFFFF
OUR RELATIONSHIP WAS ALWAYS DIFFERENT. PERSONAL.
AND YOU WERE THE ONLY ONE CAPABLE OF THE TRULY UNEXPECTED--
ENOUGH!
YOU TALK LIKE YOU KNOW ME--YOU DON'T!
OH, BUT I DO.
FWW-KRAAKK
I KNOW YOU REALIZE YOUR FIGHT IS FUTILE.
YOU KNOW I CANNOT DIE. THUS LEVIATHAN CANNOT DIE.
THUS YOU WILL NEVER BE FREE AND YOUR FAMILY WILL NEVER BE SAFE.
EXCEPT... I COULD ENSURE THEIR SAFETY.
WH-WHAT?

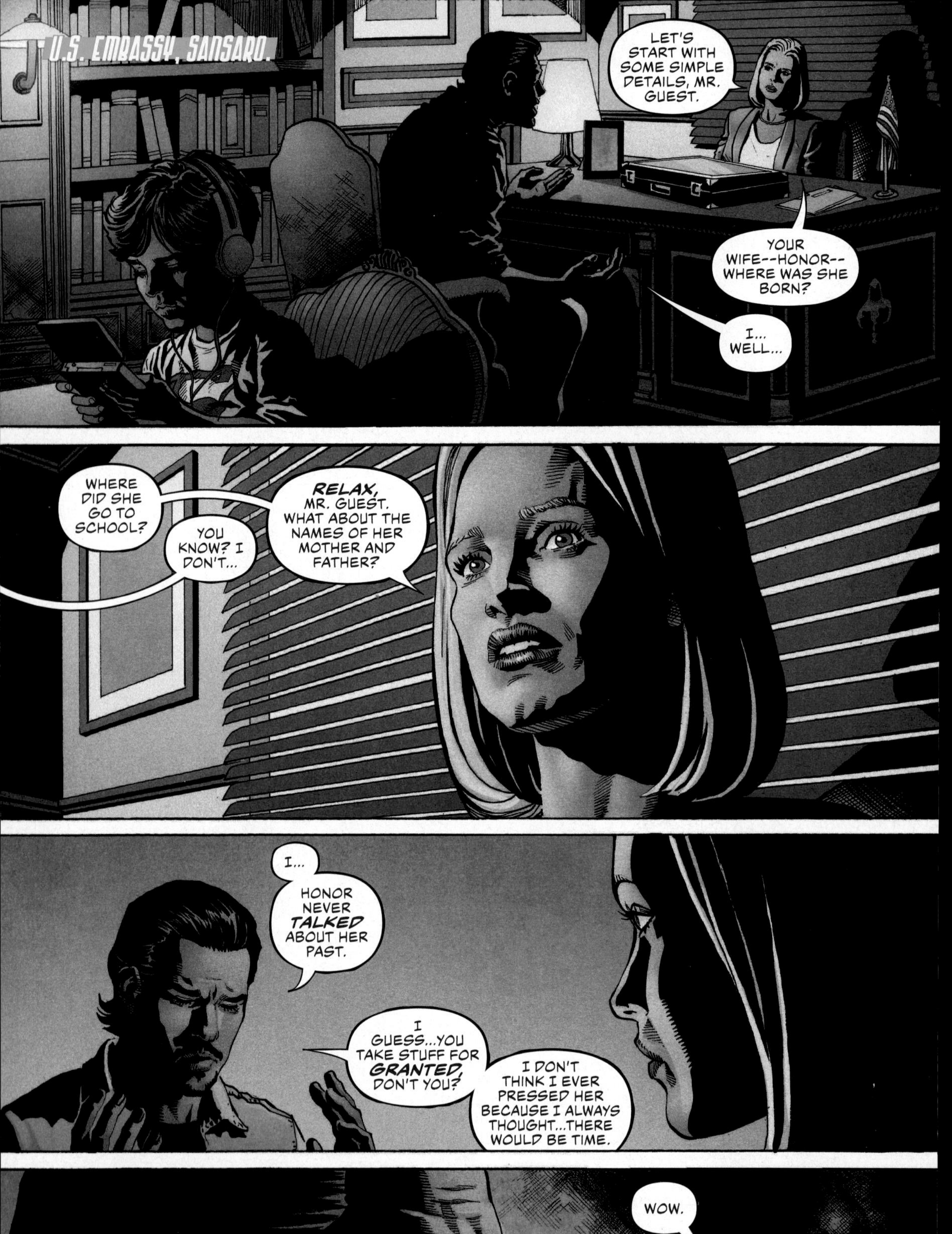
U.S. EMBASSY, SANSARO.
LET'S START WITH SOME SIMPLE DETAILS, MR. GUEST.
YOUR WIFE--HONOR--WHERE WAS SHE BORN?
I... WELL...
WHERE DID SHE GO TO SCHOOL?
YOU KNOW? I DON'T...
RELAX, MR. GUEST. WHAT ABOUT THE NAMES OF HER MOTHER AND FATHER?
I...
HONOR NEVER TALKED ABOUT HER PAST.
I GUESS...YOU TAKE STUFF FOR GRANTED, DON'T YOU?
I DON'T THINK I EVER PRESSED HER BECAUSE I ALWAYS THOUGHT...THERE WOULD BE TIME.
WOW.

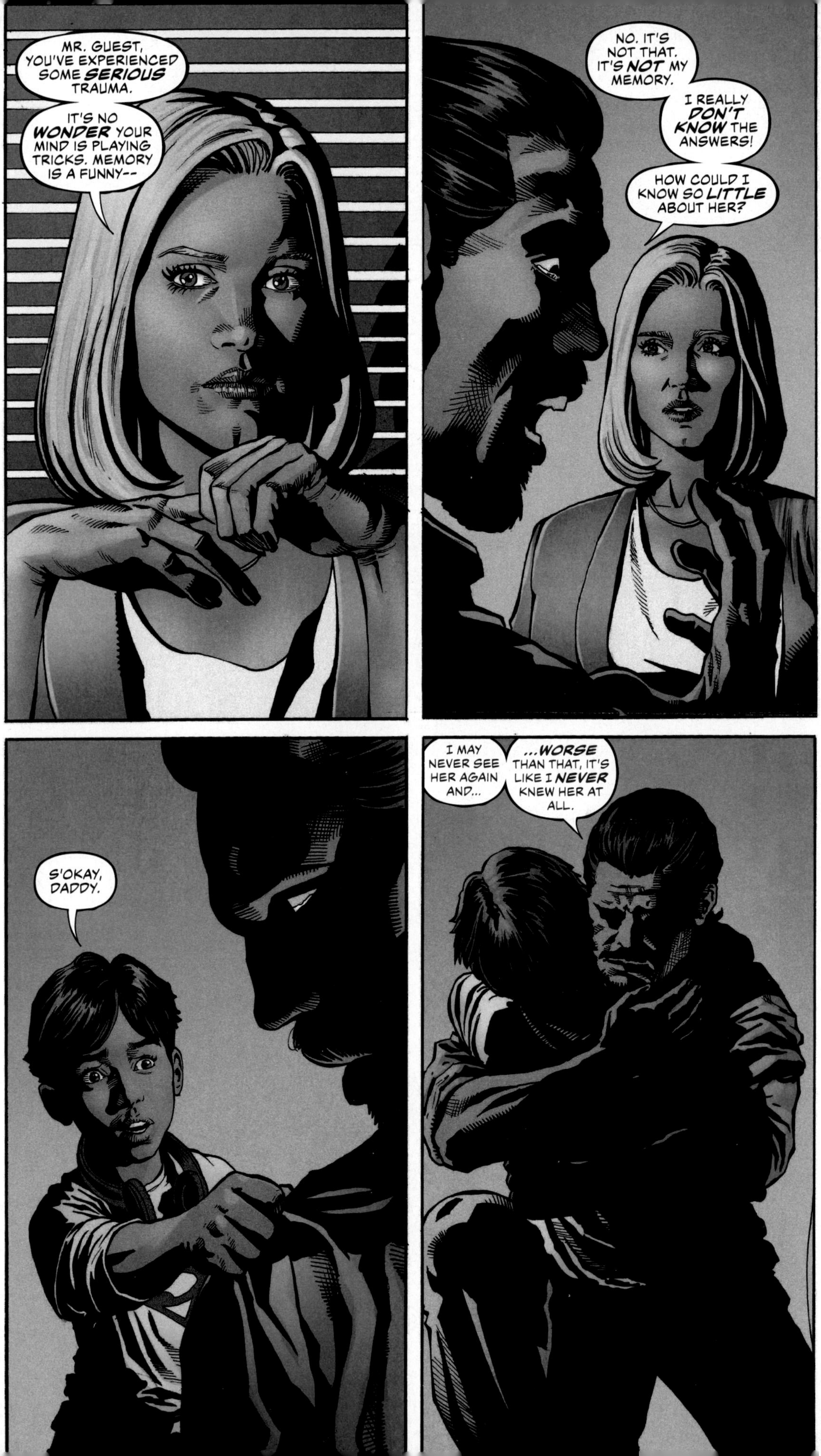
MR. GUEST, YOU'VE EXPERIENCED SOME SERIOUS TRAUMA.
IT'S NO WONDER YOUR MIND IS PLAYING TRICKS. MEMORY IS A FUNNY--
NO. IT'S NOT THAT. IT'S NOT MY MEMORY.
I REALLY DON'T KNOW THE ANSWERS!
HOW COULD I KNOW SO LITTLE ABOUT HER?
S'OKAY, DADDY.
I MAY NEVER SEE HER AGAIN AND...
...WORSE THAN THAT, IT'S LIKE I NEVER KNEW HER AT ALL.

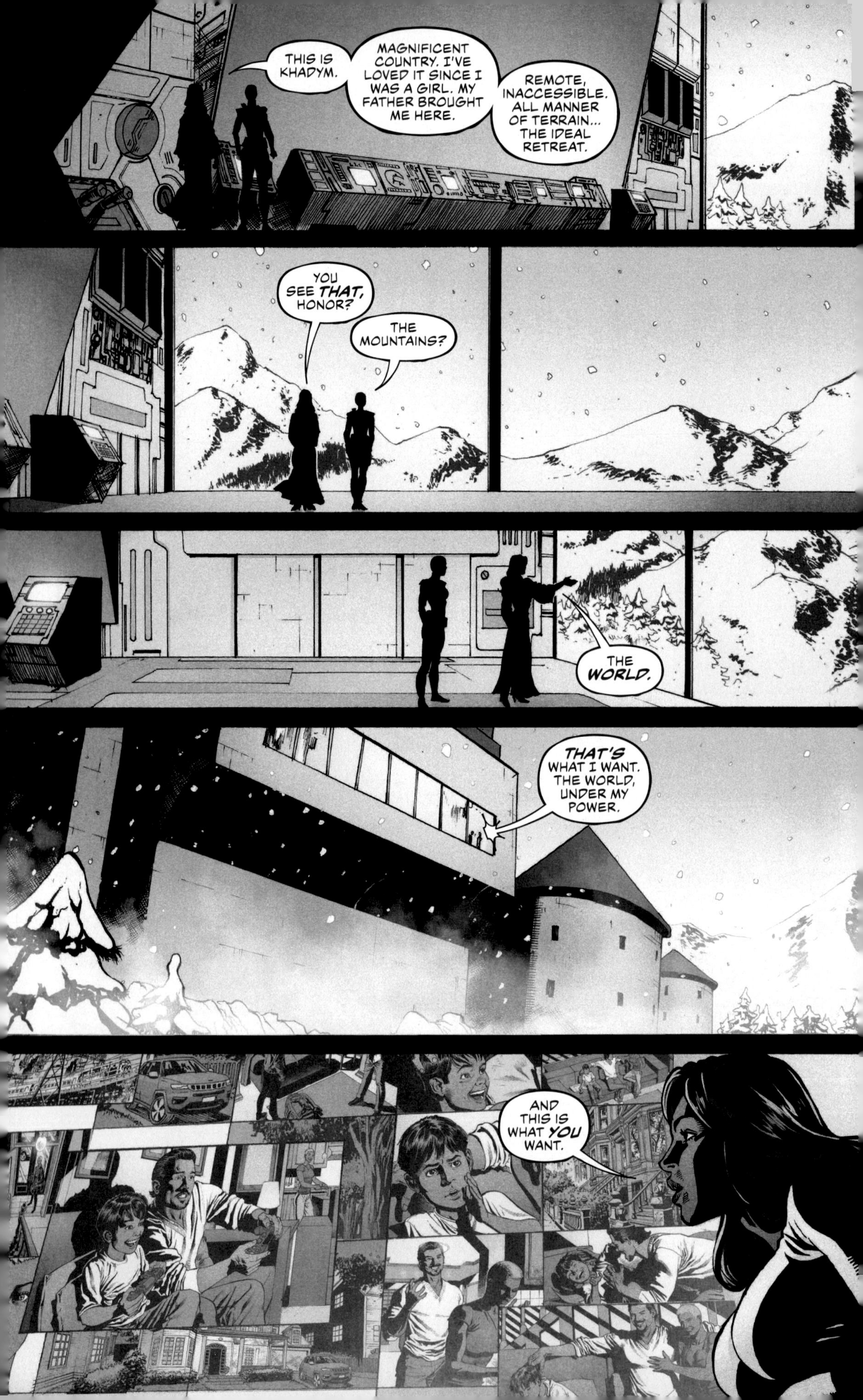
THIS IS KHADYM.
MAGNIFICENT COUNTRY. I'VE LOVED IT SINCE I WAS A GIRL. MY FATHER BROUGHT ME HERE.
REMOTE, INACCESSIBLE. ALL MANNER OF TERRAIN... THE IDEAL RETREAT.
YOU SEE THAT, HONOR?
THE MOUNTAINS?
THE WORLD.
THAT'S WHAT I WANT. THE WORLD, UNDER MY POWER.
AND THIS IS WHAT YOU WANT.

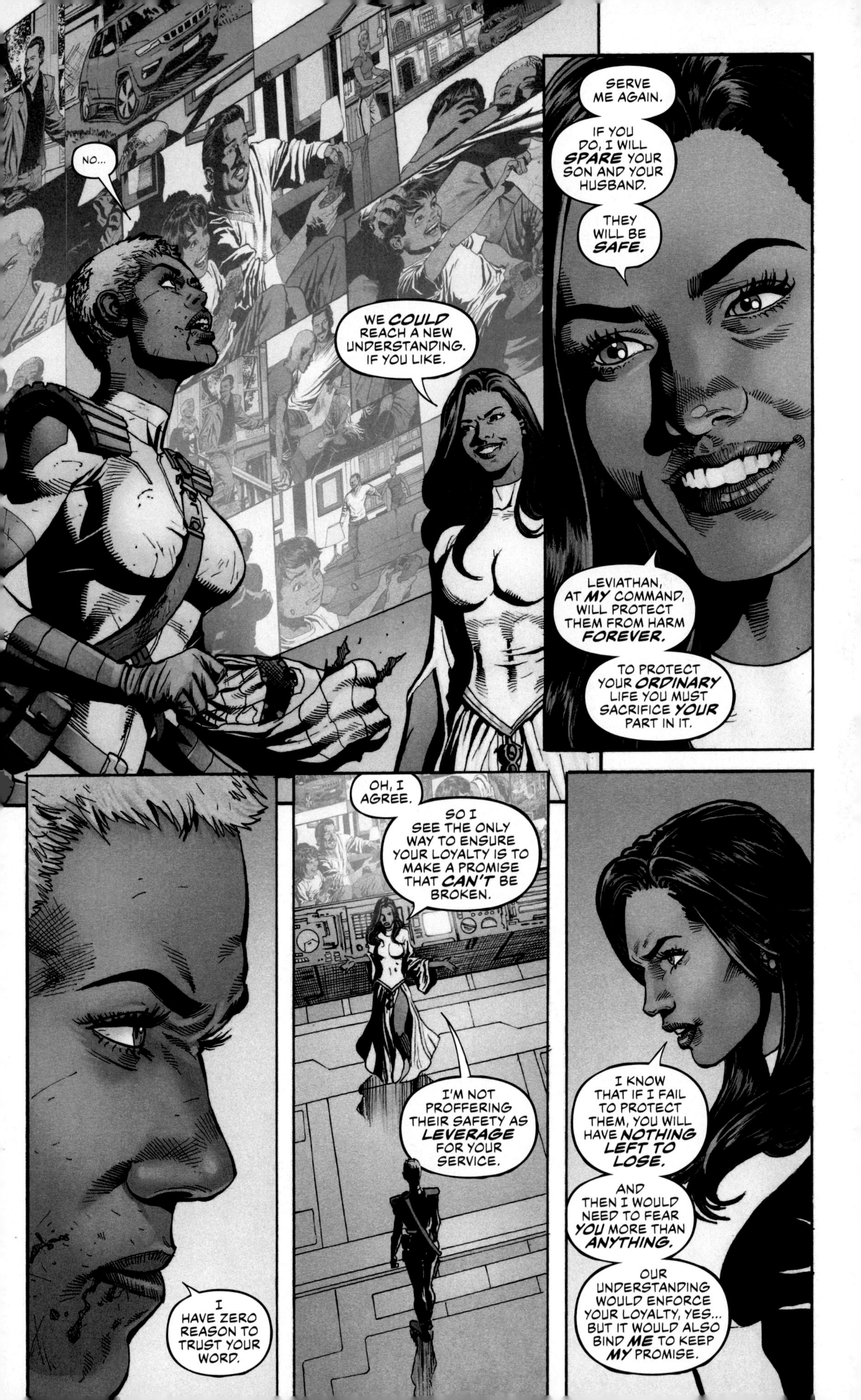
NO...
WE COULD REACH A NEW UNDERSTANDING. IF YOU LIKE.
SERVE ME AGAIN.
IF YOU DO, I WILL SPARE YOUR SON AND YOUR HUSBAND.
THEY WILL BE SAFE.
LEVIATHAN, AT MY COMMAND, WILL PROTECT THEM FROM HARM FOREVER.
TO PROTECT YOUR ORDINARY LIFE YOU MUST SACRIFICE YOUR PART IN IT.
I HAVE ZERO REASON TO TRUST YOUR WORD.
OH, I AGREE.
SO I SEE THE ONLY WAY TO ENSURE YOUR LOYALTY IS TO MAKE A PROMISE THAT CAN'T BE BROKEN.
I'M NOT PROFFERING THEIR SAFETY AS LEVERAGE FOR YOUR SERVICE.
I KNOW THAT IF I FAIL TO PROTECT THEM, YOU WILL HAVE NOTHING LEFT TO LOSE.
AND THEN I WOULD NEED TO FEAR YOU MORE THAN ANYTHING.
OUR UNDERSTANDING WOULD ENFORCE YOUR LOYALTY, YES... BUT IT WOULD ALSO BIND ME TO KEEP MY PROMISE.

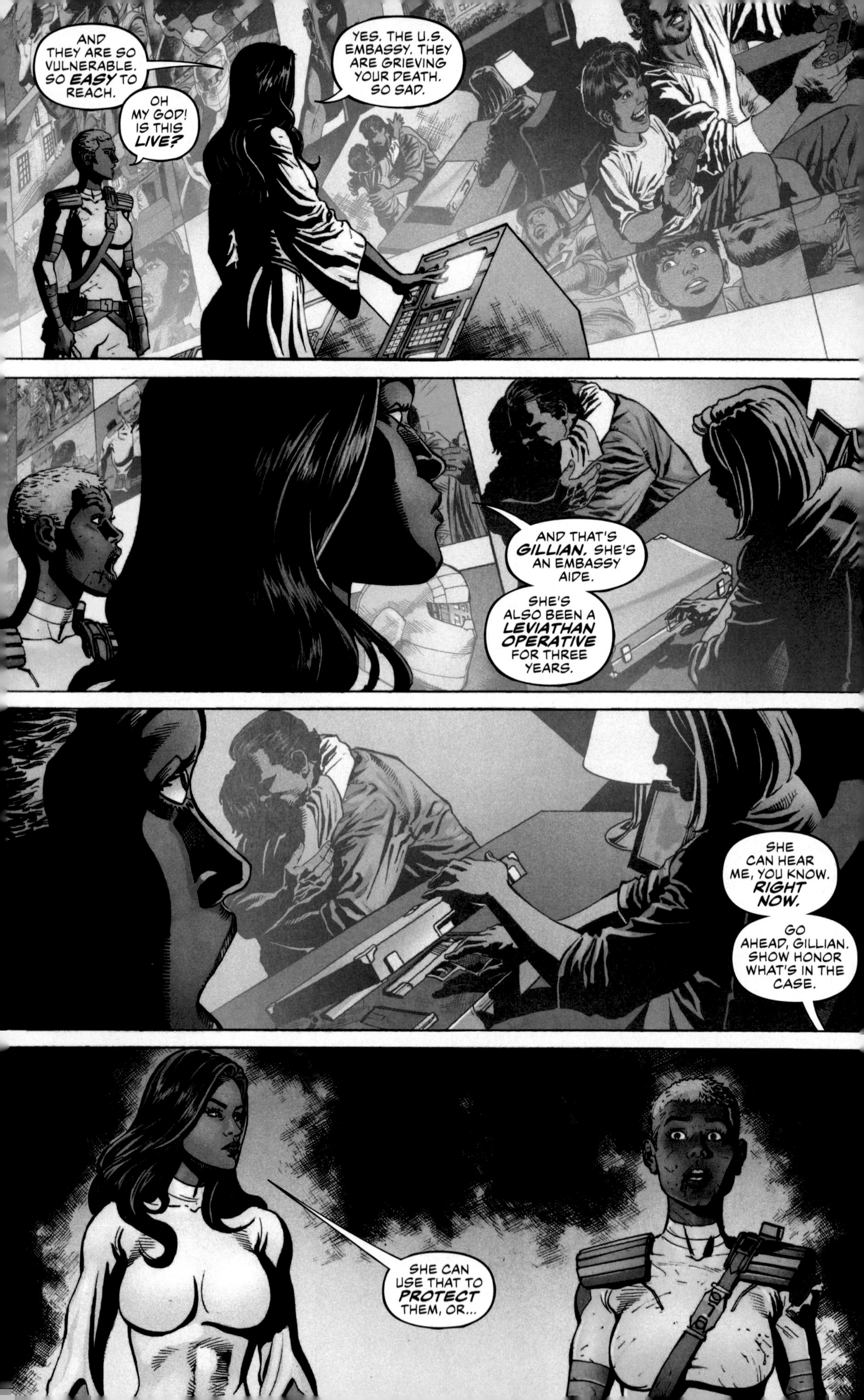
AND THEY ARE SO VULNERABLE. SO EASY TO REACH.
OH MY GOD! IS THIS LIVE?
YES. THE U.S. EMBASSY. THEY ARE GRIEVING YOUR DEATH. SO SAD.
AND THAT'S GILLIAN. SHE'S AN EMBASSY AIDE.
SHE'S ALSO BEEN A LEVIATHAN OPERATIVE FOR THREE YEARS.
SHE CAN HEAR ME, YOU KNOW. RIGHT NOW.
GO AHEAD, GILLIAN. SHOW HONOR WHAT'S IN THE CASE.
SHE CAN USE THAT TO PROTECT THEM, OR...

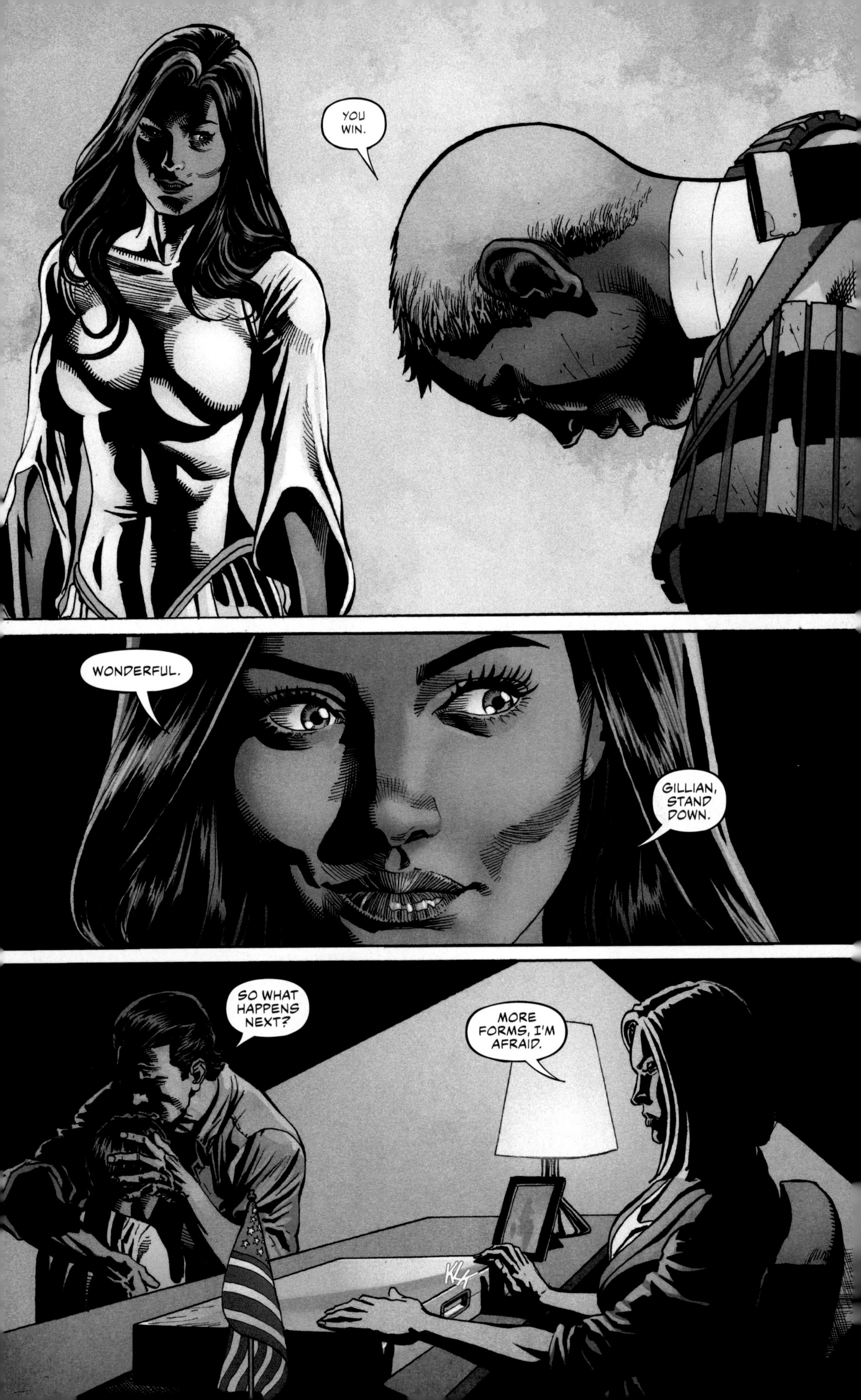
YOU WIN.
WONDERFUL.
GILLIAN, STAND DOWN.
SO WHAT HAPPENS NEXT?
MORE FORMS, I'M AFRAID.
KLK

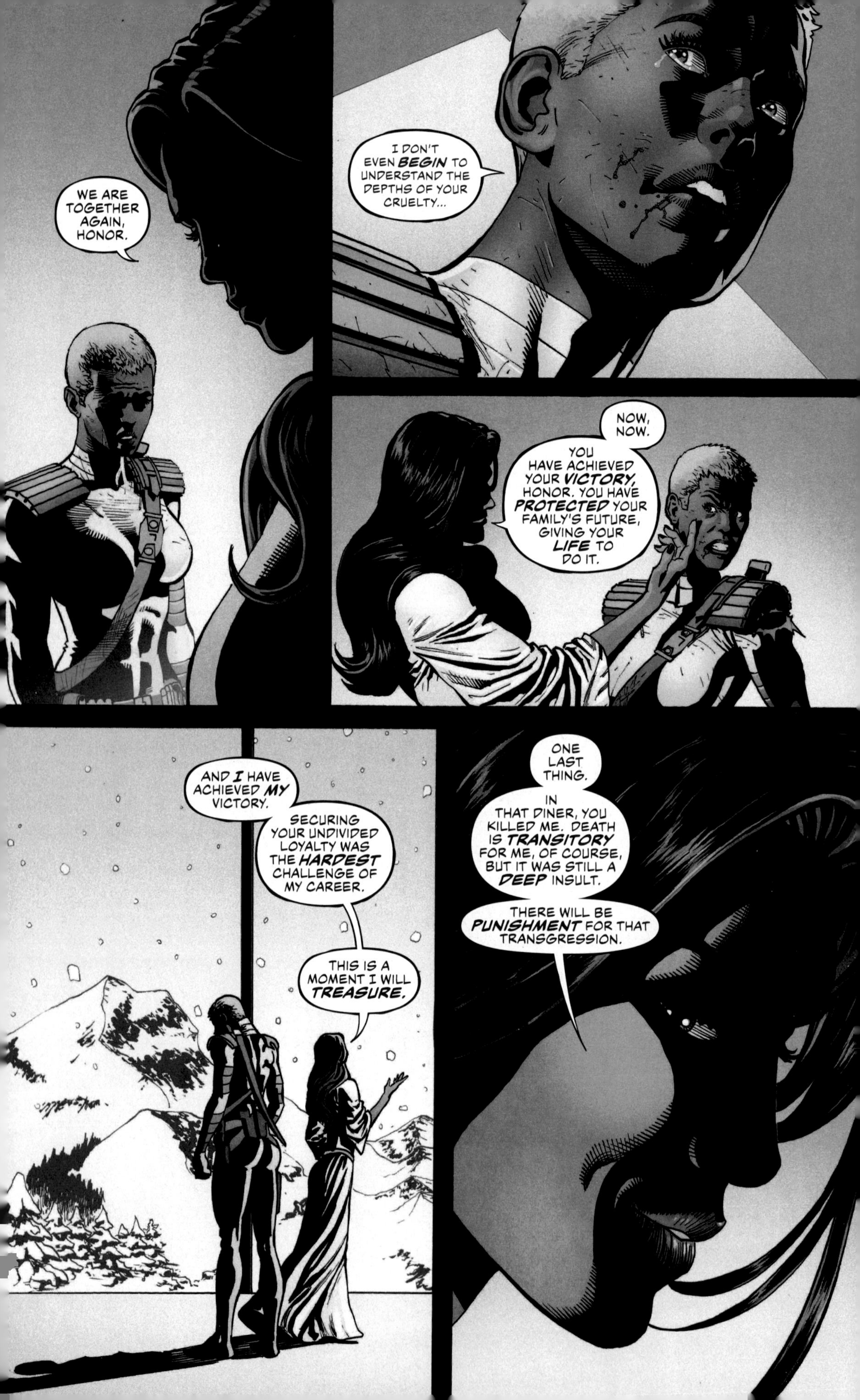
WE ARE TOGETHER AGAIN, HONOR.
I DON'T EVEN BEGIN TO UNDERSTAND THE DEPTHS OF YOUR CRUELTY...
NOW, NOW.
YOU HAVE ACHIEVED YOUR VICTORY, HONOR. YOU HAVE PROTECTED YOUR FAMILY'S FUTURE, GIVING YOUR LIFE TO DO IT.
AND I HAVE ACHIEVED MY VICTORY.
SECURING YOUR UNDIVIDED LOYALTY WAS THE HARDEST CHALLENGE OF MY CAREER.
THIS IS A MOMENT I WILL TREASURE.
ONE LAST THING.
IN THAT DINER, YOU KILLED ME. DEATH IS TRANSITORY FOR ME, OF COURSE, BUT IT WAS STILL A DEEP INSULT.
THERE WILL BE PUNISHMENT FOR THAT TRANSGRESSION.

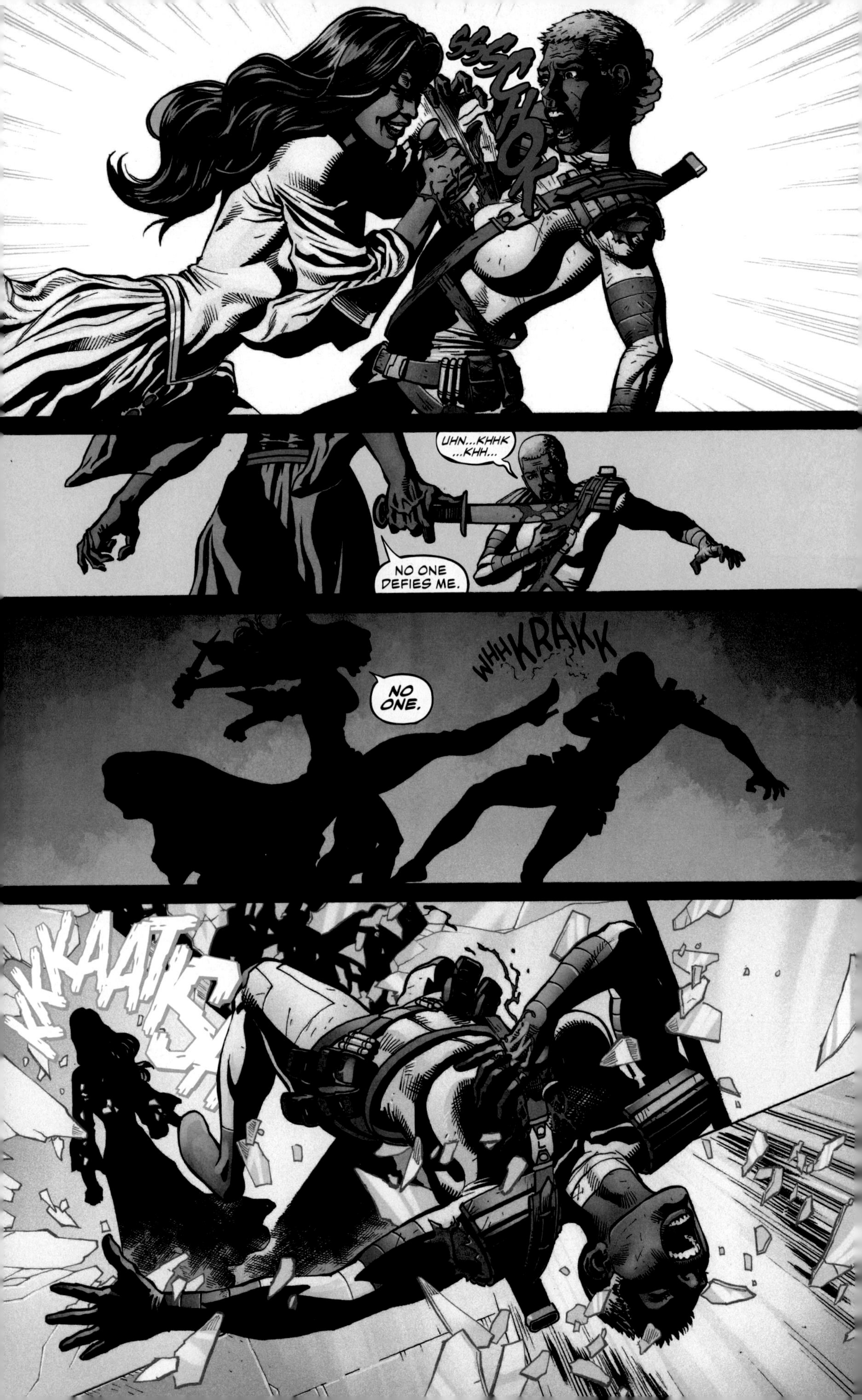
SSSCHOK
UHN...KHHK ...KHH...
NO ONE DEFIES ME.
NO ONE.
WHHKRAKK
KKAATKSH

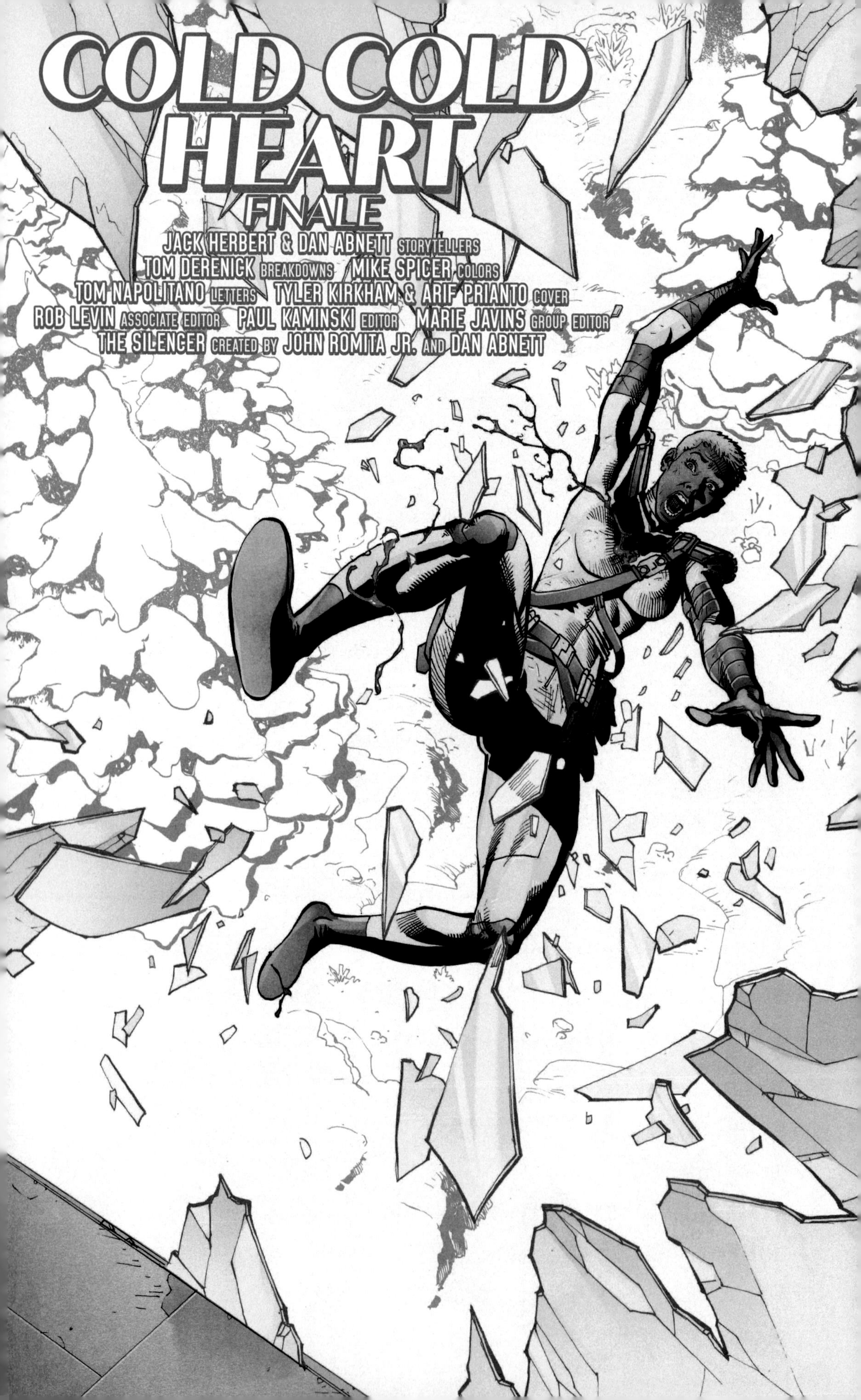
COLD COLD HEART
FINALE
JACK HERBERT & DAN ABNETT STORYTELLERS
TOM DERENICK BREAKDOWNS MIKE SPICER COLORS
TOM NAPOLITANO LETTERS TYLER KIRKHAM & ARIF PRIANTO COVER
ROB LEVIN ASSOCIATE EDITOR PAUL KAMINSKI EDITOR MARIE JAVINS GROUP EDITOR
THE SILENCER CREATED BY JOHN ROMITA JR. AND DAN ABNETT

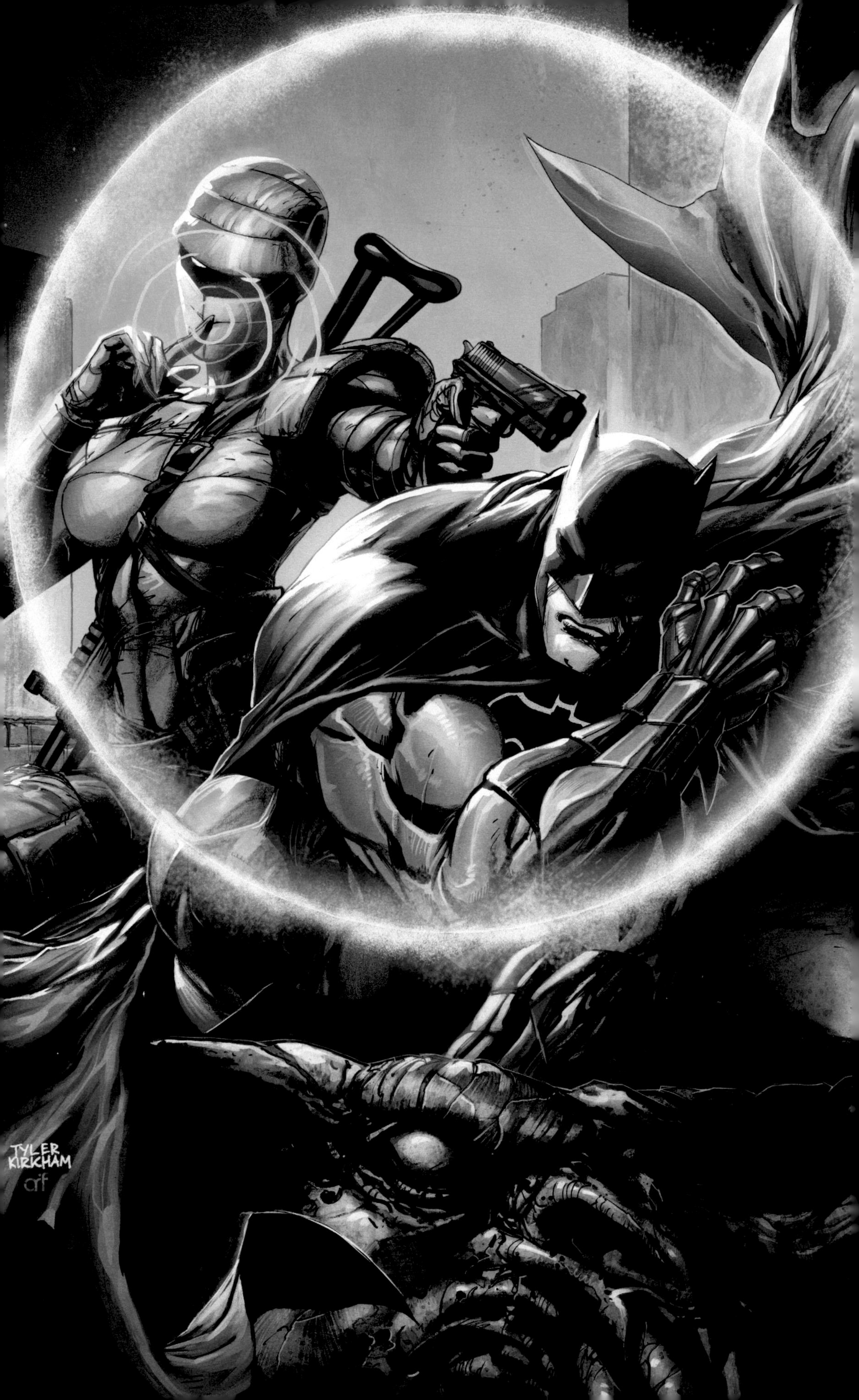
TYLER
KIRKHAM

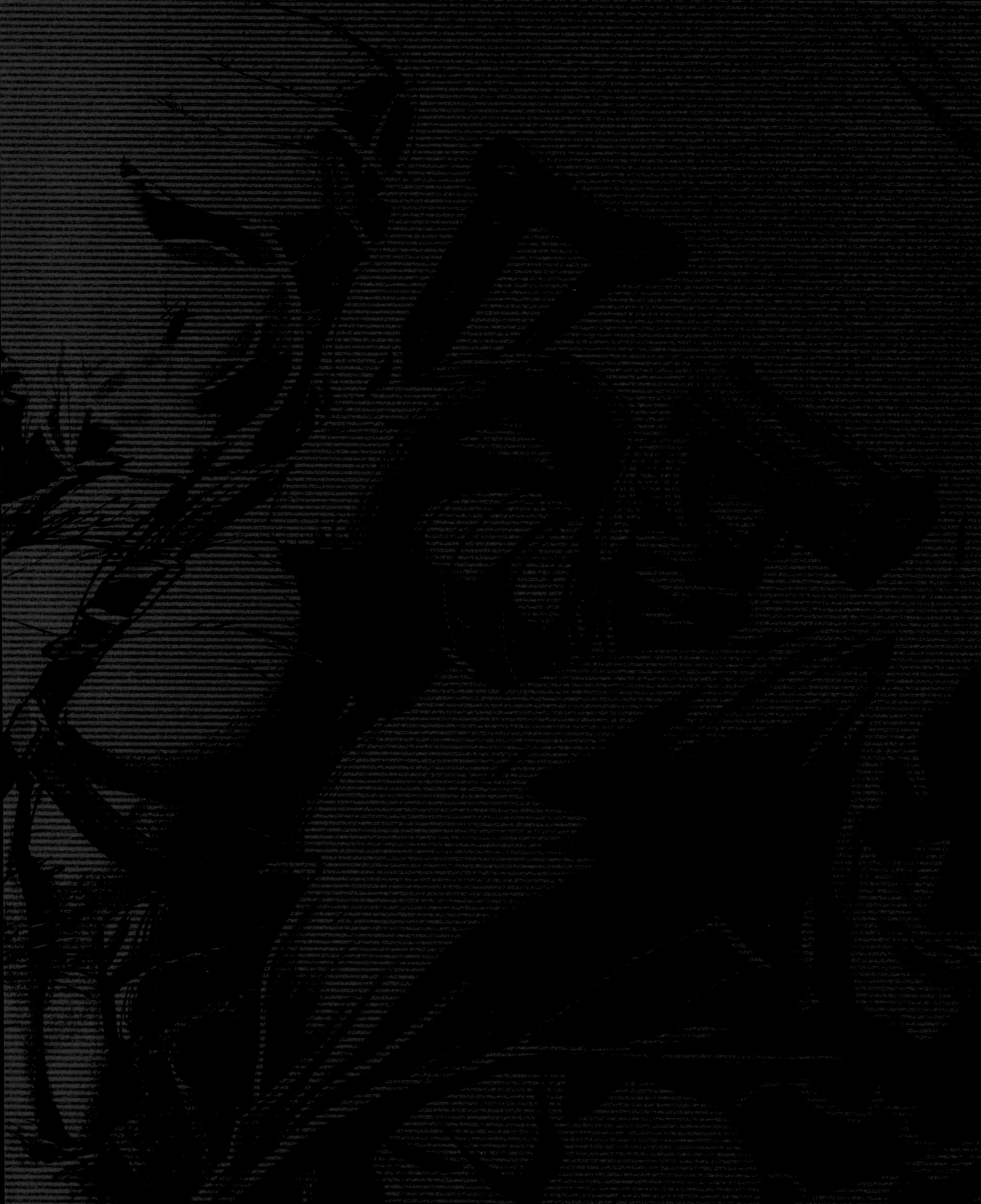

THE
SILENCER

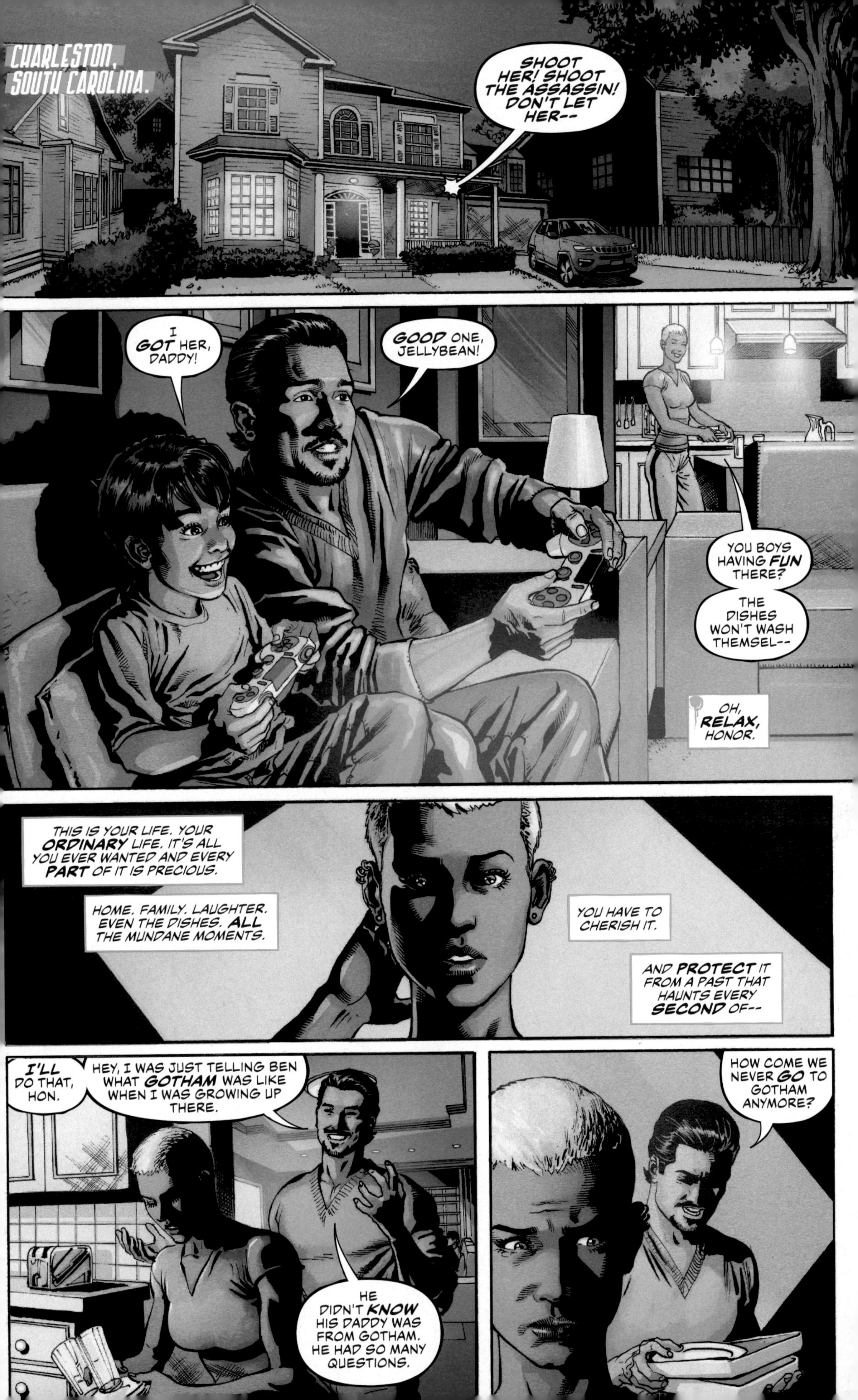
CHARLESTON, SOUTH CAROLINA.
SHOOT HER! SHOOT THE ASSASSIN! DON'T LET HER--
I GOT HER, DADDY!
GOOD ONE, JELLYBEAN!
YOU BOYS HAVING FUN THERE?
THE DISHES WON'T WASH THEMSEL--
OH, RELAX, HONOR.
THIS IS YOUR LIFE. YOUR ORDINARY LIFE. IT'S ALL YOU EVER WANTED AND EVERY PART OF IT IS PRECIOUS.
HOME. FAMILY. LAUGHTER. EVEN THE DISHES. ALL THE MUNDANE MOMENTS.
YOU HAVE TO CHERISH IT.
AND PROTECT IT FROM A PAST THAT HAUNTS EVERY SECOND OF--
I'LL DO THAT, HON.
HEY, I WAS JUST TELLING BEN WHAT GOTHAM WAS LIKE WHEN I WAS GROWING UP THERE.
HE DIDN'T KNOW HIS DADDY WAS FROM GOTHAM. HE HAD SO MANY QUESTIONS.
HOW COME WE NEVER GO TO GOTHAM ANYMORE?

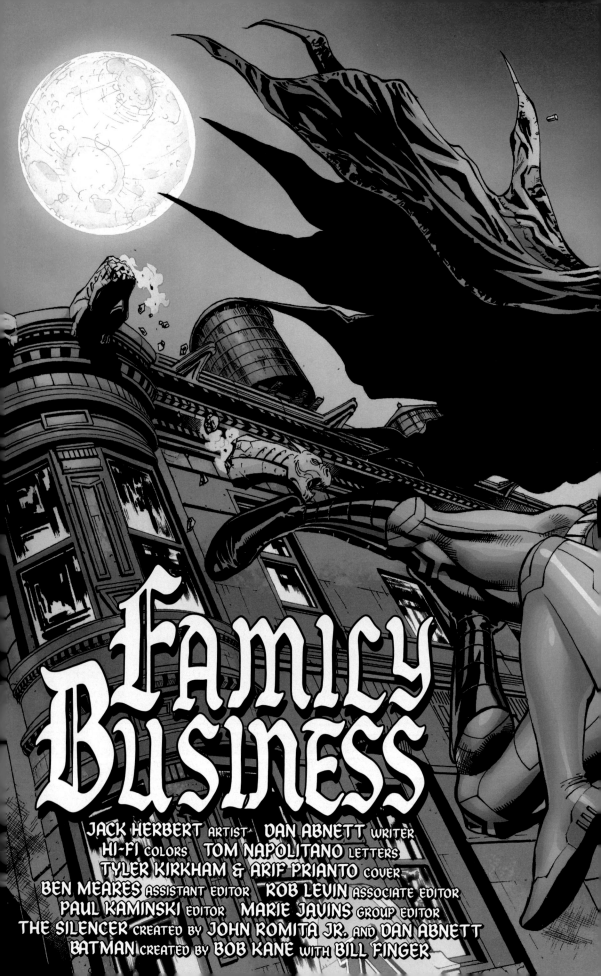

FAMILY BUSINESS

JACK HERBERT ARTIST   DAN ABNETT WRITER
HI-FI COLORS   TOM NAPOLITANO LETTERS
TYLER KIRKHAM & ARIF PRIANTO COVER
BEN MEARES ASSISTANT EDITOR   ROB LEVIN ASSOCIATE EDITOR
PAUL KAMINSKI EDITOR   MARIE JAVINS GROUP EDITOR
THE SILENCER CREATED BY JOHN ROMITA JR. AND DAN ABNETT
BATMAN CREATED BY BOB KANE WITH BILL FINGER

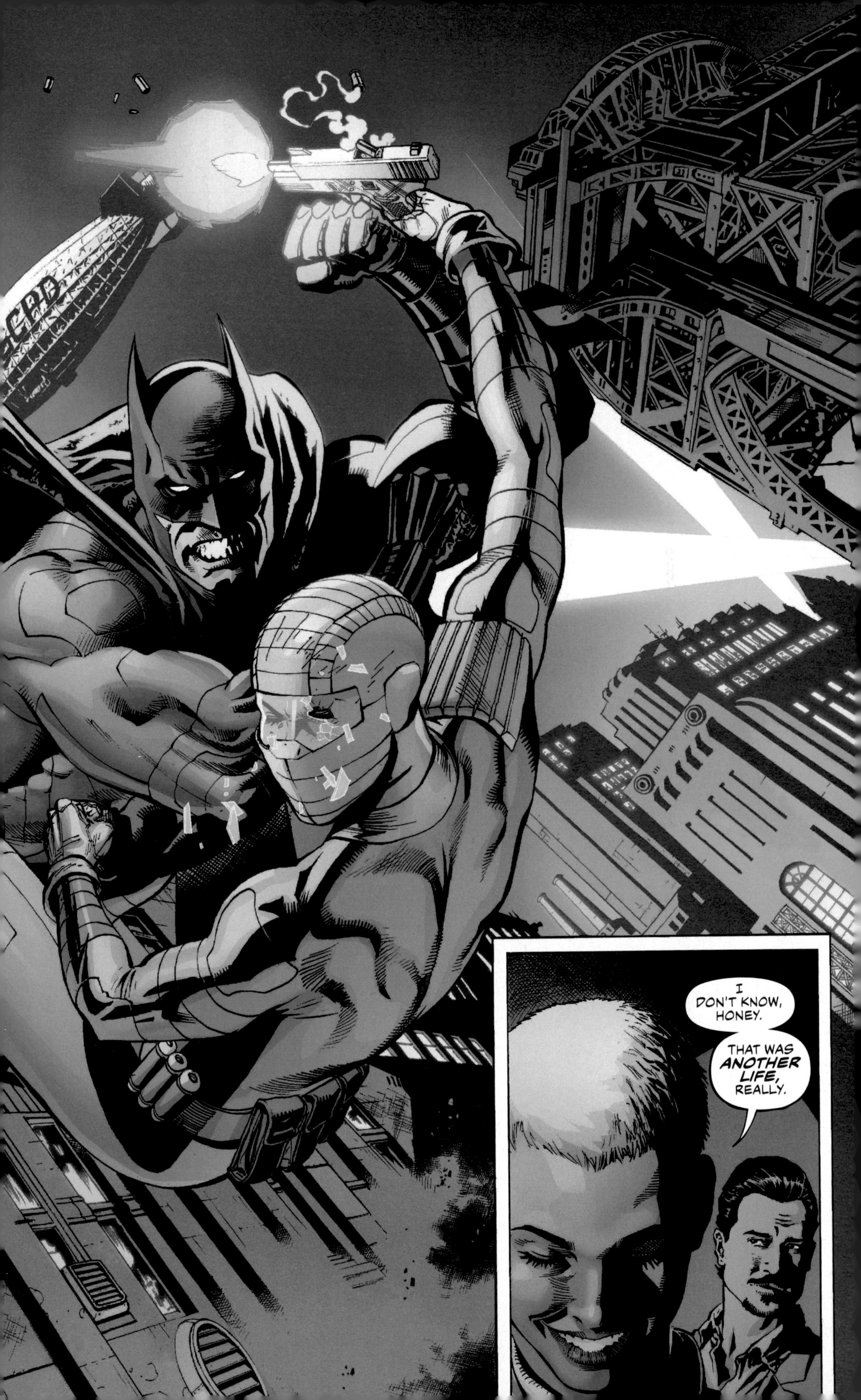

I DON'T KNOW, HONEY.
THAT WAS ANOTHER LIFE, REALLY.

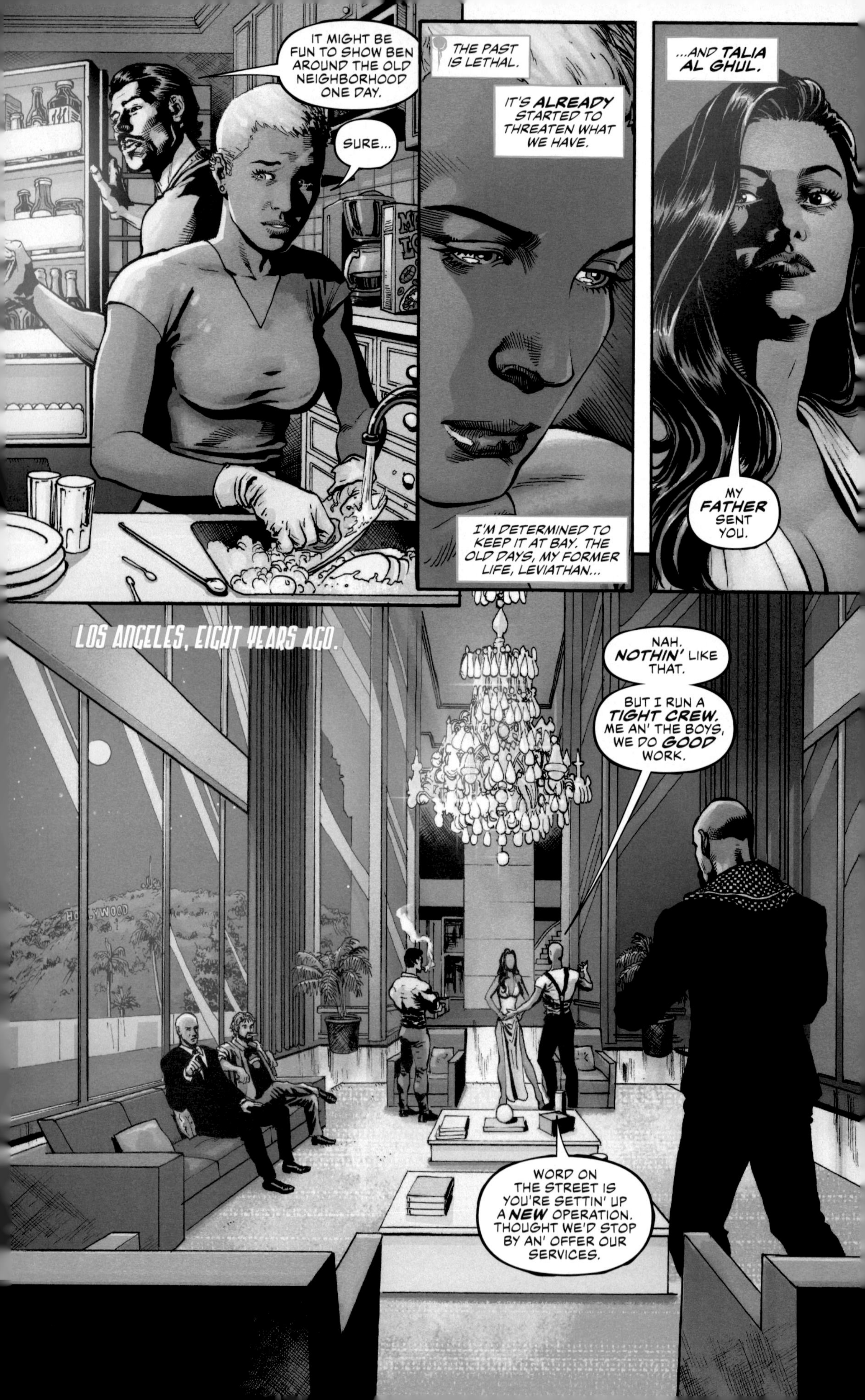
IT MIGHT BE FUN TO SHOW BEN AROUND THE OLD NEIGHBORHOOD ONE DAY.
SURE...
THE PAST IS LETHAL.
IT'S ALREADY STARTED TO THREATEN WHAT WE HAVE.
I'M DETERMINED TO KEEP IT AT BAY. THE OLD DAYS, MY FORMER LIFE, LEVIATHAN...
...AND TALIA AL GHUL.
MY FATHER SENT YOU.
LOS ANGELES, EIGHT YEARS AGO.
NAH. NOTHIN' LIKE THAT.
BUT I RUN A TIGHT CREW. ME AN' THE BOYS, WE DO GOOD WORK.
WORD ON THE STREET IS YOU'RE SETTIN' UP A NEW OPERATION. THOUGHT WE'D STOP BY AN' OFFER OUR SERVICES.
HOLLYWOOD

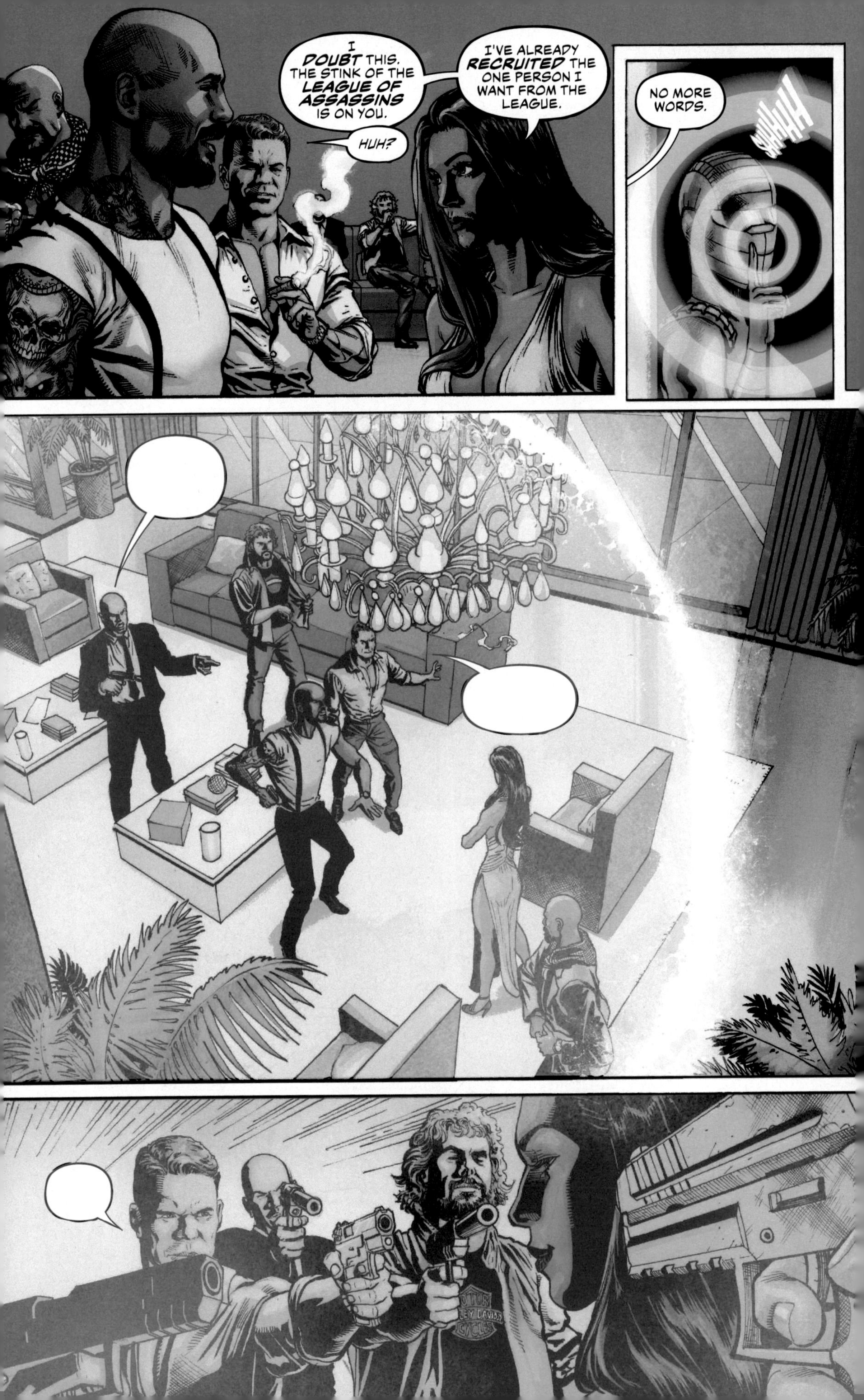
I DOUBT THIS. THE STINK OF THE LEAGUE OF ASSASSINS IS ON YOU.
I'VE ALREADY RECRUITED THE ONE PERSON I WANT FROM THE LEAGUE.
HUH?
NO MORE WORDS.

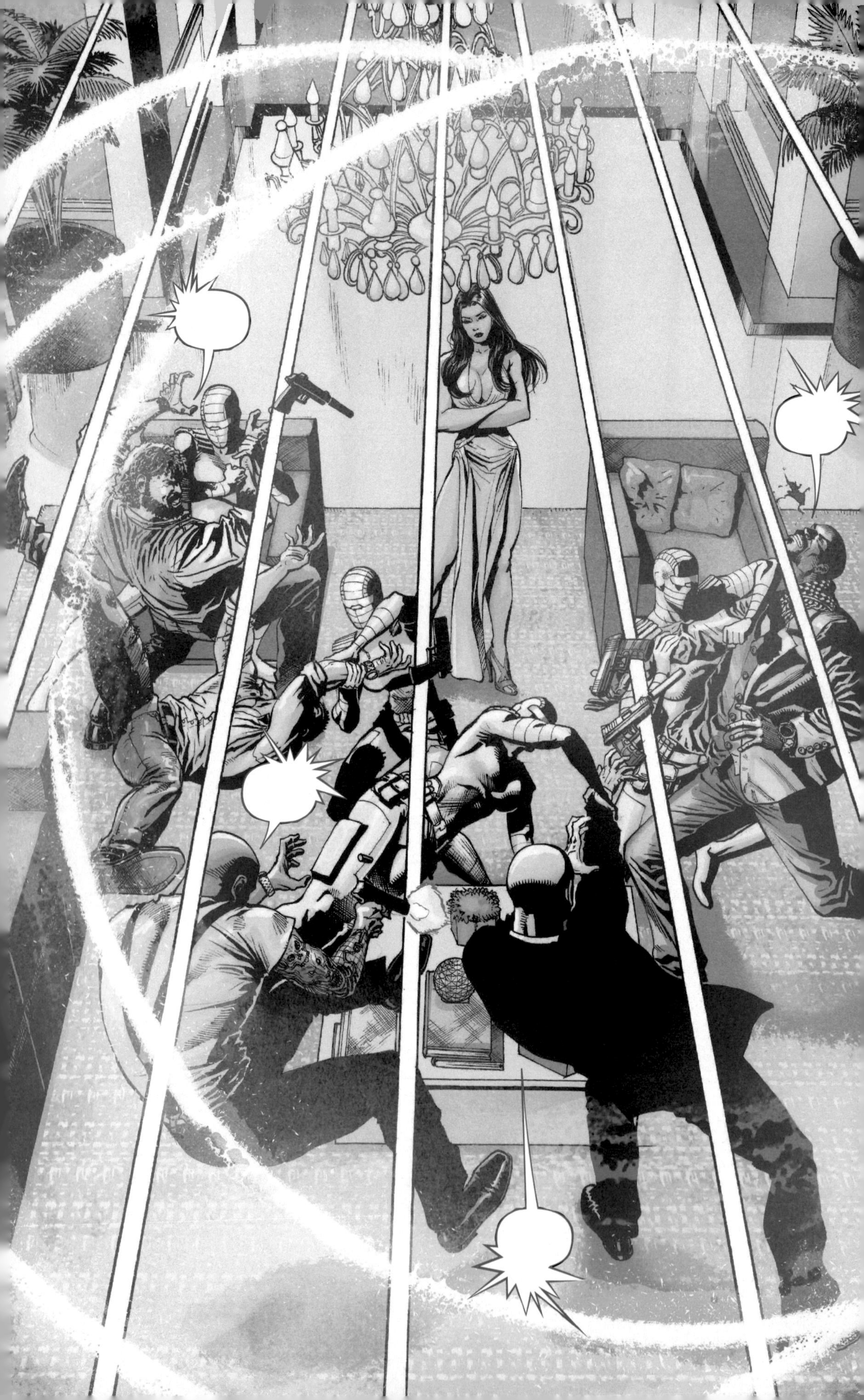

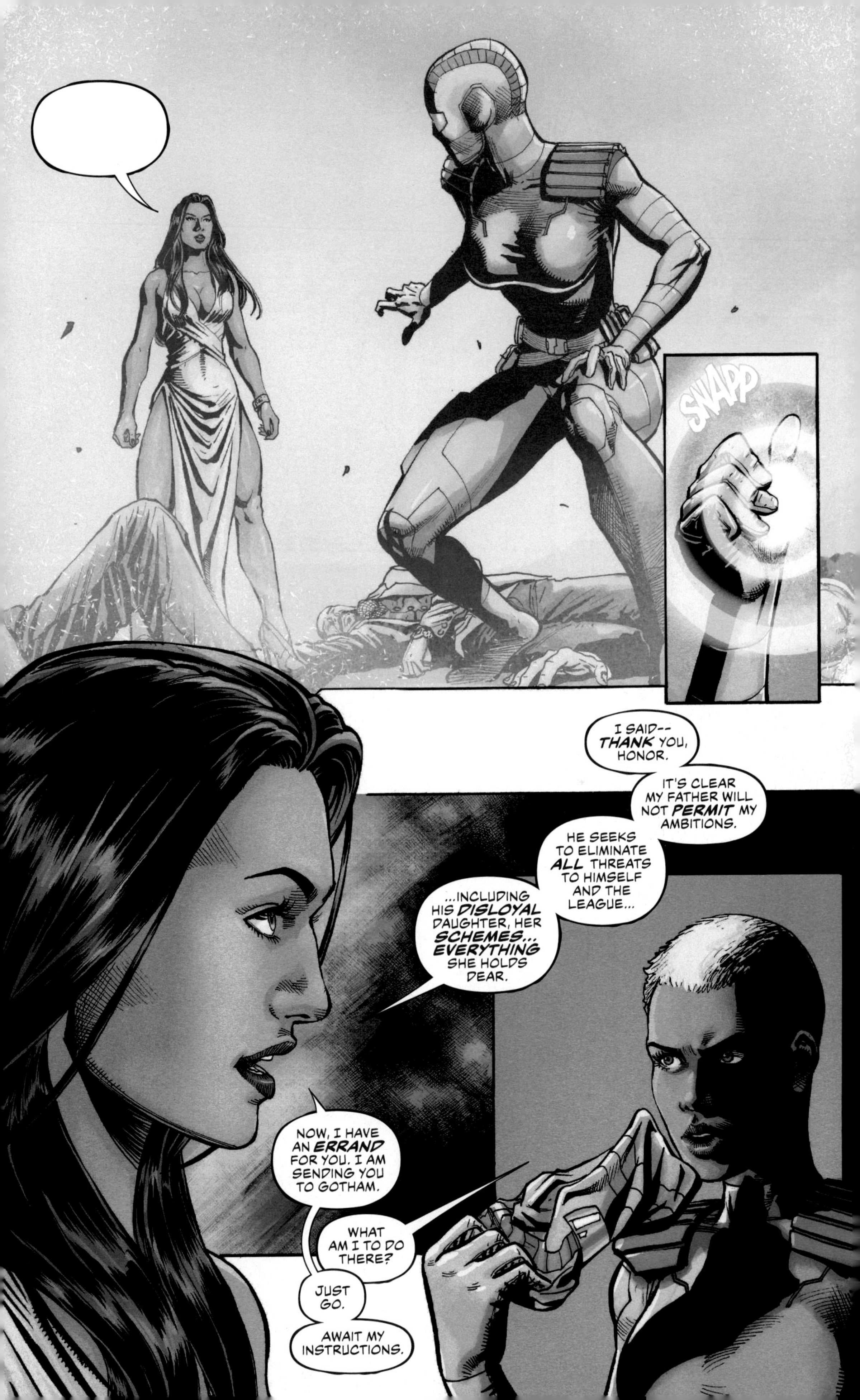
SNAPP
I SAID-- THANK YOU, HONOR.
IT'S CLEAR MY FATHER WILL NOT PERMIT MY AMBITIONS.
HE SEEKS TO ELIMINATE ALL THREATS TO HIMSELF AND THE LEAGUE...
...INCLUDING HIS DISLOYAL DAUGHTER, HER SCHEMES... EVERYTHING SHE HOLDS DEAR.
NOW, I HAVE AN ERRAND FOR YOU. I AM SENDING YOU TO GOTHAM.
WHAT AM I TO DO THERE?
JUST GO.
AWAIT MY INSTRUCTIONS.

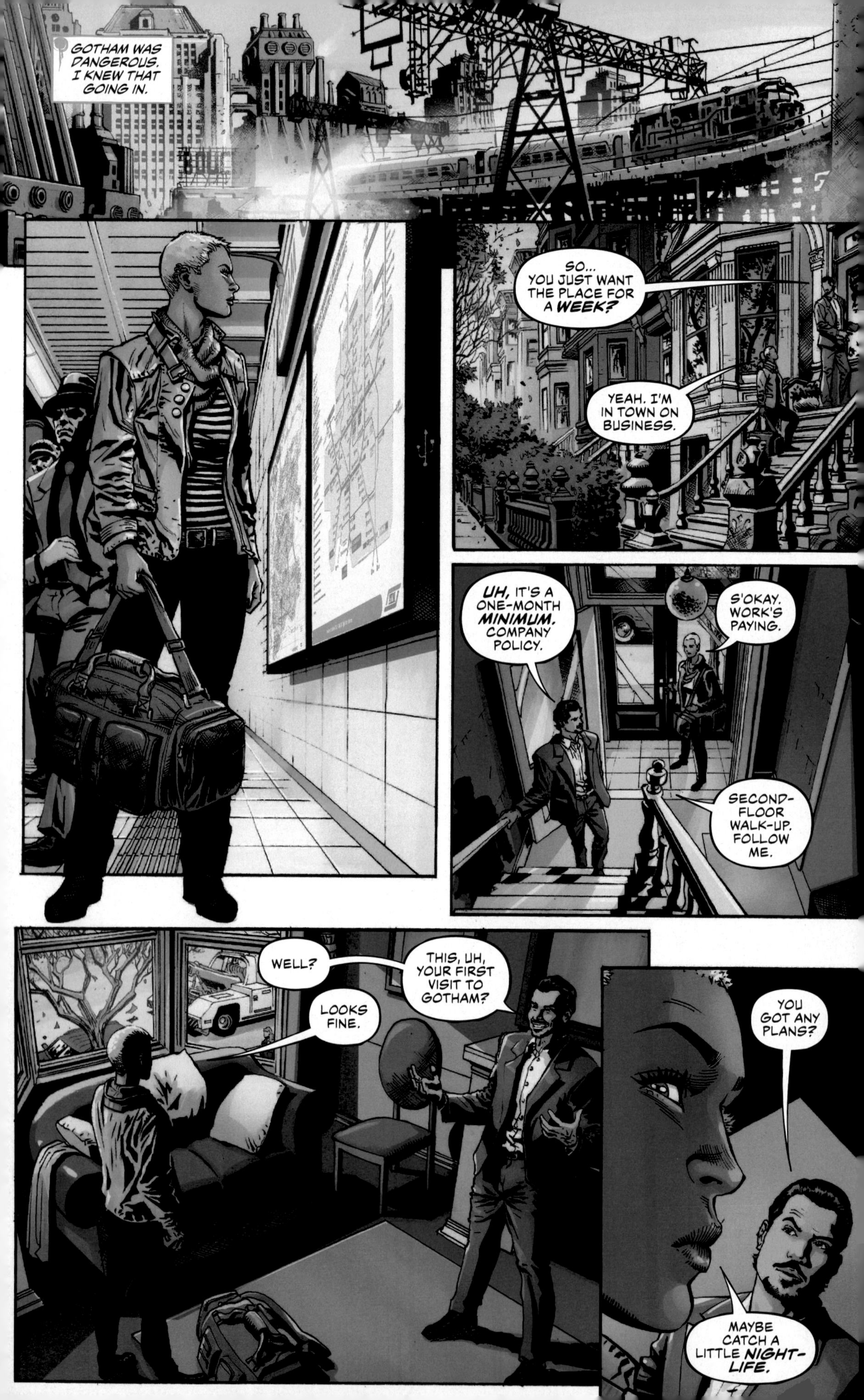
GOTHAM WAS DANGEROUS. I KNEW THAT GOING IN.
SO... YOU JUST WANT THE PLACE FOR A WEEK?
YEAH. I'M IN TOWN ON BUSINESS.
UH, IT'S A ONE-MONTH MINIMUM. COMPANY POLICY.
S'OKAY. WORK'S PAYING.
SECOND-FLOOR WALK-UP. FOLLOW ME.
WELL?
LOOKS FINE.
THIS, UH, YOUR FIRST VISIT TO GOTHAM?
YOU GOT ANY PLANS?
MAYBE CATCH A LITTLE NIGHT-LIFE.

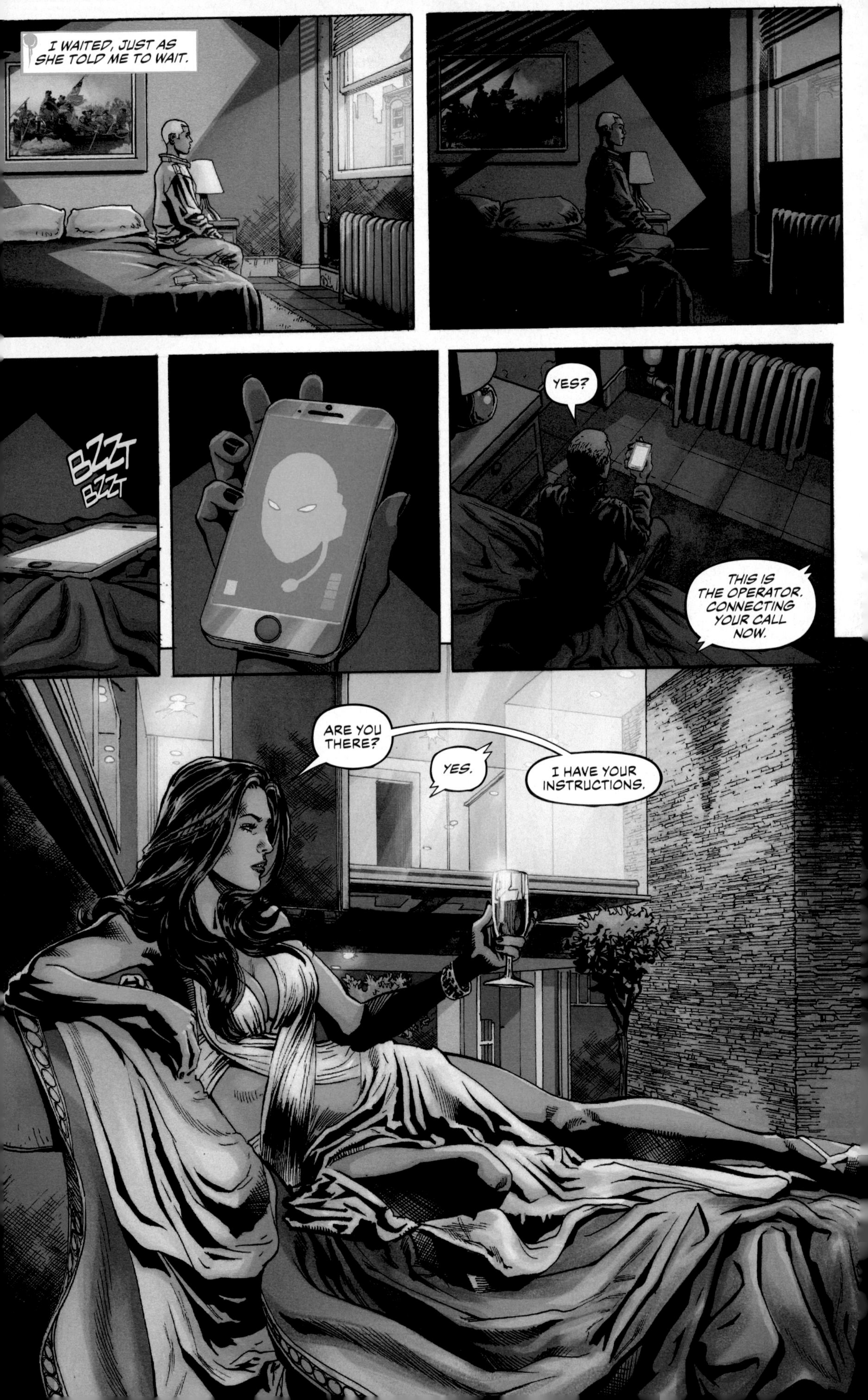
I WAITED, JUST AS SHE TOLD ME TO WAIT.
BZZT
BZZT
YES?
THIS IS THE OPERATOR. CONNECTING YOUR CALL NOW.
ARE YOU THERE?
YES.
I HAVE YOUR INSTRUCTIONS.

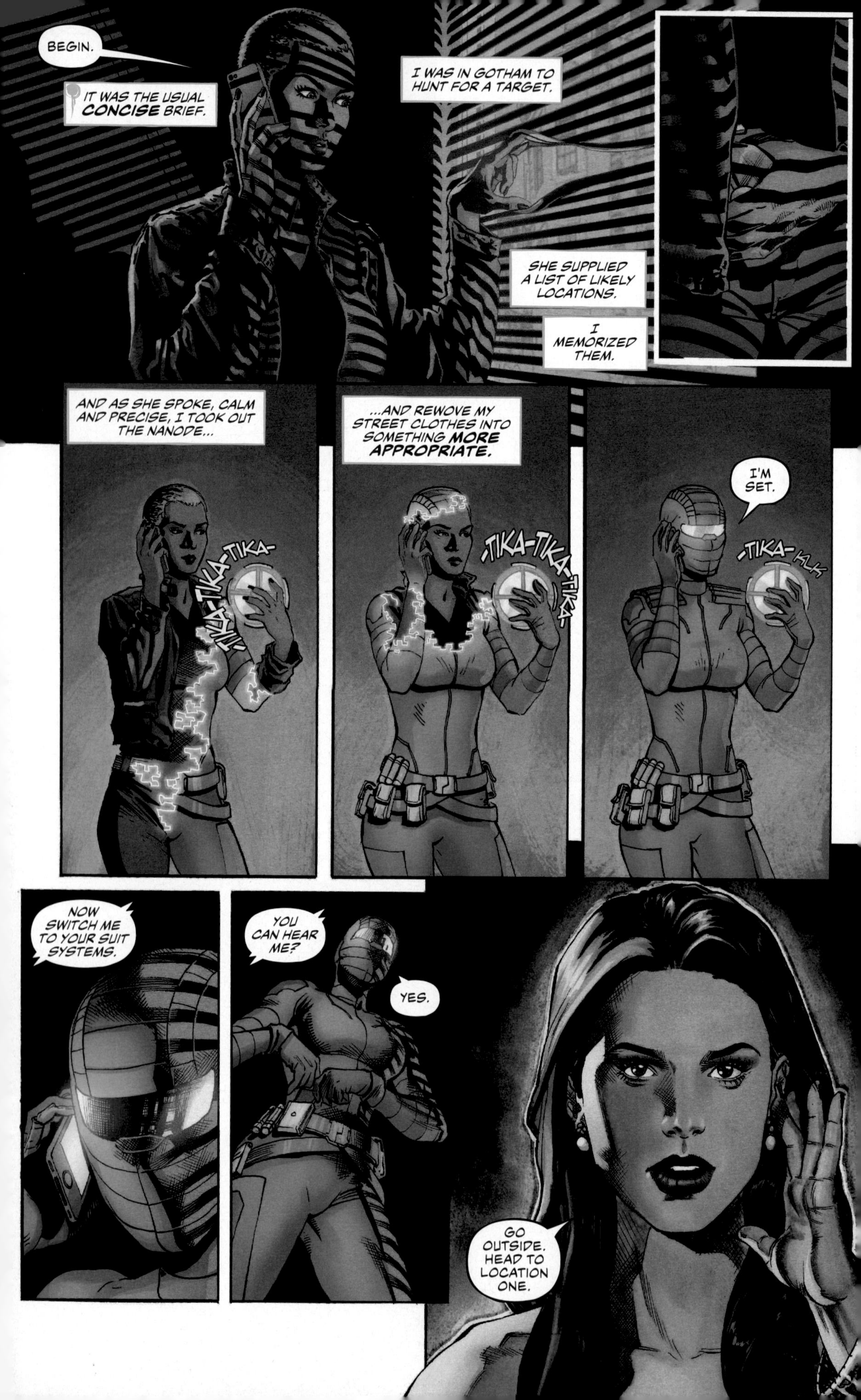
BEGIN.
IT WAS THE USUAL CONCISE BRIEF.
I WAS IN GOTHAM TO HUNT FOR A TARGET.
SHE SUPPLIED A LIST OF LIKELY LOCATIONS.
I MEMORIZED THEM.
AND AS SHE SPOKE, CALM AND PRECISE, I TOOK OUT THE NANODE...
-TIKA-TIKA-TIKA-
...AND REWOVE MY STREET CLOTHES INTO SOMETHING MORE APPROPRIATE.
-TIKA-TIKA-TIKA-
I'M SET.
-TIKA-KLK
NOW SWITCH ME TO YOUR SUIT SYSTEMS.
YOU CAN HEAR ME?
YES.
GO OUTSIDE. HEAD TO LOCATION ONE.

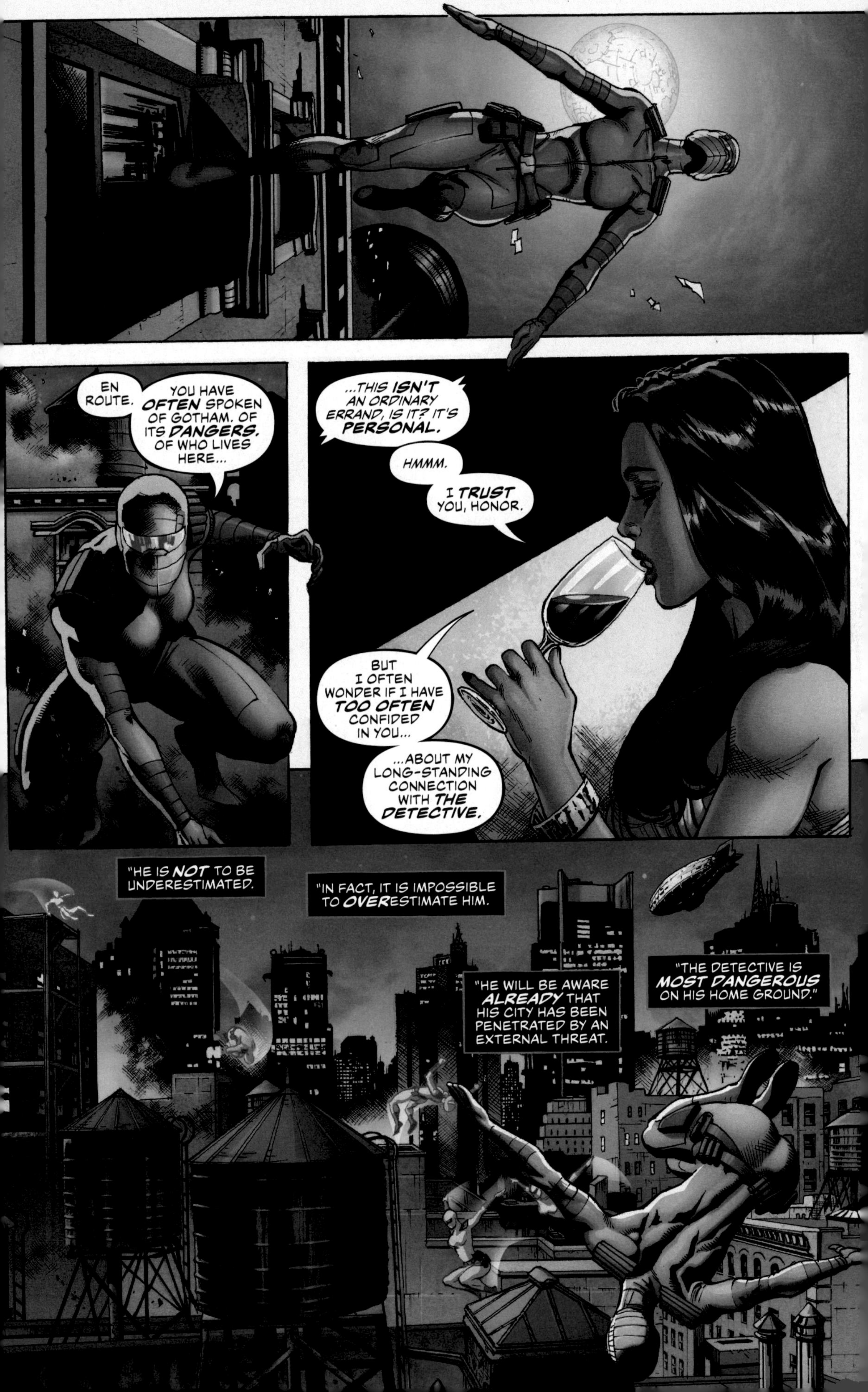
EN ROUTE.
YOU HAVE OFTEN SPOKEN OF GOTHAM. OF ITS DANGERS. OF WHO LIVES HERE...
...THIS ISN'T AN ORDINARY ERRAND, IS IT? IT'S PERSONAL.
HMMM.
I TRUST YOU, HONOR.
BUT I OFTEN WONDER IF I HAVE TOO OFTEN CONFIDED IN YOU...
...ABOUT MY LONG-STANDING CONNECTION WITH THE DETECTIVE.
"HE IS NOT TO BE UNDERESTIMATED.
"IN FACT, IT IS IMPOSSIBLE TO OVERESTIMATE HIM.
"HE WILL BE AWARE ALREADY THAT HIS CITY HAS BEEN PENETRATED BY AN EXTERNAL THREAT.
"THE DETECTIVE IS MOST DANGEROUS ON HIS HOME GROUND."

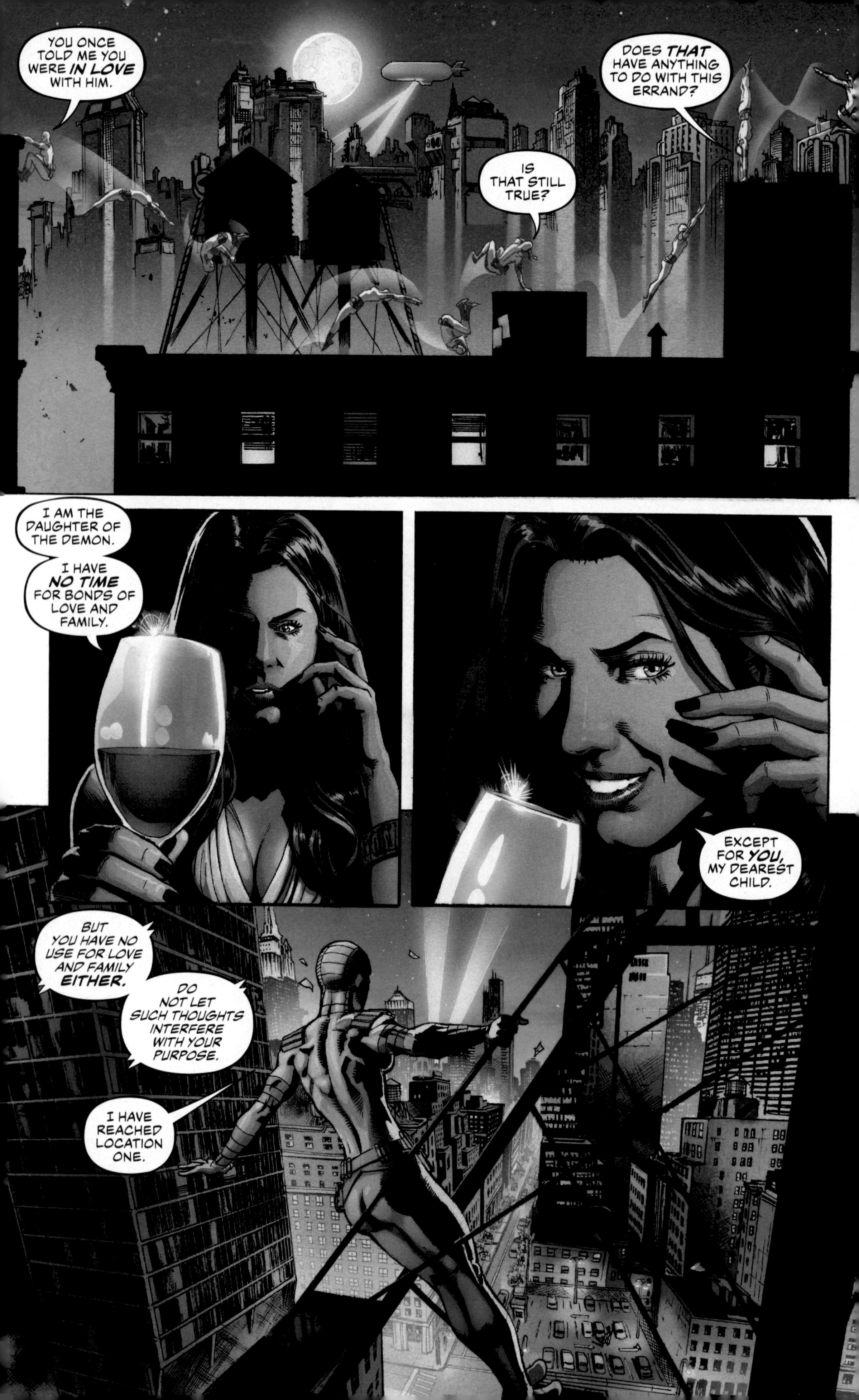
YOU ONCE TOLD ME YOU WERE IN LOVE WITH HIM.
DOES THAT HAVE ANYTHING TO DO WITH THIS ERRAND?
IS THAT STILL TRUE?
I AM THE DAUGHTER OF THE DEMON.
I HAVE NO TIME FOR BONDS OF LOVE AND FAMILY.
EXCEPT FOR YOU, MY DEAREST CHILD.
BUT YOU HAVE NO USE FOR LOVE AND FAMILY EITHER.
DO NOT LET SUCH THOUGHTS INTERFERE WITH YOUR PURPOSE.
I HAVE REACHED LOCATION ONE.

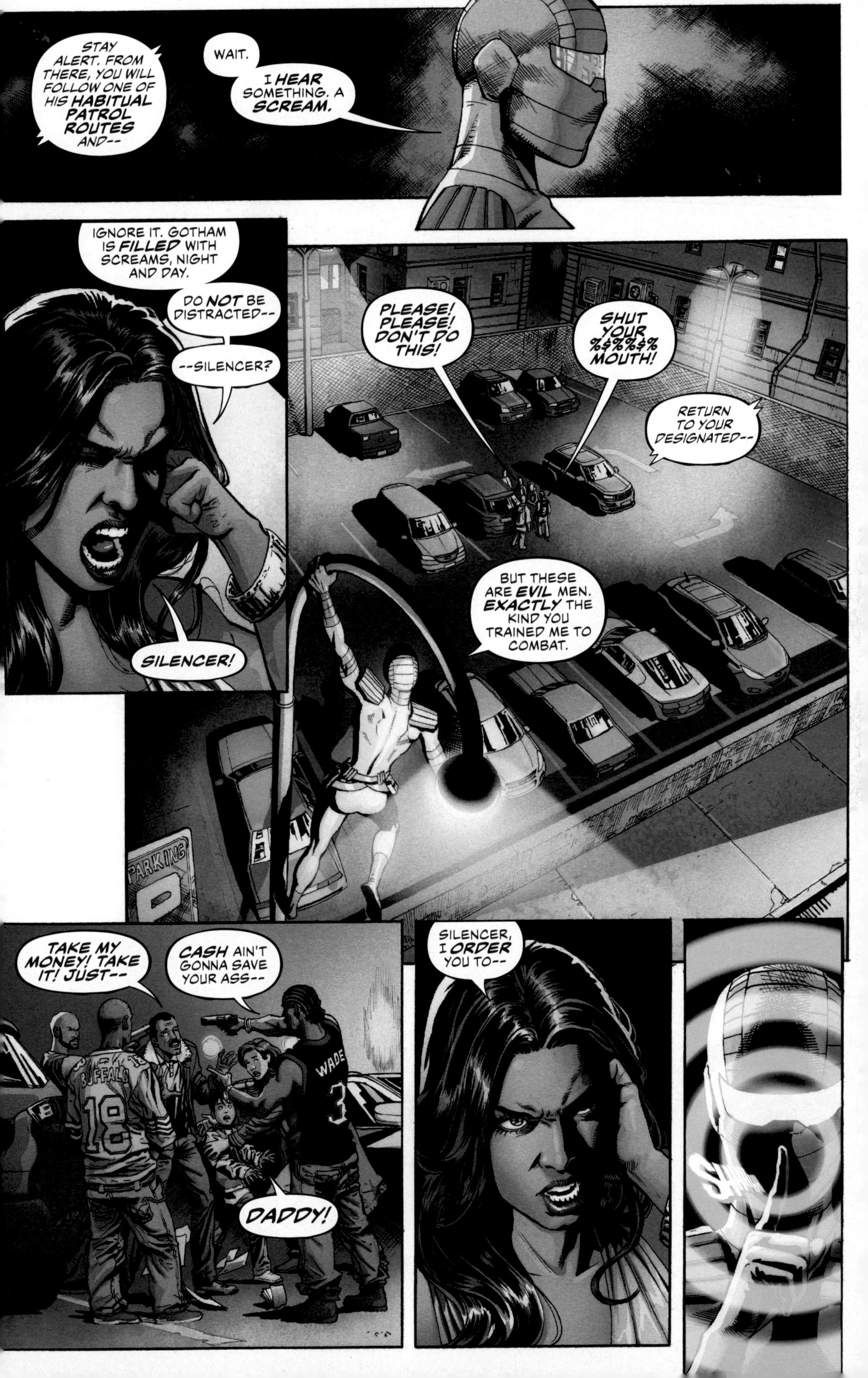
STAY ALERT. FROM THERE, YOU WILL FOLLOW ONE OF HIS HABITUAL PATROL ROUTES AND--
WAIT.
I HEAR SOMETHING. A SCREAM.
IGNORE IT. GOTHAM IS FILLED WITH SCREAMS, NIGHT AND DAY.
DO NOT BE DISTRACTED--
--SILENCER?
SILENCER!
PLEASE! PLEASE! DON'T DO THIS!
SHUT YOUR %$%%$% MOUTH!
RETURN TO YOUR DESIGNATED--
BUT THESE ARE EVIL MEN. EXACTLY THE KIND YOU TRAINED ME TO COMBAT.
PARKING
TAKE MY MONEY! TAKE IT! JUST--
CASH AIN'T GONNA SAVE YOUR ASS--
BUFFALO
18
WADE
3
DADDY!
SILENCER, I ORDER YOU TO--

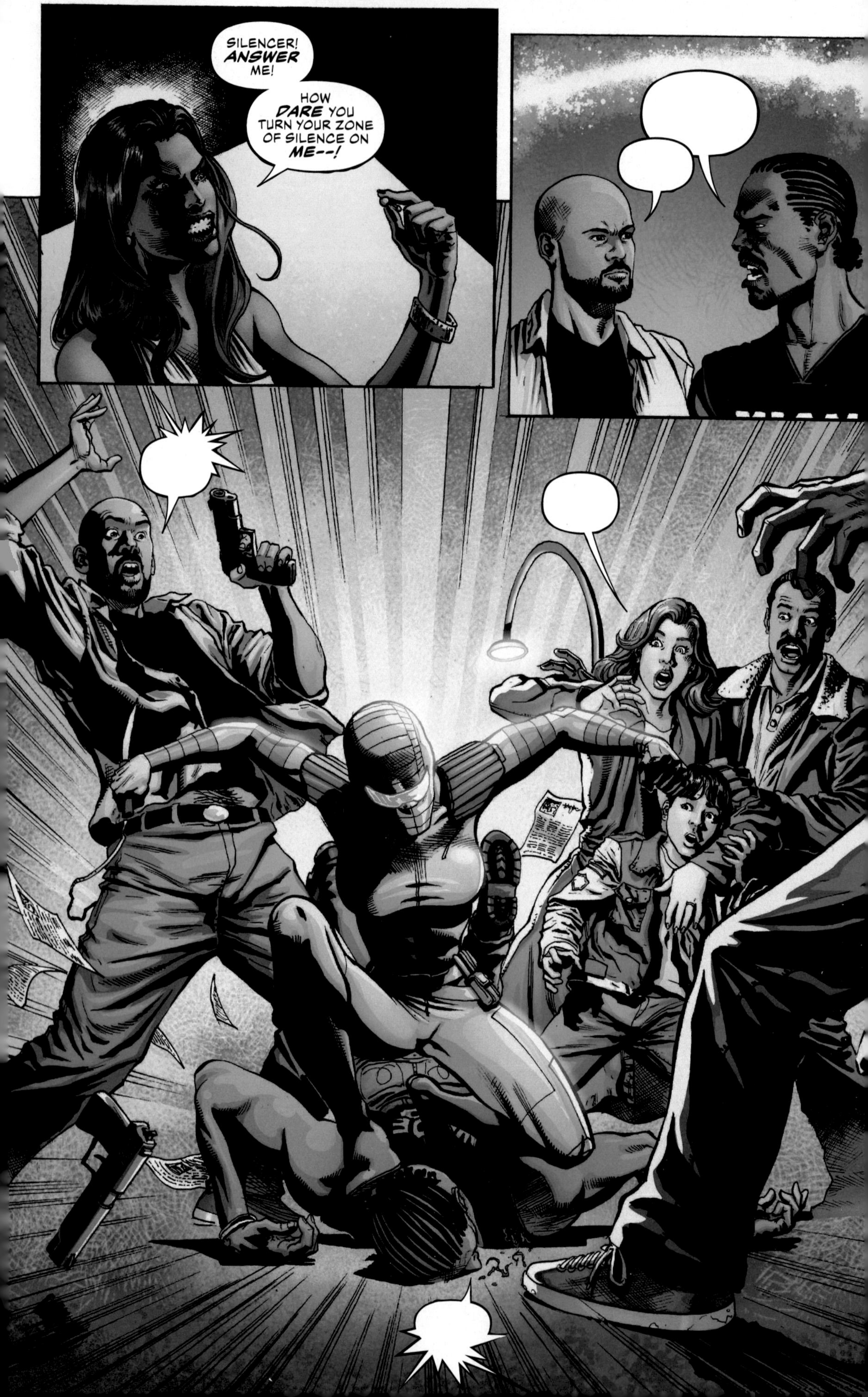
SILENCER! ANSWER ME!
HOW DARE YOU TURN YOUR ZONE OF SILENCE ON ME--!

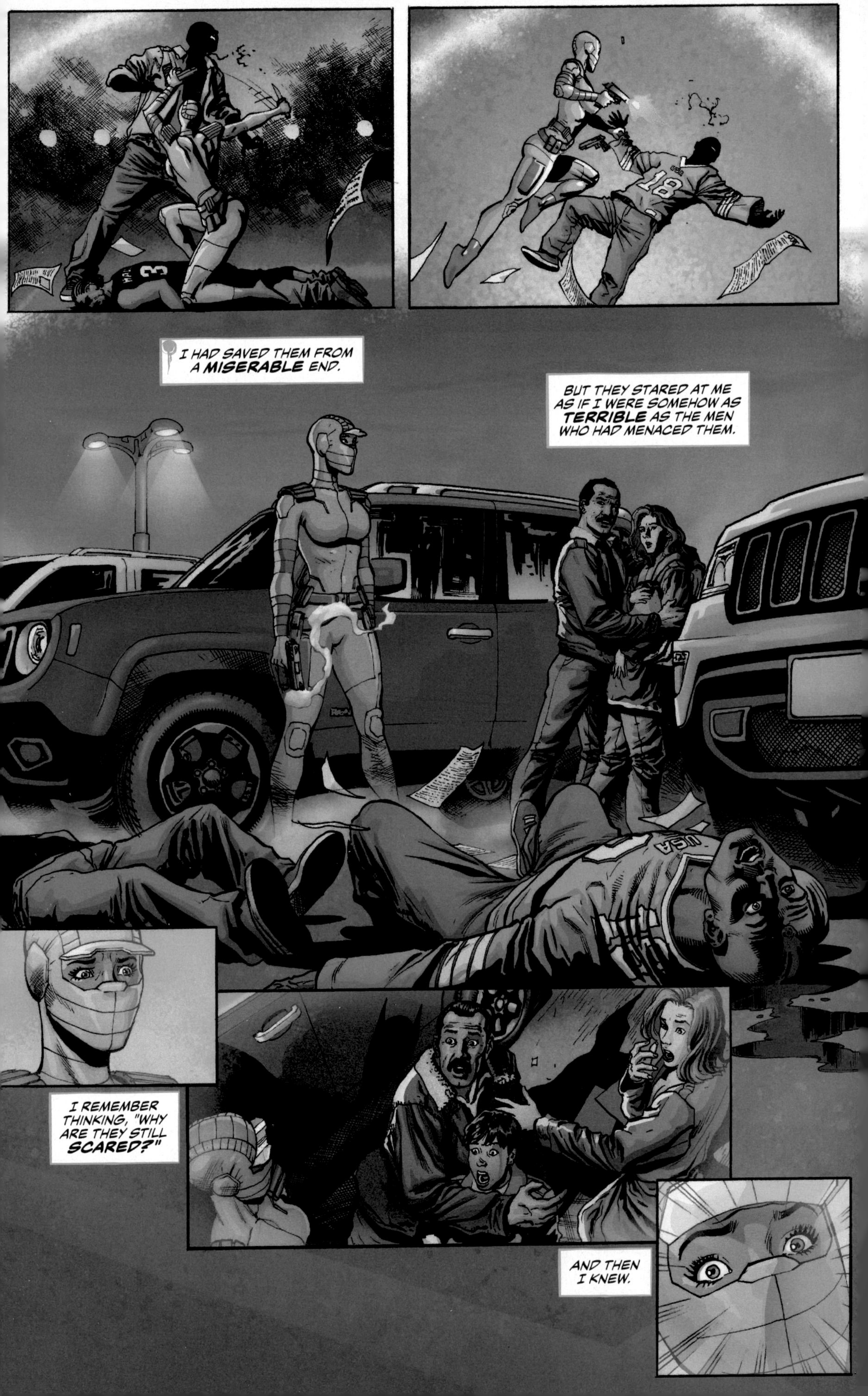
I HAD SAVED THEM FROM A MISERABLE END.
BUT THEY STARED AT ME AS IF I WERE SOMEHOW AS TERRIBLE AS THE MEN WHO HAD MENACED THEM.
I REMEMBER THINKING, "WHY ARE THEY STILL SCARED?"
AND THEN I KNEW.

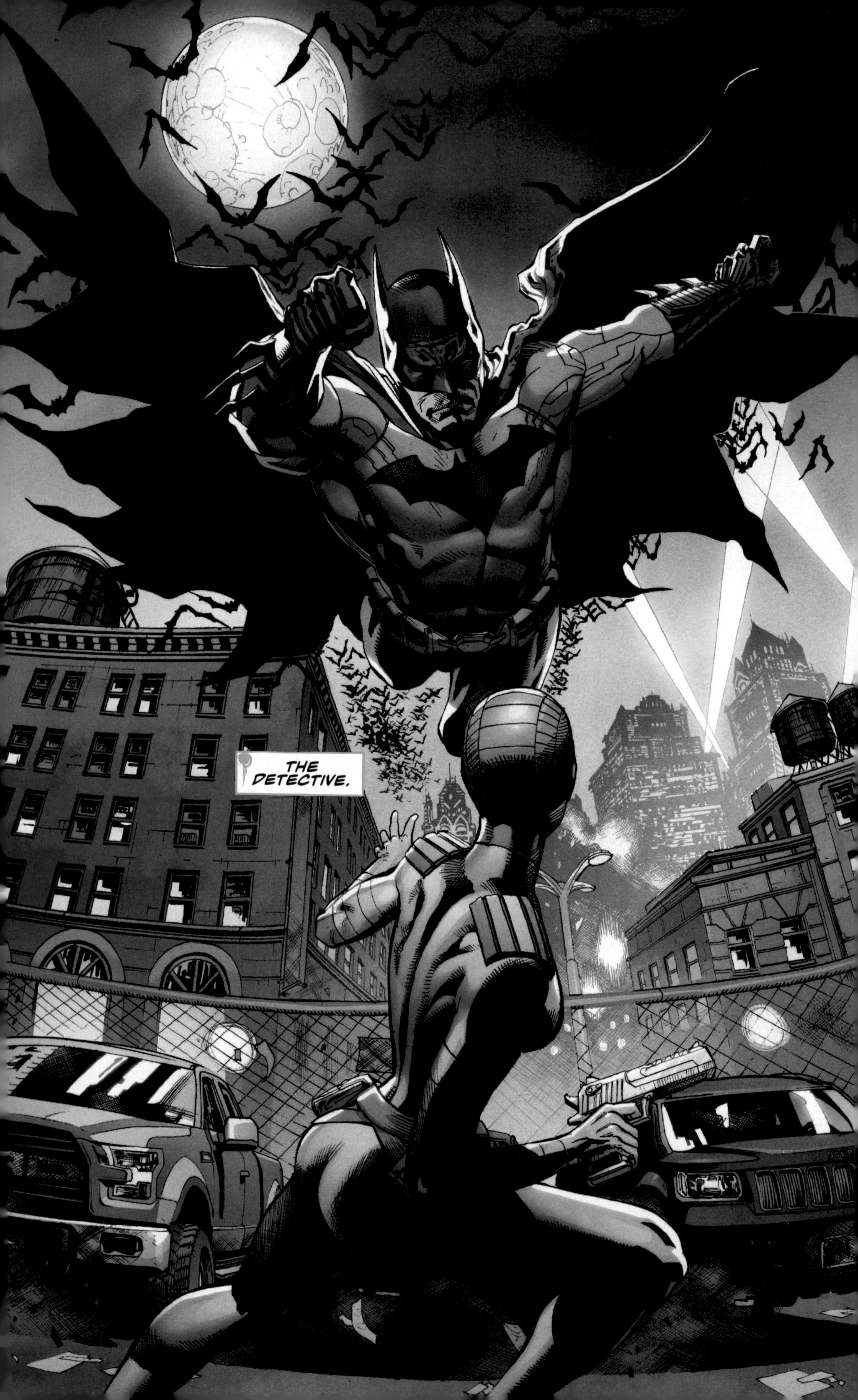
THE DETECTIVE.

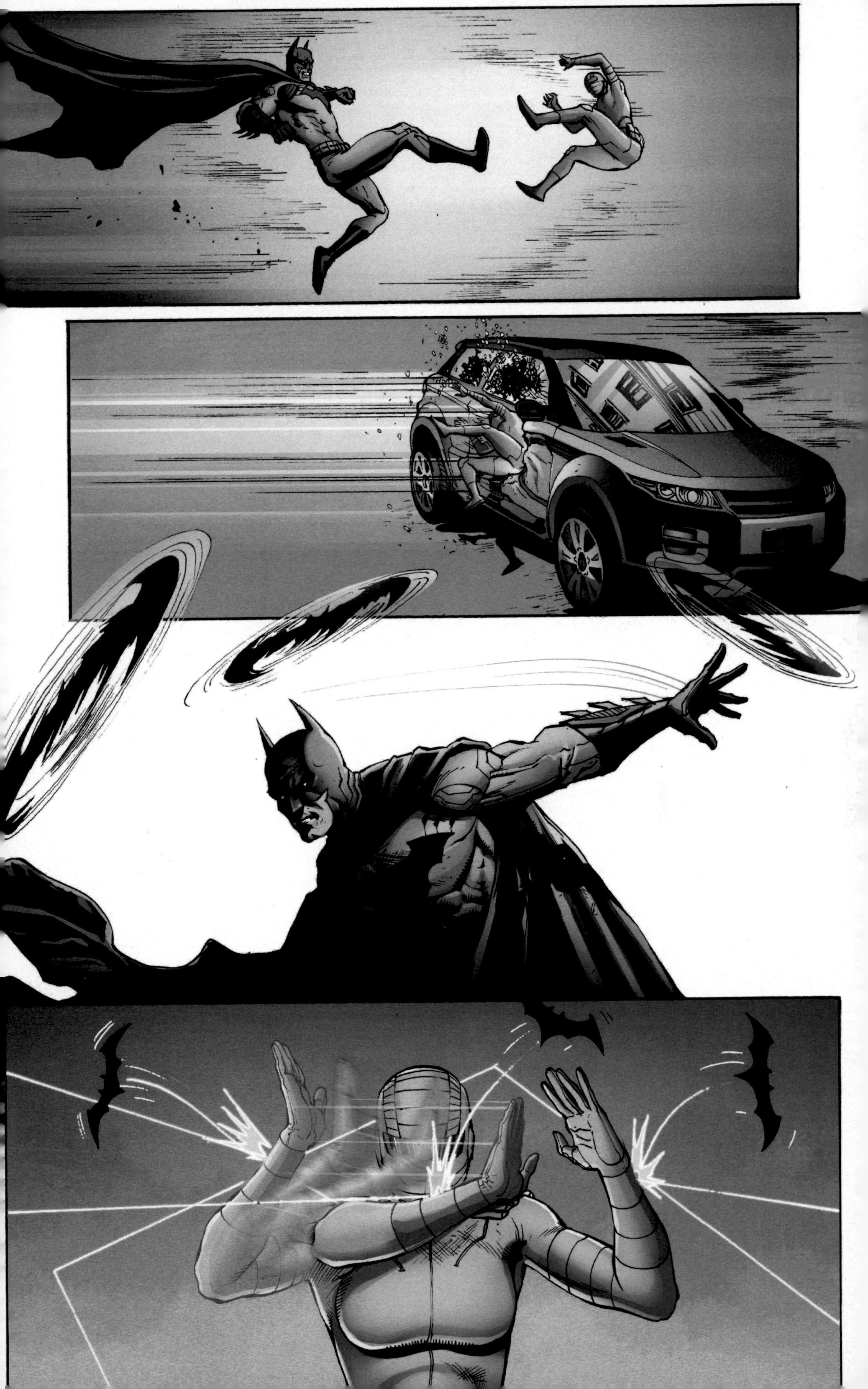

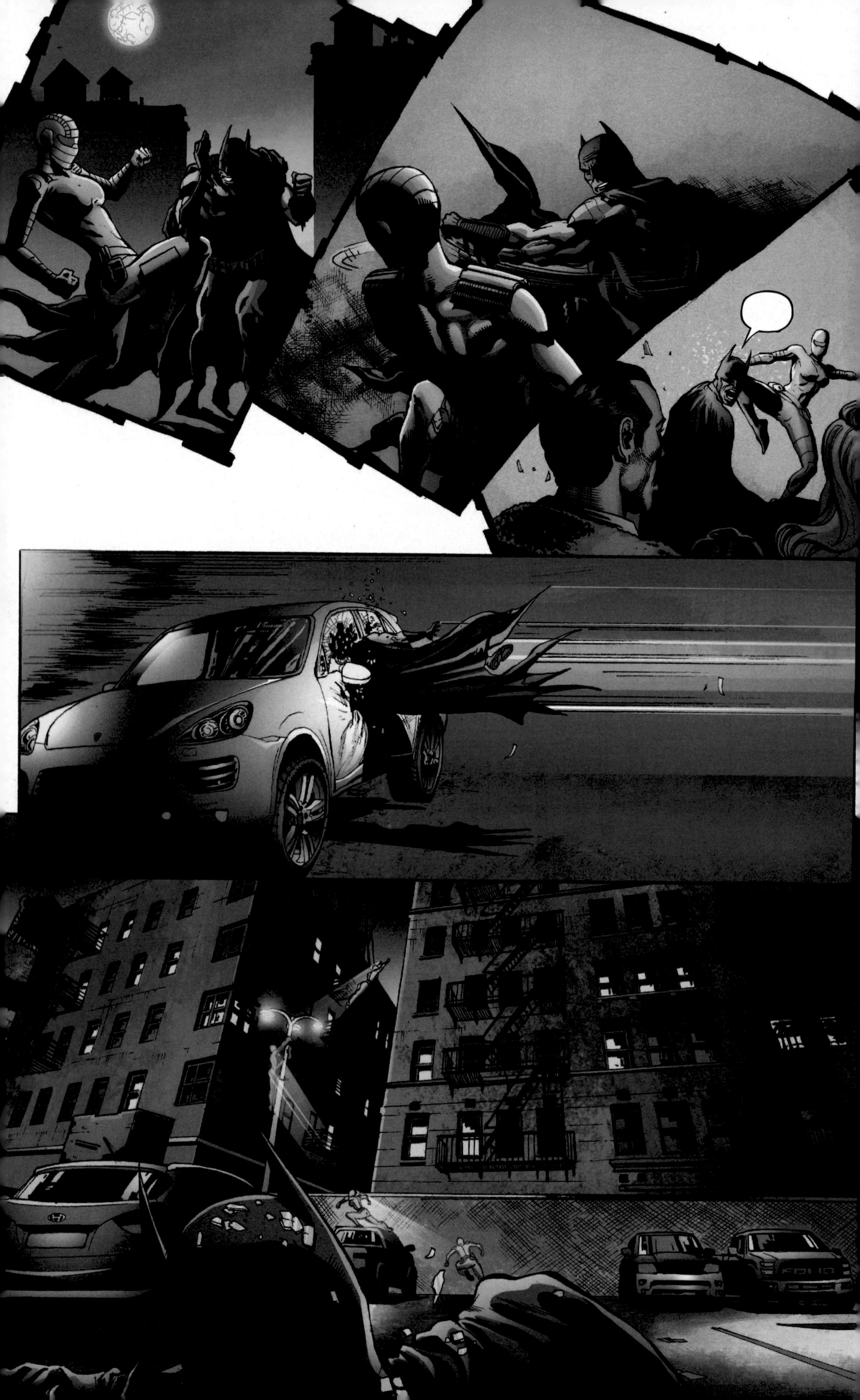

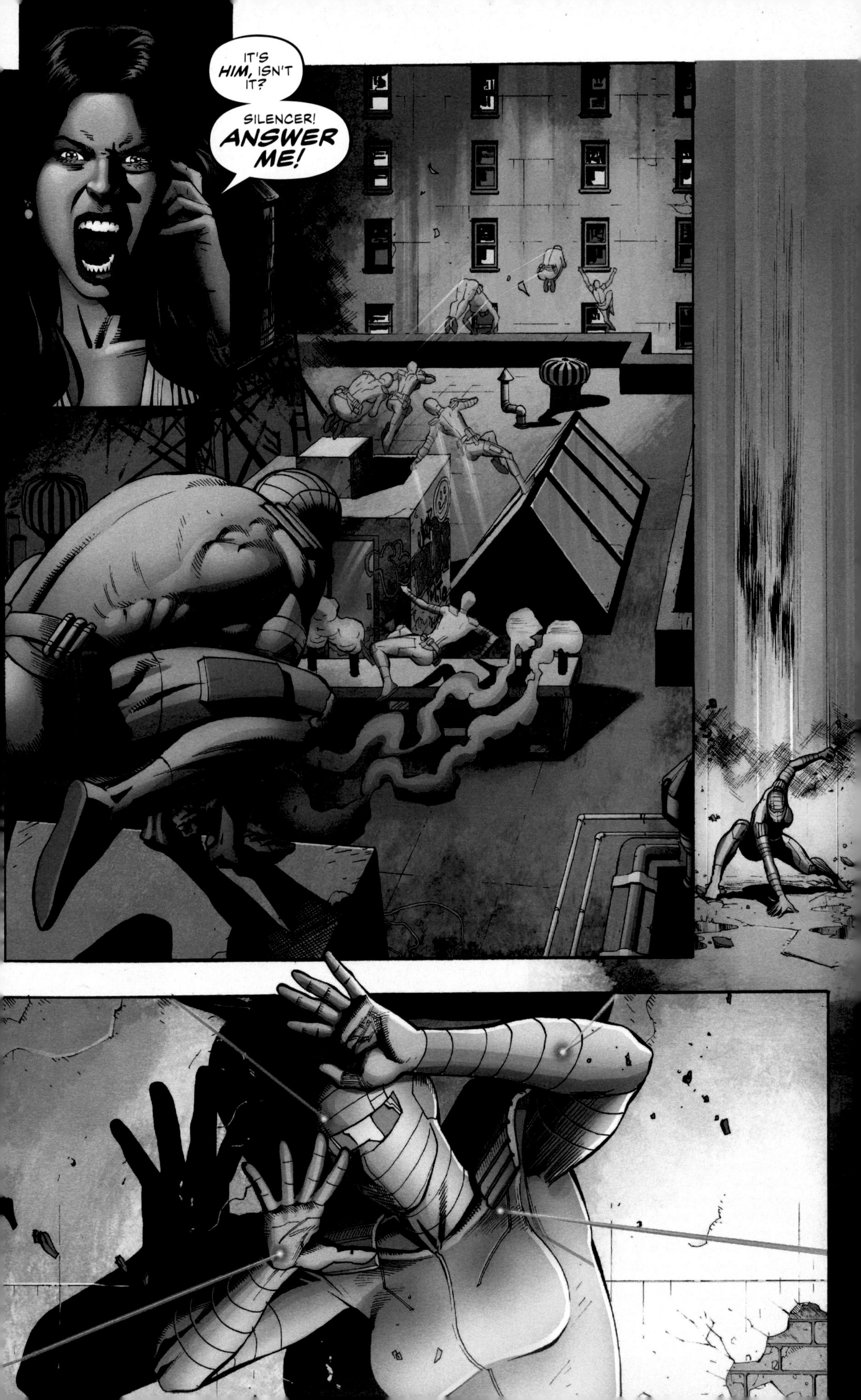
IT'S HIM, ISN'T IT?
SILENCER! ANSWER ME!

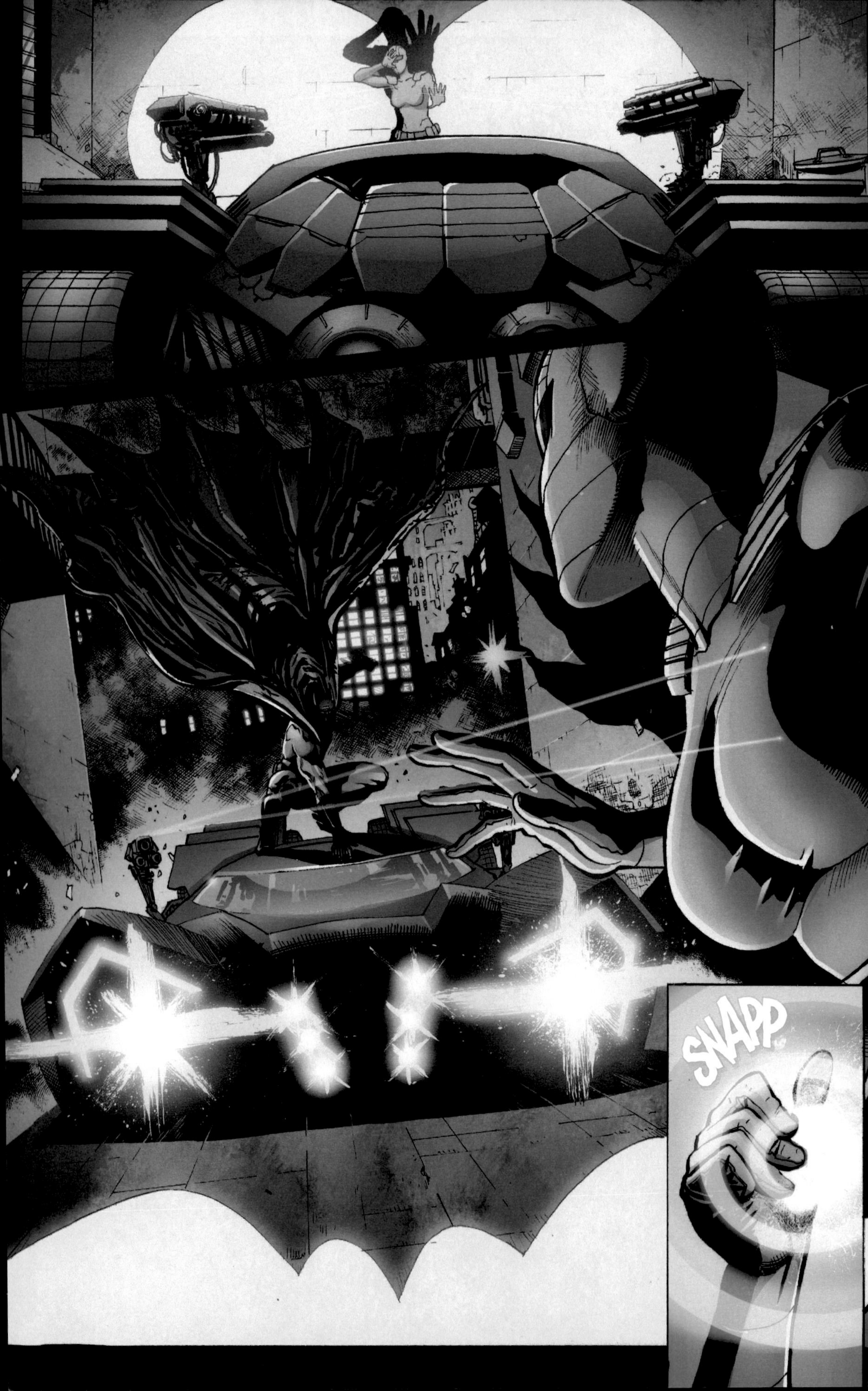
SNAPP

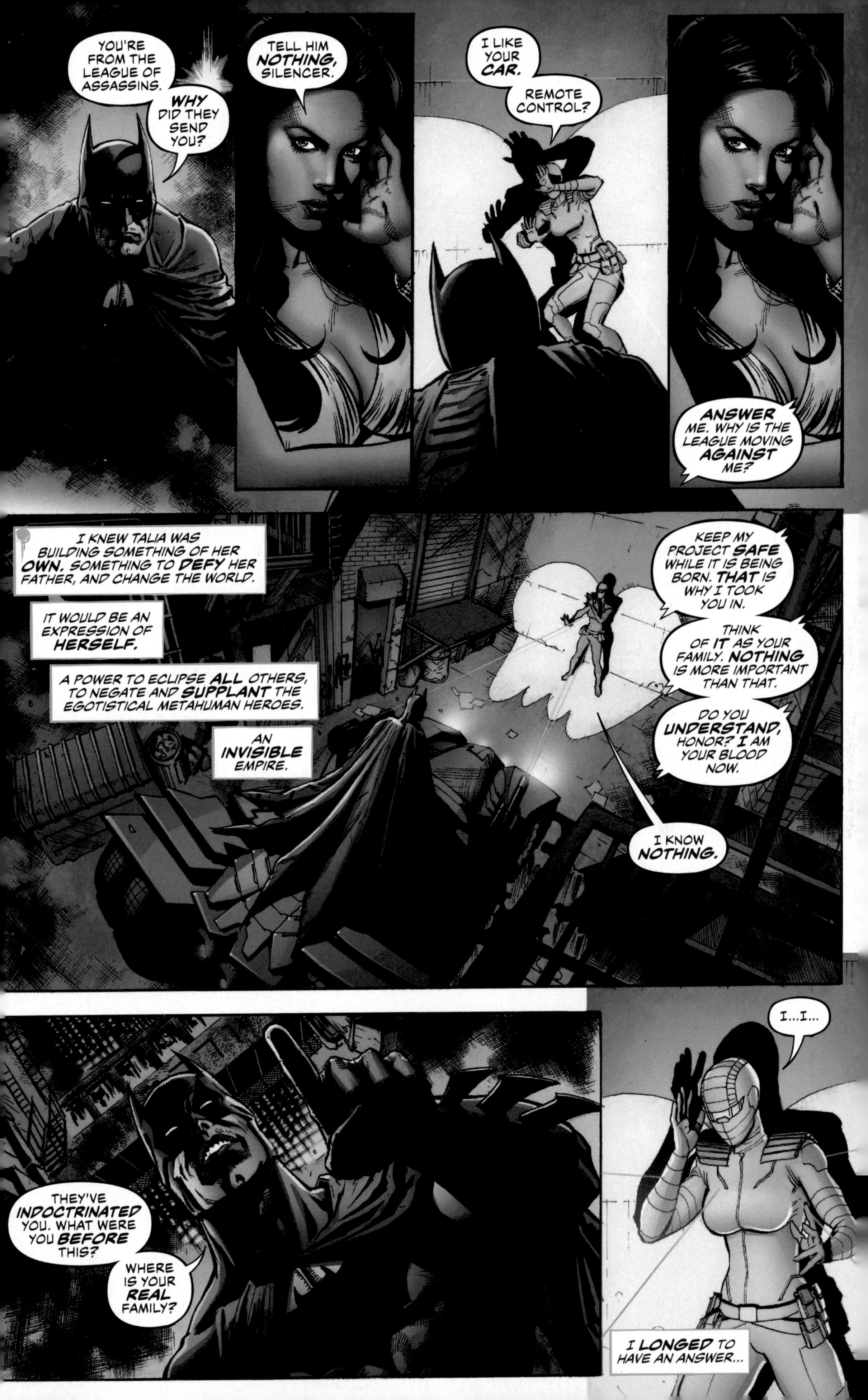

YOU'RE FROM THE LEAGUE OF ASSASSINS.
WHY DID THEY SEND YOU?
TELL HIM NOTHING, SILENCER.
I LIKE YOUR CAR.
REMOTE CONTROL?
ANSWER ME. WHY IS THE LEAGUE MOVING AGAINST ME?
I KNEW TALIA WAS BUILDING SOMETHING OF HER OWN. SOMETHING TO DEFY HER FATHER, AND CHANGE THE WORLD.
IT WOULD BE AN EXPRESSION OF HERSELF.
A POWER TO ECLIPSE ALL OTHERS, TO NEGATE AND SUPPLANT THE EGOTISTICAL METAHUMAN HEROES.
AN INVISIBLE EMPIRE.
KEEP MY PROJECT SAFE WHILE IT IS BEING BORN. THAT IS WHY I TOOK YOU IN.
THINK OF IT AS YOUR FAMILY. NOTHING IS MORE IMPORTANT THAN THAT.
DO YOU UNDERSTAND, HONOR? I AM YOUR BLOOD NOW.
I KNOW NOTHING.
THEY'VE INDOCTRINATED YOU. WHAT WERE YOU BEFORE THIS?
WHERE IS YOUR REAL FAMILY?
I...I...
I LONGED TO HAVE AN ANSWER...

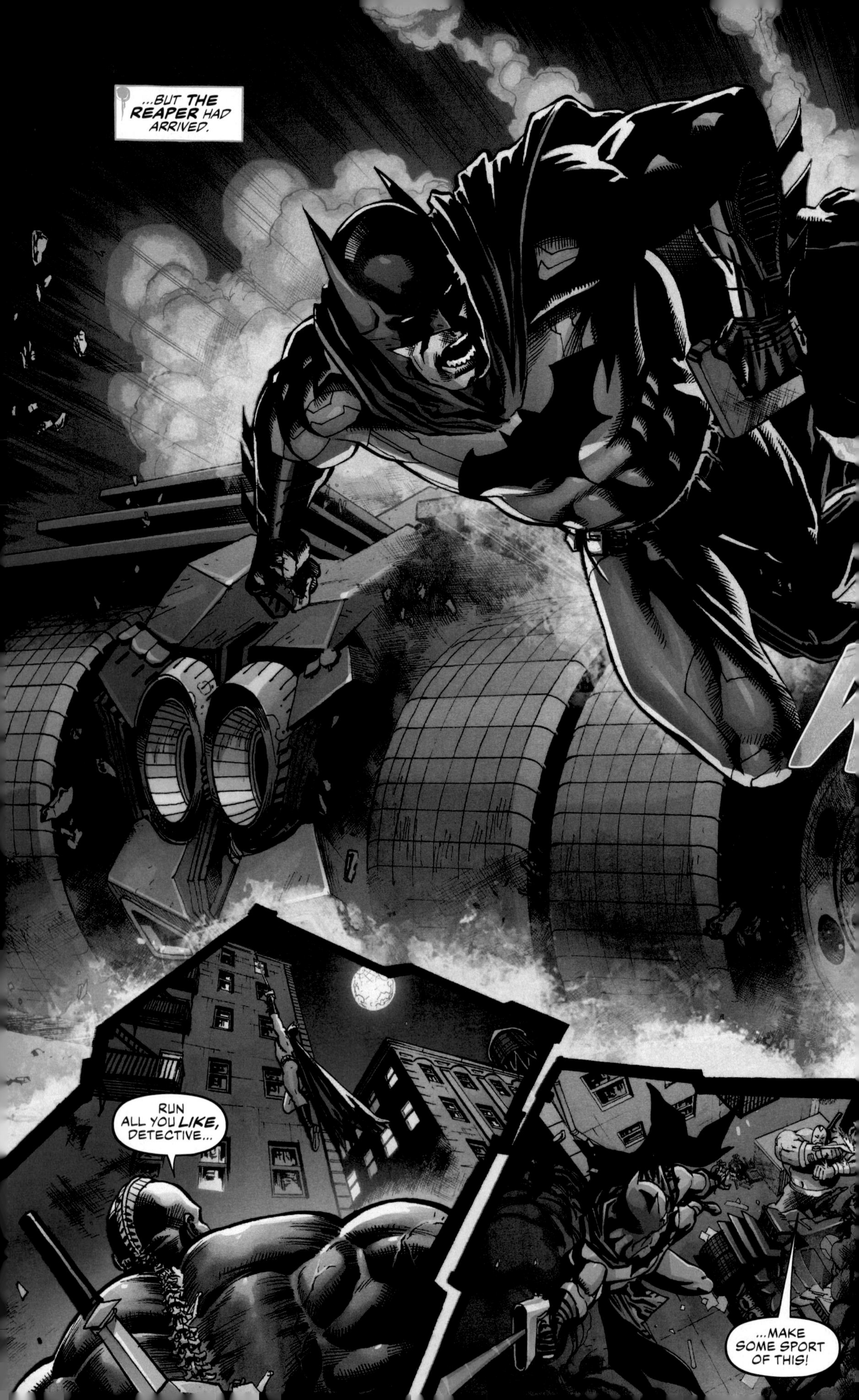
...BUT THE REAPER HAD ARRIVED.
RUN ALL YOU LIKE, DETECTIVE...
...MAKE SOME SPORT OF THIS!

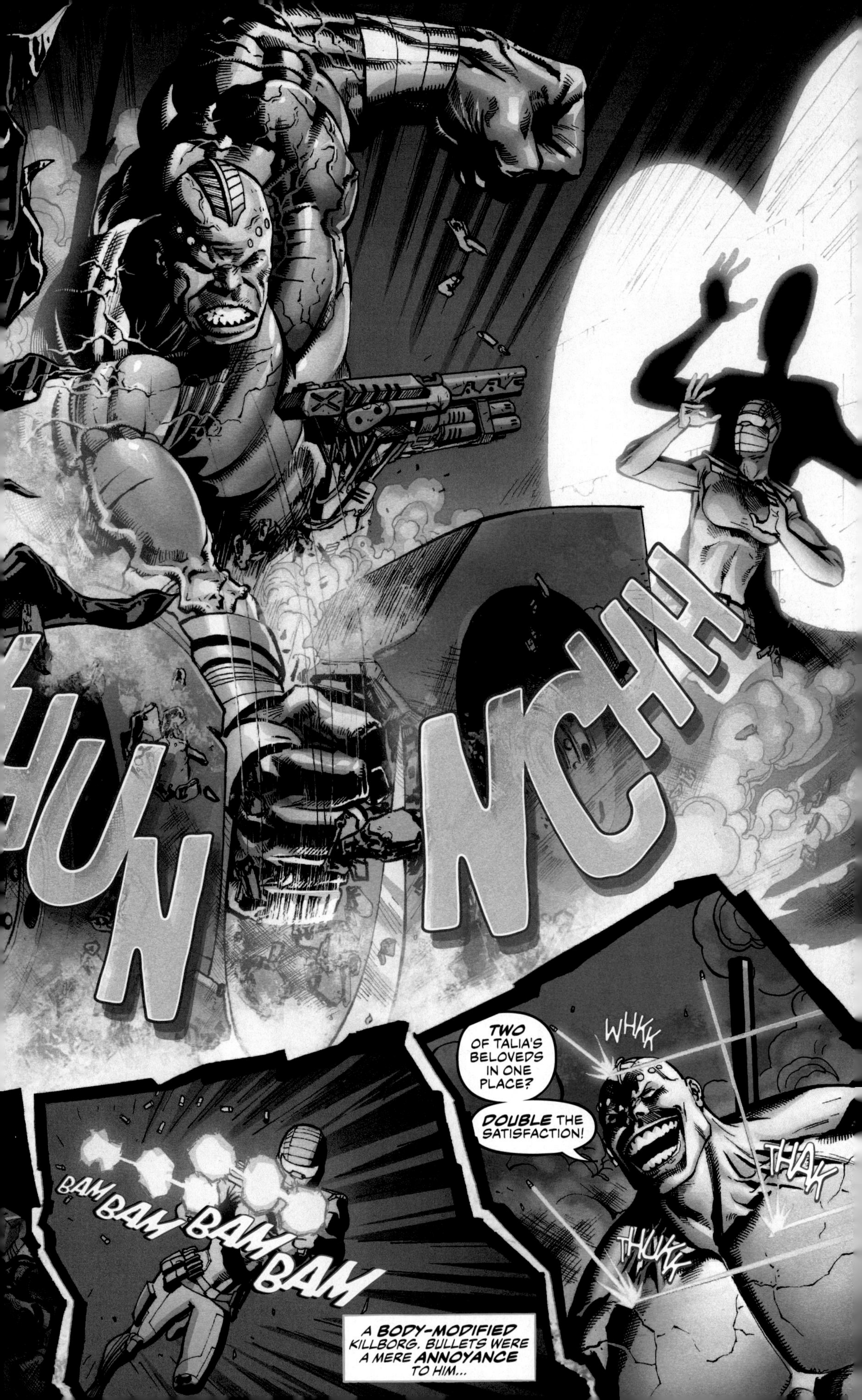
HUNNCHH
TWO OF TALIA'S BELOVEDS IN ONE PLACE?
DOUBLE THE SATISFACTION!
WHKK
BAM BAM BAM BAM BAM
THAK
THUKK
A BODY-MODIFIED KILLBORG. BULLETS WERE A MERE ANNOYANCE TO HIM...

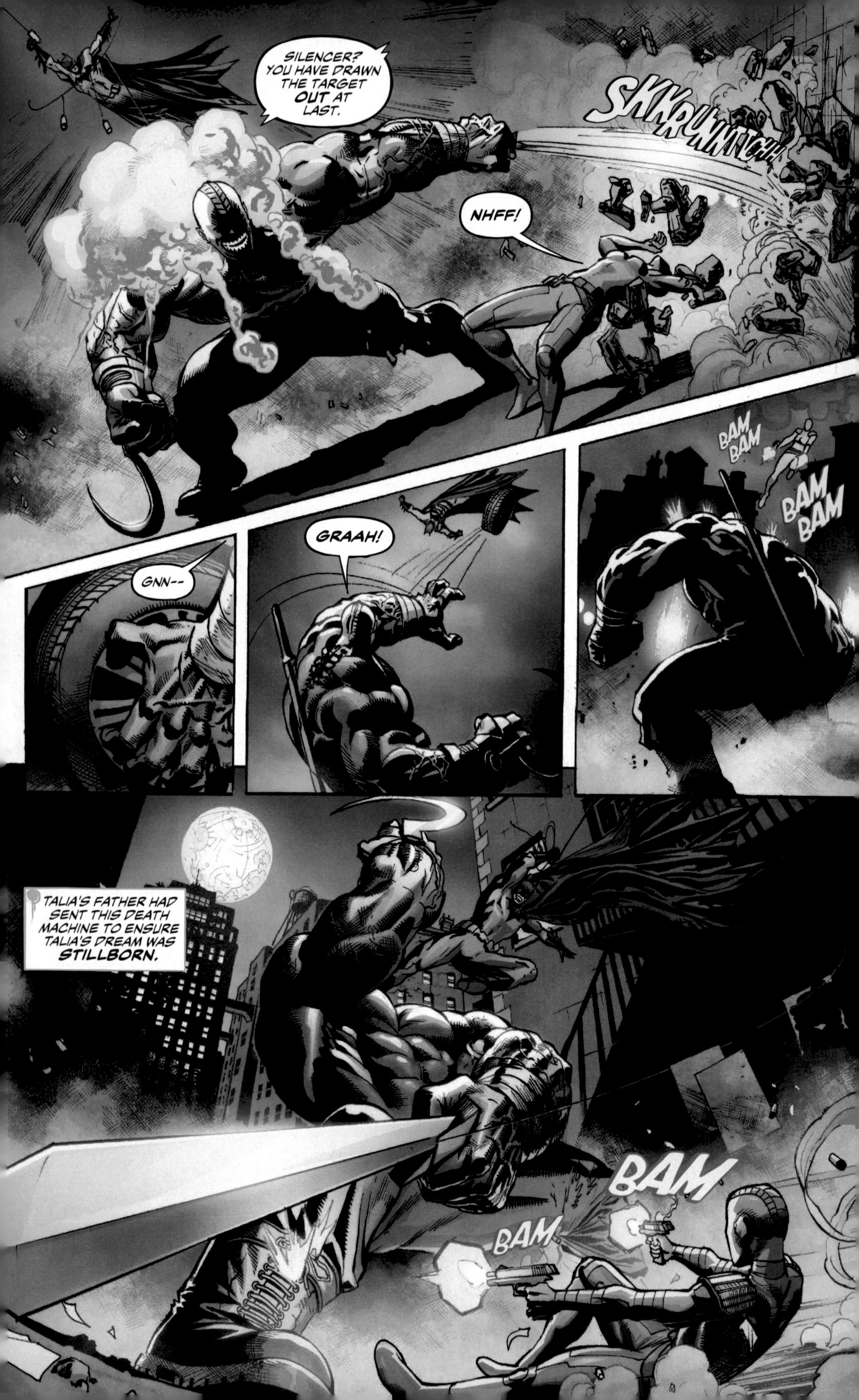
SILENCER? YOU HAVE DRAWN THE TARGET **OUT** AT LAST.
SHKRUNNTCHH
NHFF!
GNN--
GRAAH!
BAM BAM
BAM BAM
TALIA'S FATHER HAD SENT THIS DEATH MACHINE TO ENSURE TALIA'S DREAM WAS **STILLBORN.**
BAM
BAM

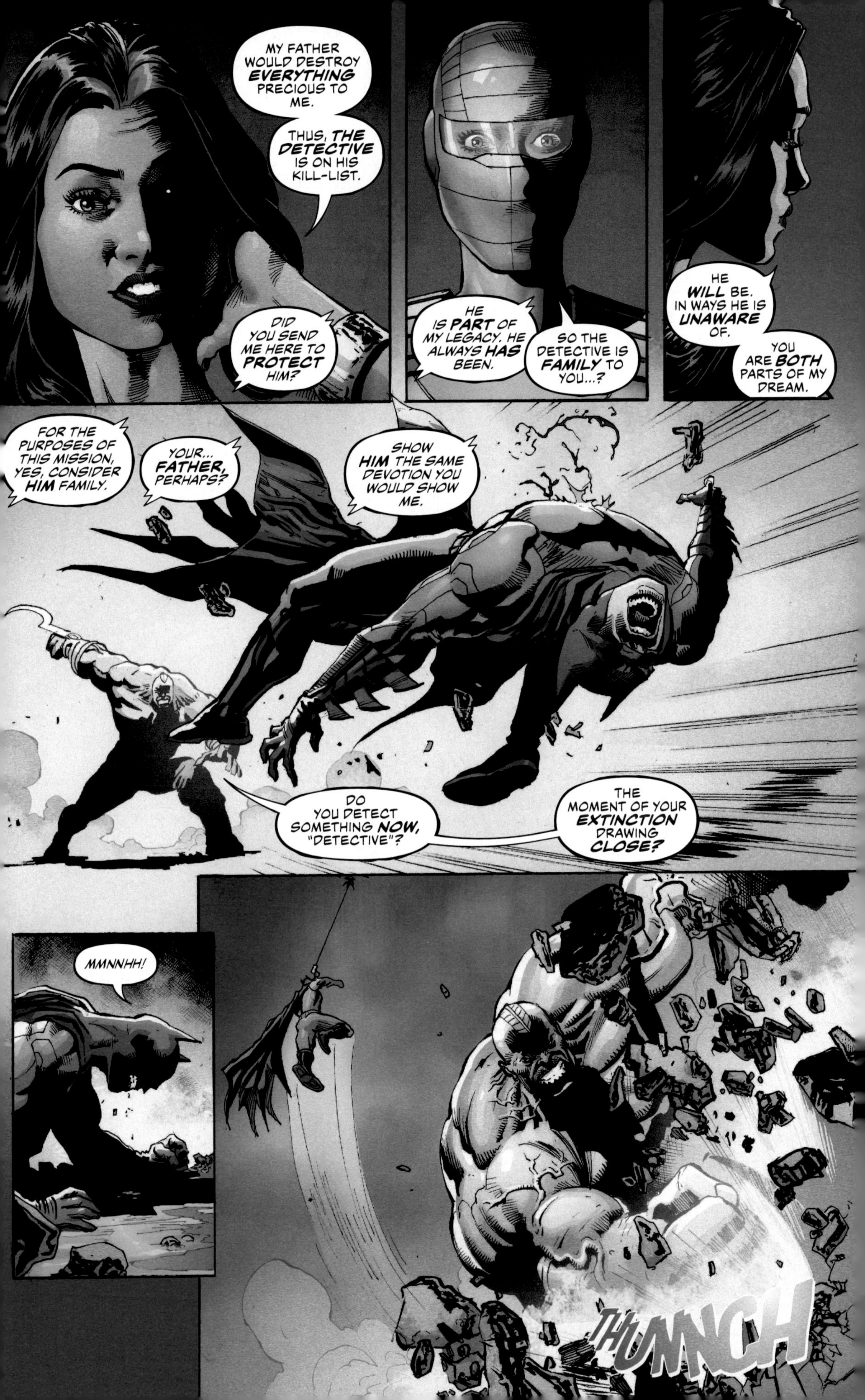
MY FATHER WOULD DESTROY EVERYTHING PRECIOUS TO ME.
THUS, THE DETECTIVE IS ON HIS KILL-LIST.
DID YOU SEND ME HERE TO PROTECT HIM?
HE IS PART OF MY LEGACY. HE ALWAYS HAS BEEN.
SO THE DETECTIVE IS FAMILY TO YOU...?
HE WILL BE. IN WAYS HE IS UNAWARE OF.
YOU ARE BOTH PARTS OF MY DREAM.
FOR THE PURPOSES OF THIS MISSION, YES, CONSIDER HIM FAMILY.
YOUR... FATHER, PERHAPS?
SHOW HIM THE SAME DEVOTION YOU WOULD SHOW ME.
DO YOU DETECT SOMETHING NOW, "DETECTIVE"?
THE MOMENT OF YOUR EXTINCTION DRAWING CLOSE?
MMNNHH!
THUNNCH

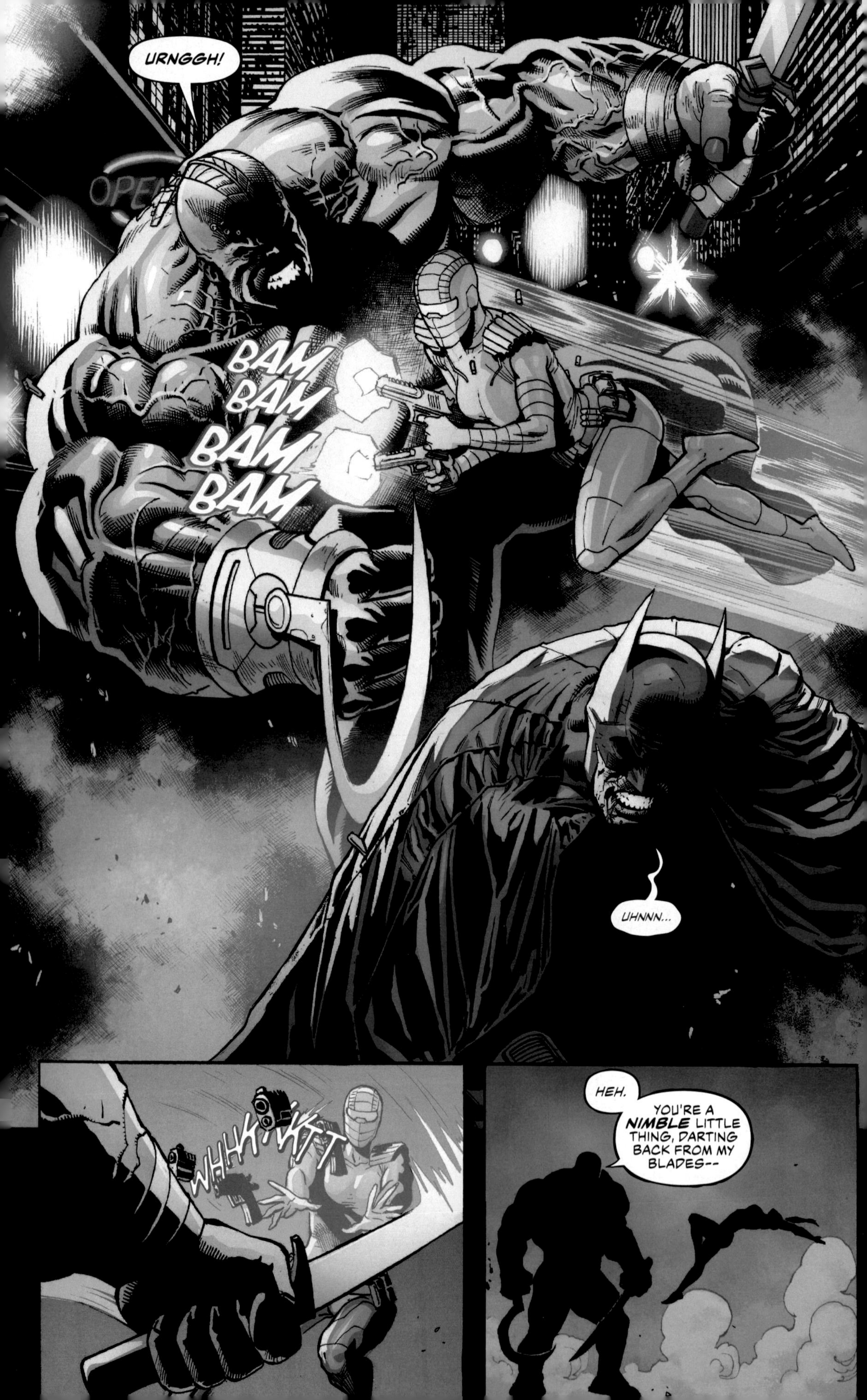
URNGGH!
BAM BAM BAM BAM
UHNNN...
WHHKKKTT
HEH.
YOU'RE A NIMBLE LITTLE THING, DARTING BACK FROM MY BLADES--

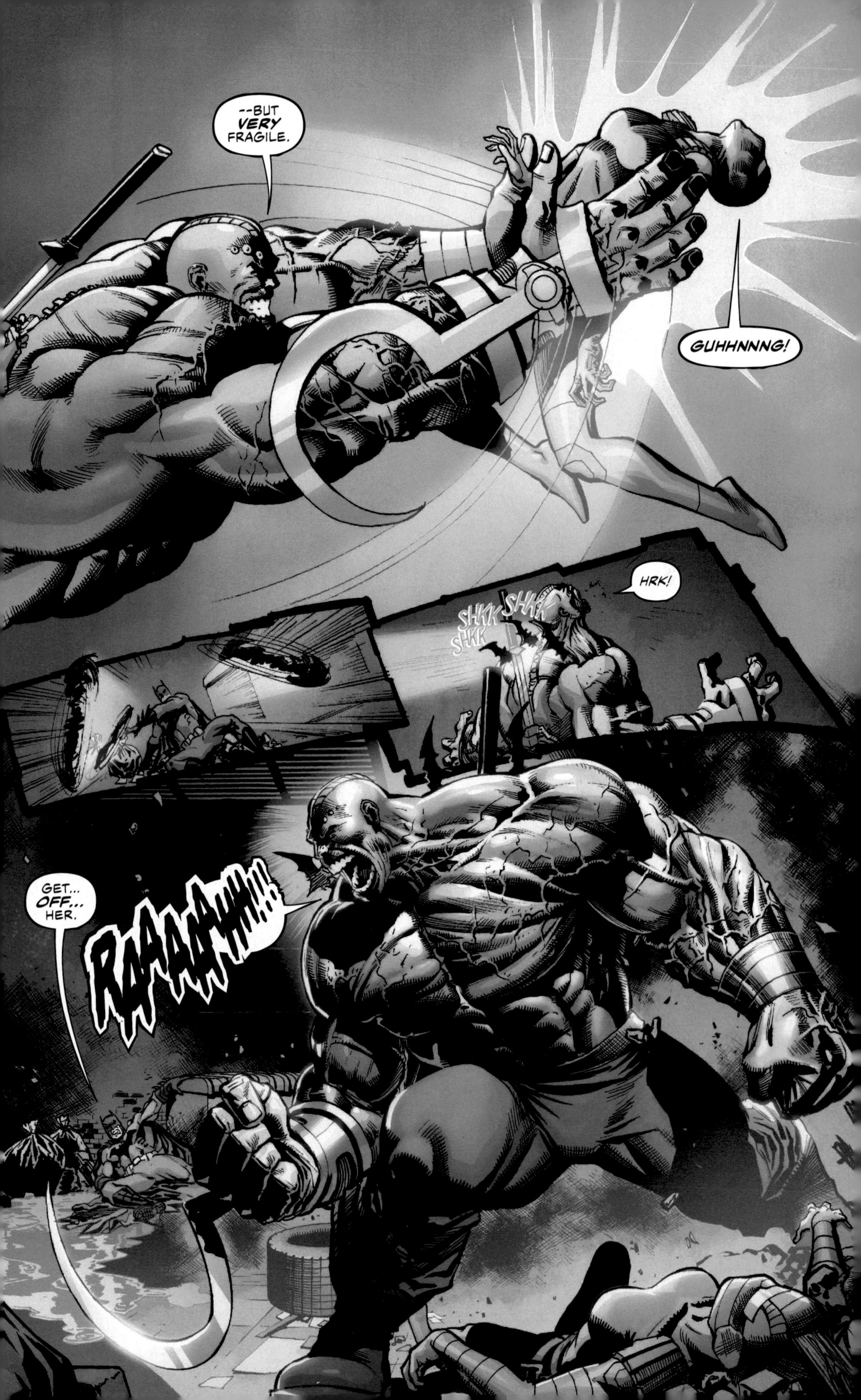
--BUT VERY FRAGILE.
GUHHNNNG!
HRK!
SHKK SHKK SHKK
GET... OFF... HER.
RAAAAHH!!!

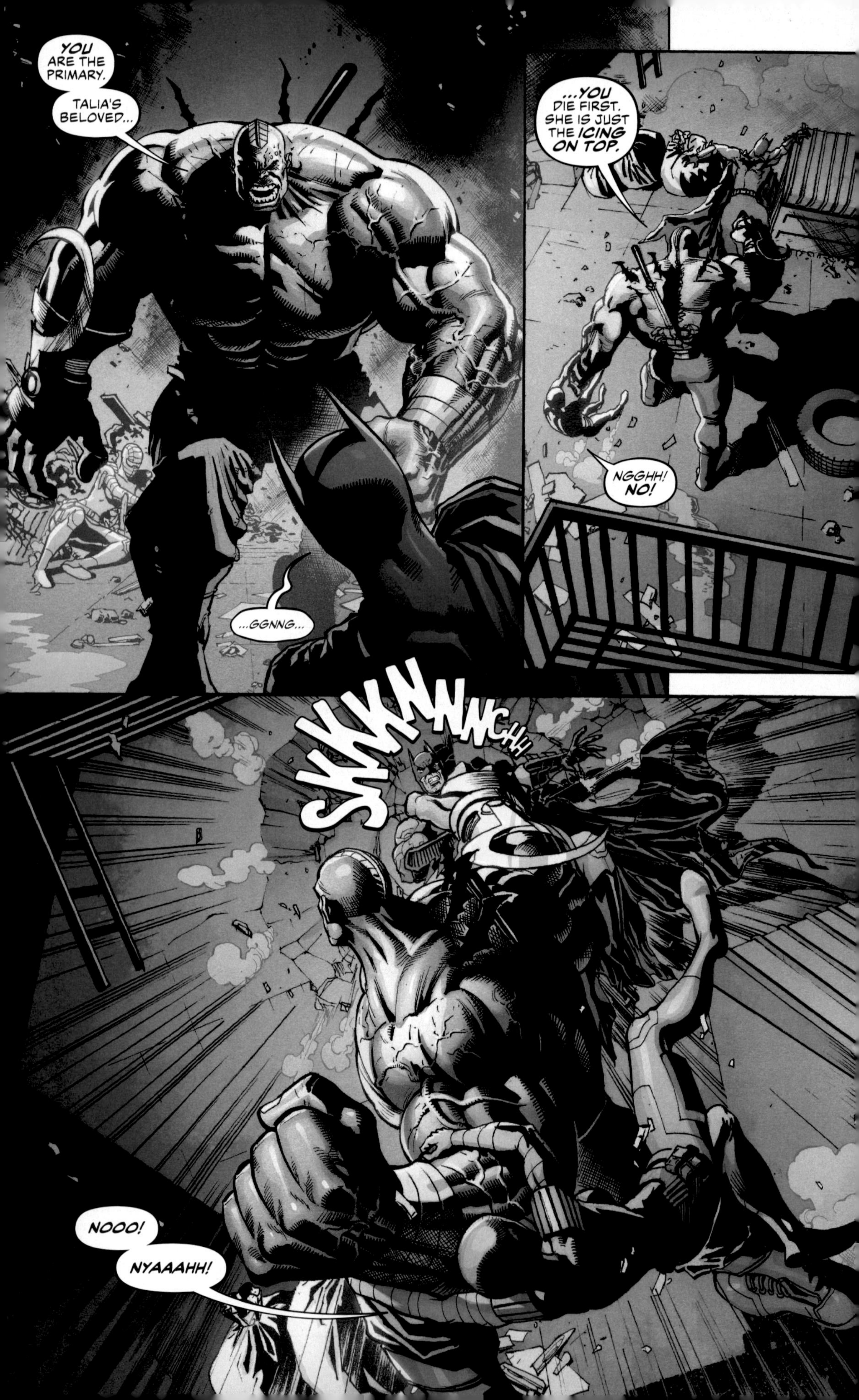
YOU ARE THE PRIMARY.
TALIA'S BELOVED...
...GGNNG...
...YOU DIE FIRST. SHE IS JUST THE ICING ON TOP.
NGGHH! NO!
SKKNNNNCHH
NOOO!
NYAAAHH!

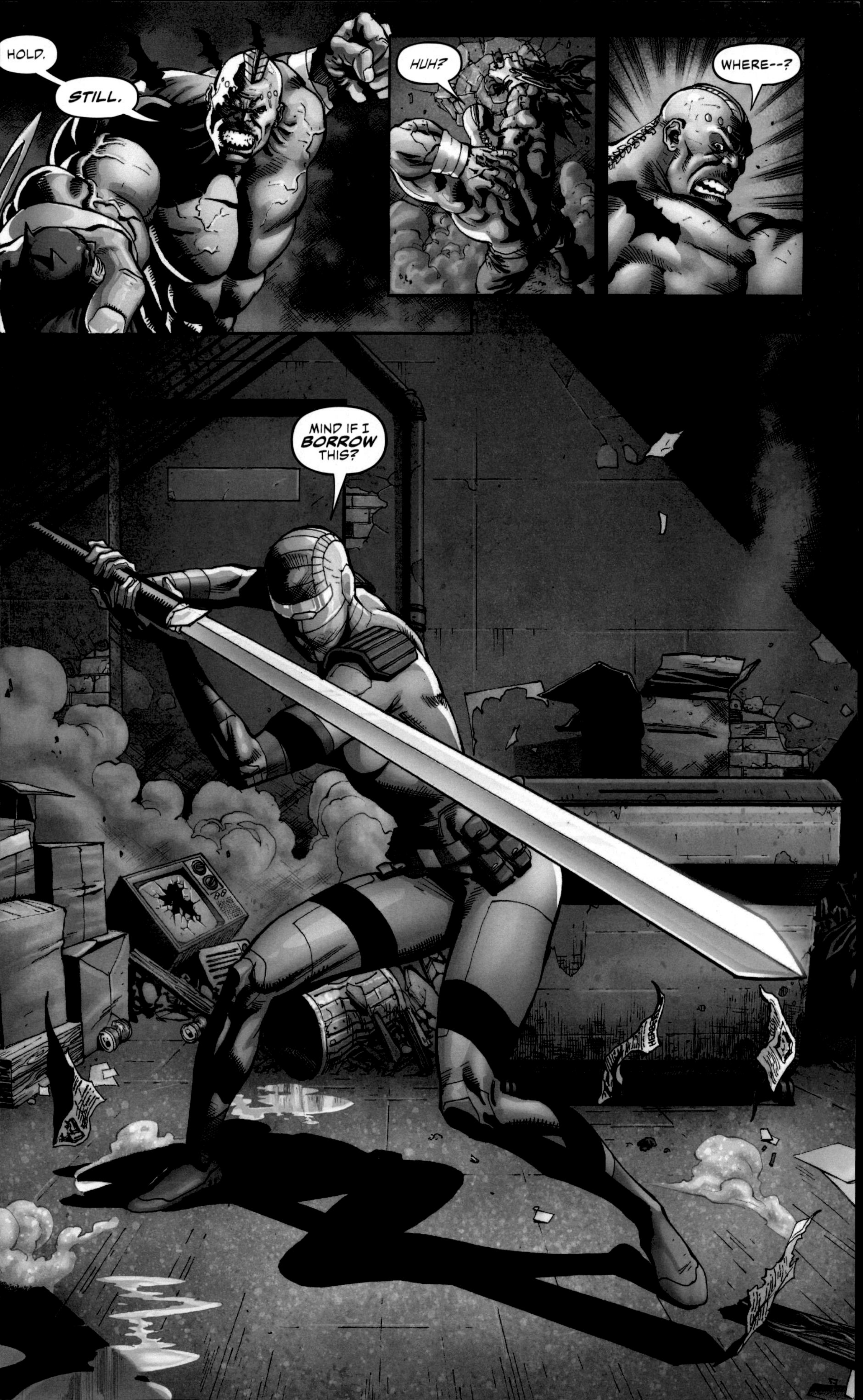
HOLD.
STILL.
HUH?
WHERE--?
MIND IF I BORROW THIS?

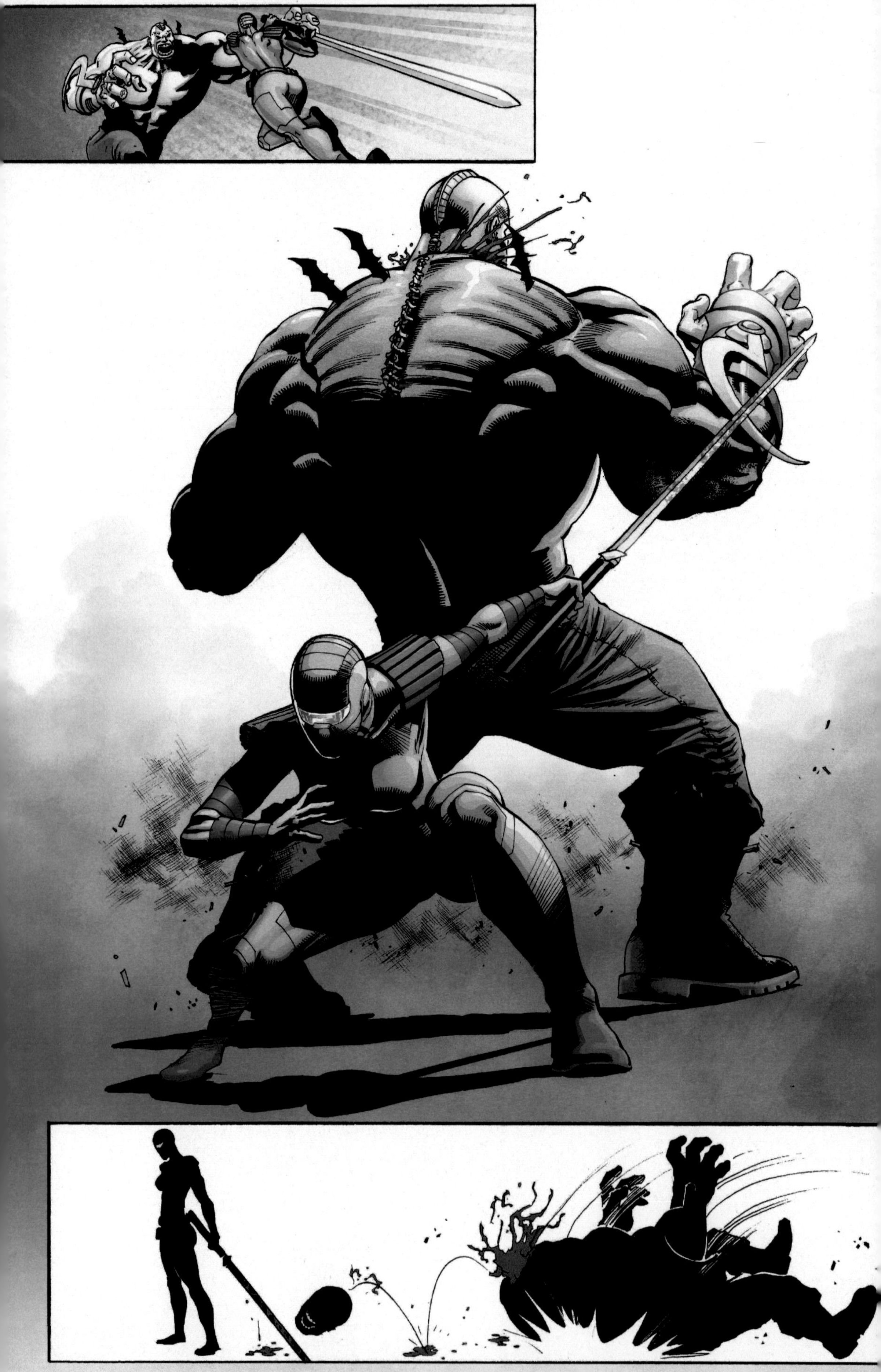

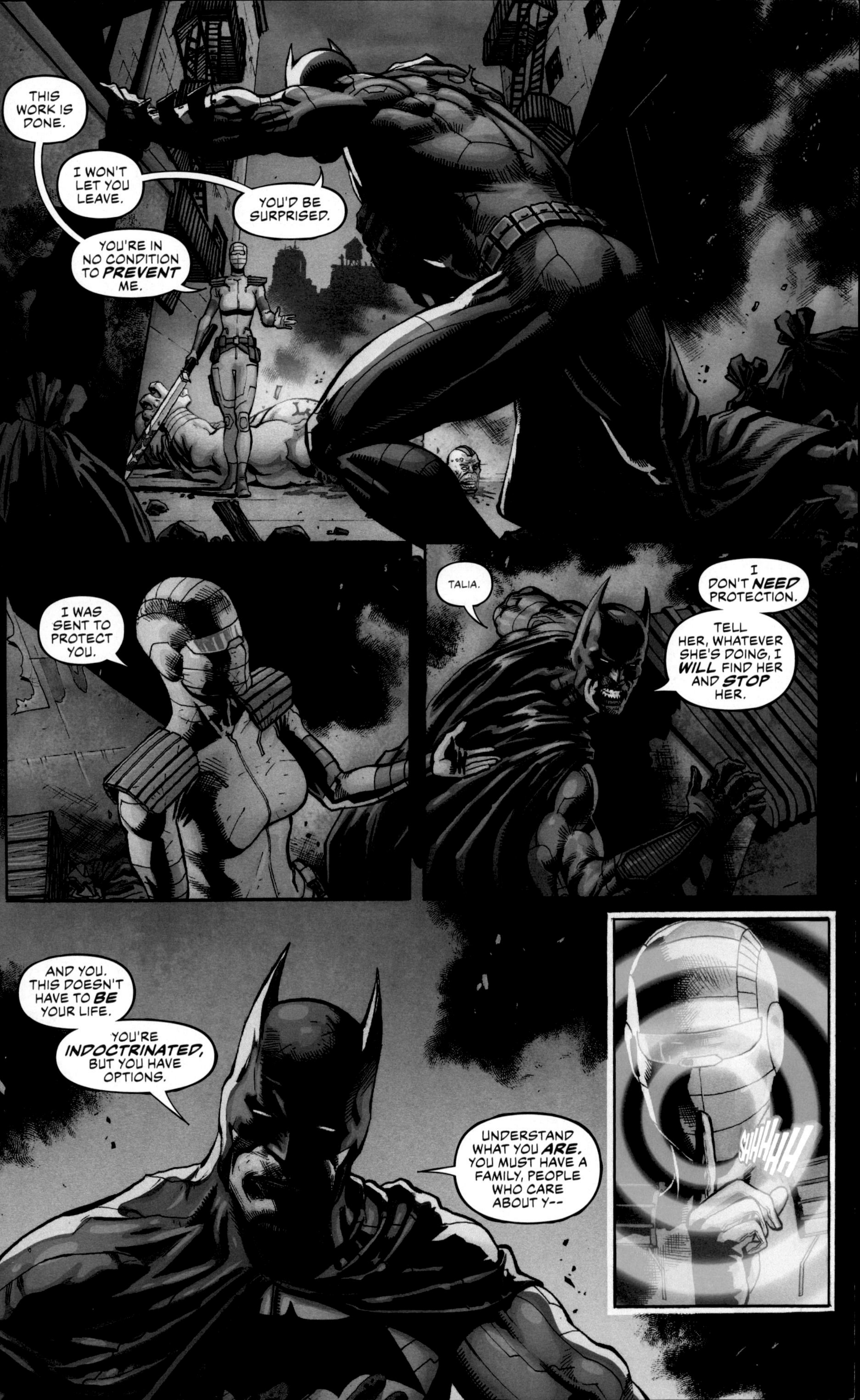

THIS WORK IS DONE.
I WON'T LET YOU LEAVE.
YOU'D BE SURPRISED.
YOU'RE IN NO CONDITION TO PREVENT ME.
I WAS SENT TO PROTECT YOU.
TALIA.
I DON'T NEED PROTECTION.
TELL HER, WHATEVER SHE'S DOING, I WILL FIND HER AND STOP HER.
AND YOU. THIS DOESN'T HAVE TO BE YOUR LIFE.
YOU'RE INDOCTRINATED, BUT YOU HAVE OPTIONS.
UNDERSTAND WHAT YOU ARE. YOU MUST HAVE A FAMILY, PEOPLE WHO CARE ABOUT Y--
SHHHHH

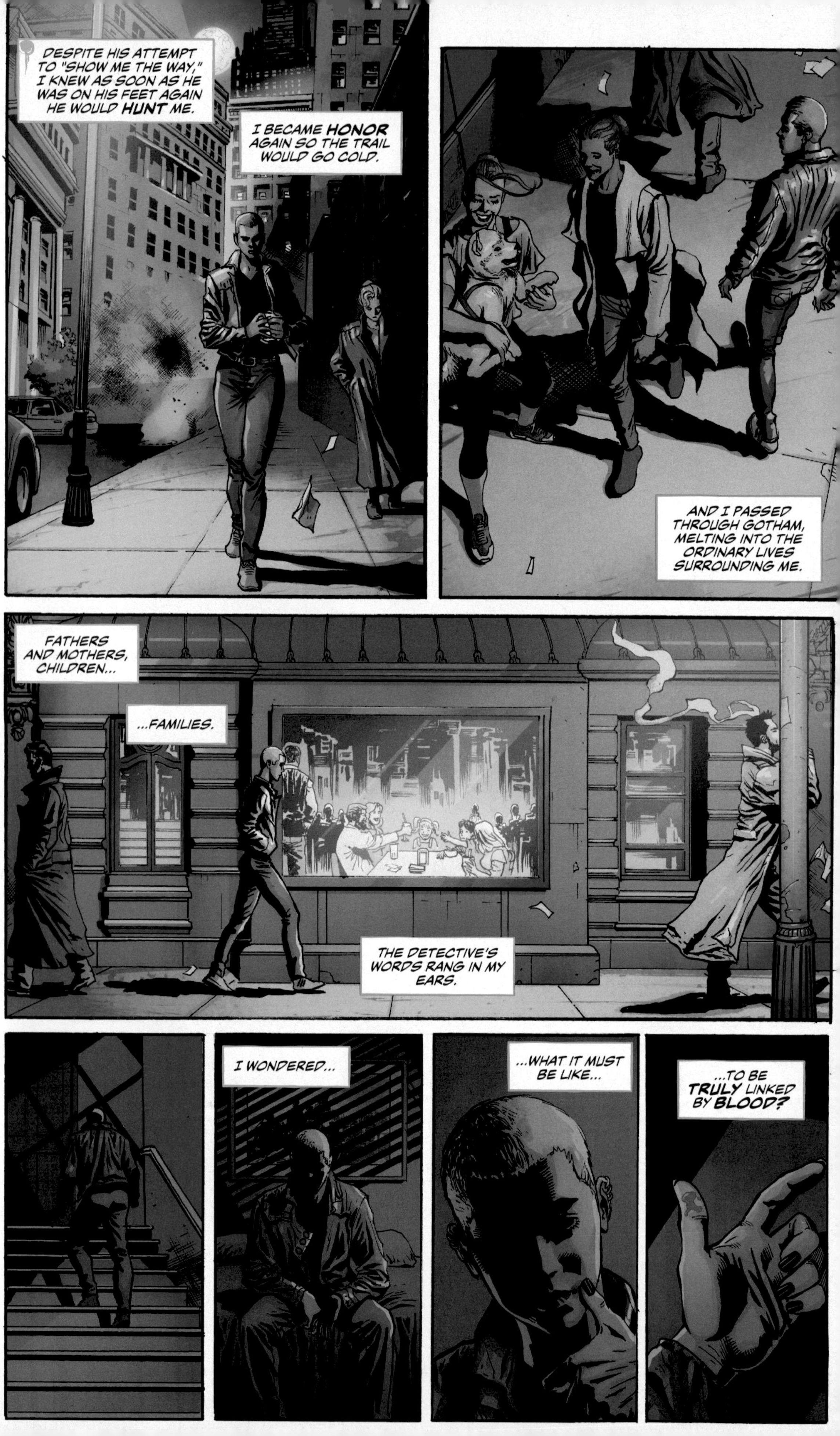
DESPITE HIS ATTEMPT TO "SHOW ME THE WAY," I KNEW AS SOON AS HE WAS ON HIS FEET AGAIN HE WOULD HUNT ME.
I BECAME HONOR AGAIN SO THE TRAIL WOULD GO COLD.
AND I PASSED THROUGH GOTHAM, MELTING INTO THE ORDINARY LIVES SURROUNDING ME.
FATHERS AND MOTHERS, CHILDREN...
...FAMILIES.
THE DETECTIVE'S WORDS RANG IN MY EARS.
I WONDERED...
...WHAT IT MUST BE LIKE...
...TO BE TRULY LINKED BY BLOOD?

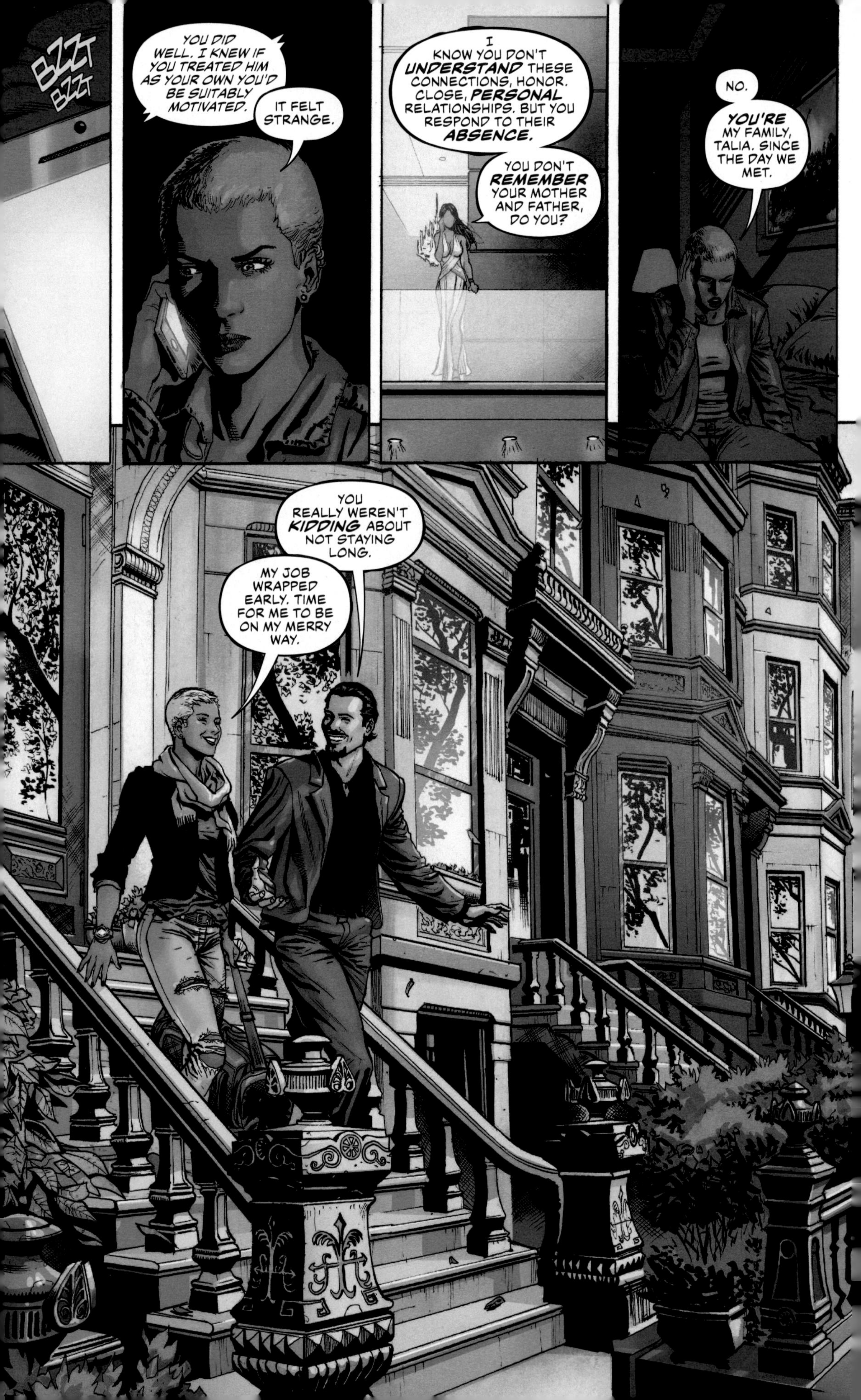
BZZT BZZT
YOU DID WELL. I KNEW IF YOU TREATED HIM AS YOUR OWN YOU'D BE SUITABLY MOTIVATED.
IT FELT STRANGE.
I KNOW YOU DON'T UNDERSTAND THESE CONNECTIONS, HONOR. CLOSE, PERSONAL RELATIONSHIPS. BUT YOU RESPOND TO THEIR ABSENCE.
YOU DON'T REMEMBER YOUR MOTHER AND FATHER, DO YOU?
NO.
YOU'RE MY FAMILY, TALIA. SINCE THE DAY WE MET.
YOU REALLY WEREN'T KIDDING ABOUT NOT STAYING LONG.
MY JOB WRAPPED EARLY. TIME FOR ME TO BE ON MY MERRY WAY.

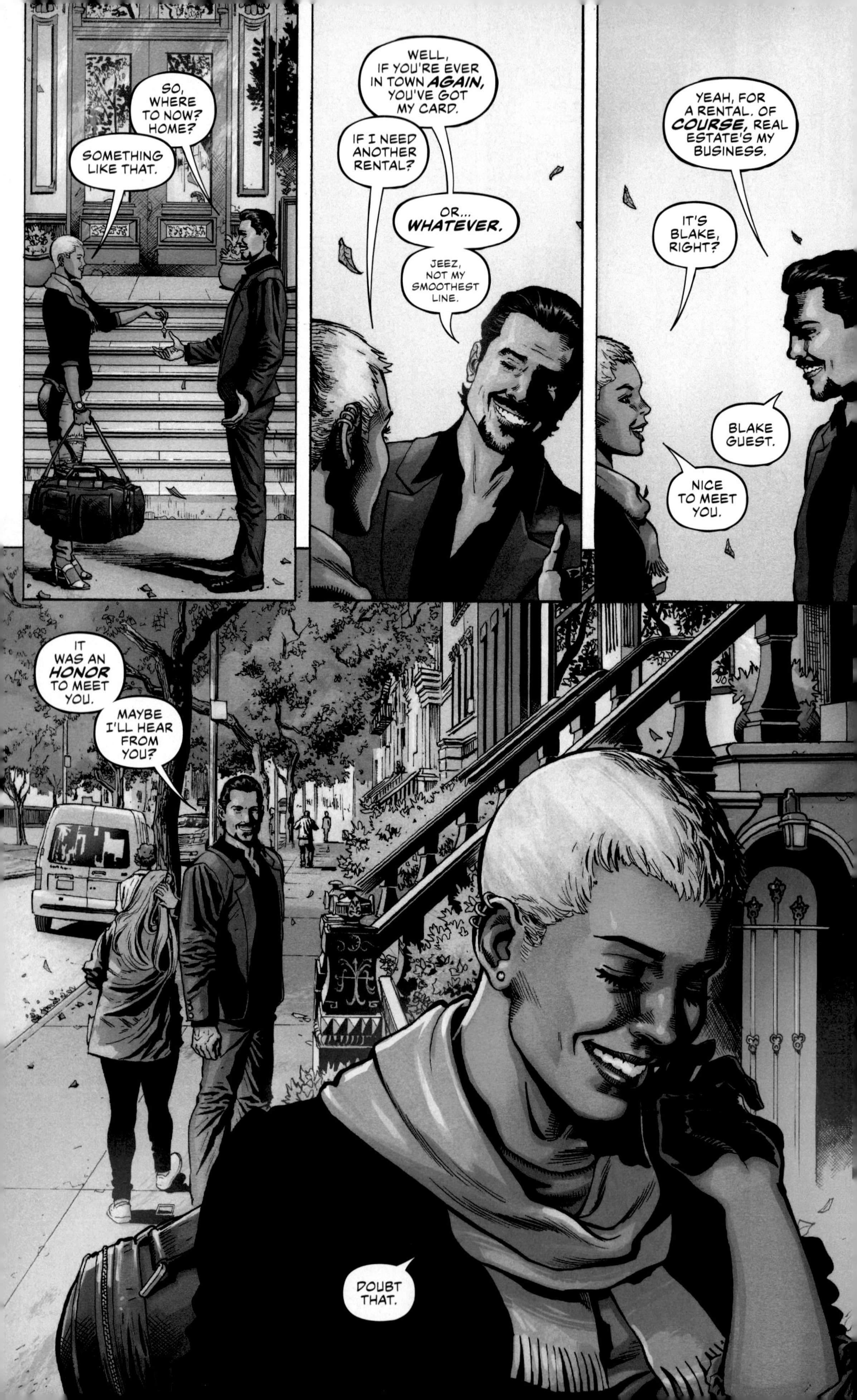

SO, WHERE TO NOW? HOME?
SOMETHING LIKE THAT.
WELL, IF YOU'RE EVER IN TOWN AGAIN, YOU'VE GOT MY CARD.
IF I NEED ANOTHER RENTAL?
OR... WHATEVER.
JEEZ, NOT MY SMOOTHEST LINE.
YEAH, FOR A RENTAL. OF COURSE, REAL ESTATE'S MY BUSINESS.
IT'S BLAKE, RIGHT?
BLAKE GUEST.
NICE TO MEET YOU.
IT WAS AN HONOR TO MEET YOU.
MAYBE I'LL HEAR FROM YOU?
DOUBT THAT.

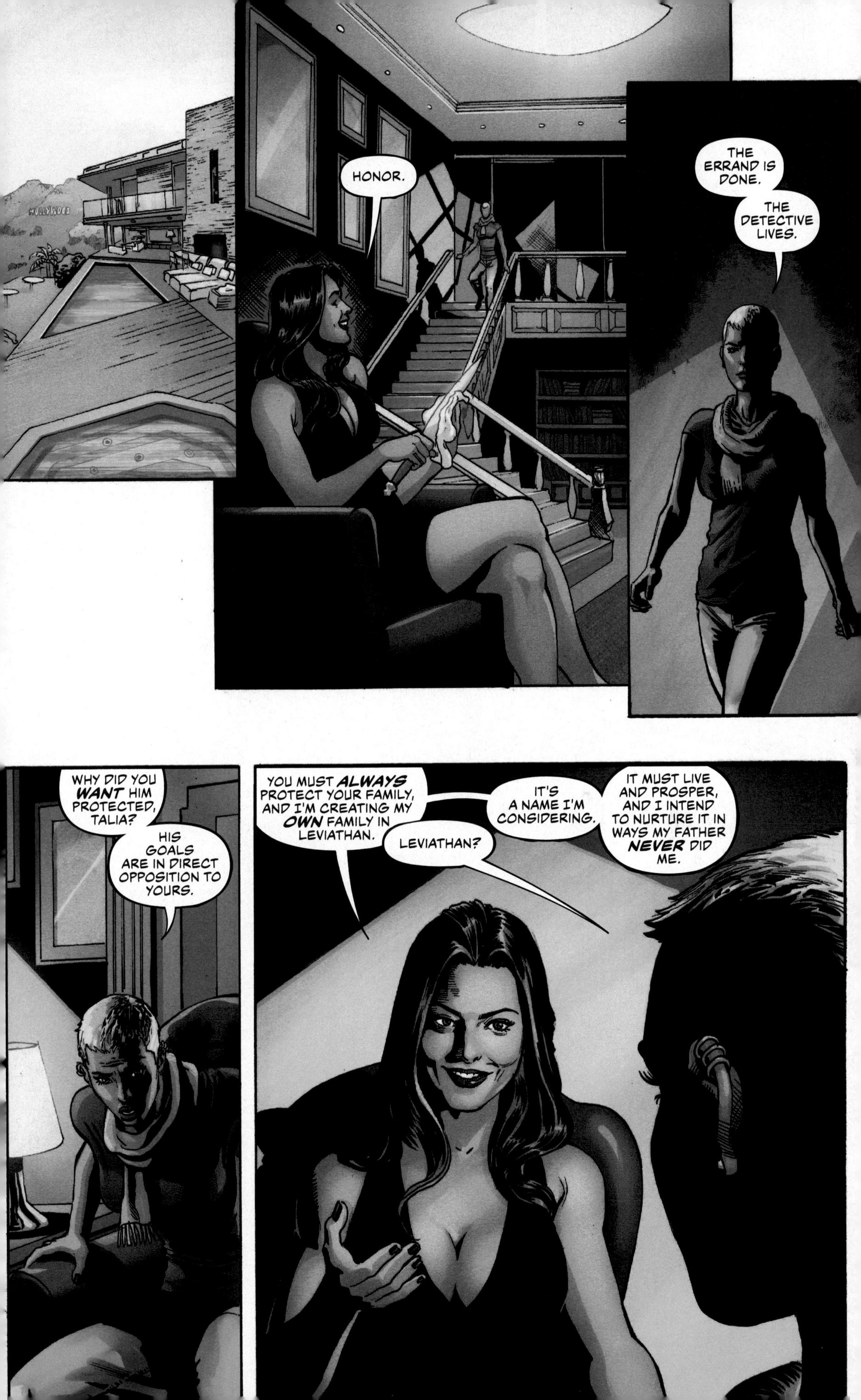
HONOR.
THE ERRAND IS DONE.
THE DETECTIVE LIVES.
WHY DID YOU WANT HIM PROTECTED, TALIA?
HIS GOALS ARE IN DIRECT OPPOSITION TO YOURS.
YOU MUST ALWAYS PROTECT YOUR FAMILY, AND I'M CREATING MY OWN FAMILY IN LEVIATHAN.
LEVIATHAN?
IT'S A NAME I'M CONSIDERING.
IT MUST LIVE AND PROSPER, AND I INTEND TO NURTURE IT IN WAYS MY FATHER NEVER DID ME.

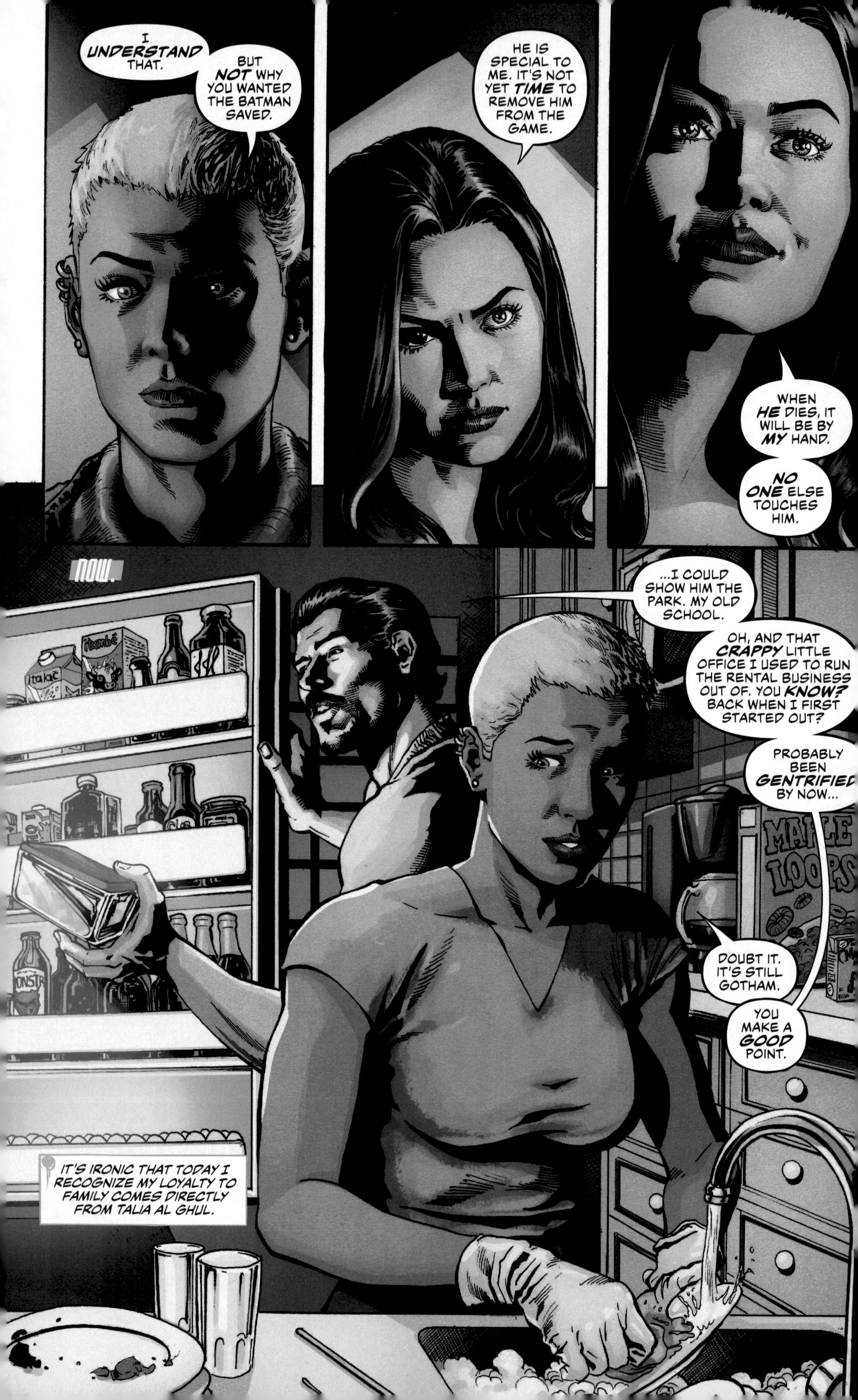

I UNDERSTAND THAT.
BUT NOT WHY YOU WANTED THE BATMAN SAVED.
HE IS SPECIAL TO ME. IT'S NOT YET TIME TO REMOVE HIM FROM THE GAME.
WHEN HE DIES, IT WILL BE BY MY HAND.
NO ONE ELSE TOUCHES HIM.
NOW.
...I COULD SHOW HIM THE PARK. MY OLD SCHOOL.
OH, AND THAT CRAPPY LITTLE OFFICE I USED TO RUN THE RENTAL BUSINESS OUT OF. YOU KNOW? BACK WHEN I FIRST STARTED OUT?
PROBABLY BEEN GENTRIFIED BY NOW...
DOUBT IT. IT'S STILL GOTHAM.
YOU MAKE A GOOD POINT.
IT'S IRONIC THAT TODAY I RECOGNIZE MY LOYALTY TO FAMILY COMES DIRECTLY FROM TALIA AL GHUL.

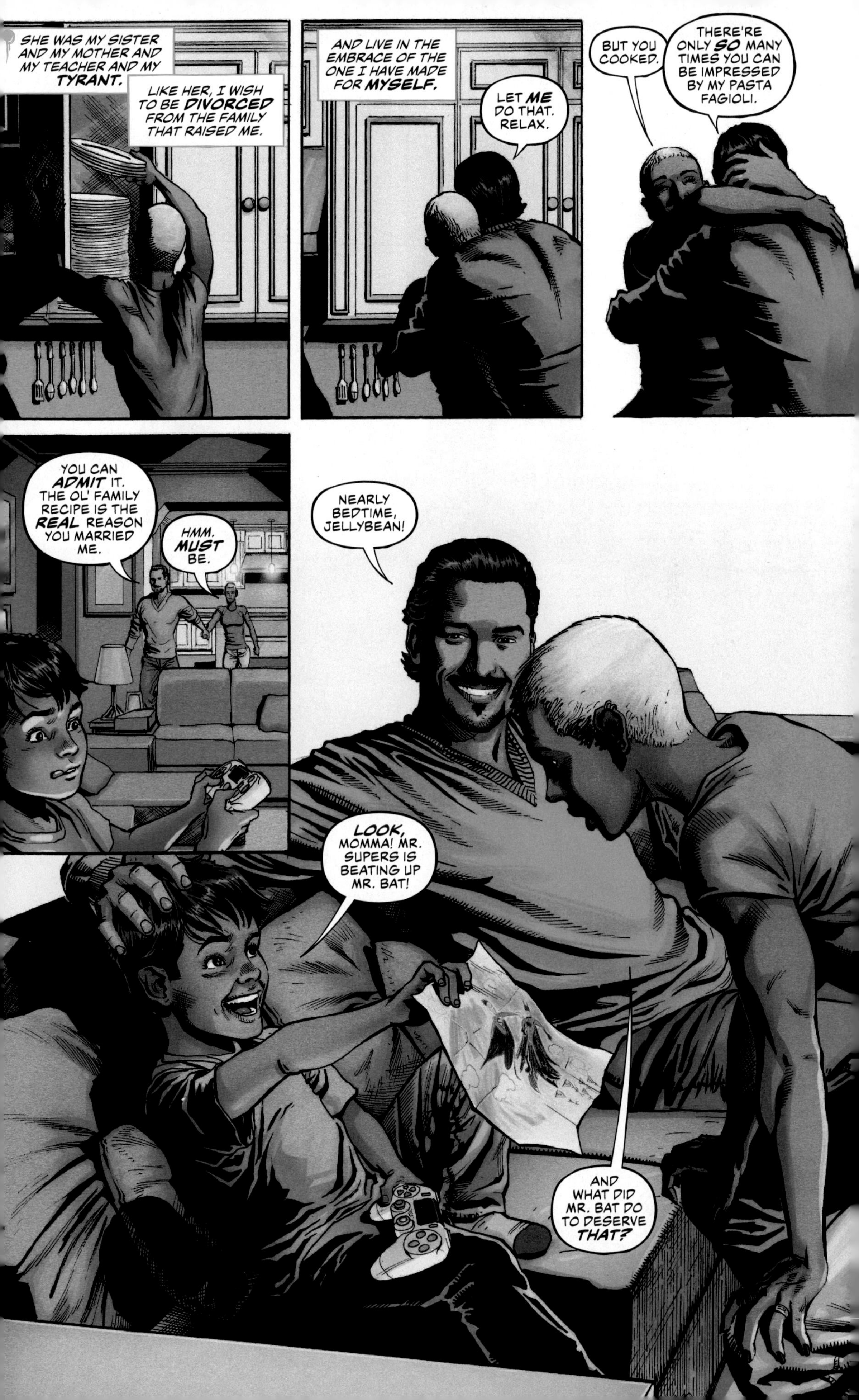
SHE WAS MY SISTER AND MY MOTHER AND MY TEACHER AND MY TYRANT.
LIKE HER, I WISH TO BE DIVORCED FROM THE FAMILY THAT RAISED ME.
AND LIVE IN THE EMBRACE OF THE ONE I HAVE MADE FOR MYSELF.
LET ME DO THAT. RELAX.
BUT YOU COOKED.
THERE'RE ONLY SO MANY TIMES YOU CAN BE IMPRESSED BY MY PASTA FAGIOLI.
YOU CAN ADMIT IT. THE OL' FAMILY RECIPE IS THE REAL REASON YOU MARRIED ME.
HMM. MUST BE.
NEARLY BEDTIME, JELLYBEAN!
LOOK, MOMMA! MR. SUPERS IS BEATING UP MR. BAT!
AND WHAT DID MR. BAT DO TO DESERVE THAT?

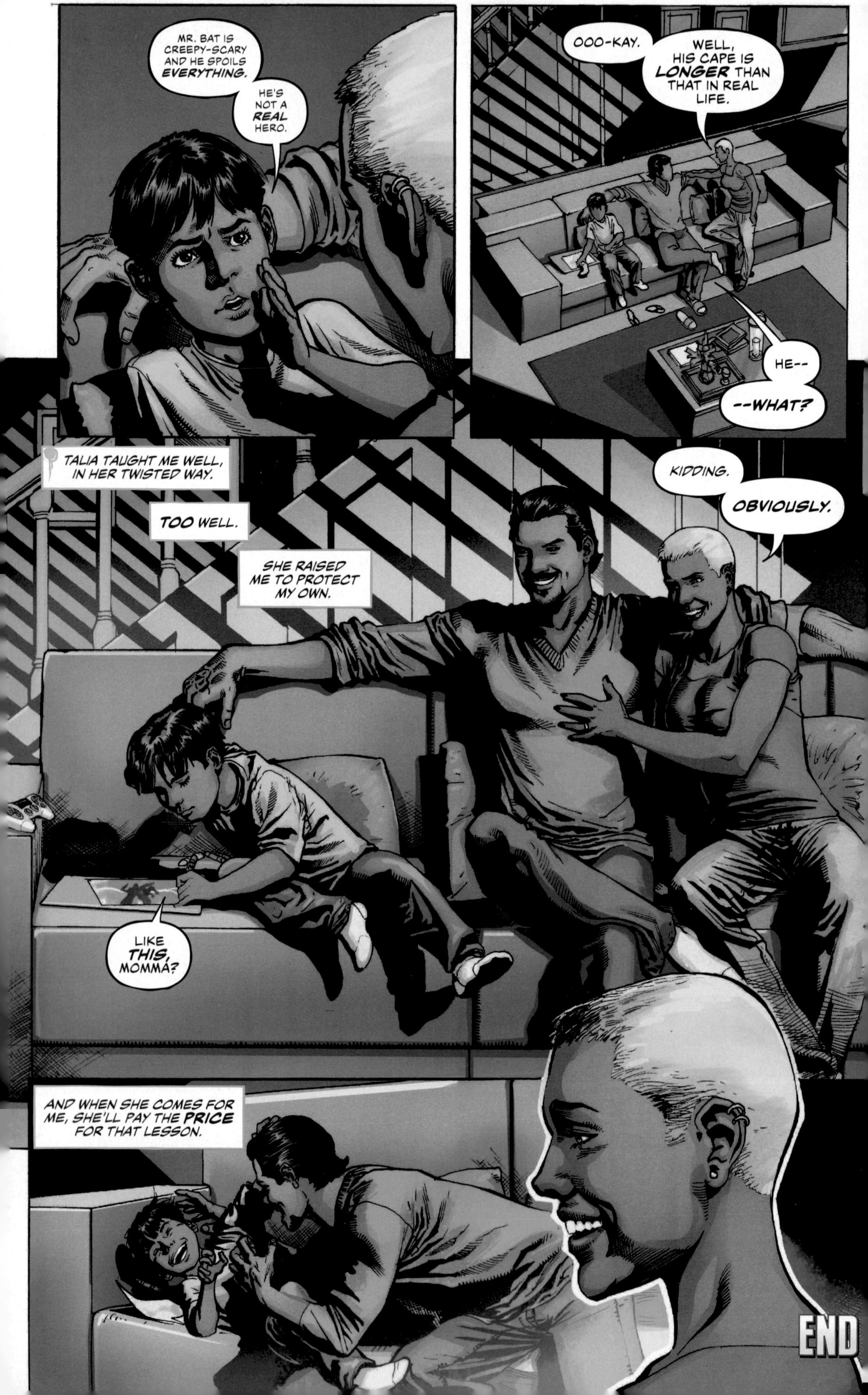

MR. BAT IS CREEPY-SCARY AND HE SPOILS EVERYTHING.
HE'S NOT A REAL HERO.
OOO-KAY.
WELL, HIS CAPE IS LONGER THAN THAT IN REAL LIFE.
HE--
--WHAT?
TALIA TAUGHT ME WELL, IN HER TWISTED WAY.
TOO WELL.
SHE RAISED ME TO PROTECT MY OWN.
KIDDING.
OBVIOUSLY.
LIKE THIS, MOMMA?
AND WHEN SHE COMES FOR ME, SHE'LL PAY THE PRICE FOR THAT LESSON.
END